Coordinating
Public Debt and
Monetary Management

Coordinating Public Debt and Monetary Management

Institutional and Operational Arrangements

Editors
V. Sundararajan, Peter Dattels, and
 Hans J. Blommestein

International Monetary Fund

Cover design by IMF Graphics Section

Library of Congress Cataloging-in-Publication Data

Coordinating public debt and monetary management : institutional and operational arrangements / editors, V. Sundararajan, Peter Dattels, and Hans J. Blommestein.

    p. cm.
Includes bibliographical references.
ISBN 1-55775-555-8

    1. Debts, Public. 2. Monetary policy. 3. Debts, External.
I. Sundararajan, Vasudevan. II. Dattels, Peter. III. Blommestein,
H.J., 1950– .
HJ8015.C66   1997
336.3′4—dc21   97–27958
                                         CIP

Price: US$27.00

Address orders to:
International Monetary Fund, Publication Services
700 19th Street, N.W., Washington, D.C., 20431, U.S.A.
Telephone: (202) 623-7430
Telefax: (202) 623-7201
E-mail: publications@imf.org
Internet: http://www.imf.org

Foreword

Institutional and operational arrangements for the coordination of monetary and public debt management play a key role in the development of government securities markets and in the adoption of indirect instruments of monetary management. The International Monetary Fund (IMF) has addressed these issues in its technical assistance work with member governments for many years.

Over the past five years, however, the massive structural changes in the transition economies have greatly increased the demand for technical assistance in all areas of macroeconomic management, including monetary and public debt management and the development of government securities markets. In response to this challenge, and at the request of major central banks, the IMF has provided a comprehensive program of technical assistance in central banking and monetary and exchange management. This assistance program has been delivered with the support of several cooperating central banks and international institutions, including the Organization for Economic Cooperation and Development (OECD). As part of this cooperative effort, the IMF joined forces with the OECD, which has had many years of experience in public debt management issues among its member states, and jointly organized workshops on coordinating monetary and public debt management. These workshops were attended by senior officials from both the central banks and ministries of finance of the Baltic countries, Russia, and other countries of the former Soviet Union, and benefited from the presentations by experts from several central banks, ministries of finance, and debt offices of industrial countries.

The purpose of these workshops was to highlight strategies for managing the public debt, developing government securities markets, and coordinating those activities with monetary management. In the context of financial liberalization and the transition to market-based financial management, the adoption of indirect instruments of monetary management and the development of government securities markets constitute a mutually reinforcing set of reforms. Implementation of these reforms is critical for the effective and efficient implementation of stabilization policies, but it requires appropriate institutional arrangements for the coordination of monetary and public debt management. This coordination process and related institutional issues were the underlying themes of the workshop papers, which have been edited and compiled into this volume.

This book illustrates the close support and cooperation that the IMF has received from central banks and ministries of finance, as well as from the OECD. The IMF is pleased to publish the product of this joint IMF-OECD endeavor. It offers policymakers a unique presentation of operational issues and practical arrangements for the coordination of monetary and public debt management, and of the institutional issues in developing government securities markets.

MANUEL GUITIÁN
Director
Monetary and Exchange Affairs Department

Acknowledgments

The editors are grateful to the contributing authors for their papers, and wish to thank them for the patience, effort, and promptness in revising their initial lectures and producing, in many cases, expanded papers in order to highlight the themes of the book. Many of the papers were presented at the seminars of the Monetary and Exchange Affairs Department of the IMF and greatly benefited from comments received from the seminar participants. Some of the papers have been issued as IMF working papers. Special thanks are due to Mr. Leite, whose earlier work in this field provided important background to many of the papers in this book, and to Mr. Baliño, who reviewed many of the papers and simplified the task of the editors. The views expressed are those of the respective authors and not necessarily those of their respective institutions.

Also to be thanked are J.R. Morrison and Martha Bonilla of the External Relations Department, who provided editorial assistance throughout the production of this book, and Magally Bernal, Margaret J. Boesch, Lourdes Z. Horton, and Eleanor G. Wood who provided excellent secretarial assistance. In addition we would like to thank Julio Prego of the Graphics Section and Alicia Etchebarne-Bourdin of the External Relations Department for composition.

Contents

The following symbols have been used in this book:

...   to indicate that data are not available;

—   to indicate that the figure is zero or less than half the final digit shown, or that the item does not exist;

–   between years or months (e.g., 1995–96 or January–June) to indicate the years or months covered, including the beginning and ending years or months;

/   between years (for example, 1996/97) to indicate a fiscal (financial) year.

"Billion" means a thousand million.

Minor discrepancies between constituent figures and totals are due to rounding.

Introduction

V. Sundararajan, Peter Dattels, and Hans J. Blommestein *

Institutional and operational arrangements for the coordination of monetary and public debt management play a key role in macroeconomic stabilization and financial market development. These arrangements constitute critical components of central bank–government relations, and the development of these arrangements is one of the essential concomitant reforms supporting the transition to indirect instruments of monetary policy. *Coordination of policies* is crucial because the policy objectives of monetary authorities, fiscal authorities, and debt managers may conflict and may require the articulation of shared objectives. Efficient achievement of policy goals and coordinated actions to pursue shared objectives both require appropriate *coordination of instruments* of monetary and debt management in terms of their technical design. Instrument coordination facilitates market development during financial sector liberalization, supports market soundness, and fosters operational autonomy of debt and monetary managers in well-developed markets. In particular, the appropriate design and operating procedures of monetary policy can help develop government securities markets and, typically, form the foundation for the liquidity and efficient functioning of these markets. Finally, the effective conduct of monetary and debt management operations requires the *coordination of information inputs* between the monetary and fiscal authorities. A lack of coordination may lead to persistent macroeconomic imbalances, slow down progress toward stabilization and market development, and raise uncertainty for the private sector, increasing the cost of funding to the government. This book examines issues and practices in the coordination of monetary and public debt management, drawing on the experience of both developing and advanced market economies, and argues that appropriate design and management of institutional and operating arrangements are important, particularly in economies liberalizing their financial systems.

The main issues and strategies for the coordination of public debt management and monetary control in both transition and market economies are surveyed in Part I. Several key findings emerge: (1) the exact scope and

*V. Sundararajan is a Deputy Director of the Middle Eastern Department and Peter Dattels is a Senior Economist at the International Monetary Fund. At the time this book was written, they were both in the Fund's Monetary and Exchange Affairs Department. Hans J. Blommestein is a Senior Financial Economist at the Organization for Economic Cooperation and Development.

content of coordination vary across countries and over time, depending upon sociopolitical factors, efficiency considerations, policy objectives, and the stage of financial market development; (2) the early stages of financial market development require close coordination of both policy objectives and technical design and operation of monetary and debt instruments, in order to support the common objectives relating to stabilization and market development; (3) in contrast, in advanced market economies, coordination can normally be achieved through market forces supported by an institutional separation of objectives, functions, and instruments of monetary and debt management; in this case, the extent to which central bank autonomy and the pursuit of price stability require autonomy and transparency of debt management and fiscal operations is a key institutional issue; (4) the relative roles of monetary, fiscal, and debt management authorities vary widely in the areas of primary debt issuance, secondary market arrangements, procedures for credit, profit transfers from central bank to government, reserve money and government debt programming, and the related sharing of information on, and management of, government cash flows and market liquidity. Legal, administrative, and operational arrangements for the delineation and coordination of responsibilities in the above areas are broadly reviewed in Part I and taken up in greater detail in Parts II and III. The review underscores the contention that coordination arrangements strongly reflect the stage of market development and the degree of central bank autonomy.

The functions of public debt management and the necessary components of a comprehensive framework for public debt management—hierarchy of objectives, range of instruments, institutions' legal underpinnings, and information and supervisory systems—are reviewed in Part II from the perspective of elucidating arrangements for coordination and their relationship to the stage of market development. Several technical issues relating to the design and operation of instruments of monetary and debt management and to the organization of secondary markets are also discussed. It is shown that careful attention to technical design and to the operating procedures of debt instruments can support effective implementation of both monetary and debt management in the initial stages of transition. The efficient organization of government securities markets is a common objective binding the monetary and fiscal authorities, and the crucial role that the authorities can play in promoting an appropriate secondary market structure is also highlighted. Analysis draws on country experiences and on the literature on the microstructure of markets and auction systems.

Part III presents case studies of selected country experiences in order to provide an in-depth discussion of important aspects of public debt and monetary management, and the evolution of institutional and operating arrangements for their coordination. Country experiences provide insights into the management of policy conflicts, the design of debt management policy, the relative effectiveness of alternative operating arrangements for debt and monetary management, the transition to market-based monetary and debt management, and the evolution of secondary markets.

In economies in transition where financial markets are underdeveloped, monetary and debt management cannot be strictly separated, while economic stabilization and the development of financial markets are common objectives linking the monetary, fiscal, and debt management authorities. These shared objectives and the nascent state of financial markets raise special issues regarding the coordination of policy objectives and instruments, and the supporting institutional and operational arrangements for such coordination. In the early stage of financial market reform, debt instruments and primary market issuance are often used for monetary purposes, calling for much closer day-to-day collaboration between the monetary and fiscal authorities than would be the case with well-developed markets. In Chapter 1, V. Sundararajan and others explore these issues, providing strategies for the successful implementation of monetary and debt management during transition. It is argued that the development of financial markets and of well-coordinated monetary and debt management procedures are mutually reinforcing processes. The adoption of market-based instruments of monetary and debt management—which initially requires arrangements for close coordination of objectives and instruments—expands opportunities for active liquidity management by the central bank, commercial banks, and the nonbanks and provides incentives for institutional development. In turn, the resulting increased depth and efficiency of money and government securities markets opens up additional opportunities to strengthen the instruments and coordination procedures of monetary and public debt policy. In the course of this interactive process, the depth of financial markets increases, the components of debt management evolve, and the scope of central bank autonomy strengthens so that details of coordination arrangements are transformed. In outlining these processes, this chapter also serves as a survey of related institutional considerations that are analyzed in greater depth in subsequent chapters.

In economies at more advanced stages of financial sector reform, with fully liberalized and well-developed financial and government securities markets, increased scope exists for the independent implementation of monetary, fiscal, and debt management policies. In this case, the alignment of policy objectives is achieved through the work of market forces with financial market rates (interest rates, exchange rates, etc.) increasingly used as inputs into decision making. The independent pursuit of objectives of fiscal, monetary, and debt management policies is supported by institutional arrangements that separate the objectives and instruments of the central bank, ministry of finance, and debt management authorities (treasury or debt agency), respectively, and that make them accountable and independent to varying degrees. The characteristics of, and preconditions for, such arrangements for market-based coordination in OECD countries are surveyed by Hans Blommestein and Eva Thunholm in Chapter 2.

Countries undergoing a transition from "captive sourcing" of government borrowing requirements (through various statutory liquidity or prudential requirements imposed on financial institutions) to "voluntary sourcing" (using market-based practices) need to build up supporting debt management functions. Placing those functions within a comprehensive framework for public debt management is important in achieving the objectives of debt and monetary management. In Chapter 3, Lars Kalderen identifies and discusses the functions that constitute public debt management and highlights the advantages and disadvantages of various possible institutional arrangements for the location of those functions.

Notwithstanding a diversity of institutional arrangements for government debt management across countries, common components that constitute a comprehensive framework for government debt management can be identified. Montserrat Ferré Carracedo and Peter Dattels (Chapter 4) survey public debt management frameworks in selected countries, identifying and comparing the components that make up the framework in these countries. A range of tactics and strategies designed both to minimize debt-service costs and to support monetary control is revealed, illustrating a high degree of convergence in industrialized countries regarding the broad strategy for efficient debt management.

In an indirect monetary policy framework, market-based monetary operations become the central bank's main instrument. In the initial stages of financial reform, the selection of a financial instrument for those operations and the design of supporting arrangements to ensure the central bank's operational autonomy when using the instrument are crucial issues. On the basis of theoretical arguments and the experience of a sample of countries that embarked on financial reforms, Marc Quintyn (Chapter 5) weighs the use of government securities as opposed to central bank securities as a monetary instrument.

Selling techniques generally vary according to the type of instruments, the target markets, and the role that the securities play in monetary management: in this regard, treasury bills are generally sold by auction. Important choices have to be made in establishing an auction system for treasury bills from the point of view of coordination with monetary management, revenue maximization, the promotion of integrity and depth in the primary market, and the authorities' other debt and monetary management goals. Carlo Cottarelli (Chapter 6) discusses the main issues that arise in the design of treasury bill auctions, including the type of auction (uniform or multiple bid format); access to, and bidders' participation in, auctions; and managing the auction process.

Efficient price discovery and liquid and deep government securities markets are common goals shared by the monetary, fiscal, and regulatory authorities. Achieving these goals depends on the existence of efficient market structures, according to the market microstructure literature and empirical evidence. Peter Dattels (Chapter 7) discusses alternative institutional structures for trading and price discovery and argues that authorities should play an active role in fostering the development of market structures for the secondary trading of government securities that are efficient and well suited to the specific circumstances of the markets. A variety of country examples illustrates different market structures and the approaches taken to encourage their development. Introducing a "primary dealer" system with special arrangements with dealers that support debt and monetary operations, as in many European countries, provides a classic example—an overview of these systems is provided. Transitional and supporting arrangements are sometimes needed, calling for a more direct role by the authorities, possibly acting as a dealer, establishing a discount house; as a market-maker, establishing a secondary market window; as an interdealer broker, establishing the infrastructure for brokering of transactions; or as a price stabilizer, participating in the market as an active auctioneer. The design and appropriate use of these arrangements are discussed.

Basic conflicts arise in the coordination of debt and monetary management, especially in a country like Italy, with its long-standing budget deficits and a large and mounting public debt. When markets lack confidence in the future value of fixed rate debt, the proportion of floating rate or indexed debt that is repriced in each time period increases. Conflicts between the monetary and debt management authorities become acute when increases in short-term rates—as part of anti-inflationary policy—have virtually immediate repercussions on the cost of servicing the public debt, exacerbating the conflict between the goal of price stability and that of containing the burden of debt-service payments and the growth in the debt stock. Carlo Santini (Chapter 8) discusses the steps taken to manage this basic conflict and to improve the coordination and effectiveness of debt and monetary management in Italy.

The fundamental link between government deficits and monetary conditions is the basis for the coordination of debt and monetary management, according to John Townend (Chapter 9), who discusses recent experience in the United Kingdom. Any excess of public sector expenditure over revenue implies, ex ante, an equivalent addition to private sector liquidity. The final economic impact will depend on how the deficit is financed, and, in particular, on whether the financing method offsets the increase in private sector liquidity. There emerges a strong case that integrating strategic decisions in these two areas improves macroeconomic management. In the United Kingdom, the Bank of England advises the treasury on these issues and conducts operations in the market for government securities on the treasury's behalf. Experience has shown this to be a highly advantageous arrangement, in terms of both smooth coordination of policy and efficient deployment of staff resources.

In a postscript to Chapter 9, the evolving new arrangements for public debt management in the United Kingdom are outlined. In response to domestic and international capital market developments, the U.K. Government has reviewed debt management procedures, and, in mid-1995, announced a new debt management framework. The new framework reorders the hierarchy of debt management objectives in order to emphasize cost minimization and reduces the emphasis on monetary policy and market stability considerations that were the dominant objectives in the past. It promotes predictability and transparency of debt issuance and proposes to foster greater liquidity in the market by developing an open repurchase market. The new arrangements imply considerable changes in the operating procedures used by the Bank of England and confirm the broad convergence of strategies in industrial countries in response to market developments.

Ireland is an example of a country in which monetary and debt management policies and operations are separate. The sole objective of national debt policy is to minimize the long-term costs of servicing the debt. To pursue this policy effectively, and in an accountable way, the National Treasury Management Agency was established in 1990. Notwithstanding the formal separation of debt and monetary management, Michael Horgan (Chapter 10) highlights the importance of coordination arrangements for the sharing of information in order to support the day-to-day execution of monetary and debt policy. Furthermore, in some circumstances, there is a need for close policy coordination; for example, in times of currency crisis such as the European exchange rate mechanism (ERM) turmoil in 1992–93, meetings were held on a regular basis at the highest level of the department of finance, the central bank, and the agency in order to coordinate the implementation of debt and monetary policy.

Creating a separate debt office does not, in and of itself, ensure an independent debt management policy. Staffan Crona (Chapter 11) discusses the initial use of domestic borrowing operations for monetary policy purposes in Sweden and the gradual evolution of the separation of debt and monetary management as markets developed. In order to develop a sound and balanced approach to debt management, establishing clear objectives and a clear organizational responsibility for the debt office was paramount, while the deregulation and development of the capital markets were prerequisites for the separation of public debt management from monetary policy.

The Spanish experience highlights the gradual transition from a highly regulated and insulated financial system to market-based arrangements for debt and monetary management. Pedro Martínez Méndez (Chapter 12) shows that, even in a highly regulated environment, the central bank can take important steps in developing instruments and operating arrangements that foster market development, thereby setting the stage for more liberalized financial markets and more efficient arrangements for debt and monetary management.

Achieving the goal of cost minimization at an acceptable level of interest rate risk exposure is discussed by Robin Miller (Chapter 13), in the case of Canada. Tactical management of the outstanding stock of debt and the strategic measures taken to improve market liquidity and efficiency of the government securities market are highlighted. The chapter discusses the evolving role of the Bank of Canada in debt management and demonstrates the high degree of planning and accountability needed in the debt management process.

Jill Ouseley (Chapter 14) describes the benefits of a regular, predictable schedule of debt issuance, which has helped to reduce the U.S. Government's borrowing costs by lessening the uncertainty surrounding treasury auctions. In addition, recent efforts to modernize the auction system have helped to increase the ease of access to the primary market and improve the treasury's market surveillance capabilities, thereby improving the efficiency and integrity of the auction system. The U.S. experience with the uniform-price auction format for two- and five-year note auctions is analyzed, finding benefits from a broadening of the number of direct participants consistent with reducing the "winner's curse" predicted by auction theory.

Bjarne Skafte (Chapter 15) discusses the development of highly automated and sophisticated trading systems in Denmark and the role of transparency of information in supporting efficient markets. Drawing on this experience, he considers the development of market microstructure and suggests that order–matching systems rather than primary dealers may be appropriate in some of the less-developed markets.

I

Coordinating Public Debt Management and Monetary Control: Issues and Strategies

1

Coordinating Public Debt and Monetary Management in Transition Economies: Issues and Lessons from Experience

V. Sundararajan and Peter Dattels*

The coordination of policy objectives, instruments, and institutional and operational arrangements of public debt and monetary management assumes particular significance in the process of financial sector reform and stabilization of economies in transition.[1] In market economies, such coordination can be achieved through either (1) the sharing of common objectives and pursuit of joint actions to achieve those objectives or (2) the work of market forces in cases where there is strict institutional separation of objectives, functions, and instruments. In the latter case, coordination is achieved with the central bank exercising operational autonomy in designing and implementing monetary policy, and the monetary and fiscal authorities operating in different segments of well-developed financial markets, supported by a separation of debt and monetary instruments. In either case, arrangements exist for the sharing of needed information and of responsibilities to support the day-to-day execution of monetary and debt policy and the effective pursuit of stabilization goals.

In economies in transition, where financial markets are underdeveloped, the development of such markets is a common objective linking

*V. Sundararajan is a Deputy Director of the Middle Eastern Department and Peter Dattels is a Senior Economist at the IMF. Ian S. McCarthy, Marta Castello-Branco, and Hans J. Blommestein also contributed substantially to this chapter. Mr. McCarthy and Ms. Castello-Branco are Senior Economists at the IMF; Mr. Blommestein is a Senior Financial Economist at the OECD.
[1]This chapter was originally issued as IMF Working Paper 94/148 (Washington: International Monetary Fund, December 1994); while the paper was written in the context of reforms in economies in transition, many of the issues addressed apply more generally to economies undertaking financial sector liberalization

the monetary and fiscal authorities, and monetary and public debt management cannot be strictly separated. This raises special issues regarding the coordination of policy objectives and of instruments, and the supporting institutional and operational arrangements for such coordination. Indeed, it is not uncommon in the early stages of financial reform for debt management instruments to be used for monetary purposes, calling for much closer day-to-day collaboration between monetary and fiscal authorities than would be the case in well-developed financial markets.

The development of financial markets and well-coordinated monetary and debt management procedures are mutually reinforcing processes. The development of market-based instruments of monetary and public debt management supports and stimulates the growth of money and government securities markets, because the use of market-based instruments expands the opportunities for active liquidity management (for the central bank, the commercial banks, and other nonbank institutions) and provides incentives for institutional development (for example, more active asset-liability management by commercial banks or the development of new institutions to support secondary trading). In turn, the resulting increased depth and efficiency in money and government securities markets open up additional opportunities for effective and efficient implementation of monetary and public debt policy; moreover, the growth in government securities markets serves as a catalyst for the development of markets in other, more risky securities (such as enterprise bonds and stocks).

In the course of such an interactive process, a number of operational and institutional aspects of coordination between monetary and public debt management assume increased importance. In particular, the relative roles of the monetary and fiscal authorities need to be delineated in organizing and managing primary issuance of government securities; in monitoring, forecasting, and planning reserve money and government borrowing programs; and in regulating and fostering secondary markets in government securities (including the supporting clearing and settlement system). In addition, certain institutional arrangements between the central bank and the finance ministry may have to be underpinned by appropriate legal provisions relating to limitations on central bank credit to the government, the distribution of central bank profits, and procedures to deal with central bank losses.

The specific objectives of coordination arrangements derive from the broader goals of stabilization and financial sector reform. These objectives include (1) the effective and efficient conduct of monetary and debt management, (2) the development of deep and liquid government securities markets, and (3) the enhancement of central banks' operational independence in the conduct of monetary policy. A lack of close coordination between the monetary and fiscal authorities could limit the effectiveness of monetary policies and slow the development of secondary markets.

The actual division of responsibility between central banks and ministries of finance and other statutory institutions in coordinating and implementing monetary and public debt policies depends, in part, on a variety of historical and sociopolitical factors. However, as discussed below, certain parallels in the approach to coordination can be derived from the underlying economic linkages and common objectives that bind monetary, fiscal, and debt management.

The following issues in coordination are discussed in this chapter (subsequent chapters provide in-depth focus and case studies on particular topic areas and aspects of coordination):

- The rationale for coordination, the objectives of public debt management, and the scope of institutional arrangements to achieve coordination.
- Strategies for the development of primary markets in government debt and their role in indirect monetary management, with emphasis on technical aspects of the coordination of primary market operations with other instruments of indirect monetary control.
- Strategies for the development of secondary markets in government securities, and explanation of the role of central banks.
- Organizational and institutional arrangements to support monetary and debt management operations and their coordination.
- Issues arising from the macroeconomic impact of debt management policies.

Rationale for Coordination and Associated Institutional Arrangements

In the context of economies in transition, this section discusses the rationale for coordination, the objectives of debt management, and the evolution of supporting institutional arrangements.[2] The transition from direct monetary controls and limited financial markets to market-based arrangements for monetary and debt management is illustrated in Chart 1. It presents a stylized sequence of critical steps in debt and monetary management in the course of transition to market-based arrangements and highlights areas requiring coordination between the monetary and fiscal authorities.

---

[2]For further elaboration of these issues, see Chapters 2, 3, and 4.

Chart 1. Transition to Market-Based Debt and Monetary Management

Undeveloped Stage
- Limited or no domestic government debt outside the central bank
- Fiscal deficits accommodated by money creation

Preparatory Stage
- Introduction of marketable securities, typically treasury bills sold in auctions
- Interest rates insufficiently flexible and largely controlled by the authorities
- No secondary market, weak interbank markets
- Development of debt management objectives
- Introduction or testing of other indirect instruments of monetary policy (credit auction, bill rediscount, etc.)

Transitional Stage—Fostering Markets
- Further development of market-based debt and monetary management instruments, with greater flexibility in interest rates and more active liquidity management by the central bank
  — use of treasury bills for monetary management
  — coordination of treasury bills and credit auctions for monetary management
  — securitization of outstanding claims on government
  — replacement of bad loans with government securities
  — sterilization of excess reserves
- Introduction of a comprehensive public debt management regime, including medium-term debt securities, with rates set administratively or tied to treasury bill rates. Buildup of volumes and widening of the range of holders
- Strengthening reserve money and debt programming, and related treasury and monetary operations
- Planning of regulatory and institutional arrangements for secondary trading (the central bank remains the major source of liquidity to government debt instruments)
- Strengthening of interbank markets and clearing and settlement arrangements
- Review of the adequacy of banking supervision relating to asset-liability management

Developed Stage—Strengthening Markets
- Interest rates fully flexible
- Expansion of institutional arrangements for secondary markets strengthened by appropriate regulatory and supervisory arrangements
- Liquidity of government debt instruments, ensured by the market, with the central bank managing liquidity in the market at its own initiative, using more flexible market-based instruments (repos, interventions in secondary trading)
- Auctions of medium- and long-term debt instruments
- Further expansion of book-entry clearing and settlement system, consistent with overall reforms of the payment system

Source: IMF staff.

Rationale for Coordination

The basic rationale for coordination and the associated institutional and operational arrangements derive from the following interrelated objectives:

- to set internally consistent targets and objectives of monetary and debt management, with a view to achieving stabilization goals;
- to contribute to the development and liberalization of financial markets; and
- to facilitate efficient implementation of the objectives of monetary and public debt management through mutually supportive information sharing and structural policies.

Table 1 highlights the government's consolidated (treasury and the central bank) budget constraint, which will be used to demonstrate the need for and kinds of coordination arrangements.

Table 1. Government Budget Constraint and Policy Coordination

Fiscal Policy		Debt Management		Monetary Policy	
D_t	$=$	$[B_t - B_{t-1}]$	$+$	$[M_t - M_{t-1}]$	(1)

The budget constraint highlights the fact that the main elements of fiscal policy (the size of the budget deficit), debt management (the issuance of public debt), and monetary policy (the rate of expansion of monetary base) are linked. Expression (1) shows that the government's deficit in the current period (D_t) must be financed either through net bond sales $(B_t - B_{t-1})$ to the public (banks, corporations, or persons), or through central bank credit to government, resulting in a rise in the monetary base $(M_t - M_{t-1})$ held by the public in the form of currency or bank reserves.[3] Since all three policies cannot be independently determined, a need arises to coordinate policy. There are three possible cases with different implications for the scope of coordinating arrangements.

Case (1): The monetary authorities are in a position to determine the supply of base money M_t, $t = 1, 2, 3, \ldots$, consistent with an inflation target. The deficit path is then determined in relation to monetary objectives and financing possibilities. Clearly, this arrangement requires a central bank with operational autonomy to set a path for the monetary base (at

---

[3]In this simple model of the interactions between the private sector, the fiscal authority, and the monetary authority, it is assumed that the entire government debt consists of one-period debt. For simplicity also it is assumed that other sources of increase in base money—credit to banks, changes in net foreign assets, and so forth remain unchanged.

least the domestic component of the monetary base if the exchange rate is fixed) and sufficient policy coordination and fiscal discipline to align the fiscal balance.

Case (2): The fiscal authorities determine the deficit path D_t, $t = 1, 2, 3, \ldots$, and the monetary authorities then supply whatever volume of base money is required to finance government deficits. Consequently, the central bank's mandate for delivering the desired level of price stability may be jeopardized, particularly when the fiscal deficit is large in relation to stabilization goals and the scope for debt issuance outside the central bank is limited. This case is typical of many economies in transition in the undeveloped stage.

Case (3): The fiscal authorities and monetary authorities take independent decisions about the size of the fiscal deficit and the path for the monetary base, respectively. Debt management operations in well-developed government securities markets finance the deficit in a noninflationary manner through bond sales B_t, $t = 1, 2, 3, \ldots$, outside of the central bank to banks and the nonbank public. In this arrangement, interest rates—and also exchange rates, depending upon the exchange system—adjust in well-developed financial markets and bring about the alignments needed to satisfy the government budget constraint.

In economies in transition, the coordinating arrangements under Case (3) are not realistic—with undeveloped financial markets, it is impossible to set the deficit and the supply of money independently, as the budget constraint demonstrates. Hence, if the plans of the fiscal and monetary authorities prove incompatible with the budget constraint and stabilization goals, then either the government or the central bank has to modify its targets.

This discussion also suggests that for economies in transition, which are typically characterized by Case (2), coordination of monetary and fiscal policies should encompass not only the reconciliation of targets for fiscal balances and monetary growth, but also the development of financial markets, particularly government securities markets.

Achieving the market development goal would create the scope for more independent fiscal and monetary policies. In due course, the signals for policy adjustments would be provided by market prices rather than by explicit operational coordination arrangements, which could be limited to essentials such as information sharing.[4]

---

[4]It is important to note, however, that even in countries with developed financial markets, a lack of coordination between the fiscal and monetary authorities can cause volatility in financial markets and create uncertainty about the future real value of bond and money holdings of the private sector. See Chapter 2 for a discussion of issues and strategies for coordination of debt and monetary management for countries with well-developed markets.

Coordination of Debt and Monetary Management Objectives, and the Development of Financial Markets

The pace of financial market deepening will depend greatly on the strategies for developing primary securities markets (the choice of debt and monetary instruments and their management) and of secondary markets (the role played by the central bank in market development). Moreover, absent secondary markets, the primary market for government securities may be used for *both* debt and monetary management purposes.

In these circumstances, the objectives and operations of monetary and debt management cannot be strictly separated, requiring coordination to achieve the goals of financial market development, on the one hand, and liquidity management, on the other hand. In this context, it is vital to articulate a debt management objective so that the design of the debt program may be consistent with harmonizing debt and monetary management and attaining financial market development goals.

The objectives of debt management and hence the details of coordination arrangements are likely to vary with an economy's stage of development. (Chapter 4 provides a survey of objectives and institutional arrangements for public debt management in selected countries.) In modern market economies, a widely accepted debt management objective is to minimize the expected cost of debt service. This presupposes that debt management policies are part of a system (Case (3)) that includes macroeconomic policies (fiscal and monetary) geared toward economic stabilization, well-developed financial markets, a regulatory framework that supports voluntary holdings of government debt, constraints that limit central bank financing of the government (and the requirement of maintaining positive cash balances), and a central bank that determines the overall monetary stance (i.e., the debt managers treat interest rates as a variable exogenous to the debt management strategy).

This debt management objective can be illustrated by expanding expression (1) to form equations (2) and (3). Given an exogenously determined financing requirement (government spending on goods and services (G_t), less revenues (R_t), plus debt service (S_t)), what mix of debt instruments—short-term bonds (B_t^s) and long-term bonds (B_t^l)—minimizes the expected debt-service costs (S_{t+1})? This cost-minimization problem depends on the shape of the yield curve—short-term interest rates $(I^s{}_{1/2})$ versus long-term interest rates (I^l)—and the expected future course of interest rates $(I^s{}_{2/2})$.[5]

---

[5] Although this is a one-period model with all bonds due at the end of the period, short-term bonds can be thought to roll over (principal amount matures and is reissued) with the same bond holder whose interest from the first half of the period $(I^s{}_{1/2})$ accrues at the interest rate for the second half of the period $(I^s{}_{2/2})$. At the start of the period, the interest rate for the second half of the period $(I^s{}_{2/2})$ is unknown.

$$[G_t - R_t] + S_t \quad = \quad [B_t - B_{t-1}] + [M_t - M_{t-1}] \tag{2}$$

$$S_{t+1} \quad = \quad [B^s_t * I^s] + [B^l_t * I^l] \tag{3}$$

where:

$$B_t \quad = \quad B^s_t + B^l_t$$

$$I^s \quad = \quad [(1 + I^s_{1/2}) * (1 + I^s_{2/2})] \; ^{1/2} - 1.$$

In economies lacking well-developed financial markets or with high deficit-financing requirements, a debt management framework of cost minimization of this type is unsuitable. Possible conflicts between the goals of monetary policy—which may call for higher interest rates—and debt management—which seeks to contain debt-service costs—are discussed for the case of Italy in Chapter 8. Given a scarcity of market sources of financing (there will not likely exist a long-term bond market, let alone a short-term market), such an objective could encourage the government to borrow from the central bank (at the expense of fostering inflation). Or, as illustrated by equation (4), private sector borrowing—loans from banks (B^{cb}_t) and nonbank financial institutions (B^p_t)—would likely be at nonmarket interest rates $[(I^{cb})$ and $(I^p)]$, enforced by statutory regulations such as high liquid asset requirements on these captive sectors.

$$S_{t+1} = [B^{cb}_t * I^{cb}] + [B^p_t * I^p] \tag{4}$$

where I^{cb} and I^p are typically unequal and fixed at below the rate of inflation.

Such a segmented market approach to debt management would undermine the development of financial markets and exacerbate the costs of stabilization through distortions in the interest rate structure. Thus, the challenge for economies in transition is to articulate and adopt a debt management objective that is compatible with the broader goals of monetary stabilization and the development of financial markets. One broad objective might be as follows:

> To enhance economic stabilization and promote financial system development, to be accomplished by (1) government borrowing from noninflationary (noncentral bank) sources; (2) inducing voluntary holdings of government debt through establishing market-related rates of return; and (3) minimizing the cost of debt service by enhancing the liquidity of government debt instruments through the development of a government securities market, while taking actions to increase investor confidence.

This objective may also involve trade-offs. For example, a larger fiscal deficit—or larger fiscal adjustment—would be needed to recapitalize and restructure banks. But such bank structuring is often needed to promote interest rate flexibility and financial market development. In this case, the additional debt issuance for bank restructuring could be designed as part of the overall strategy to develop government securities markets; in this strategy, refinement of monetary operations plays a crucial role by fostering liquid markets in government debt instruments. (For a survey of debt management objectives, see Chapter 4.)

In summary, in economies in transition, stabilization and the development of financial markets are common objectives binding monetary and fiscal authorities, while monetary and public debt management policies cannot be strictly separated. Therefore, coordination of policy has to be achieved through the sharing of common objectives and the pursuit of joint actions—involving stabilization and institution-building measures—to achieve those objectives.

Institutional and Operating Arrangements

The coordination of fiscal, debt, and monetary policies has to be supported by concrete institutional and operating arrangements. Types of arrangements, their rationales, and their likely evolution are discussed briefly here and more fully below.

First, institutional arrangements that limit central bank credit to the government can reduce conflicts between the central bank and the finance ministry in decisions regarding the sources of deficit financing and enhance the operational autonomy of the central bank.

Second, institutional arrangements, such as a debt and monetary management committee, can play an important role in coordinating the volume of debt issuance in the primary market with monetary policy goals and help resolve conflicts concerning the stance of interest rate policy.[6]

Third, operational arrangements to share information and to forecast variations in government balances with the central bank or in expected changes in the government's overdrafts can help to facilitate appropriate day-to-day adjustments of instruments and the attainment of both the reserve money and debt issuance objectives.

Fourth, arrangements and rules for the treatment of central bank profits and losses will be important for maintaining central bank operational autonomy through the preservation of the central bank's capital, while removing incentives for inflationary spending that may result from transference of profits to the budget.

Fifth, the central bank and the finance ministry have a joint interest in developing secondary markets in government securities. Well-functioning secondary markets are important for the finance ministry since they stim-

---

[6]See Leite (1992) for a detailed discussion of the role of coordinating committees.

ulate demand and render the absorption of relatively large issues less problematic. Thus, the central bank may need to consider institutional arrangements to enhance secondary markets, such as establishing a secondary market window or developing market-makers, while arrangements in the primary market will need to be designed to enhance market deepening by improving the auction system.

Such institutional arrangements will generally evolve along with the stages of transition. In the initial stage (the *undeveloped stage* in Chart 1), regulatory changes may be required: for example, central bank legislation may need to be altered to permit the central bank to issue its own securities, or to purchase and sell government securities in the open market; changes may also be needed to permit it to act as a fiscal agent for the finance ministry. In addition, a ministerial decree or a public debt act may be needed to permit the government to issue securities or to allow investors to trade in securities.

In the *preparatory stage*, the coordination of debt and monetary instruments will probably require the formal establishment of a high-level policy coordination committee, comprising finance ministry and central bank officials. The placement of limits on central bank credit to the government, and the introduction of debt instruments and selling techniques to serve both monetary and fiscal objectives would be important aspects of coordination.

In the *transitional stage*, the promotion of a secondary market should make it possible for the central bank to further develop open-market-type operations; this would require the establishment of an open market committee and direct-dealing relationships with market participants, and more intensive day-to-day coordination of primary issues with other instruments of monetary management (e.g., credit auctions). At the same time, greater emphasis would need to be given to short-term liquidity forecasting for the conduct of open market operations, which would, in turn, require more frequent information about the central bank's balance sheet. In addition, increased information sharing between the central bank and the finance ministry would be needed to monitor and project government cash balances. Arrangements for primary auctions might also become increasingly market-based to further market development: for example, the authorities might switch from a minimum price tender (setting the cutoff rate) to a market-clearing auction (setting a fixed supply).

Given deepening financial markets in the *developed stage*, institutional arrangements may delineate separate objectives for debt management and monetary management policies, supported by greater reliance on market operations and market signals to ensure coordination, and further development of institutional arrangements to reduce policy conflicts. Such arrangements could include stricter limitations on direct central bank financing of the government, permitting only indirect purchases of government securities in the secondary market. In some countries, a separate statutory institution—a debt management office—has been established to pursue the objective of cost minimization in a market environment. (See Chapters 10 and 11 for a discussion of the role of debt management offices.)

Development of Primary Markets and Their Role in Indirect Monetary Management

This section discusses the development of primary markets for government securities and central bank securities and their role in indirect monetary management, and their interface with other monetary instruments.

Primary Markets in Government Securities: Designing an Appropriate Strategy

The design of an appropriate program of debt sales and debt instruments, and the choice of selling mechanisms, will depend upon the overall strategy for stabilization and the strategy for the development of government securities markets. The choice of strategy, and aspects of instruments and selling mechanisms, are discussed in detail in Chapters 3, 5, and 6. For a market-based strategy, there are four main elements:

First, the debt sales program should form part of the overall process of stabilization by seeking noninflationary sources of financing. If debt sales are seen as an opportunity to increase expenditures and run larger fiscal deficits, they will raise inflationary expectations and, at a minimum, raise borrowing costs to the government.

Second, in the context of developing efficient financial markets to support stabilization and broader structural reform objectives, debt management policies should avoid creating distortions in capital and credit markets, which, as country experiences have shown, will tend to slow the development of secondary markets. Thus, the primary issuance of government debt should be based on selling arrangements that are market-based with flexible and competitive interest rate determination, inducing voluntary holdings of securities by investors, rather than based on involuntary holdings by captive market segments using statutory reserve and liquid asset requirements and interest rate restrictions.

Third, an overall strategy for the development of the government securities markets should be developed and agreed upon. Typically, most countries embarking on financial reform have placed the initial emphasis on treasury bill markets, as part of money market development, and gradually extended the maturity spectrum of government securities to encourage capital market development. (It is easier to develop secondary markets in short-term instruments than in long-dated securities whose investment risk, for a majority of institutions and investors, is much greater.) The parallel development of market-based monetary management has helped to stimulate money and interbank market activity by inducing banks, in particular, to manage their liquidity actively, using short-term liquid instruments such as treasury bills.

Fourth, as part of the strategy for economic stabilization and overall market development, the central bank and the finance ministry will need to decide whether to use the primary market for treasury bills strictly as a means of financing the fiscal deficit (and smoothing short-term fluctuations in treasury cash flows), or to use it also as a significant monetary management tool.

Coordination of Primary Market Issuance of Government Debt

In the absence of secondary markets in treasury bills or other market-based instruments to manage bank reserves, many countries have used treasury bill auctions as a substitute for open market operations. Since indirect monetary management consists of targeting the level of bank reserves in order to control the lending capacity of banks and short-term interest rates, and thereby the overall monetary expansion and the general interest rate level, primary issues of government debt can, in principle, be used not only to meet debt management objectives but also to implement indirect monetary management.

The use of primary issues of treasury bills to regulate the level of bank reserves—also known as open-market-type operations—requires that the volumes sold be varied from time to time in response to variations in autonomous factors affecting bank reserves, while ensuring that sufficient amounts of treasury bills always remain outstanding in the market to permit liquidity management by holders and foster market development.[7] In general, using treasury bills as a monetary management tool requires that an auction technique be adopted to sell the bills regularly, frequently, and at market-clearing interest rates; that the volume of sales be used as a means to regulate the level of bank reserves; and that the interest rate resulting from the auctions be used to signal the authorities' intentions and thereby guide other interest rates in the financial system.

The coordination of policies insofar as they relate to the primary issuance of securities is typically done in a joint committee (or working group) of central bank and finance ministry officials. If deficit financing is

---

[7]This can be achieved by maintaining standard amounts of treasury bills offered with a predictable regularity to assist buyers in their investment planning. On top of this standard amount, the authorities could vary the quantity offered for monetary purposes.

the primary objective, then central banks will essentially play an advisory role, while the finance ministry will normally have the final authority concerning the terms of primary issues including, in particular, the volume of issue, but also the interest rates and maturities. In the case where issuance is for monetary management purposes, the central bank will normally be granted much greater discretion in choosing the volume of securities to issue. In addition, arrangements may be required, and agreement sought, to sterilize the proceeds from the sale of securities on the balance sheet of the central bank to eliminate the attendant risk that an increase in government cash balances could induce an expansion in government expenditures. Finally, the central bank and the finance ministry should also agree on, or permit the central bank to determine, various technical aspects of treasury bill sales, such as frequency of offerings, settlement times, the range of bidders, type of auctions, items to be preannounced, and so forth. (See Chapter 6 of this book for a discussion of the design of treasury bill auctions.)

If fiscal deficits are sizable, debt financing solely through sales of treasury bills may not be sufficient. In this case, either the fiscal deficits will have to be reduced or efforts will need to be made to sell a wider range of government debt instruments to tap different markets (or a combination of both). It is therefore important that, in parallel with introducing treasury bill auctions, the fiscal and monetary authorities agree on a comprehensive program of government debt management, including the use of a range of debt instruments and selling techniques, and a phasing-in strategy for the various debt instruments.

Development of Additional Monetary Instruments

In practice, the use of treasury bill auctions for monetary management will not be sufficiently flexible, and the development of additional monetary instruments will often be necessary to facilitate monetary management, especially in cases where liquidity fluctuations are volatile and large, or permanent. For example, if a liquidity shortage suddenly develops, owing to short-term capital outflows, the authorities may wish to contain the resulting increases in short-term interest rates. However, an injection of liquidity would be difficult to achieve solely through the maturing of treasury bills at discrete intervals. At the same time, sharp reductions in the amounts offered may disrupt market development and investment planning by buyers. Therefore, in many countries, refinance/rediscount instruments or repurchase agreements or both are used to inject or withdraw liquidity for short periods. This raises technical issues regarding the coordination of treasury bill auctions with other instruments, which are discussed later in this section. The development of monetary instruments and their coordination with debt management during transition is discussed in general below and is illustrated for the case of Spain in Chapter 12.

In cases in which the initial situation is one of high excess liquidity in the banking system (or if such a situation develops), it may not be feasible or desirable to absorb this excess by treasury bill issues alone. Reserve requirements could be raised, but this could be inefficient if the required reserves are already high and are not adequately remunerated. In such a case, it may be preferable to sterilize the excess liquidity, if feasible, through the issuance of medium-term government debt. Another possibility is the issuance of central bank securities, especially if the issuance of government securities would lead to an excessive buildup of government deposits.[8] Yet another possibility is restraining the volume of central bank credit to banks, which, in combination with an increase in the volume of treasury bills sold, could also be used to offset the excess liquidity. Such control in the volume of central bank credit at the initiative of the central bank would require additional instruments, such as credit auctions. The appropriate choice (or combination) of instruments, naturally, would depend upon the circumstances.

Typically, the authorities need an arsenal of instruments used in some combination to regulate the level of bank reserves or the level of interest rates in the treasury bill and interbank markets. The use of primary issuance of treasury bill auctions alone would not normally be enough and would have to be supplemented by other instruments, such as credit auctions, short-term repurchase agreements, special issues of securities (central bank or government) for monetary purposes, adjustments in government deposits, reductions in central bank credit to priority sectors, and variations in reserve requirements (see Appendix 1). A few of these instruments that have an impact on government securities markets are discussed below.

Central Bank Securities

It has been assumed that treasury bill issuance through auctions—both the volume of issuance and interest rates determined by auction—is the main monetary policy instrument, which is supplemented by other instruments to manage bank reserves; in addition, the central bank is given sufficient operational autonomy to manage the treasury bill auction volumes for both debt and monetary management purposes. Insofar as such an approach—and the implied cooperation between monetary and fiscal authorities—proves difficult to achieve, the central bank could choose to

---

[8]Alternatively, a large buildup of government deposits could be appropriately sterilized on the balance sheet of the central bank in a "special account" that would not be available for government expenditure but would be remunerated by the central bank.

issue its own securities strictly for monetary purposes. In that case, treasury bill auctions would be used mainly to support debt management objectives. The experience of countries where central bank securities (or securities issued solely at the discretion of the central bank) have been used for monetary management is summarized in Appendix 2, while the choice of monetary instrument—central bank versus treasury securities—is discussed in detail in Chapter 5.

When central bank bills and treasury bills coexist, coordination of the maturity of issuance can be a factor limiting potential conflict between the debt and monetary authorities. Thus, it may be desirable to limit central bank bills to a fairly short initial maturity (say, one month to three months), given the objective of liquidity management, and issue treasury bills in longer maturities (three to six months). Such an institutional arrangement minimizes the direct competition between treasury and central bank bills.

In principle, at the initial stage of transition, it would be preferable to use one type of security for both budgetary and monetary management. This would avoid segmentation of the secondary market, promote faster development of short-term markets in the initial stages of financial sector reform, and avoid complications arising from possible differences in yields on otherwise identical instruments. However, if the needs of monetary management are pressing and cannot await the resolution of coordination issues between the finance ministry and the central bank, it may become necessary to issue central bank bills. This has been the case in many countries. Central bank bills can be seen as a useful transitional arrangement until secondary markets in treasury bills (as in Poland) or other instruments to manage bank reserves, such as credit auctions and repurchase agreements, are fully developed.

Central Bank Credit Auctions

In most transition economies, for a variety of historical reasons, commercial banks depend heavily on central bank credit. Providing a significant portion of such direct credit through auctions can be used as an important and indirect monetary instrument.[9] The need to rely mainly on treasury bill auctions for monetary management may then be less pressing, and treasury bill issues may be managed simply from a budgetary perspective. In this case, credit auctions would be the main monetary instrument to transmit the authorities' monetary policy intentions. The auction volumes would be varied from week to week as needed to influence bank reserves, and the credit auction rate would provide the key signal to the

---

[9]For a discussion of credit auctions, see Saal and Zamalloa (1995).

market and thus influence other short-term interest rates. It is important to note that credit auctions may be partially or wholly collateralized using treasury bills that would, in turn, support the further development of the treasury bill market.

Government Deposits

In the absence of well-developed secondary markets and given the limit on the use of treasury bills for monetary purposes, the authorities in some countries (e.g., Malaysia) have used the transfer of government deposits from the central bank to commercial banks (and vice versa), either occasionally or on a regular basis, to influence the level of bank reserves and conditions in short-term money markets. Among developed countries, the Bank of Canada uses daily transfers of government balances as its principal monetary tool. This instrument is also used in some countries (e.g., the United States) to facilitate monetary management to "neutralize" reserve changes arising from government operations, in conjunction with other market-based instruments. While the transfer of government balances to commercial banks can be determined by an allocation formula, in order to encourage to a greater extent market-based arrangements in general and money market development in particular, using auctions (as in Canada), or placing deposits in interbank markets through brokers or agents, would be preferable.

The main advantage of this instrument is that changes in the level of reserves and banking system liquidity can be determined with precision. However, there are significant drawbacks. First, detailed arrangements are required to determine the allocation of government deposits in the banking system. Usually, this requires complex negotiations between the government and banks, and sufficient technical capacity of the government and banks to support a broad distribution of deposits in the banking system. Second, the banking system must be sound (otherwise, the government may be subject to considerable credit risks) and well developed (otherwise, banks would be unable to manage the effect on banking system liquidity of volatile changes in government cash balances). Third, the use of switching government balances as a regular instrument may not encourage the holding and trading of treasury bills. Finally, effective use of this instrument requires special arrangements and agreements between the central bank and the ministry of finance.

Central Bank Participation in Primary Auctions

In the early stages of financial sector reform, a common question in the management of primary issues of treasury bills (and other government securities) is whether the central bank should participate in the auction and, if so, how. In general, an arrangement whereby a minimum price is set beforehand (which may or may not be preannounced) and the central bank is required to take up the amounts that remain unsold is an undesirable practice. At the least, it complicates monetary management; at the worst, it creates pressures to finance the government, undermining the stabilization efforts as well as the progress toward market-based mechanisms. It is preferable, therefore, for the central bank to refrain from participating in the auctions and to acquire treasury bills through the secondary market. If the market's limited absorptive capacity requires the central bank to participate, it should not do so as a competitive bidder, since this will reduce the confidence in and transparency of the auctions. Instead, the central bank should participate on a noncompetitive basis at the weighted average auction price; preferably, the central bank should preannounce the amount to be purchased or, at the least, the market should be informed at the time the auction results are announced of the amounts purchased by the market and by the central bank. Such arrangements will help to convince market participants that awards at the auction are truly based on market-clearing prices, which will build up confidence and encourage more active participation in markets.

The use of both credit auctions and treasury bill auctions for monetary management requires coordination of technical aspects. Experience suggests that the maturity of credit auctions should generally be less than the minimum initial maturity of treasury bills. This improves control over bank reserves and short-term interest rates, permitting smoother management of treasury bill auctions. The synchronization of settlement for treasury bills and credit auctions and the timing of auctions in relation to banks' reserve maintenance periods are both important for efficient management of money markets. The management of the interest rate structure—the relationship between the credit auction rate, the interest rates on direct central bank credit, the treasury bill auction rate, and the central bank's bid/offer rate for treasury bills in the secondary market—also requires careful coordination. For example, under normal market conditions, credit auction rates should be higher than treasury bill yields of similar maturity; if not, central bank financing may be used for market arbitrage. In addition, the rediscount rate or the bid rate quoted by the central bank in the nascent secondary market for treasury bills might be less than the credit auction rate, in order to foster liquidity in the secondary market, particularly in the initial stages; it might also encourage the establishment of yield spreads reflecting differences in credit risk. (Chapter 6 provides a full discussion of the technical aspects of the organization of treasury bill auctions; Chapter 14 discusses the design and use of auction systems in the United States.)

Secondary Market Development—The Role of Central Banks and Coordination Issues

Secondary markets in government securities provide liquidity for investors (the ability to move from securities to cash, and vice versa, at a reasonable cost) and continuous interest rate determination (price discovery). These functions are supported by the financing and arbitrage activities of market participants, bringing about closer links between the various segments of financial markets and facilitating the transmission of monetary policy. The development of secondary markets supports interest rate liberalization, so that the authorities achieve progressively greater flexibility in interest rates by strengthening monetary operations and money and interbank markets and by promoting competitive and closely integrated markets. Secondary market development also helps to widen the range of holders of government securities and facilitates more efficient (primary market) pricing of debt securities and more flexible debt management operations.

The central bank and the finance ministry will need to help create a supporting framework for secondary markets. This involves introducing appropriate legislation and regulations facilitating the emergence of sound institutions (e.g., dealers, brokers, clearing systems, and custodial arrangements), instruments (e.g., intervention arrangements, rediscount and repurchase facilities), and information systems (for transparency of price and other information, and for monitoring and supervising markets and market participants).

Active and sound secondary markets in government securities are typically associated with the following features:

(1) An absence of price and tax distortions or other inefficient portfolio regulations that foster market segmentation and the involuntary holdings of government securities;

(2) Efficient primary market arrangements in which both the central bank and the finance ministry are willing to sell securities at market-clearing prices;

(3) A sufficient volume of outstanding government securities with a broad distribution among a large number of holders;

(4) Active liquidity management by the central bank—supported by appropriate fiscal policies—designed to manage the overall liquidity of the banking, money, and securities markets and ensure adequate flexibility in interest rates, while avoiding excessive volatility or instability;

(5) Strong interbank and money markets supported by an efficient clearing and settlement system for interbank transactions. Well-functioning money and interbank markets—and the supporting clearing and settlements system—provide the foundation on which secondary markets are built;

(6) The existence of a well-defined microstructure for the secondary market—where buyers and sellers can become aware of each other or where competing market-makers (dealers) in government securities quote firm bid and ask prices and are prepared to deal in sufficient volumes at the stated prices; and

(7) A transparent and equitable regulatory and supervisory framework to foster sound institutions and well-capitalized dealers, and to support the components (1) to (6) above.

In light of these considerations, the authorities' actions to stimulate the secondary market can be viewed either as affecting the market value and the process of price discovery, that is, how the price and interest rates are determined by coordinated monetary and fiscal policies and primary market arrangements (items (1) to (4) above), or as affecting the secondary market structure and its operational efficiency, that is, how the buyers and sellers interact through the microstructure of secondary markets (items (5) to (7) above). A number of measures can be taken.

Measure I. Provide a transparent and equitable system for regulation and supervision of secondary markets

A transparent and equitable regulatory framework is essential. In recent years, most countries have tended to favor establishing a single centralized authority—such as a securities commission (by various names)—that is responsible for promulgating securities laws and is the primary and final authority on securities market regulation and supervision. Some of its powers are formally delegated, by specific acts, to either the treasury or the central bank, or to self-regulatory organizations, which may have a comparative advantage in terms of expertise, information, resources, and independence.[10] Specific institutional arrangements are established regarding the participation and interaction of the central bank or the finance ministry, or both, with other bodies involved in securities market regulations and supervision.

The key objectives of securities market regulation and supervision are to monitor and enforce sound operations, ensure that there is adequate capital in relation to risk, create efficient trading systems, and at the same time, encourage competition and innovation. These objectives require that the regulatory constraints on specific activities be applied uniformly across various institutions and in a flexible manner so as not to stifle innovation.

Typically, countries have endeavored to modernize their government securities markets by adapting the basic regulatory framework to the needs of investors and market professionals for liquidity, transparency, and

---

[10]The government and the central bank are normally exempted from the various provisions in securities laws related to public offerings and disclosure.

adequate and efficient trading facilities. These adaptations have often led to the creation of a new securities commission or a broadening of the supervisory powers of the existing commissions and a clearer delineation of responsibilities among various official bodies.[11] Appendix 3 summarizes the regulation of securities markets in a selection of countries. While the overall regulatory and supervisory framework for securities markets and the powers delegated to central banks and to ministries of finance vary from country to country, central banks are typically involved in the prudential supervision of securities activities and the asset-liability management of commercial banks and nonbank financial institutions with whom central banks directly interact in implementing monetary policy.

Measure II. Develop an efficient and secure clearing and settlement system for transactions in government securities

As lender-of-last-resort to the banks and the authority responsible for the soundness of the payments system, the central bank has a strong interest in ensuring that clearing and settlement systems for securities are designed to control credit, liquidity, and operational risks and to minimize systemic risks. As fiscal agent of the government, the central bank has to help ensure the marketability and distribution of securities. Finally, as a market participant, the central bank, just like any other player in the market, is concerned that securities trades are completed properly, with delivery of securities matched by receipt of payments.

There are four key elements for a clearing and settlement system for securities: (1) trade comparison and clearing arrangements; (2) a depository, which handles securities and maintains a book-entry securities transfer system; (3) a money transfer system; and (4) a custodial/safekeeping arrangement so that members of the depository can safely keep securities on behalf of clients.

The central bank may participate in the clearing and settlement system by providing all or some of these services. However, regardless of which services, if any, the central bank provides it should make certain that the architecture of the system is sound. In particular, the movement of securities by the depository and the opposite movement of funds through the money transfer system should be simultaneously combined so that the clearing and settlement system ensures "delivery versus payment" (DVP). This eliminates "principal risk," which can arise when either securities are transferred before funds are received or vice versa. Appendix 4 outlines the systems of a number of countries.

---

[11]Countries that have, in recent years, created new regulations (or reformed existing ones) or created new regulatory bodies include Australia, France, Greece, Italy, Luxembourg, the Netherlands, Norway, Portugal, Spain, the United Kingdom, and the United States.

Since, typically, central banks organize and operate large-value transfer systems (LVTS) for interbank funds, the development of clearing and settlement of government securities in book-entry form could be integrated with the large-value transfer system to ensure delivery versus payments and to support security market development.

Measure III. Foster an appropriate microstructure of money and securities markets, and support the role of market-makers in government securities

The central bank and the finance ministry should play active roles in fostering an appropriate market microstructure and price discovery process. Chapters 7 and 15 discuss in detail the role of the authorities in promoting efficient market structures.

Most secondary markets for government securities have in recent years tended to be modeled on that of the United States, where authorized primary dealers are charged with making continuous markets in government securities through continuous bid and offer quotations and are given certain privileges to match their market-making obligations. Primary dealers are also required to keep the government debt manager and the central bank (in its function as fiscal agent) up-to-date on market developments, assisting the authorities in the design of market-based debt and monetary operations and the smooth functioning of the market, thereby increasing the depth and breadth of the government securities market. The role of such dealers is highlighted in Table 2.

Dealers provide "immediacy of execution" by purchasing and selling securities as principals, at quoted prices. Thus, successful dealer markets tend to be characterized, and sometimes dominated, by institutional investors who transact in large block sizes and attach a premium on immediacy of execution. At the same time, the promotion of dealers that are prepared to transact at quoted prices facilitates the central bank's liquidity management using open market operations, which also require immediacy of execution. The licensing of market-makers, the definition of their privileges and obligations, and their supervision are, in many countries, the responsibilities of the central bank, in view of the importance of such market-makers in the implementation of monetary policy.

Government securities may also be traded on exchanges (e.g., in Ireland and Denmark; see Chapter 15), which provide a secondary "auction" market. These markets direct buy-and-sell "orders" (limit orders or market orders) to a single location (or an exchange floor or electronic order matching system), where they are executed at the market-clearing or "best" price. Auction markets rely on the flow of buy-and-sell orders to assure that markets are continuous and that sufficient market depth exists.

Table 2. Roles of a Primary Dealer in the Secondary Market

Role	Description
Price stabilizer	Maintains an elastic inventory of securities (expandable and contractible) to absorb imbalances in the supply and demand for securities in order to keep markets continuous and maintain pricing of the security close to its equilibrium value.
Information processor	Incorporates available information into the pricing of securities by taking trading (principal) positions in the market; the market price thus reflects all relevant information and is efficient.
Supplier of immediacy	Provides firm bids and offers and is prepared to take principal positions, thereby providing traders with immediacy of execution.
Active sales distributor	Maintains a sales unit that actively solicits buying interest in the securities.
Educator	Educates investors as to the characteristics of securities and their suitability, and the advantages of holding and trading securities.

When order flow is insufficient, a large block order can destabilize auction markets, resulting in "execution risk" for the buyer or seller.

In nascent markets, sufficient order flow is likely to be lacking. In such a case, the encouragement of a group of dealers to support, maintain, and promote secondary markets will benefit market development and enhance secondary market liquidity. Alternatively, auction markets can be organized along the lines of a "call auction," where securities are traded at a particular time of the day or week (e.g., Israel). The concentration of orders in a batch (periodic) market helps stabilize prices and ensures liquidity to the investor through the accumulation of orders over time. In addition, the costs of execution and settlement are lower, while the existence of a single price each day, or each trading period, reduces the risk of settlement errors.

In the initial stages of market development, when the size of the market is insufficient to support several market-makers, central banks have often established a secondary market window by standing ready to buy and sell government securities. In these cases, the central bank either can set the buy-and-sell prices itself or can respond at its discretion and on a dynamic basis, depending on market developments and in response to quotes provided by the market. The latter method is generally preferable, since it permits the central bank more flexibility and encourages the development of market-making by participants. Importantly, the development and experience gained in setting up and operating a secondary market window prepare the central bank for full-fledged open market operations as the market develops.

In some countries, the authorities have established a discount house, which is jointly or wholly owned by the central bank, to act as market-maker. A line of credit is extended to the discount house to help provide financing for inventory. This approach is an extension of the secondary window method and has the advantage of clearly separating monetary policy functions from dealer functions. However, as a monopoly market-maker, the discount house could discourage the emergence of competing market-makers in the nongovernment sector. In general, transitional secondary market arrangements should be replaced as soon as possible by a more competitive structure of secondary markets, with central banks indirectly supporting the market through monetary operations.

Where transparency of price information or communication systems are problematic, some central banks (e.g., in Italy and Poland) have supported secondary markets by providing a trading system, often as part of facilities to clear and settle government securities transactions. This approach can offer greater transparency relative to telephone over-the-counter markets and provide operational efficiency by linking the trading system with the clearing and settlement system. Chapter 7 discusses in full the design of transitional arrangements that support the development of the secondary government securities market and the role of central banks in the supporting arrangements.

Measure IV. Manage liquidity actively with market-based instruments using government securities

Central banks should manage bank reserves actively to minimize excessive volatility in banking system liquidity, while maintaining sufficient flexibility in interest rates. Excessive volatility in banking system liquidity, and consequently in short-term interest rates, will discourage market participants from taking positions in longer-term treasury bills given the increased liquidity risk (the risk of being unable to borrow overnight, or short-term, in order to fund longer-term securities positions).

In the initial stages, central banks use simple market-based instruments, as discussed earlier, to manage the level of bank reserves in line with monetary policy objectives, and in the process build up active interbank markets, laying the foundation for secondary markets in government securities. (Chapter 12 illustrates such a transition for the case of Spain.)[12] While the specific mix of indirect monetary policy instruments will vary according to the evolution of bank reserves, the state of development of money markets, and the details of the clearing and settlement system, the

---

[12]As already noted, effective management of bank reserves and interest rates requires a monetary programming and debt programming framework that calls for close coordination between the central bank and the finance ministry.

authorities can use their monetary operations to stimulate markets in treasury bills. For example, treasury bills (or other government securities) may be required as collateral for credit auctions, or equivalently, the central bank may auction repurchase agreements (repos) against treasury bills. Either would stimulate the treasury bill market. The central bank would also maintain a sufficient stock of treasury bills in its own portfolio, if necessary by converting part of its outstanding claims on government into treasury bills, which could then be sold on a repurchase basis for a short period; this would be a supplementary means of sterilizing bank reserves, in addition to outright sales of treasury bills and adjustments in the volume of credit auctioned. Thus, progressively greater use of government securities in monetary operations—as indicated above—would foster further development of government securities markets.

The use of repurchase operations in treasury bills to manage money market liquidity is an important way in which central banks can support the development of interbank and treasury bill markets. As markets develop, central banks mostly use repurchase agreements in government securities—and occasionally outright sales and purchases—to influence overall liquidity conditions in the money markets and to provide financing support to dealers in government securities, thereby influencing the level and volatility of interest rates. The central banks' monetary operations have an immediate impact on interest rates in interbank markets and money markets, which will, in due course, influence long-term rates, since dealers in long-term government securities typically finance their securities holdings for distribution and market-making activities in the money markets, and investors adjust their portfolio of assets in response to changes in relative yields. During the initial stages of market development, some central banks may intervene in securities markets directly through a secondary window or a discount house.

Some countries have agencies that intervene in the secondary market, on behalf of the government, for price stabilization purposes. In these cases, intervention is carried out either by the central bank or through a joint body involving both the central bank and the finance ministry. In several countries, the finance ministry (or a national debt office charged with the role of debt manager) also intervenes in the secondary markets occasionally, to buy up illiquid securities and replace them with more liquid securities with desirable technical features.

Supporting Arrangements for Monetary and Debt Management Operations

Effective coordination of monetary and debt management requires a variety of supporting organizational, legal, and operational arrangements.

The operation and settings of indirect monetary instruments have to take into account projections of government cash flows based on programmed debt sales. Appropriate organizational arrangements are needed to facilitate such projections and related decisions on instruments. Effective coordination also requires legal and operational arrangements relating to constraints on central bank credit to the government, the disposition of central bank profits, and a division of various debt management functions between different agencies.

Coordination of Debt and Monetary Policies

Coordination Committees

The establishment of coordination committees—either formal or informal—for debt management purposes is common in most countries. These committees meet on a regular basis to exchange information on the government's financing requirements, to discuss and analyze the results of the government's cash balance projections, to monitor overall liquidity and market developments, and to discuss strategies for achieving debt and monetary management objectives. Committees (or groups) to coordinate monetary and public debt management issues take different forms in different countries, but they normally include officials of the finance ministry, the treasury or debt office, and the central bank. The exact mandate of these coordinating bodies varies across countries—(Chapter 11 discusses the role of coordination committees for the case of Sweden) but the following items are representative of the practice in several OECD countries:

(1) planning the regular sale of securities, including setting quarterly and yearly targets; the setting of these targets requires estimates of government cash-flow needs and assessments of the absorption capacity of the market (i.e., the likely development of the demand for government securities), taking into account monetary policy considerations;

(2) discussing the results of consultations with financial institutions (including dealers) and their customers regarding their preferences on existing and planned debt instruments;

(3) changes in secondary market arrangements, including clearing and settlement systems, issues concerning automation, and regulatory and supervisory questions;

(4) changes in primary market arrangements, including auction procedures, the frequency of offerings, and the introduction of new instruments; and

(5) studies and recommendations on medium- and long-term issues, such as the use of distinct debt instruments for monetary management purposes, modernization of the government securities market, and so forth.

In addition to this interinstitution coordination committee, central banks generally establish a monetary management committee to ensure that various factors affecting bank reserves and money supply are consistently projected and to derive the implications for the stance of monetary policy. Thereafter, the translation of monetary policy stance into the day-to-day settings of monetary policy instruments and the daily strategy for market intervention is typically entrusted to a monetary operations department (or committee) of the central bank (see Chapter 9 for a fuller discussion of such arrangements for the case of the United Kingdom). As markets develop, the day-to-day sharing of information between the market operations department and the treasury on government cash flows assumes increasing importance. Such coordination of debt and monetary policy and operations is highlighted in a stylized example in Chart 2, and Part III of this volume discusses coordination arrangements in detail for several countries.

Intervention Instruments for Monetary Management

Coordination of operating arrangements helps to achieve debt and monetary policy goals. In particular, in countries with rudimentary financial markets, a high degree of coordination is required, since both the monetary authorities and the fiscal authorities operate in the primary market and, in many cases, government securities may serve a dual purpose—monetary and debt management.

Three general types of operating arrangements for the conduct of debt and monetary management can be described. *Arrangement I (same market—different instruments)* uses the primary market for both monetary and debt management but different securities—for example, central bank securities, special deposits at the central bank, special-issue treasury securities, or credit auctions for monetary management, while government securities are used for debt management purposes only. *Arrangement II (different markets—same instrument)* uses the primary market for new-issue government securities for debt management purposes, while the central bank operates in the secondary market through open market operations in outstanding government securities; this is the dominant arrangement in developed countries. *Arrangement III (same market—same instrument)* uses the primary market for government securities for both debt and monetary management purposes, in some cases because of the absence of developed secondary markets. Table 3 shows the operating arrangements for the conduct of debt and monetary management in a sample of countries.

These arrangements differ according to the extent of day-to-day coordination required of volumes, prices, and forecasts by monetary and fiscal authorities. Arrangement II, typical of OECD countries, requires a lower degree of coordination than Arrangement III, because debt and monetary

Chart 2. Stylized Structure of Institutional Arrangements for Monetary and Debt Management

Joint Monetary and Debt Management Coordination Committee[1]
(Central Bank and Ministry of Finance)
Joint determination of auction program and parameters for size and rate determination to meet operating targets for monetary management and debt management goals. Government cash balances are endogenous subject to upper and lower bounds.

Monetary Management
Committee (Central Bank)
• Formulate policy goals in relation to inflation, interest rates, and balance of payments
• Establish short-term operating targets (e.g., reserve money) in order to achieve ultimate targets

Debt Management Committee
(Ministry)
• Formulate overall debt management program including debt instruments, size, and timing
• Establish short-term auction program to meet debt management objectives and maintain positive cash balances

Monetary Operations
Unit/Committee (Central Bank)
• Analyze liquidity projection and money market developments
• Determine stance of open market operations (buy/sell) and size of operations to meet operating targets set by Joint Committee

Treasury Unit (Ministry)
• Monitor fiscal position

Liquidity Projection Unit
(Central Bank)
• Monitor changes in the accounts of the central bank balance sheet
• Project autonomous changes in the supply of liquidity

Government Cash Balance Unit
(Central Bank and/or Ministry)
• Monitor and project path of government cash balances

Auction Management Unit
(Central Bank)
• Manage auction process —tenders, acceptance, etc.

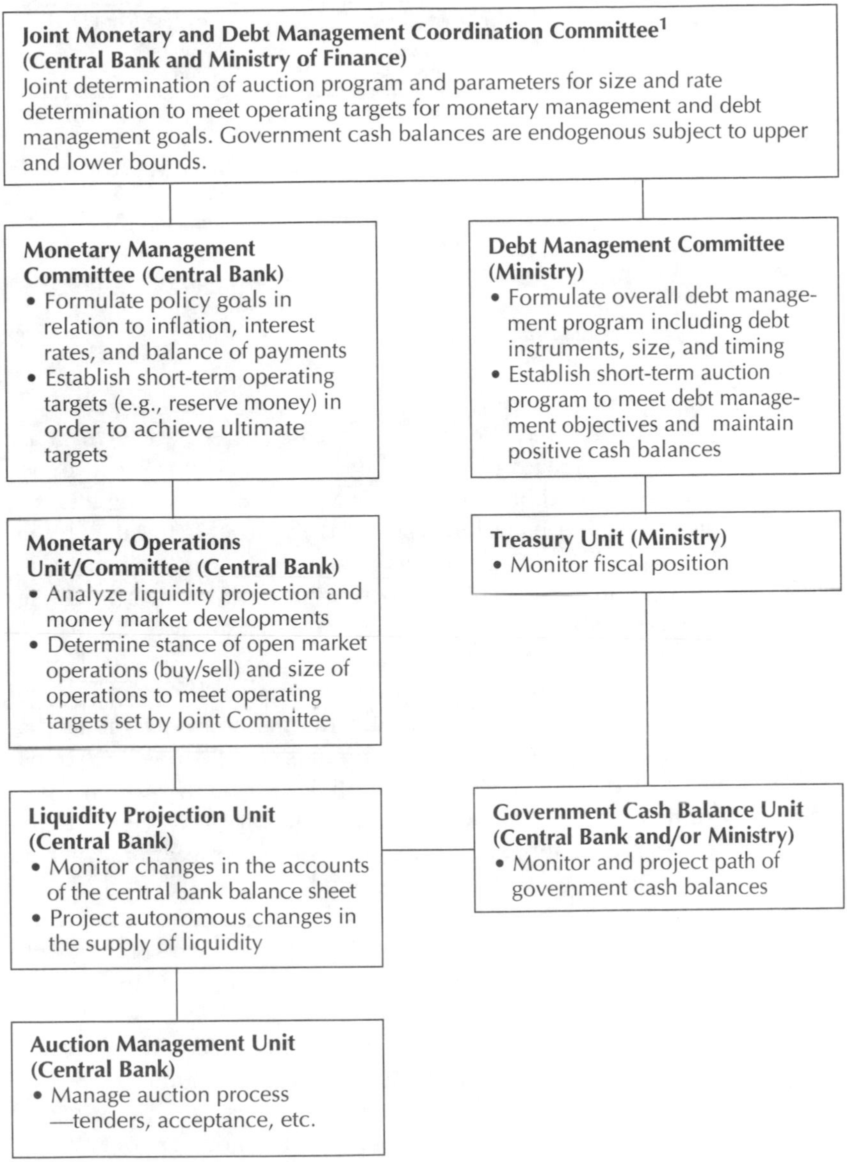

Source: IMF staff.

[1]A *committee* is defined as a decision-making body composed of various members of the institution. A *unit* is defined as operations-oriented, with decision-making capabilities circumscribed by the institution, and can represent either a department or division of the institution.

Table 3. Operating Arrangements for Debt and Monetary Management in Selected Countries

Arrangement I: Different Instruments, Same Market	Arrangement II: Same Instrument, Different Markets	Arrangement III: Same Instrument, Same Market
Russia	United States	United Kingdom
Romania	France	(tap issuance of gilt-
Poland	Spain	edged securities)
New Zealand	Most developed	Pakistan
United Kingdom (use of	economies	India
treasury bills)		Many developing
Nepal		countries
Many economies in transition		

Source: IMF staff reports.

instruments are differentiated—deficit financing takes place in primary markets and monetary management in secondary markets. It can be argued that the need for coordination is also minimal in Arrangement I, under which the central bank intervenes either through specifically designed instruments like nongovernment paper (i.e., central bank bills, such as those used in New Zealand) or through distinct government securities (i.e., treasury bills of a specific maturity that are used exclusively for monetary management purposes, such as those used in the United Kingdom until recently). Although specifically tailored instruments require a lower degree of day-to-day coordination, clear arrangements that specify the joint and individual responsibilities are essential for transparency and effectiveness. The need for both policy and day-to-day operational coordination is clearly the strongest in Arrangement III, common in many developing countries in the process of liberalization (such as Pakistan and India); also in the United Kingdom, where the short-term management of issuance (tap sales) of gilt-edged securities in part serves as a monetary management tool, although recently this aspect of debt management has been de-emphasized.[13] An important principle, essential for the effectiveness of all three arrangements, is that the treasury regards the interest rate (price) as endogenous, that is, influenced jointly by monetary management of the central bank and by market conditions.

In many economies in transition, two key factors need to be considered when deciding on the most suitable arrangement for monetary operations: (1) the undeveloped primary and secondary markets for government se-

---

[13]See the discussion of the U.K. Debt Management Review of 1995 and the Note from the Editors at the end of Chapter 9.

curities; and (2) commercial banks' heavy dependence on central bank credit. These considerations suggest that it may be best to use Arrangement I, under which the finance ministry initially develops the primary treasury bill market to finance the deficit, while the central bank uses credit auctions—together with other instruments such as central bank securities on deposits—to implement monetary policy.

However, sales of government securities, regardless of their purpose, may still have a monetary effect that needs to be taken into account, for instance when proceeds or subscriptions for sales of government securities are temporarily deposited with the central bank. Also, on occasion, debt can be issued to serve a monetary objective, for example, the sterilization of excess reserves. Thus, government securities would supplement monetary management, coordinated with the finance ministry, as in Arrangement III. Moreover, where appropriate, Arrangement III is preferred in order to avoid the market segmentation created by introducing two similar but different instruments.

Institutional Arrangements for Public Debt Management and Central Bank–Treasury Relations

The legal framework for public debt management generally authorizes the treasury or the finance ministry to borrow on behalf of the government. In addition, the treasury or finance ministry is empowered to delegate debt management functions to the central bank.[14] In this way, the treasury can focus on its primary responsibilities—financial planning of government operations, control of budget execution, and cash management—while delegating other aspects of debt management to the central bank or, alternatively, to a separate statutory agency such as the "debt management office."

The rationale for dividing various debt management functions between the finance ministry and the central bank is discussed below, followed by a brief discussion concerning the establishment of a debt management office. See Chapter 3 for a full discussion of debt management functions and institutional arrangements.

The allocation of debt management functions. Public debt management comprises a number of separate but related functions; these are highlighted in Table 4. Different institutional arrangements for the division of labor are allocated among the treasury, the finance ministry, the central bank, and, where applicable, the debt management office. The allocation is likely to be influenced by historical and sociopolitical factors, but economic factors can be equally important. For example, the allocation of debt management

---

[14]See Chapter 4 for a discussion of the legal aspects of establishing the government's borrowing program and Chapter 13 for the case of Canada.

Table 4. Debt Management Functions

Function	Description
Policy	• Formulation of debt management objectives • Setting of instruments to meet those objectives • Coordination with monetary management • Approval of debt program
Planning	• Projection of fiscal requirements • Formulation of debt program regarding frequency, volume, and issuance by instrument
Primary issuance	• Short-term management of primary market including management of issuance volumes and borrowing calendar
Fiscal	• Management of cash balances • Short-term projection of cash balance requirements
Selling	• Management of selling arrangements (auctions, subscriptions, etc.)
Secondary market	• Management of outstanding stock in secondary market for active debt management policy • Development of secondary market depth and liquidity
Advisory	• Advising the treasury (or finance ministry) on debt management functions
Issuance/redemption	• Administration of delivery and redemption of security versus receipt/payment
Accounting	• Management of records of debt instruments and stock of debt

Source: IMF staff.

functions among institutions may depend on economies of scale in performing a particular function, thereby minimizing the operational cost (in terms of hiring personnel or purchasing resources): in a number of countries, post offices are used to distribute debt instruments as well as mail to the public; similarly, the central bank's agency network, which is used for servicing currency distribution, may also be used for issuing and redeeming debt. In addition, comparative advantage is an important economic factor. For example, in light of its monetary policy role, the central bank may be made responsible for the secondary market function, given its greater access to information about money, bond, and credit markets, and its developed expertise in interpreting and analyzing market developments.

The dominant debt management objective may also determine the location of debt management functions. Where development of the secondary markets or monetary control is the primary objective of debt management (as in the United Kingdom until recently; see Chapter 9), or where debt issuance is tailored to institutional maturity preferences or subject to "timing of market developments," the central bank may have considerable scope in determining debt management decisions concerning issuance type, size, and timing. On the other hand, where debt service or interest cost minimization is the primary objective, or where debt is issued according to a regular and invariant program, the finance ministry or treasury generally manages most aspects of the debt policy (as in the United States and France, discussed in Chapter 14). It can also be argued that these arrangements avoid the issue of moral hazard for a central bank of providing indirect support to government debt issues through monetary management (by easing market conditions); they therefore enhance the independence of the central bank, as well as of the debt manager. Finally, the operating arrangements for monetary management previously discussed will play a key role in the allocation of debt management functions.

The minimum responsibilities a central bank normally performs in debt management fall into three categories. First, as *advisor*, the central bank informs the finance ministry of the liquidity situation in the banking system, interest rate movements, and the evolution of money and credit aggregates. The advice of the central bank on the volume, structure, and timing of government securities is important both for the financing of the budget deficit and achieving monetary policy targets. Coordination between the central bank and the finance ministry to maintain orderly market conditions—by neutralizing unanticipated changes in the supply of reserve money—is important to the government debt manager for ensuring the continued flow of funds from investors to the government securities market, notably the new issue market. Second, as *issuing agency and redemption agent*, the central bank sets procedures for issuing government securities (e.g., auctions), for the delivery of securities, and collection of payments for the finance ministry, and for redemption of securities on maturity. Finally, as *fiscal agent*, the central bank makes payments (including the servicing of principal and interest payments to investors) and receives payments. The government cashier role of the central bank is an additional reason for government deposits to be held at the central bank. The second reason is based on monetary policy considerations.

In summary, a diverse combination of institutional arrangements and allocation of debt management functions exists and is influenced by sociopolitical as well as economic factors, such as economies of scale and comparative advantage, the debt management objective, and the intervention instrument for monetary policy.

Establishment of a debt management office. In economies with well-developed markets, there is increased scope for more "micro" objectives of debt management, such as cost minimization. In general, pursuit of such an objective is supported by a separation of debt and monetary instruments and/or by institutional arrangements that enable the monetary and fiscal authorities to operate in different segments of well-developed financial markets (for example, Arrangements I and II discussed earlier). In addition, a separate debt management office may be established to achieve a more formal institutional separation of objectives, instruments, and functions.

New Zealand, Sweden (see Chapter 11), and Ireland (see Chapter 10) have established debt management offices, and offer examples of the institutional separation of debt and monetary management objectives and responsibilities. However, this separation does not lessen the need for coordination arrangements in these countries. For example, the Reserve Bank of New Zealand makes recommendations regarding the volume, terms, and timing of primary market operations. In addition, it acts as fiscal agent and cashier of the government. In Sweden, senior officials of the central bank and of the debt office are members of two advisory groups (one for domestic currency operations and one for foreign exchange borrowing operations) that discuss the financing of government borrowing requirements. In Ireland, the debt office keeps the central bank fully informed of its day-to-day transactions in order to ensure that its operations do not conflict with central bank monetary operations. In times of currency crisis, the debt office and the central bank, together with the finance ministry, will coordinate their intervention and other market activities.

Collecting the Required Information

For monetary and debt management operations, reliable projections of the major components of the central bank balance sheet, as well as of government cash balances and net credit to the government, are essential.

Central Bank Balance Sheet

For day-to-day liquidity management, the central bank needs timely information on changes in the components of its balance sheet. These will include discretionary changes in central bank assets or liabilities, such as auctions of credit or sales of securities in the open market, and autonomous changes over which the central bank exercises little direct control (changes in credit to government and net foreign assets) or elements that are essentially demand-determined (the provision of credit to banks at preannounced terms, and the demand for currency). These autonomous changes will need to be projected—the liquidity forecast—by the central bank with inputs from the finance ministry (for example, in developing projections for net foreign assets and government cash balances).

The liquidity forecast serves two important purposes: (1) it provides an indication of the size of the required withdrawal/injection of bank reserves—that is, discretionary changes needed—and thus helps to guide the use of indirect monetary instruments by the central bank, and (2) it is an important indicator of the likely demand for government securities by the banking system.

In most countries, variations in government accounts with the central bank are a critical factor affecting day-to-day liquidity conditions in the money markets, requiring a focus on information systems for monitoring and forecasting, on a daily or weekly basis, the evolution of the government accounts (claims on government and government deposit balances at the central bank). Such information systems, and forecasts of bank reserves based on them, are the basis for day-to-day management of money markets by the central bank. Also, timely provision of information on commercial bank balances in current accounts at the central bank is important for the effective functioning of interbank money markets, including the treasury bill market.[15]

Outstanding Government Debt and Activities in the Secondary Market

The development of a database covering the type and volume of outstanding government securities and their maturity profile facilitates the formation of public debt management policy and offers important information to market participants. Although arrangements vary from country to country, the central bank is typically responsible for maintaining such a database in its public debt department, when appointed as fiscal agent for the government. Also, data on the volumes and prices of transactions in the secondary market need to be closely monitored as part of information systems for both monetary and debt management. The latter is also typically undertaken by central banks.

Government Cash Balances

A projection of the government's cash flow based on the execution and control of the budget and government operations accounting is essential to plan the issuance of government debt, to monitor and control the

---

[15]In many transition economies, central bank policy concerning the account structure of commercial banks has undergone significant changes. This has a major impact on demand for reserves and money market securities, such as treasury bills. The consolidation of current accounts of banks into a single or limited number of accounts per bank (instead of separate accounts for each branch) reduces the demand for excess reserves, increases the demand for treasury bills, and facilitates the establishment of efficient and timely interbank funds transfer systems in support of money and treasury bill markets.

growth in central bank credit, and to manage the balances in the treasury account with the central bank. It is important, therefore, both for debt and for monetary management. In some countries, such as Canada, the central bank and the finance ministry independently forecast government net disbursements. In other countries, such as the United Kingdom, the central bank relies on the treasury for projections of government net disbursements. In either case, regular meetings between the finance ministry and the central bank should be held to discuss whether forecast errors are the result of temporary shortfalls or surpluses or due to more fundamental and permanent events. The preparation of such projections also facilitates regular public disclosure of the size of the government's financing requirements and its plans for meeting them. Such disclosure can enhance the credibility of stabilization plans and promote forward planning.

The finance ministry typically prepares monthly forecasts from the annual budget, on the basis of the historical and expected spending and revenue patterns. This monthly projection can be used to monitor progress on the implementation of the budget, while also providing the basis for the daily or weekly projections of government cash balances. Short-term projections can be undertaken by either or both the treasury and the central bank. As the clearing agent for the government, the central bank generally maintains government accounts, into which government receipts and disbursements flow. On the basis of the information provided by these movements, the central bank can prepare daily or weekly projections of the government's cash balances and net central bank credit to the government. Whether daily or weekly, information on the short-term forecast will need to be shared: the central bank will be primarily concerned with the liquidity management consequences of changes in government cash balances, while the treasury is responsible for managing cash balances so as to minimize the cost of debt service.

Other Operational and Legal Arrangements

Legal and operational arrangements relating to the management of government cash balances, central bank credit to the government, and the treatment of central bank profits and losses have special significance for central bank government relations; they can also have an impact on the effectiveness of monetary and debt management.

Arrangements for the Management of Government Cash Balances

The effect on liquidity of changes in government deposits and its importance depend on two factors: (1) the absolute variability of government cash balances relative to the variability in bank reserves, and (2) the institutional arrangements for the management of government cash balances. Although in principle the effect on the level of bank reserves of changes in government deposits with the central bank can be offset by other monetary policy operations, special arrangements for the management of government cash balances exist in some countries where the impact of variability of these balances on bank reserves has been found to be substantial, such as in the United Kingdom, the United States (see Chapter 14), Canada, and Malaysia. Typically, the central bank act gives the bank the role of fiscal agent for the government's banking arrangements. From this point, further arrangements can be negotiated with the government and commercial banks for the purposes of addressing the monetary and the government debt management issues that arise in the management of cash balances. See Appendix 5 for a summary of practices in selected countries.

Institutional Arrangements for Central Bank Credit to the Government

Borrowing from the central bank is one of the ways governments can satisfy their financial requirements; indeed, it is usually the main source of domestic financing when securities markets are undeveloped. If central bank lending is at more favorable terms than other domestic financing, it may appear to be a very convenient means of financing budget deficits. However, extending unlimited credit to government at below-market rates will fuel inflation, limit the independence of the central bank, and adversely affect the bank's financial position. Moreover, the availability of cheap central bank credit may encourage governments to spend more, thereby further exacerbating inflation.

To avoid the adverse consequences of excessive government borrowing from the central bank, it is common practice to include in the central bank laws a provision limiting the total amount of outstanding central bank credit to the government. The establishment of such limits is an important institutional arrangement designed to enhance central bank autonomy and contain the risk of inflation.

Statutory ceilings are typically imposed on government advances or overdrafts or both and on purchases of newly issued government debt by the central bank. Indirect credit is usually not explicitly limited, in recognition of the fact that the central bank may need to buy government securities in the open market for monetary management purposes. A formal constraint on central bank credit to the government can be expressed as a fixed amount (including zero), which can be revised by the legislature from time to time, or as a percentage of some aggregate (such as government revenues, government expenditures, or central bank liabilities). In other cases, explicit limits are not established, but approval by the legislature for any funding of the government by the central bank is required.[16]

The effectiveness of such statutory ceilings in achieving central bank independence is diminished, however, when the fiscal stance is inconsistent with stabilization objectives and the capacity of markets to absorb government debt is strained. Experience has shown that there are various ways in which statutory ceilings can be circumvented: for example, a central bank may provide the required credit in an indirect manner by lending to banks that on-lend funds to the government. Therefore, in economies in transition with rudimentary financial markets, quantitative ceilings must be strictly enforced in the context of stabilization efforts and, as markets develop, progressively tightened. Instituted in this manner, ceilings are a key component of coordination arrangements, promoting monetary restraint and helping to establish central bank credibility and operational autonomy. Access to central bank credit should be extended only at market rates and preferably through the purchase by the central bank of government securities, which could then be sold into the market.

The Maastricht Treaty offers a good example of an institutional arrangement designed to enhance the independence of central banks when economies are at the developed stage. It prohibits the establishment of overdraft facilities or any other type of credit facility from the (future) European Central Bank (ECB) or with existing central banks of the European Union (EU) in favor of EU governments. Moreover, the Maastricht Treaty forbids the direct purchase of government securities in the primary market by the ECB or EU central banks.

The Maastricht Treaty allows only indirect central bank credit to the government, that is, by voluntary purchases of government securities in the secondary market (e.g., outright open market operations, repurchase agreements, the acquisition of government paper as collateral for the refinancing of the banking system). In most advanced market economies, there is no formal constraint on indirect central bank credit to the government. However, in many countries, the creation of indirect central bank credit is informally constrained (1) by a requirement that open market operations can be performed only for monetary policy reasons (e.g., in Austria, Germany, and Portugal); or (2) by a prohibition on the transfer of seigniorage to the government (in most countries, part of the seignorage is transferred to the government, that is, central bank profits are used to maintain the real value of capital and reserves, and legal provisions in sev-

---

[16]Cottarelli (1993) and Leone (1991) have surveyed practices and experiences in a large sample of developed and developing countries and note that the most commonly used base for the statutory ceilings is government revenues.

eral countries stipulate that central bank profits should also be credited against the central bank's holdings of government securities; in almost all countries, the remainder of the profits are transferred to the government).

Table 5 highlights institutional arrangements to limit central bank credit to the government in some industrial countries. The importance of such institutional arrangements for the independence of the central bank is discussed in Chapter 8 for the case of Italy.[17]

Institutional Arrangements for the Treatment of Central Bank Profits and Losses

Central banks are not—and should not be—profit-maximizing entities. Nonetheless, in the course of the pursuit of their primary objective, or objectives, they will make profits and, more occasionally, losses. These profits and losses can be substantial, and their treatment can have important implications, sometimes perverse, for monetary policy and public debt management. Because it is important that appropriate arrangements be made, preferably in advance, to ensure that profits and losses and their subsequent treatment do not interfere with primary objectives, many central bank laws and regulations contain provisions regarding the treatment of profits and losses;[18] losses should normally be covered by the government, since such losses are generally the result of the central banks exercising various quasi-fiscal functions or of the implementation of monetary policy.

With high inflation, nominal interest rates tend to rise at the same pace. The central bank's interest income received on loans will increase as a result, but most of the monetary base (e.g., currency in circulation) will continue not to be remunerated. The central bank may, therefore, make substantial profits. However, if these profits were to be transferred to the government and then spent, the effect could be perverse, since it could further exacerbate inflation. Profits from earnings on foreign exchange reserves, expressed in local currency, will also tend to rise rapidly in an inflationary environment, since the currency will tend to depreciate at the same pace as inflation.

At the other extreme, in some cases, often in an economy in transition, the central bank may have few or no foreign exchange holdings—it may not even be the repository of the foreign exchange reserves. At the same time, the central bank may be forced to carry out some fiscal or quasi-fiscal functions. For example, in several countries (e.g., Chile), central

---

[17]See Cottarelli (1993) for an in-depth discussion and survey of central bank credit to government.

[18]However, out of a sample of 60 central bank laws, one-third did not have any explicit provisions regarding the treatment of profits and losses (Vaez-Zadeh (1991)).

Table 5. Central Bank Financing of the Public Sector in Selected Countries[1]

Item	Belgium	Greece	France	Ireland	Italy	Sweden	United Kingdom
Overdraft or other credit facilities by central bank to public entities							
Legally possible	Yes	Yes	Yes	Yes	Yes	Yes	Yes
Automatic access or on application	Automatic	Automatic	Automatic	Automatic	Automatic	Automatic	Automatic
Ceilings on outstanding amount	Yes	Yes	None	Yes	Yes	None	None
(in billions of national currency or as a percentage of government expenditure/revenue)	(BF .20)	5%	n.a.	IR£.25	14%	n.a.	n.a.
Actual use (in percent of GDP)							
Flow in 1991	−1.6	1.0	−0.2	0.0	0.1	1.1	−0.1
Flow in 1992	n.a.	n.a.	n.a.	0.0	n.a.	0.0	−1.0
Outstanding amount end-1991	0.0	3.4	0.4	0.0	4.8	0.0	1.3
Outstanding amount end-1992	n.a.	n.a.	n.a.	0.0	n.a.	0.0	0.3
Direct purchases of public entities' debt by central banks in primary market							
Legally possible	Yes	Yes	Yes	Yes	Yes	Yes	Yes
Gross direct purchases in 1991 (in percent of GDP)	0.0	2.0	0.0	0.0	0.7	3.7	1.3
Gross direct purchases in 1992 (in percent of GDP)	n.a.	n.a.	n.a.	0.0	n.a	4.8	2.8

Sources: OECD; Cottarelli (1993).

Note: n.a. denotes "not applicable."

[1]On January 1, 1994, European Union central banks had to comply with Article 104 of the Maastricht Treaty, which states that overdraft and other credit facilities by central banks to public entities as well as direct purchases of public entities' debt in the primary market are prohibited.

banks have issued securities to recapitalize commercial banks. In some cases, governments have required the central bank to assume foreign liabilities, whether through guarantees of foreign borrowing or by assuming responsibility for servicing government and government-guaranteed external debt. Similarly, central banks have been required to service domestic government and government-guaranteed debt. In addition, sometimes the central bank is the only credible issuer of securities; in order to undertake effective monetary policy, it may need to issue substantial amounts of its own paper at high interest rates. In these situations, the central bank can suffer substantial losses.[19]

Profits. Central banks in developed economies typically make profits. This is so because of the seigniorage that they receive, since they issue non-interest-bearing liabilities, namely currency, while typically receiving income from interest on credits to the government and to banks, as well as interest and other earnings from foreign exchange reserves. A basic principle is that, in a high-inflation environment, the allocation of residual central bank profits (after replenishment of the central bank's capital and reserve funds to offset their erosion by inflation) should not give rise to additional spending (spending that would not take place otherwise).

When profits accrue from real output growth, spending central bank profits reinjects into the economy the liquidity that was withdrawn when interest payments on central bank credit were made. This liquidity is needed to ensure a neutral monetary stance. However, under high inflation, central bank profits typically result from an "inflation tax" on money balances, rather than from the increase in demand for money that would accompany an increase in real income. If central bank profits are transferred to the government and spent, this expenditure will contribute to an inflationary spiral. Thus, such "inflation profits" should not be transferred. Instead, the interest income received on central bank credit is sterilized, helping to stabilize inflation.

To support stabilization goals, central bank profits, when distributed to the treasury, should be immediately netted out against treasury debt to the central bank rather than deposited into the treasury's current account at the central bank. The budget law, on the other hand, should consider central bank profits as extraordinary revenue that should be used only to repay treasury debt to the central bank.

When the central bank can conduct an active and flexible monetary policy, central bank profits can be used to repay government debt outside

---

[19]For example, during the second half of the 1980s, the Bank of Jamaica's (BOJ) losses exceeded 5 percent of GDP each year. These losses resulted from both foreign and domestic operations. The BOJ issued domestic certificates of deposit to contain inflation and also accumulated substantial foreign liabilities at a time when the currency was depreciating sharply.

the central bank as well. In this case, the central bank can sell its holdings of treasury securities to third parties to offset the expansionary impact of debt repayments. The public would then end up holding these treasury securities instead of the original claims on government. The macroeconomic impact would be essentially the same as in the alternative situation, in which the government repurchases debt directly from the central bank. In practice, however, in an economy in transition, the alternative in which the government can repurchase only debt owed to the central bank should be preferred, at least initially.

The general principle is that profits above those "necessary" to maintain the resources of the central bank should normally be transferred to the government.[20] However, transfers should be based upon realized (cash) profits, not notional (accrued) profits; "paper" profits on the central bank's foreign exchange holdings should not be transferred. Moreover, profits that are needed to reconstitute reserve funds in real terms should also not be transferred.

Losses. Although central banks typically make profits, sometimes they have substantial outgoings (e.g., interest payments on securities that they have issued or liabilities for credits that they have guaranteed on behalf of the government, or real losses on their foreign exchange operations), while, at the same time, they have only limited income (e.g., if they have little or no foreign exchange holdings).[21] As with profits, it is important to distinguish between the "cash" and "accrual" positions of central banks where losses are concerned. As a general rule, the "cash" position should determine whether transfers to cover losses should be made.

The basic principle is that central bank cash losses generally lead to a monetary injection that should be offset. Moreover, if these losses are not covered, the day-to-day operations of the central bank can be hampered. Therefore, central bank losses should be charged to the treasury, typically in the form of a loan or placement of securities carrying market rates to be repaid within a specified period. Appendix 6 shows the treatment of central bank profits and losses in a sample of countries.

Key Policy Coordination Issues

Structural debt management policies—measures to induce changes in the structure of domestic debt in terms of holders, maturity, and other nonprice characteristics—influence the demand for and supply of liquid-

---

[20]Robinson and Stella (1988) argue that "if central bank net profits go to the Government, then central bank net losses should result in a transfer from the Government."

[21]For example, the central banks of Argentina, Brazil, Chile, The Gambia, Ghana, Jamaica, Malaysia, the Philippines, and Turkey have all, at one time or another, recorded substantial losses.

ity, the flow of funds to different financial markets, and the level and term structure of interest rates. For example, a shift away from central bank financing tends to strengthen the balance of payments and reduce inflation but can temporarily raise short-term interest rates. The buildup of markets for treasury bills sold primarily to banks and other financial institutions will reduce the demand for unremunerated excess reserves and raise the money multiplier, and hence the growth in money supply for any given growth in reserve money. How increases in interest rates on government securities and changes in the maturity structure of government debt affect the demand for money needs to be closely followed.

Insofar as the authorities wish to limit the growth in credit to the government from the banking system—to avoid the crowding out of bank credit to other sectors—the fiscal authorities will need to target potential nonbank markets for government securities, including small savers and institutional investors. The pricing and other technical features of government securities for such specific target markets should be closely coordinated with interest rates on other government securities, and with monetary policy objectives generally, and should strive to avoid segmentation of markets by types of holders. Otherwise, it will become difficult to widen the range of holders and build up secondary markets. In particular, the tax treatment of incomes and capital gains from securities should be uniform across various types of instruments and holders. Interest rates and buy-back facilities for nonmarketable securities sold to small savers (who are averse to price risks) should not be so attractive that they cut into deposit markets and counteract interest rate policy.

Excessive reliance on short-term securities such as treasury bills increases the size and frequency of refunding operations, causing instability in the debt program (particularly when markets are not wide and depend upon a limited range of holders, mostly banks), increases the volatility of debt-service costs, adding uncertainty to budget management, and may lead to monetary consequences, creating an unanticipated drop in the demand for money or an increased money multiplier. Therefore, the authorities should also encourage medium-term securities and strive to build up a balanced maturity profile (see Chapter 13 for a discussion of issues in balancing the level and volatility of interest cost as a debt management objective).

In higher-inflation countries, medium-term securities would need to be based either on adjustable rates (rates periodically adjusted according to treasury bills or other money market rates) or on an indexation of principal (principal adjusted in line with a price index) or of stepped-rate bonds (different rates in different subperiods in the life of the bond). Instruments of this design can lower debt-service costs by reducing the inflation premium (the premium that investors demand for the risk of unexpected increases in the rate of inflation) (see Shen (1995)). Furthermore, by reducing the scope for the government of imposing an "inflation tax" (reducing ex post the real value of debt through unexpected inflation), the credibility of the government's stabilization program may be enhanced (see United Kingdom (1995)). In devising such instruments in conditions of high or variable inflation, however, considerable care should be exercised to ensure that they are part of a well-articulated stabilization program. If not, extensive reliance on indexed instruments may precipitate a confidence crisis, and raise debt-service costs and the costs of containing inflation, for example, as in the case of Mexico. The experience with commodity bonds in the states of the former Soviet Union, which are effectively equivalent to indexed bonds, suggests that such instruments should *not* be introduced until a credible stabilization program is in place. Moreover, while adjustable rate instruments can be a cost-effective way of extending the maturity profile of debt, they increase the variability of interest costs, which complicates treasury and budget management and may constrain interest rate policy. (See Chapter 8 for the use of floating rate instruments in Italy and the consequences for monetary management.)

The authorities should thus strive to anticipate the monetary and fiscal consequences of structural debt management policies and take these into account in designing their debt management and monetary policy instruments and operations to ensure macroeconomic stability.

Appendix 1
Indirect Instruments of Monetary Policy

Non-market-based instruments
  Reserve requirements
  Liquid asset requirements
  Conventional central bank credit facilities at preannounced interest rates (e.g.,
    Lombard facility, overdrafts, bill rediscount facility)
  Drawdown/redeposit of government deposits between the central bank and
    commercial banks based on an allocation formula for placing deposits with
    commercial banks

Market-based instruments
  Primary market
    Auctions of government securities
    Auctions of central bank bills
  Secondary market
    Open market operations in government securities through outright purchase and
      sales, and repurchase agreements in government securities (repos)
    Credit auctions using bills or securities as collateral (equivalent to repos)
    Deposit auctions using bills or securities as collateral (equivalent to reverse repos)
  Interbank deposit market
    Credit auctions without collateral
    Auctions of government deposits
    Drawdown and redeposit mechanism with market–based allotment ratios
    Intervention in interbank markets using government deposits funds
  Foreign exchange market
    Foreign exchange swaps
    Outright purchases and sales of foreign exchange

Appendix 2
Debt Securities Issued by the Central Bank: Experience in Selected Countries

Country	Instrument	Purpose
Germany (Bundesbank)	Short-term treasury bills (three, six, and nine months) issued by the Bundesbank through auction to banks with operational accounts at the Bundesbank in accordance with Section 42 of the Bundesbank Act and up to a maximum amount of DM 25 billion.	Introduced in February. 1993 to stimulate short-term secondary markets and discontinued in July 1994 with the enactment of regulation permitting money market mutual funds.
Ghana (Bank of Ghana)	Short-term central bank bills, introduced in late 1988. The underdeveloped state of financial markets at the time, combined with the ineffectiveness of treasury bills to absorb the required amount of liquidity, prompted the Bank of Ghana to issue its own debt instruments. In late 1989, medium-term Bank of Ghana bonds were issued (180 days, one and two years) in an effort to address the persistent situation of liquidity overhang. Medium-term securities were found not to be attractive to holders and the Bank of Ghana has relied more on short-term central bank bills. Short-term central bank bills have been effective in the conduct of monetary management.	Introduced to absorb excess domestic liquidity, owing to the prolonged use of credit ceilings. Central bank bills became the main intervention instrument for monetary policy, with decreasing policy intervention through primary markets for government securities.
Korea (Bank of Korea)	The Bank of Korea began issuing its own debt instruments, Monetary Stabilization Bonds (MSBs), as early as 1961. MSBs carry maturities of one year or less. Under the Monetary Stabilization Act (1961), the Bank of Korea is authorized to issue them in its own name. However, the terms are set by the Monetary Board. Rigidities in the market for MSBs, as well as their narrow purpose, have limited MSBs' use as the main instrument for monetary control.	For monetary management purposes, to deal with the liquidity absorption requirements at the time.

Appendix 2 *(concluded)*

Country	Instrument	Purpose
Nepal (Nepal Rastra Bank (NRB))	Short-term NRB bonds (three-month and one-year central bank bills), introduced in February 1992, issued through competitive auction simultaneously with auctions of three-month treasury bills; at the discretion of the central bank. NRB bonds have been effective in sterilization operations.	For monetary management purposes—primarily the sterilization of foreign exchange transactions by the NRB.
New Zealand (Reserve Bank of New Zealand)	Short-term Reserve Bank bills (63 days—changed from 91 days in February 1991) issued twice weekly by auction, nontraded and discountable with 28 days remaining to maturity. Because of the discount feature, the Reserve Bank bills yield slightly less than treasury bills. Reserve Bank bills have been effective in separating debt and monetary management operations.	For monetary management purposes, used in conjunction with the discount margin (penalty) and open market operations (OMOs).
Philippines	Medium-term securities (three to five years), introduced in 1970, issued by auction and phased out in 1981. Short-term bills introduced in 1984 and phased out in 1986. Phased out in part due to central bank losses.	Introduced to absorb excess liquidity in the banking system and increase central bank operational autonomy.
Poland (National Bank of Poland (NBP))	Short-term NBP bills (one month), introduced in July 1991, issued through auction. With the introduction of one-month treasury bills, NBP bills of three-month and six-month maturities were introduced.	Introduced as a monetary instrument and replaced by OMO repurchase and reverse repurchase auctions in January 1993. Reintroduced in November 1994 to sterilize banking system liquidity.

Source: IMF staff.

Appendix 3
Secondary Market Regulations in Selected Countries

Canada
Canada's regulatory framework is characterized by substantial institutional variety. Securities markets, dealers, and brokers are regulated at the provincial level by provincial securities commissions. The Canadian Securities Administration is an umbrella organization for these provincial authorities. It has issued a series of national policy statements in order to encourage a uniform approach to securities regulations.

France
Activities of primary dealers in government securities are regulated by the treasury, but supervision is left to the Banking Commission. Money market brokers are regulated by the Bank of France. The Paris Stock Exchange and brokers active in the Stock Exchange are regulated by the Stock Exchange Commission (an official agency) and by the Association of the French Stock Exchange, a self-regulatory body.

Germany
Securities business of banks, that is, securities trading for the account of clients, will be subject to supervision by the newly created Federal Securities Supervisory Office. Brokers and stock exchanges are supervised by the stock exchange supervisory authorities, in most cases, the Ministries of Economics in the local governments. The liabilities of stock exchange brokers deriving from own-account trading will be governed by regulations issued by the Federal Securities Supervisory Office.

United Kingdom
The Bank of England (BOE) is responsible for supervising the discount houses, the Gilt-Edged Market-Makers, and other participants in the gilt market. The BOE also supervises certain brokers and principals active in a variety of wholesale markets. Regulations are distinguished by institution, namely discount house or Gilt-Edged Market-Maker.

United States
The United States Treasury has rule-meeting authority for the government securities market. As such, dealers and brokers in the government securities market must register with the treasury or the Securities and Exchange Commission (SEC) and meet certain capital and other requirements. Enforcement of the regulations is carried out by the entity's relevant regulatory authority. The Federal Reserve Bank of New York carries out market surveillance and monitors the activities of dealers, but it does not have formal regulatory authority over them. The SEC enforces antifraud regulation under the securities acts.

Appendix 4
Key Features of Securities Transfer Systems in Selected Countries

Canada: Securities Settlement Service of the Canadian Depository for Securities (CDS)

1. Date operations commenced	1981 for equities; 1989 for government debt securities
2. Instruments	Debt securities, including government issues and "strips"; equities
3. Ownership	Six major banks; five trust companies; Investment Dealers' Association, Toronto and Montreal Exchanges—in three equal groups
4. Operator	CDS
5. Securities depository	CDS
6. Settlement bank for funds	Royal Bank of Canada
7. Participants	Regulated financial institutions (including dealers, banks, trust companies, insurance companies, clearing and depository companies); investment institutions (credit unions, unit trusts, pension funds, etc.)
8. Separation of accounts	Customer securities segregated en bloc by dealers only
9. Overseer or regulator	No federal regulatory agency; but Office of the Superintendent of Financial Institutions has been developing a Memorandum of Understanding with provincial securities commissions and CDS to establish cooperative regulatory arrangements

France: Saturne

1. Date operations commenced	September 1988
2. Instruments	Treasury bills, certificates of deposit, CP, medium-term notes
3. Ownership	A department of the Bank of France
4. Operator	Bank of France
5. Securities depository	Bank of France
6. Settlement bank for funds	Bank of France
7. Participants	Banks, securities houses, brokers, insurance companies, pension funds, foreign central banks, international financial institutions, Cedel/Euroclear
8. Separation of accounts	Customer securities can be separately identified by system en bloc (or a series of blocks) or individually at participant's discretion
9. Overseer or regulator	No official oversight; Bank of France provides day-to-day management oversight

Appendix 4 *(continued)*

France: Regalement-Livraison de Titres (RELIT)

1. Date operations commenced	October 1990
2. Instruments	All securities quoted on the stock exchange (shares, bonds, government bonds), nonquoted securities for primary and gray market, SICAVs (mutual funds)
3. Ownership	A non-profit-making intercompany syndicate (GIE RELIT) has been set up with three tasks: developing and testing the system, informing participants of project requirements, and financing the whole project
4. Operator	Operational responsibility rests with SICOVAM (the French central securities depository) and Société des Bourses Françaises (SBF)
5. Securities depository	SICOVAM
6. Settlement bank for funds	Bank of France
7. Participants	Commercial banks, securities houses, stockbrokers
8. Separation of accounts	The securities holdings of participants include securities held for customers as well as the participant's own holdings. The customers' securities can be separately identified in the system's records
9. Overseer or regulator	SBF and Conseil des Bourses de Valeurs (CBV)

Germany: Deutscher Kassenverein AG (DKV)

1. Date operations commenced	1937 (legal arrangement for book entries); 1969/1970 (implementation of Delivery versus Payment (DVP) system)
2. Instruments	Listed fixed interest and dividend-bearing securities
3. Ownership	Stockholders (banks)
4. Operator	DKV (seven branches)
5. Securities depository	DKV
6. Settlement bank for funds	Central bank (Bundesbank)
7. Participants	All banks active in trading or custody of securities; securities brokers and trading firms in respect of own holdings. Admission criteria must be met
8. Separation of accounts	DKV holds and identifies customer securities separately or collectively; the customer's rights are fully protected, and his or her securities cannot be pledged for liabilities of the intermediary
9. Overseer or regulator	DKV is a specialized bank subject to official supervision by the Federal Banking Supervisory Office

Appendix 4 *(concluded)*

United Kingdom: Central Gilts Office (CGO)

1. Date operations commenced   1986

2. Instruments   Stocks registered at Bank of England

3. Ownership   Office of Bank of England, responsible to JMC, a joint Bank of England and Stock Exchange committee

4. Operator   CGO

5. Securities depository   CGO

6. Settlement bank for funds   Intraday claims on assured payment (or guarantor) banks; end-of-day settlement at Bank of England

7. Participants   All participants in gilt-edged market, including market-makers, brokers, discount houses, banks, nominee companies

8. Separation of accounts   Separation not required, unless under Financial Services Act. CGO cannot identify owners of participants' stock

9. Overseer or regulator   CGO governed by Stock Transfer Act of 1982; no formal external supervision; JMC provides oversight

United States: Fedwire (Federal Reserve Book-Entry Transfer System)

1. Date operations commenced   1967

2. Instruments   U.S. dollar-denominated securities of the treasury, federal agencies, and international organizations

3. Ownership   The 12 Federal Reserve banks

4. Operator   Federal Reserve

5. Securities depository   Federal Reserve banks

6. Settlement bank for funds   Federal Reserve banks

7. Participants   Commercial banks, thrift institutions, federal agencies, and international organizations

8. Separation of accounts   System can support a limited number of segregated accounts but does not attribute special significance to them or require segregation

9. Overseer or regulator   Federal Reserve, overseen by the Board of Governors. U.S. Treasury also oversees Fedwire operation with regard to transfer and safekeeping of U.S. Treasuries

Source: Bank for International Settlements.

Appendix 5
Arrangements for Dealing with Variations in Government Cash Balances in Selected Countries

Canada

The government maintains accounts in both the central bank (Bank of Canada) and the commercial banks. The central bank exercises discretion over how much is placed in its accounts and the accounts of commercial banks through the drawdown and redeposit mechanism, and the Bank of Canada actively uses this mechanism to "neutralize" the effect of government transactions and other central bank transactions. In addition, the payment system and the timing of the drawdown and redeposit permits the Bank of Canada to achieve a target change in the level of reserves with precision. The drawdown/redeposit mechanism is the main instrument used to effect "dynamic" or policy-induced changes in bank reserves. The discretion granted to the Bank of Canada (as fiscal agent to the Government of Canada) to alter the distribution of government deposits between itself and the commercial banks is an example of a supporting operational arrangement for monetary management.

Malaysia

In 1981, a money market operation account (MMO) was created, enabling Bank Negara Malaysia to shift government deposits to and from the commercial banks and to and from the government's current account at the central bank. Since then, the instrument has been refined and coordination between the central bank and the fiscal authority has intensified. The central bank is given the authority to recycle the funds in the MMO account, by placing them directly with the market or through principal dealers, consistent with monetary policy objectives. As such, the central bank enjoys full control over the use of this policy instrument for short-term liquidity management.

New Zealand

Neutralization of the impact of government cash flows by the Reserve Bank of New Zealand is done through the issuance of seasonal treasury bills. Although these bills are a government debt instrument, the central bank decides autonomously on their maturities, taking into account the forecast of liquidity flows.

United Kingdom

The government maintains its cash balances primarily in an account with the Bank of England (BOE). Net disbursements of the government are a major determinant of changes in bank reserves. The BOE forecasts changes in the government's position and announces at 9:45 a.m. each day its projection of net reserves for the system, while clearing banks give the BOE their target reserve balances. Intraday open market operations are then conducted to "neutralize" or sterilize the effect of government operations on bank liquidity. In addition, credit facilities are available to discount houses for end-of-day extension of liquidity when required.

United States

The Federal Reserve is the clearing agent for the government. However, the treasury maintains cash balances with the Federal Reserve and the commercial banks (treasury tax and loan accounts). Each day, the treasury shifts balances between these two accounts in sufficient amounts to cover any expected net debit/credit changes in the account at the Federal Reserve while aiming to maintain a low balance at the Federal Reserve because it does not pay interest, while the commercial banks do. Hence, the "expected" change in reserves owing to government transactions is neutralized by the treasury. Nonetheless, variability in reserves from government transactions is significant because of "unexpected" changes in government transactions.

Appendix 6

Treatment of Central Bank Profits and Losses in Selected Countries

Country	Description
Argentina	After replenishment of reserve funds, profits are transferred to the treasury. Losses are earmarked to the reserves; if that is not possible, they are earmarked to capital. The government has no obligation to replenish the capital.
Brazil	Central bank profits are distributed twice a year and, owing to inflation, are generally large.[1] Profits are immediately credited against the central bank's holdings of treasury securities. Losses are charged to a provision account and treated as an interest-bearing claim against the treasury to be repaid during the following fiscal year, before any distribution funds are set aside to maintain the real value of capital and reserves.
Chile	Profits may be allocated to building up reserves (up to 10 percent of total surpluses) and to taxable profits. The bank may ask the ministry of finance for a capital increase or for the transfer of funds to its assets. Any losses are to be first absorbed by the constituted reserves.
Germany	Twenty percent of profits, or DM 20 million, whichever is higher, is transferred to the legal reserves until they reach 5 percent of the total amount of banknotes in circulation; the legal reserves may be used only to offset decline in value and to cover other losses. Up to 10 percent of the remaining net profit may be used to form other reserves. These reserves cannot exceed the Bundesbank's capital. DM 30 million are transferred to a special fund for the purchase of equalization claims (to carry out open market operations). The balance is transferred to the federal government.
Japan	One twentieth of profits is appropriated for a reserve fund to cover losses and for dividends. Special reserve funds may be opened with the permission of the finance ministry. Dividends for the year cannot exceed 5 percent of paid-in capital. After deducting from the surplus, the reserve funds, and dividends, the Bank of Japan must transfer the remainder to the government within two months after the end of the fiscal year.
United States	Stockholders of the Federal Reserve Fund are entitled to receive an annual dividend of 6 percent on the paid-in capital stock. After these dividends have been met, net earnings are paid to the surplus fund of each Federal Reserve Bank. At the discretion of the Secretary of the Treasury, the earnings can be used to supplement the gold reserves or can be applied to the reduction of the outstanding bonded indebtedness of the United States.

Appendix 6 *(concluded)*

Country	Description
Venezuela	Ten percent of the net income is allocated to the General Reserve Fund until it reaches a limit established by the Board of Directors of the central bank. The remainder of profits are paid to the treasury. If the bank's equity capital declines, the Republic is responsible for replenishing the equity capital in the following fiscal period. If this is not possible because of the fiscal situation, the congress may authorize the issuance of a special security at market terms with a maturity of five years or less.

[1]The Central Bank of Brazil has assumed, however, a large foreign debt portfolio, which reduces its profits substantially, because foreign exchange valuation adjustments are charged against profits.

Bibliography

Amihud, Yäkov, Thomas Ho, and Robert Schwartz, 1985, *Market Making and the Changing Structure of the Securities Industry* (Lexington, Massachusetts: Lexington Books).

Auernheimer, Leonardo, 1974, "The Honest Government's Guide to the Revenue from the Creation of Money," *Journal of Political Economy*, Vol. 82 (May/June), pp. 598–606.

Bank for International Settlements, 1990, *Report of the Committee on Interbank Netting Schemes of the Central Banks of the Group of Ten Countries* (Basle).

Bredenkamp, Hugh, 1993, "Conducting Monetary and Credit Policy in Countries of the Former Soviet Union: Some Issues and Options," IMF Working Paper 93/23 (Washington: International Monetary Fund).

Cottarelli, Carlo, 1993, *Limiting Central Bank Credit to the Government: Theory and Practice*, IMF Occasional Paper No. 110 (Washington: International Monetary Fund).

de Fontenay, Patrick, Gian Maria Milesi-Ferretti, and Huw Pill, 1995, "The Role of Foreign Currency Debt in Public Debt Management," IMF Working Paper 95/21 (Washington: International Monetary Fund).

Feldman, Robert A., and Rajnish Mehra, 1993, "Auctions: Theory and Possible Applications to Economies in Transition," IMF Working Paper 93/12 (Washington: International Monetary Fund).

Fischer, Stanley, 1992, "Seigniorage and the Case for a National Money," *Journal of Political Economy*, Vol. 90 (April), pp. 295–313.

Fry, Maxwell J., 1990, "Can a Central Bank Become Insolvent?" (unpublished; Washington: Fiscal Affairs Department, International Monetary Fund).

Hilbers, Paul, 1993, "Monetary Instruments and Their Use During the Transition from a Centrally Planned to a Market Economy," IMF Working Paper 93/87 (Washington: International Monetary Fund).

Leite, Sergio Pereira, 1992, "Coordinating Public Debt and Monetary Management During Financial Reforms," IMF Working Paper 92/84 (Washington: International Monetary Fund).

Leone, Alfredo, 1991, "Effectiveness and Implications of Limits on Central Bank Credit to the Government," in *The Evolving Role of Central Banks*, ed. by Patrick Downes and Reza Vaez-Zadeh (Washington: International Monetary Fund).

MacArthur, Alan, 1990, "Monetary Operations, Financial Market Development, and Central Bank Independence" (unpublished; Washington: Central Banking Department, International Monetary Fund).

Molho, Lazaros, 1989, "European Financial Integration and Revenue from Seigniorage: The Case of Italy," IMF Working Paper 89/41 (Washington: International Monetary Fund).

Robinson, David J., and Peter Stella, 1988, "Amalgamating Central Bank and Fiscal Deficits," in *Measurements of Fiscal Impact: Methodological Issues*, IMF Occasional Paper No. 59, ed. by Mario I. Blejer and Ke-Young Chu (Washington: International Monetary Fund).

Saal, Matthew I., and Lorena M. Zamalloa, 1995, "Use of Central Bank Credit Auctions in Economies in Transition," *Staff Papers*, International Monetary Fund, Vol. 42 (March), pp. 202–24.

Shen, Pu, 1995, "Benefits and Limitations of Inflation-Indexed Treasury Bonds," *Economic Review*, Federal Reserve Bank of Kansas City, Vol. 80, No. 3, pp. 41–56.

Storkey, I., 1993, "Institutional Arrangements of Government Debt Management in New Zealand," paper presented at the OECD/IMF Workshop on Public Debt Management and Government Securities, Paris (July).

Sweden, National Debt Office, 1993, *A Guide to the Swedish Government Securities Market* (Stockholm).

Swinburne, Mark, and Marta Castello-Branco, 1991, "Central Bank Independence and Central Bank Functions," in *The Evolving Role of Central Banks*, ed. by Patrick Downes and Reza Vaez-Zadeh (Washington: International Monetary Fund).

United Kingdom, 1995, *U.K. Debt Management Review*.

United States, Department of the Treasury, Securities and Exchange Commission, and Board of Governors of the Federal Reserve System, 1992, *Joint Report on the Government Securities Market* (Washington: Government Printing Office).

Vaez-Zadeh, Reza, 1991, "Implications and Remedies of Central Bank Losses," in *The Evolving Role of Central Banks*, ed. by Patrick Downes and Reza Vaez-Zadeh (Washington: International Monetary Fund).

2

Institutional and Operational Arrangements for Coordinating Monetary, Fiscal, and Public Debt Management in OECD Countries

Hans J. Blommestein and Eva C. Thunholm*

The possibility that the objectives and operations of fiscal policy, monetary policy, and public debt management may, at times, conflict requires that an efficient institutional framework for coordination and cooperation be in place to resolve differences. Otherwise, lack of coordination between these three policy areas may lead to macroeconomic imbalances and create major uncertainties for the private sector. Insofar as lack of coordination leads to higher-than-targeted inflation, policymakers will lose credibility. The institutional and operational arrangements for the coordination of these policy components have evolved significantly in the countries of the Organization for Economic Development and Cooperation (OECD), influenced by several factors. Central banks in the OECD area have become more autonomous in pursuing the goal of price stability, while fiscal policy has become more transparent and accountable. Debt managers also have become more autonomous in pursuing their objectives, and the objectives themselves have evolved to emphasize minimizing the costs of financing deficits over the long run, for specified levels of risks, in highly liquid market settings. The liberalization of financial markets, including government securities markets, has enabled the necessary coordination of monetary and fiscal authorities and debt managers to take place, in part, through policy adjustments in response to market signals.

*Hans J. Blommestein is a Senior Financial Economist and Eva C. Thunholm is a Senior Economist at the Organization for Economic Cooperation and Development.

This chapter surveys institutional arrangements in a sample of OECD countries and highlights the broad characteristics that govern the design and largely market-based coordination of monetary, fiscal, and debt management policies.

Institutional Framework for Coordination

The state of financial market development, the degree of central bank independence, the degree of accountability of the government authorities, and the transparency of fiscal institutions are interdependent and influence the rationale and operational details of coordination arrangements. Broadly speaking, such arrangements include formal and informal arrangements for cooperation and information sharing between monetary and fiscal agencies, as well as explicit and implicit coordination arrangements. Implicit coordination includes the use of financial markets (by extracting information or giving signals) to align monetary and debt management objectives.

Clearly, the coordination of monetary policy and public debt management is more difficult when the financial system is repressed. In that situation, the financing options for the government are limited, and this, in turn, limits central bank independence. As discussed more fully in Chapter 1, in the early stages of transition to a market economy, in particular when the borrowing needs of the government are substantial, strong coordination is required to attain both monetary stability and market development.

The pursuit of price stability has triggered institutional changes in central banking, in fiscal governance, and in debt management practices. Effective central bank independence is an important institutional factor in bringing about low inflation and maintaining credibility in the anti-inflationary stance of policies.[1] Central bank independence necessarily constrains options for public debt management, calling for institutional arrangements in support of market-based debt management. In addition, it has been argued that the degree of transparency and accountability of fiscal and budgetary institutions may be even more important than the formal independence of central banks in maintaining price stability.[2] The lack of political support for or social consensus about a low-inflation environment may manifest itself in nontransparent fiscal and budgetary institutions. In the OECD area, many countries have introduced an institutional framework for efficient governance in the public sector, particularly more trans-

---

[1]See Cukierman, Webb, and Neyapti (1992); Pollard (1993).
[2]See Zarazaga (1992, 1993) for examples and a theoretical model.

parency and accountability in fiscal and budgetary institutions.[3] The world-wide trends toward financial sector deregulation, the liberalization of cross-border capital flows, and the resulting internationalization of financial markets have led to a reorientation of public debt management policies. A key feature has been the strengthening of the role of market principles in government debt management. This reorientation has been accompanied by structural changes in government securities markets, including a strengthening of market microstructure (see Chapter 7) and of the regulatory framework.[4] Against this background, the coordination of monetary and public debt management policies in OECD countries has reflected the common goal of price stability and the emerging trend toward transparency and accountability and autonomy of fiscal and monetary institutions.

In this institutional setting and given the shared macroeconomic objectives of the policymakers, the *strategic parameters* for the conduct of monetary control, fiscal policy, and public debt management are defined by the institutional separation of objectives and instruments:

- monetary authorities pursue price stability without political interference by operating market-based instruments in liquid money markets that are closely linked to government securities markets;
- fiscal authorities pursue transparent tax and expenditure policies and are held accountable to the budget and budgetary process; and
- public debt managers act with considerable autonomy to meet the gross borrowing requirements of the government, based on well-specified risk-return parameters, in liberalized money and securities markets that are liquid and efficient.

With each agency pursuing its own strategy—within a macroeconomic policy framework—less explicit coordination is required at the level of policy objectives, beyond the setting of broad parameters within which objectives are pursued, except in exceptional circumstances (e.g., during systemic crisis) when macroeconomic policy priorities have to be reset. On the other hand, explicit coordination regularly takes place at the tactical or operational level. Moreover, indirect or implicit coordination via the market is an important institutional feature of the conduct of monetary control, fiscal policy, and public debt management in OECD countries. Financial market rates (interest rates, exchange rates, prices on futures markets, secondary market prices of debt instruments), as well as bond credit ratings by private sector agencies, are used as important input into

---

[3]There is a clear parallel with the conditions for effective corporate governance in the private sector.

[4]Financing government deficits through foreign currency debt is not covered in this paper. See, for details, e.g., Guidotti and Kumar (1991) and de Fontenay, Milesi-Feretti, and Pill (1995) and references therein.

the decision making of the central bank, ministry of finance, and debt management agency. Under ideal circumstances, a smooth adjustment process leading to an alignment of policy goals and actions—needed to satisfy the government budget constraint—would take place. In this way, financial markets would act as a disciplinary mechanism by giving timely and correct signals to policymakers to adjust their policies. Thus, making explicit coordination at the strategic level is unnecessary in normal circumstances.[5]

In reality, adjustments usually take place in a less orderly fashion, characterized by sudden and major changes in financial market rates, as well as over- or undershooting of equilibrium rates. Financial market turbulence provides an important rationale for explicit coordination at the tactical level and in extreme circumstances, such as an exchange rate or balance of payments crisis, at the policy level.

Overview of Institutional Arrangements for Monetary, Fiscal, and Public Debt Policies

The Appendix at the end of this chapter provides a concise overview of institutional arrangements for monetary and debt management in ten OECD countries whose government securities markets are at different levels of development. The information is provided on six attributes that characterize monetary and debt management objectives and operations: the authority responsible for debt management; funding sources for public sector deficit; instruments of monetary policy; institutional coordination arrangements; instruments and selling techniques in the primary issue market; and secondary market arrangements. Information in the Appendix supports the notion that both central bankers and public debt managers have become more autonomous. Central bank credit to government has been abolished or sharply contracted. Both monetary policy and public debt management have become more market-oriented. Markets have become more liquid and efficient.

Central Bank Independence and Credit to Government

In recent years, many OECD countries have adopted legislative proposals to make central banks more independent and less subject to government directives. Formal constraints on central bank credit to government are a key component of bank independence and, therefore, of (implicit) coordination arrangements between the monetary and fiscal authorities. In fact, automatic and unlimited access to central bank credit

---

[5]Similar arguments have been used to explain why the nature of international economic policy coordination has changed in response to an increase in international capital mobility (see Blommestein (1991)).

would subordinate both monetary policy and public debt management to the government. The Maastricht Treaty envisages an independent central bank with strict constraints on direct central bank credit to European Union (EU) governments: overdraft facilities and other types of credit facilities for governments are prohibited, and the Treaty also forbids the direct purchase of government securities in the primary market by the future European Central Bank or EU central banks. The majority of OECD countries do not place *formal* constraints on indirect central bank credit to government, that is, on the bank's voluntary purchases of government securities in the secondary market (e.g., outright open market operations, repurchase agreements ("repos"), acquiring government paper as collateral for refinancing the banking sector). Nevertheless, there are often *informal* constraints on creating indirect central bank credit. One way this is accomplished is by stating that open market operations can be performed only for monetary policy reasons (e.g., in Austria, Germany, and Portugal). Another way is to restrict the transfer of seigniorage to the government—in most countries, central bank profits are used to maintain the real value of capital and reserves; in several countries, legal provisions stipulate that central bank profits should also be credited against the bank's holdings of government securities; and in the great majority of countries the rest of the profits are transferred to the government.

Central Bank as Advisor, Issuing Agency, and Fiscal Agent to the Government

The central bank should not be assigned responsibilities that could (potentially) conflict with its price stability mandate. This means that the tasks assigned to the central bank in public debt management should not be in (potential) conflict with its monetary policy responsibility. The precise role of the central bank in public debt management varies across OECD countries, but it generally involves the following activities:

- As advisor, the central bank provides advice on the design of the debt program, the mix of debt instruments, and the structure of the stock of debt. These aspects provide stability to the overall debt program, which in turn facilitates the smooth functioning of markets, creating a stable environment for the conduct of monetary operations and thus enhancing the scope for monetary control.
- As issuing agency, the central bank organizes rules and procedures for selling and delivering securities and for collecting payments for the government.
- As fiscal agent, the central bank makes and receives payments (including the servicing of principal and interest payments to investors).

The bank's role of cashier is an important reason for the government to have deposits with it.

These activities can largely be considered part of the policymaking process and administration of public debt management but not the management of public debt or the implementation of the debt program. The administrative role of the central bank in public debt management can be justified on the basis of comparative advantage, as long as it is recognized that only these tasks should be assigned and as long as it does not interfere with the central bank's monetary management. Indeed, it has been argued that involvement of central banks in managing public debt can reduce the independence of central banks in pursuing the appropriate monetary policy in support of price stability (Roll (1993)). At the same time, as debt stocks have mushroomed in OECD countries, pursuing independent debt management strategies has gained importance in government policymaking, leading to a more restricted operational role of central banks in debt management.[6] In many cases where central banks play an active role in debt management, formal institutional arrangements have been introduced to clarify the relative role of the central bank in conducting debt management operations on behalf of the treasury.[7]

Organization of Debt Management Agency

The strengthening of the role of market principles has been an important feature of public debt management in OECD countries. This trend has been accompanied by a process of making the authorities of debt management operations more independent from political decision making. In some countries—Sweden, Ireland, Austria, and New Zealand—this has taken the form of separate debt management agencies, which are directly responsible for achieving the goals of debt management, principally cost minimization, within well-specified policy parameters generally set by the ministry of finance. These agencies are not constrained by civil service salary scales and other conditions of employment. More autonomous debt management agencies may increase the institutional resistance to the proclivity of governments to generate inflation.

Intervention Instruments for Monetary Management

Most central banks in OECD countries use government securities as an instrument of monetary intervention. The fact that government securities

---

[6]See Chapters 3 and 4 for a discussion of institutional arrangements for debt management and the Note by the Editors at the end of Chapter 9 for a summary of recent changes in debt management practices in the United Kingdom.

[7]For a recent example, see Bank of England and H.M. Treasury (1995).

may serve a dual purpose—monetary and debt management—is an important reason for establishing coordinating arrangements between the monetary and fiscal authorities. The degree of coordination is a function of the degree of development of the money and government securities markets. A relatively low degree of coordination is required in countries with liquid money and capital markets, because deficit financing takes place in the primary market and monetary management can be conducted effectively in the money market and the secondary market for government securities. Analysis suggests that the need for coordination is also low or minimal when the central bank intervenes using specifically designed instruments such as nongovernment paper (e.g., central bank bills) or specifically designated government securities (e.g., treasury bills of a specific maturity that are used exclusively for monetary management). Even in this case, arrangements must clearly indicate the joint and separate responsibilities of the central bank, finance ministry, and debt management agency.

Coordination Committees or Groups

Committees or working groups to coordinate monetary policy and public debt management can play a useful role in reducing or eliminating (potential) conflicts between the objectives of the central bank, finance ministry, and debt management agency. They may also contribute to the design and implementation of institutions and operating procedures to improve the functioning of money and government securities markets. The mandate (advisory, policy design, and planning), status (formal or informal, high-level or working-level), and operations of these committees or groups vary across countries (see the Appendix to this chapter).

Monitoring and Auditing Fiscal Objectives

Many OECD countries have taken measures to increase the transparency and accountability of fiscal institutions. Key elements of such a framework include proper fiscal accounts, strict disclosure requirements, explicit targets for budget balance as well as the stock of debt, and auditing procedures. For example, the New Zealand Government has passed a Fiscal Responsibility Act that seeks to provide an institutional framework with incentives to avoid lax fiscal policies. Several countries have introduced institutional constraints on governments to prevent them from running large and persistent deficits. For example, the protocol on the excessive deficit procedure annexed to the Maastricht Treaty stipulates government deficit and public debt criteria.

Government Securities Market Infrastructure

Government securities markets have become more efficient as part of financial liberalization more generally. An important feature of the reorientation of public debt management has been the strengthening of market principles. This has led to a strong interest of debt managers for efficient financial markets, including more efficient primary and secondary markets. Most government paper is being sold under competitive conditions, with auction techniques playing a dominant role. A second important indication of the trend toward the implementation of market principles has been the progressive abolition of privileged access by the government to domestic sources of finance. The number of OECD countries that have mandatory investment regulations in favor of government securities and liquidity ratio requirements has declined sharply. The central bank's role as the "underwriter-of-last-resort" of new government issues has been abolished or sharply reduced. In countries where the central bank, in its capacity as fiscal agent for the government, takes up new issues of government paper for resale to the market, it is now standard practice that such "tap issues" can be sold only into the secondary market if competitive yields are offered.

The introduction of market principles has led to more transparency for the framework of public debt management. In particular, more transparent and predictable issuance policies have led to clearer public statements about the allocation of roles among the central bank, finance ministry, and debt management agencies. It has also made debt managers more independent and sophisticated. The trend toward more active cash management provides an example of this growing sophistication. A second reason for more independent and sophisticated debt management practices is that governments are increasingly denied access to central bank credit.

The market infrastructure for trading government securities has been improved. Improved market functioning and market management support the government's debt management objectives, including the fixing of terms of new issues, securing continued market access, and achieving orderly market conditions. Sound secondary markets are typically associated with a substantial volume of outstanding government securities widely distributed among a large number of holders; safe and efficient clearing and settlement systems; a transparent and equitable regulatory and supervisory framework; the presence of "market-makers" (primary dealers or specialists in government securities); and reliable automation systems. In practice, the major OECD government securities markets are converging on a model characterized by the following main features:

- a market-making structure based on primary dealers;
- regular and predictable issuance, entirely or predominantly through auctions;
- development of a repo market to help fund securities positions by dealers; and
- a strips market to adapt the features of the securities to investors' needs.

Concluding Remarks

Although considerable diversity still exists among OECD countries in the area of institutional arrangements for monetary and debt management and their coordination, reflecting principally the state of development of financial markets, a distinct convergence of institutional arrangements for coordination is also evident. As monetary and debt management have become more market-oriented, and as markets have become more liquid, more efficient, and more integrated globally, the need for transparency and accountability of both monetary and fiscal institutions has grown.

Appendix
Overview of Institutional Arrangements in Ten OECD Countries

Debt Management Authorities	Funding Sources for Public Sector Deficit	Instruments of Monetary Policy	Institutional Coordination Arrangements	Markets	
				Primary	Secondary
Finland					
The MOF is responsible for the formulation of monetary and debt management policy. Monetary policy is executed by the Bank of Finland, by focusing on the impact of its operations on liquidity and interest rates. Debt management policy is executed by the State Treasury Office, which, acting as agent for the ministry, is responsible for issuing government securities.	Issuance of securities in domestic and foreign markets. The Bank of Finland has only rarely and under exceptional circumstances extended credit to the government.	The Bank of Finland conducts open market operations, buying and selling banks' certificates of deposit. Treasury bills are also used in money market interventions. The bank does not intervene in the treasury bond market.	A joint working group consisting of officials from the Bank of Finland, the MOF, and the State Treasury Office meets regularly for purposes of coordination. Its mandate is primarily consultative. Main topics of discussion are the division of the borrowing requirement between markka-denominated and foreign-currency-denominated issues, and the timing of the issues.	The State Treasury Office issues 1- to 12-month treasury bills, 2- to 8-year yield bonds for personal investors, and 2- to 10-year serial bonds for institutional investors. T-bills are sold at weekly auctions and both noncompetitive and multiple price bids are accepted. There are regular auctions for serial bonds, while yield bonds are sold to banks for resale to the general public. A primary dealer system has been in operation since 1992.	Government securities are traded on the OTC market, which operates a phone- and screen-based multiple quotation system. The Bank of Finland plays a central role in the clearing and settlement of government securities, through the Helsinki Money Market Center, of which it is a principal shareholder.

Germany

The Bundesbank is responsible for the formulation of monetary policy and legally independent of the government. The government prepares the budget and decides on appropriate ways to cover the deficit and which instruments should be used to raise funds, within a legally set limit on the annual increase in new government debt. The Bundesbank acts as the fiscal and selling agent for government securities issues.	Issuance of federal long-term bonds and other debt instruments. Prior to the Maastricht Treaty ratification, short-term credit lines to the government were extended, with interest charged at the Lombard rate.	Weekly repurchase operations, and reserve requirements.	There are no institutional coordination arrangements. An advance approval from the Bundesbank for issues of bonds by public authorities is required. The terms of individual issues are agreed upon through a committee with representatives of the MOF (or other public sector issuer), the Bundesbank, and market participants.	The Bundesbank manages the Federal Bond Consortium through which all government bonds are launched. Federal long-term bonds are the most important instrument, issued up to 8 times a year through a combination of bank syndicate and auction, with a separate tranche reserved for the Bundesbank for later resale on the secondary market. The tap technique is used for 5-year special notes, and private placements are sometimes arranged directly between the federal government and investors.	Most marketable government securities are traded on the stock exchanges. The Bundesbank intervenes to support prices and ensure liquidity and thus performs a role that, in other countries, is carried out by market-makers.

Overview of Institutional Arrangements in Ten OECD Countries *(continued)*

Debt Management Authorities	Funding Sources for Public Sector Deficit	Instruments of Monetary Policy	Institutional Coordination Arrangements	Markets	
				Primary	Secondary
Greece					
Fiscal policy and public debt management are the responsibility of the MOF. The CB formulates and implements monetary policy and acts as fiscal agent for public debt issues.	Issuance of marketable securities. CB credit to the government was discontinued as of January 1, 1994. Until 1992, it amounted to 10 percent of budget expenditure and was thereafter gradually scaled down.	Rediscount rate and Lombard facility were introduced in 1993 as means of controlling market liquidity. Open market operations and repurchase agreements in the interbank market.	A joint committee of the MOF and the CB decides on matters concerning public debt management based on proposals submitted by the CB.	Auction techniques for placing government securities were experimentally introduced in 1993 for 6-month treasury bills and 2-year drachma bonds, but have not yet replaced the more common subscription method using commercial banks as intermediaries.	The secondary market for government securities is still relatively thin, although progress toward a more efficient market has been made in the past 2 years, during which period issues in book-entry form and certain other innovations were introduced. All government securities are listed on the Athens Stock Exchange, but the volume of transactions is small in proportion to total amount outstanding.

Ireland

The CB is independent in carrying out its functions, including the formulation and implementation of monetary policy. Government debt management is carried out under legislation by the National Treasury Management Agency (independently of the CB), subject to the ultimate control and general supervision of the MOF. The CB acts as fiscal agent to the agency, as well as banker to the government.

In principle, issuance of government securities is on the domestic and foreign markets; but in practice, net funding is restricted to domestic borrowing.

Repurchase agreements and fixed-term deposit operations on the interbank market, mostly overnight or at one-week terms.

Formal day-to-day information transmission from the agency to the CB. Essentially, an information exchange is supplemented by formal policy coordination in crisis situations.

The government funding program is met through sales on "tap," supplemented by occasional auctions. The bond market operates through the stock exchange, and the government broker acts as the interface between the agency and the market. Neither the MOF nor the CB has any role in relation to the day-to-day issuance of securities by the agency.

Trading in government bonds occurs through the Irish Stock Exchange with bid and offer prices posted by authorized stockbrokers. Dealt prices are announced through the Stock Exchange information system within 15 minutes of dealing. The agency maintains a presence in the secondary market through a trader who manages a small fund for purposes of improving liquidity, stabilization, and market intelligence. The CB does not operate in the secondary market for government securities but is responsible for all aspects of registration and settlement.

Overview of Institutional Arrangements in Ten OECD Countries *(continued)*

Debt Management Authorities	Funding Sources for Public Sector Deficit	Instruments of Monetary Policy	Institutional Coordination Arrangements	Markets	
				Primary	Secondary
Italy					
Monetary policy is formulated and implemented by the Banca d'Italia. The treasury is responsible for debt management policy, but the Banca d'Italia fulfills a number of debt management functions, such as fiscal agent, issuing manager, and financial advisor.	Issuance of treasury bills and treasury notes. Foreign borrowings. Prior to January 1994, the treasury obtained short-term funding from Banca d'Italia in the form of a credit line limited to 14 percent of budgetary expenditure.	Primarily open market operations, overnight and term in government securities.	No formal arrangements, but in advising the treasury on its recourse to the market, the Banca d'Italia takes into account the amount of available free bank reserves, money supply growth, and interest rate levels.	The amount and type of securities the treasury can issue is regulated by law; lately treasury bills (2, 6, 12 months), floating rate treasury certificates (7 years), ECU-denominated treasury credit certificates (5 years). T-bills are sold by competitive bid auction while T-bonds and credit certificates are sold at uniform-price auctions according to a regular schedule. Since the early 1980s, the Banca d'Italia no longer acts as a residual purchaser of securities at issue.	The bulk of open market operations are carried out on a screen-based wholesale market, which includes 30 primary dealers committed to quote continuous bid and offer prices. Since 1994, there have been specialist market-makers (12).

Spain

The Bank of Spain is fully independent in its monetary management. The treasury decides on public debt management policy issues after consultation with the Bank of Spain, which acts as fiscal agent and is entrusted with the responsibility for organizing and managing primary and secondary market activity.

Issuance of marketable securities in domestic markets, as well as various forms of external borrowings. The former system of central bank credit to government was curtailed in 1990 and discontinued as of January 1, 1994.

Open market operations in government securities, mainly through 10-day (maximum) repurchase agreements.

A committee, formed in 1983 with members from the CB and the treasury, meets regularly in advance of auctions to resolve possible conflicts regarding desirable levels of interest rates. The final decision is legally the prerogative of the treasury but operationally becomes subordinate to the Bank of Spain monetary policy conduct.

The maximum number of issues is regulated by the budget law. Within that limit, the range of instruments and their characteristics are decided on by the treasury. Auctions are held according to a published, regular schedule, although extraordinary issues are allowed. Treasury bills (3, 6, 12 months) are exclusively auctioned while treasury bonds (3–5, 5–10 years) are auctioned, followed by subscription periods at a fixed price for small investors. A primary dealer system is in operation.

A highly efficient OTC screen-based market is operated in part by primary dealers charged with maintaining active and continuous two-way trading. There is sizable direct participation by nonresidents (very little trade in Spanish government securities takes place abroad).

Overview of Institutional Arrangements in Ten OECD Countries (continued)

Debt Management Authorities	Funding Sources for Public Sector Deficit	Instruments of Monetary Policy	Institutional Coordination Arrangements	Markets	
				Primary	Secondary
Sweden					
The Riksbank is responsible for formulation and implementation of monetary policy. The National Debt Office, an independent government agency subordinate to the MOF, is the sole institution authorized to borrow on behalf of the Kingdom. It is solely responsible for debt management both in terms of policy and issuing functions.	Issuance of government securities in domestic and foreign markets. For short-term cash management purposes, the debt office until July 1994 maintained a credit line with the Riksbank, as a complement to the issuance of treasury bills. Interest on drawings was paid at the market overnight rate. In preparation for compliance with the Maastricht Treaty, this credit line was canceled.	Open market operations, cash reserve requirements for banks and finance companies. Regulatory instruments with specially obtained consent of the government.	The debt office must inform the Riksbank on direction of borrowing activities. This takes place informally through two advisory groups (composed of officials from the bank, the debt office, and the MOF) for foreign currency and for krona borrowings. In principle, monetary policy considerations would prevail over debt policy considerations in case of conflict. However, the bank is now normally able to carry out its monetary policy without recourse to debt management and, as a consequence, the advisory groups now take a more passive role, mainly serving as a forum for the exchange of information.	Treasury bills (3, 6, 12 months) and treasury bonds (2–16 years) are issued by the debt office at multiple-price auctions according to a fixed calendar published in advance. Only authorized primary dealers can participate directly in the auctions. A predetermined share of the total stock issued was traditionally offered to the Riksbank at the average auction price, but since March 1995, the Riksbank has made all its purchases in the secondary market. To improve secondary-market liquidity, the debt office also carries out a modest volume of tap issues, for which the Riksbank acts as agent.	OTC market built on a market-maker system with an interbank market and an investors' market. Dealers acting as market-makers are approved by the debt office and have agreed to quote each other continuous two-way prices. The debt office intervenes only to withdraw old illiquid issues and replace them with more liquid T-bills or T-bonds.

Turkey

Monetary policy is formulated and implemented by the CB. The treasury is the sole authority in debt management, but the CB acts as fiscal agent for the government.	Liquidity and reserve requirement ratios, discount window. Open market operations.	Official coordination through joint working groups only as regards auction procedures in the primary market. Informal coordination on other matters takes place between the CB and the treasury.	Both auction and tap techniques are used: 3-, 6-, and 9-month T-bills and 1-year T-bonds are sold at weekly multiple-price auctions; 2- to 5-year variable rate T-bonds are issued on tap to investors. Auctions are open to all participants but guarantees asked from participants favor financial institutions. Direct sales of T-bills to the public via banks were introduced in 1992.	Government securities are traded on the Istanbul Stock Exchange, through a fully computerized system. There is also a very active OTC market, dominated by re-purchase operations.
Short-term advances from the CB, as well as sale of marketable securities. The maximum amount of such advances is stipulated by law (15 percent of total budgetary appropriations), but the actual amount as well as interest charged is determined by the CB and the Prime Minister.				

Overview of Institutional Arrangements in Ten OECD Countries (continued)

Debt Management Authorities	Funding Sources for Public Sector Deficit	Instruments of Monetary Policy	Institutional Coordination Arrangements	Markets	
				Primary	Secondary
United Kingdom Ultimate responsibility for both monetary policy and debt management rests with the treasury, advised by the Bank of England on both a regular and an ad hoc basis. The Bank of England implements policy in both areas, thus ensuring consistency from the onset. It acts as the government debt manager, giving advice on the choice of securities for issue and amounts involved, but new issues of government securities require the prior approval of a treasury minister.	Under the full fund policy in force since 1985/86, the public sector borrowing requirement plus maturing debt and any net increase in foreign exchange reserves must be funded by sales of longer-term government debt to the private sector. The bank makes short-term advances to cover shortfalls in the government's current account at the bank and also purchases government debt at issue for subsequent sale on tap to investors in the secondary market.	Open market operations; repurchase agreements.	Debt management policy is discussed at regular monthly meetings between the treasury and the Bank of England, chaired by a treasury minister. Monetary policy is likewise discussed at joint meetings by officials, highlighted by a separate monthly meeting between the Chancellor of the Exchequer and the Governor of the Bank of England.	Two methods of issue are used: (1) public offers of larger amounts by auction and, infrequently, tender; and (2) placing with the Bank of England for subsequent sale on tap to primary dealers in gilts. Auctions are conducted on a multiple-price basis and follow a regular timetable, although no preannounced calendar is published.	All secondary market operations are carried out by the bank from its own dealing room, and the treasury thus has no operating presence. There are 19 major gilt market makers (GEMMs), 8 stock exchange money brokers (SEMBs), and 3 interdealer brokers (IDBs) participating in various capacities in the secondary market keeping in close relationship with the Bank of England, which ensures an orderly and liquid market, as well as undertakes the financial supervision of these separate institutions.

United States

The United States Treasury and the Federal Reserve Board have traditionally maintained independence in their respective tasks of debt management and conduct of monetary policy. The goal of the treasury is to finance increasing amounts of federal debt with minimum disruption to financial markets, observing regularity and predictability of an issuance. The Federal Reserve acts as fiscal agent for the treasury and in this capacity conducts all auctions, collects proceeds, and maintains the commercial book-entry system.	Issuance of marketable securities. Treasury statutory authority to borrow from the Federal Reserve expired in 1981.	Open market operations in government securities.	There are no formal arrangements, but periodic meetings of senior staff of the treasury and the Federal Reserve take place for exchange of information and the coordination of operational issues.	The treasury issues bills (13, 26, 52 weeks), notes (1–10 years), and bonds (over 10 years). Bills have been auctioned since their introduction in 1929, while notes and bonds have been auctioned since 1970, having been sold through subscription previously. All auctions are now conducted on a yield basis, according to the multiple-price system with a few exceptions. Thirty-eight primary dealers participate in the auctions on a nonexclusive basis.	In its conduct of open market operations, the Federal Reserve is an active participant in the secondary market. Secondary-market book-entry transactions are cleared and settled over Fedwire on delivery-versus-payment basis. The CHIPS system settles participants' net debits and credits at the close of each business day, as opposed to the gross settlement of each individual transaction executed by Fedwire. There is also the GSCC, a private clearing organization whose member organizations are netted multilaterally, greatly reducing the volume of Fedwire activity at the end of a day.

Source: Organization for Economic Cooperation and Development.
Note: CB = central bank; MOF = ministry of finance; OTC = over the counter; T-bills = treasury bills; T-bonds = treasury bonds.

Bibliography

Bank of England and H.M. Treasury, 1995, *Report on the Debt Management Review* (July).

Blommestein, Hans, ed., 1991, *The Reality of International Economic Policy Coordination* (Amsterdam: North-Holland).

Cukierman, Alex, Steven B. Webb, and Bilin Neyapti, 1992, "Measuring the Independence of Central Banks and Its Effect on Policy Outcomes," *World Bank Economic Review*, Vol. 6 (September), pp. 353–98.

de Fontenay, Patrick, Gian Maria Milesi-Ferretti, and Huw Pill, 1995, "The Role of Foreign Currency Debt in Public Debt Management," IMF Working Paper 95/21 (Washington: International Monetary Fund).

Guidotti, Pablo E., and Manmohan S. Kumar, 1991, *Domestic Public Debt of Externally Indebted Countries*, IMF Occasional Paper No. 80 (Washington: International Monetary Fund).

Pollard, Patricia S., 1993, "Central Bank Independence and Economic Performance," *Federal Reserve Bank of St. Louis Review*, Vol. 75 (July–August), pp. 21–36.

Roll, Erie, and panel, 1993, *Independent and Accountable—A New Mandate for the Bank of England*, Report of an Independent Panel chaired by Eric Roll (London: Center for Economic Policy Research).

Zarazaga, Carlos, 1992, "Hyperinflations, Institutions, and Moral Hazard in the Appropriation of Seigniorage" (doctoral dissertation; University of Minnesota).

——— , 1993, "Hyperinflations and Moral Hazard in the Appropriation of Seigniorage," Federal Reserve Bank of Philadelphia Working Paper No. 93–26 (Philadelphia).

II

Institutions and Operating Arrangements for Public Debt Management and Monetary Control

3

Debt Management Functions and Their Location

Lars Kalderen *

This chapter considers the functions that governments should perform in order to manage the public debt in a satisfactory way. While the perspective is that of a government debt manager—rather than a central banker—a section toward the end of the chapter discusses the issue of coordination of debt management with monetary control. As used in this context, the term "government debt manager" covers all the officials—from the minister of finance down—who have the responsibility for proposing the government's debt management objectives and instruments and for implementing them after their acceptance by the country's highest constitutional authority, usually the parliament.[1]

Like the rest of the book, this chapter is concerned with *domestic* public debt in contrast to *external* debt. In fact, it is the latter that has received most of the attention in the literature; a wide measure of agreement has emerged among experts with regard to how governments should perform their role of international debtor, the technical capacity and staff competencies needed, and so forth. Agreement is less advanced on the administrative and institutional arrangements that are desirable in the area of domestic public debt.

For many countries the concept of domestic debt is less clear-cut today than it was some years ago, and particularly before the dismantling of exchange restrictions and the deregulation of financial markets in the 1980s. Earlier, domestic public debt could be defined as loans to the government from residents of its own country and denominated in its own

---

*Lars Kalderen is a former Director General, Swedish National Debt Office, Sweden.
[1]For an elaboration of the role and position of the government debt manager, see Bröker (1993), especially Chapter 4.

currency. Inconvertibility of the local currency made such debt unattractive to nonresidents—sometimes they were even forbidden to hold such debt—while residents were prevented from investing in currencies other than their own. There was a simple identity between debt issued in local currency and the financial claims on the public sector held by residents. But today, in most countries in the Organization for Economic Coordination and Development (OECD) and many others, nonresidents are major holders of local currency debt, while the savings of residents may be freely invested in the public debt of other countries, as well as in the foreign currency debt of their own government. The development of computerized information and communications systems and of financial technology has further reduced the barrier between international and domestic markets. Reflecting these new realities, debt administration units in some countries are becoming more integrated in their handling of external and domestic debt, somewhat reversing the trend of the 1970s and 1980s. Nonetheless, in this chapter we are only concerned with debt instruments issued in the domestic market primarily for domestic investors, and with the arrangements necessary for relations with that market.

Objectives

A discussion of domestic debt management in a particular country should begin with a statement about the objectives to be achieved (see Chapter 4 for a survey of countries' objectives). These should be clear and noncontradictory, in order to allow for the design of a borrowing program that can be monitored and evaluated against stated aims. A number of such objectives, classified in various ways, are offered by the literature (see Bröker (1993), Chapter 3). There is agreement that the debt manager's basic objective must be to cover the government's borrowing needs. A common primary objective is to minimize the cost of debt (at a given level of risk or, alternatively, to minimize risk within acceptable cost limits). However, in economies in transition, cost minimization may lead to undesirable effects, such as excessive borrowing from the central bank (fueling inflation) or from "captive markets" at below-market interest rates (retarding the development of secondary markets) (see Chapter 1). Instead, other, secondary motives should have priority: the use of government debt to strengthen monetary management (i.e., to coordinate debt activities with the monetary policies of the central bank, including more borrowing from nonbank sources) or improving the functioning of financial markets, particularly the treasury bill and bond market, through interest liberalization and the integration of various market segments. A special objective, which has sometimes been permitted to override the cost-effectiveness target, is the promotion of private household financial savings through the offer of attractive retail instruments.

Such a collection—or, rather, hierarchy—of objectives of domestic debt management will vary across countries at any one time, and over time for a particular country. Thus, any map of the "landscape" of motives and national institutions for debt management will present a wide variety of models, and for many countries the map will tend to become obsolete in only a few years because of rapid evolution of its economic and financial conditions. What is more, aims as defined in public documents—with language often inspired by international models—may not correspond to actions as observed "on the ground," because the exact allocation of roles to debt management institutions is determined not only by rational considerations but also by various sociopolitical factors with their roots in the history and traditions of a particular country. Nonetheless, establishing an appropriate hierarchy of objectives is an important task of the authorities: the examples given in the following sections should be regarded as illustrations of some of the choices that newcomers to debt management may have to confront rather than as ideal models.

Functions

For a description of public debt management in terms of functions and the institutions that perform them, we need an agreed-upon list, similar to the ones adopted in the field of external debt.[2] Although no such list exists as yet, we can start with a number of functions that are clearly fundamental for a public debt management operation, namely, *accounting*, which provides a firm basis for all other activities, and *payment of debt service* (interest and redemption). New borrowings will be planned according to needs established by *forecasting* of the budget deficit and of debt repayments and other relevant transactions, and will be undertaken subject to established guidelines for *policy and planning*, which will determine volume of issue as well as the choice of markets and instruments. New funds for the government will be raised by *primary issuance*, which requires special *selling arrangements* and which will benefit from deep and liquid *secondary markets*, where both the debt manager and the monetary authorities can intervene to promote their individual and joint objectives. In many countries, separate arrangements have been created for the functions of *payment and settlement* of trades in securities, and for *information* to and among market participants. Finally, the sound development of a financial market requires an effective supervisory function.

---

[2]See, for example, United Nations Conference on Trade and Development (UNCTAD) (1989).

Accounting Function

The debt crisis of the 1980s focused attention on the need for determining in detail the extent of, and for controlling, a country's external debt in general and that of the public sector in particular. To this end, a large number of countries have installed microcomputer-based systems for recording and reporting external debt and for triggering debt-service payments. These systems can also be used for the sophisticated management of liabilities. Moreover, they can be equipped to handle domestic debt. The development of these systems and the building up of the necessary database in each country have typically taken place alongside the existing systems of government accounts, budgeting, and cash management. Recently, however, and especially in Latin America, considerable effort has been devoted to combining these four systems into an *electronically integrated financial management system*, in which data entered into any one of the four subsystems will be immediately available in all four, with consequent savings in time and effort and with a significant reduction of the potential for human error in manual data entry. Thus, a complete and up-to-date debt system will not only ensure accurate debt reporting and timely payment of debt service, including redemption, but will also enhance the reliability of the accounting information system as well as the budget system, both providing key inputs for the calculation of borrowing requirements. Needless to say, all subsystems will have to satisfy the standards for audit and control that are set for the accounting system. These improved financial statistics will aide in the formulation of monetary policies and promote the dialogue between the state as an issuer and the market for government securities. The efforts to introduce integrated financial management systems are being supported by the World Bank and a number of other donor agencies.

Forecasting Function

The treasury's borrowing requirements are a function of the flows of government revenue and expenditure over time. Such flows should be forecast on a weekly and monthly basis, so that cost-effective arrangements can be put in place for the financing of cash deficits and for the investment of temporary surpluses. Forecasters depend heavily on projections based on the accounting system but must often supplement them with analytical work on specific issues, surveys among government agencies, and so forth. In the latter case, the quality of the information received is clearly influenced by the ability of the treasury to engage in a constructive dialogue with the suppliers of data and forecasts. Calculating debt-service payments when a large share of the debt stock has been raised in the form of short-term borrowings, or at floating rates of interest, further complicates forecasting. Thus, governments must have a satisfactory capacity to analyze and project trends in the global and national economy and in the financial markets.

The size of the borrowing requirement can be reduced by the treasury's use of liquidity management techniques. Drawings on the treasury account should be matched with actual expenditures by the agencies, while revenues should be collected as promptly as possible. The establishment of a "single account" is the fundamental characteristic of a modern cash management system; into this account all government revenues should be immediately deposited, and from it all expenditures should be paid.

For short-term cash requirements, most treasuries have a credit line with the central bank (although in the United States and Canada, for example, the government borrows sufficiently to maintain positive cash balances with the central bank and banking system). In some cases credit is provided interest-free, whereas in others, governments pay market or near-market rates. However, under the Maastricht Treaty, members of the European Union may no longer indulge in central bank financing of budget deficits, and those countries are now gradually winding down previous arrangements, replacing them with borrowings in the money market. Again, this will increase demands on treasury staff to keep in touch with and skillfully handle deals in the short-term markets.

Policy and Planning Function

For each country, the objectives of domestic debt management must be translated into *operating policies* and *borrowing programs*. Gross borrowing requirements will determine the size of the program, and the volume to be raised will influence the policy framework. If the needs are large, the government debt manager must try to tap all pockets of savings in the economy more or less at the same time; on the other hand, if they are small, he or she can afford to take a longer view and to develop and use one or two market segments at a time. Which subsector will have priority depends as much on tradition and national institutions as on macroeconomic and financial conditions. Clearly the availability of funds and the market conditions will be important for the choice of sector and the design of borrowing instruments. Thus, familiarity with the investment habits and preferences of each category of savers, and with the market for the kind of instruments that might attract them, becomes a significant element in policy formulation.

Broadly speaking, there are two separate groups of savers and investors: individuals ("households") and institutions. *Individuals* are generally attracted by low-risk nonmarketable instruments that provide them with a steady stream of income, like savings certificates, but they will also buy lottery bonds (the chance of winning big payoffs compensates for a comparatively low yield) and standard government bonds if available in small denominations. Developing appropriate policies for a successful program of borrowings from this sector should not be too difficult—there are many such national programs around the world that can be used as sources of inspiration—and should involve easier choices and less intricate coordination problems vis-à-vis the monetary authorities than borrowing from financial institutions. On the other hand, tapping the household market may involve more administrative costs than targeting the large-scale institutional investor, and may also require certain safeguards against inflation, like indexation. Banks and the postal system, which are often used to retail the borrowing instruments, are likely to ask for some remuneration for their services. For policy development and programming in this area, debt managers must keep in close touch with the household market and be prepared to adapt their instruments to meet competition from other established forms of private savings.

In an economy in transition, the group of *institutional investors* may initially consist of little more than the banks. The policies required to develop a program of treasury bill financing in the banking system have been fully documented in earlier chapters, in which the need for close coordination between the debt manager and the central bank was stressed. As the pool of institutional savings outside the banking system grows, however, the government will wish to attract the financial surpluses of social security systems, pension funds, insurance companies, money and capital market funds, foreign investors, and others. Naturally, various categories of investors will have different preferences, which the government debt manager should strive to identify and, if possible, satisfy. Generally speaking, the government will want to issue and market medium- and long-term bonds, which will also support the noninflationary financing of the stabilization program.

Some years ago, the predominant pattern in many countries, particularly in the developing world, was to prescribe by law that a certain percentage of the assets of institutional investors be invested in government securities, often at below-market rates. In addition, there was differentiation between segments of investors in terms of the kind of government paper they had to hold as statutory reserves or liquid assets. Naturally, such securities had no secondary market because their low yield made them difficult to sell except at prices well below their nominal value, and the group of eligible buyers was restricted. With governments increasingly desirous of deep and efficient markets for their securities, restrictions of this kind have been progressively lifted and markets deregulated, in order to create incentives for more active trading. In such policy packages, emphasis is frequently given to the creation of sufficiently large volumes of a few standardized debt instruments (e.g., coupon bonds with maturities of five and ten years). The growth of derivatives based on government securities has helped to build interest in so-called benchmark issues. By such actions, the government can spearhead the development of capital markets that can also serve the needs of private sector issuers.

In a number of OECD countries, government debt management is seen as a two-tier operation: strategic guidelines for raising and administering government debt are decided—usually on an annual basis—by the highest political authority of the country (parliament or council of ministers or both). The implementation of such guidelines through day-to-day operations is then left to a specialized body such as a department in the ministry of finance or central bank, or an autonomous state agency reporting to the minister of finance (or to parliament, as was the case in Sweden until 1989). The tasks of formulating and obtaining decisions on such guidelines, in the form of performance benchmarks for the year ahead or otherwise, and of monitoring their implementation (including revising them if need be) are often the responsibility of a high-level committee of the government, chaired by a minister or the central bank governor and assisted by a small staff unit.[3]

The amount and quality of work under the policy and planning function will vary not only with the volume and diversity of the debt but also with the government's degree of ambition in setting goals for its debt policy. In several countries, a debt issuance and management strategy is adopted each year at the time of budget finalization and then revised as conditions change during the year (Australia is a case in point). In recent years, it has become fashionable to set specific targets for the cost of carrying the debt portfolio, with measurement methods drawn from portfolio management theory and practices of evaluating asset managers. Thus, if the debt manager is asked to minimize the cost of debt (within certain limits), his or her degree of success is measured against a *benchmark portfolio*, based on a "neutral" or normal pattern of debt issuance, embodying considerations of the long-run composition of the debt stock and the authorities' tolerance for risk. In this approach, the debt manager exercises a degree of discretion in the choice of instruments and duration. Evaluating the performance of the debt manager against a benchmark (if used) is sometimes entrusted to an outside agency—a private investment bank in the case of Ireland, the Cour de Compte in the case of France.

---

[3]In Sweden, for example, advisory groups were established for foreign currency borrowing and domestic currency borrowing. The former was chaired by the Governor of the Central Bank and the latter by the Undersecretary of State of the Ministry of Finance (see Chapter 11 for more details).

Primary Issuance Function

Strictly speaking, this function should be limited to the decisions and activities of the government debt manager leading up to the time that a loan or bond issue is ready for launching. In some OECD countries, the task of actually selling the issue into the market is undertaken not by the treasury but by the central bank, and the objectives may be as much those of monetary management as of debt management for the government. However, in other countries, the responsibility for placing the issue in the market remains with the issuer—the treasury or a separate debt office— and the issuing function must then be seen as a continuum, that is, it covers the whole relationship between the state borrower and the primary market for government paper.

Characteristics of the primary issuance function vary from country to country partly because of administrative structures and national traditions but more significantly because of differences in government objectives and policies, with regard to the markets that the government wants to tap, the variety of instruments used, selling techniques (such as auctions), and so forth. We have already made the broad distinction between the household market, with its preference for small denomination issues that are normally nonnegotiable and often made attractive through tax advantages, and the institutional market, with its appetite for large, standardized issues. Within the institutional market, there are many ways of raising funds. Using a syndicate of banks to place a public issue in the market during a limited selling period can be a useful first step, and many governments continue to use this method as their standard practice. If the market is dominated by a few major institutional investors, a private placement may be recommended, usually arranged with the help of one or several banks. A large public issue can be offered widely to banks, pension funds, insurance companies, and the like through a system of auctions; this is the normal practice for treasury bills. Finally, bills and bond issues can be placed in the market through a more or less continuous selling process ("on tap") whenever the selling agent deems it appropriate. A government with a substantial borrowing requirement may decide to use all these techniques in pure or intermediate forms, usually starting with a syndicate and then adding other techniques as the market grows and deepens.

Some state issuers rely on a *government broker* to communicate with market participants. The real home of this practice was and remains the United Kingdom even if, since 1986, the famous top hat is no longer worn by representatives of a private stockbroking firm but by a senior official of the Bank of England.

A widespread practice among OECD countries is that of appointing *primary dealers* as market-makers for state debt. These are banks or firms that have undertaken to participate regularly and in a significant way in auctions of newly issued government securities. The government thus creates a public or private sector network to perform the issuing function. The use of primary dealers has been the established practice for many years in countries such as the United Kingdom and the United States. Of more recent origin is the French system of Spécialistes en Valeurs du Trésor (SVT), which has served as a model also for Belgium, Italy, Portugal, and Spain. But not all governments have found such formal networks desirable; Denmark is among the countries that prefer to do without a system of primary dealers (see Chapter 15).

Whether or not the network is formal, the government will find primary dealers (under any name) useful as its advisors on issuing matters and its "eyes and ears" in the marketplace. The primary dealers may also enjoy special privileges in return for their undertaking to participate in auctions of government securities. Particularly in the early stages of such a system, it may be necessary to offer the dealers fairly generous selling commissions, which can then gradually be reduced or abolished entirely, depending on the success of the system. The dealers can also be given an exclusive right of tendering for government securities (rather than having to share it with major investors) and loan facilities to enable them to build up their stocks (see Chapter 7, Appendix 2, for an overview of primary dealer arrangements).

Almost regardless of the placing and selling techniques adopted, a number of conditions appear necessary for the issuing function to work smoothly. One is the existence of a secondary market for government debt, discussed below. Another is the need to establish a reasonably stable calendar of issuing activities, although opinions differ as to exactly how stable and explicit it should be. Big borrowers like the U.S. Treasury usually have a rather fixed schedule, announced far in advance as to maturities and coupons; the only element of surprise (announced just before the auction) is the volume to be auctioned. At the other extreme we find the tap issue technique, which is wholly opportunistic in satisfying current "market appetites" and therefore sets no fixed calendar (Ireland and Denmark). In both cases, however, the market will have a reasonably accurate picture of the government's total borrowing needs for the coming fiscal year. In addition, experts agree that the government should publish all details of loans issued and currently available, the result of auctions, and so on.

Because households may well account for the largest pool of investable savings in the country, particularly when the institutional market is in its infancy, they are a source that governments often wish to tap. To circumvent the obstacle of high distribution costs for special instruments in small denominations, some governments (Denmark, Sweden) have created special computer systems through which small investors can participate in the issuing activities of the government and enjoy market rates that are otherwise available only to holders of securities in large denominations.

Finally, it is obvious that the success of the issuing function is very much dependent on a smoothly working *accounting and payments system*. If securities are issued in registered form, an accurate registry must be kept by the issuer or by some other agency, preferably by the authority in charge of the clearance and settlement system. Where bearer bonds are sold, a good printing shop for such paper is necessary. Payments of debt service can be arranged through a separate office (Ireland has a Gilt Settlement Office and the United Kingdom has its Central Gilt Office at the Bank of England).

Secondary Market Function

The secondary market function is normally performed by players other than government debt managers but can be of vital importance to the success of their operations, particularly if government borrowing needs are high and expected to remain so, and if the securities markets are dominated by professional investors. For them, the secondary market will guarantee the liquidity of their investments and set prices on a day-to-day basis. Naturally, they will be more willing to take up new issues if they know that they can liquidate some of their holdings at any time for cash and at reasonable prices.

But a secondary market may not spring up by itself—experience shows that it typically requires both active intervention from the authorities and the reduction of various regulatory obstacles (see Chapter 7 for a discussion of the role of the authorities in promoting efficient market structures). A recent study (OECD (1993)) enumerates some of the obstacles identified in countries like Korea and Malaysia, where primary markets are fairly large:

- a controlled or administered structure of interest rates through which the effective yields on government bonds are kept below the levels of the credit market;
- protection by the commercial banks of their privileged position as lenders to the private sector;
- legal restrictions on the issuance of corporate debt by enterprises;
- high minimum denominations of new issues, which bar individual investors from participating; and
- the lack of a securities infrastructure in the form of a competitive auction system, rating agencies, and clearing and settlement systems.

The study makes a general observation that corporate bond trading receives a stimulus from an active government bond market—and vice versa.

The role of the authorities must therefore be twofold: on the institutional side, to reduce the legal and regulatory obstacles and create a supporting framework for the secondary market and on the operational side, to adopt issuing policies and techniques that will facilitate wholesale trading of government securities.

To start with the latter: the most important consideration—which is often the most difficult one from the political point of view—is that the government as an issuer must decide to allow the market to set the price of its debt instruments. Second, government debt managers must try to avoid fostering market segmentation, which will generally tend to make borrowing more expensive; instead, they should opt for a few standardized issues that are reopened periodically to create really large volumes of securities with high liquidity. In this connection, the central bank will play a crucial role by providing rediscounting and repurchase facilities for treasury bills.

While the central bank will use the secondary market for government debt for the purpose of monetary policy, debt managers want to stimulate the market's appetite for their instruments generally and thus create greater demand in the primary market. To this end, some debt offices are prepared to offer "switches" of illiquid stocks (loans of small volumes or loans due for redemption within a year or two and therefore trading near par) for benchmark or other major issues. In some countries, the debt office has a separate department with its own funds and the authority to operate in the market, for example, to shore it up before a new issue is launched, to round out the total of an issue that has not been fully taken up by the market, or to buy back small volumes of outstanding debt that are too labor-intensive to handle.

In countries with advanced capital markets, a range of institutions perform roles of importance for the secondary market in government securities. While the creation and improvement of such institutions—for example, advisory groups on debt issuance, market associations, selling and underwriting groups, and dealer groups—is often beyond the reach of the debt manager alone, he or she can assist the government in pointing out their potential benefit and actively cooperate in establishing them. A case in point is the development of a group of primary dealers into a network of market-makers who are obliged under contract with the debt manager to provide continuous two-way (i.e., buy and sell) quotes that are binding for indicated amounts of specified government securities (particularly so-called benchmark issues). This ensures that liquidity is provided to the market under adverse as well as favorable market conditions. For large volumes of transactions, an efficient secondary market may require a book-entry system rather than the movement of securities in paper form.

Clearing and Settlement Function

In small and undeveloped secondary markets, clearing and settlement (i.e., the transfer of ownership of securities and the transfer of sales proceeds) are normally undertaken by the banks (each bank making such transfers between the accounts of its own customers, and banks also making transfers among themselves), or by the central bank in case of transactions involving government securities held by different banks. However, this structure is not likely to foster a high-turnover market, and other solutions have therefore come to dominate more developed markets. While all of them feature a *central depository center*, there is a rather rich variety of models to consider (see Chapters 1 and 4 for a survey of arrangements). In some countries, the central bank has agreed to enlarge its role as agent for the government debt manager by operating a computerized debt registry and payments scheme for the secondary market. In other countries, the government as market participant has joined hands with the banks and the dealers to create a separate securities depository center, which effects legally binding transfers of ownership and which may or may not also make payment transfers through a clearing process. To guard investors against counterparty risk (i.e., the failure of a party to a securities transaction to fulfill his obligations), the center may have the right and the resources to step in and meet the failing party's obligation. Through sophisticated legal and technical means, countries strive to achieve a fail-safe application of the principle of "delivery against payment," this being a prerequisite for the success of transactions involving a chain of separate deals. In some countries, trading is done through the stock exchange, which may have a separate bond market and an electronic clearing system. Clearing and settlement can be carried out also by a separate institution jointly owned by the government and other market participants, such as banks and dealers, and specializing in bonds and money market instruments; this model can be found in Nordic countries such as Finland and Sweden and variations on this theme are common in many countries.

Information Function

The importance of timely and correct information from government debt managers to the market has been highlighted in previous sections of this chapter. Equally important is that debt managers receive relevant information from the market in order to tailor their issuing activities to the goals set by policymakers. Increasingly, the debt manager is also a participant in electronic information systems that have been set up by electronic information services (Reuters, Telerate), by banks and dealers, or occasionally by the authorities (see Chapter 7 for examples) to facilitate the functioning of the primary and secondary markets. Thus, in a number of countries, traders are connected to other traders, to issuers, and to investors through screen-based information and market-making systems that allow quick execution of sell and buy orders (and can be used to call for bids at a primary auction). The advent of fiber-optic cables and other technical advances are likely to allow a very rapid growth of such information systems, facilitating the role of debt managers but also making demands on their time.

Supervisory Function

For all its activities as a market participant, the government must always play a central role in *market surveillance*. Different models can be followed to implement this subfunction: some countries have separate agencies for the supervision of banks and of capital markets, reporting to parliament through the ministry of finance. In other cases, the ministry has delegated certain tasks and powers to the central bank, to the stock exchange, or to self-regulatory organizations. Recent experience has taught many countries the lesson that the supervisory function requires forethought and vigilance, which can only be achieved with staff resources in sufficient numbers and of the right quality.

Location of Functions

Among OECD countries, the functions outlined above are performed by staff units within the central bank, the ministry of finance, and the government debt office, which may be a department of either of the two or an autonomous agency normally reporting to the ministry. Little systematic knowledge is as yet available about the specific tasks of such units, their size, and the composition of their staff (education, training, and competencies). Naturally, such data would vary enormously between countries, if only because of the diverse sizes of their debt operations.

As regards the exact location of the various functions in debt management, there is no clear pattern among OECD countries. Ministries of finance and central banks are everywhere engaged to a greater or lesser degree, and in some countries there is also an autonomous agency located outside both the ministry and the bank that is charged with day-to-day operations in debt management. Defining the status of that agency is not always easy, as the degree of independence may vary over time, and written instructions or laws defining its powers may be less important than informal structures. Nevertheless, at one end of the spectrum are certain countries where the central bank is the sole agent of the government in carrying out the policies and instructions laid down by the highest constitutional authority and transmitted to the operating level through the ministry of finance (which then has a small unit to serve as a link with the bank). Denmark, Italy, Turkey, and the United Kingdom are examples of that model. Their central banks serve as fiscal agent to the government and sell securities into the primary market through auctions or tap sales. They print and distribute bearer bonds, keep accounts, and handle the payment of debt service to investors. Because they are in daily contact with the market, they advise the government on market conditions, borrowing strategies, and financial techniques for new issues. In practice, they have the dominant role in government borrowing and debt management.

At the other end of the spectrum, the ministry of finance either does the work itself (through a department staffed with specialists in external finance and equipped with appropriate computers and software) or relies for the execution of its decisions (particularly loan administration matters) on a treasury agency under its direct supervision (Austria, Finland, Germany, the Netherlands, and the United States all have agencies of this kind, with varying degrees of independence). The needs of the central bank with regard to government securities with which to conduct open market operations are then made known to the ministry through a coordinating committee of some kind.

Agencies with a somewhat greater-than-average degree of autonomy—typically called debt management offices—are found in Sweden (where one was set up under parliamentary authority some 200 years ago but recently brought under the ministry of finance) and in Ireland and New Zealand (where they are of more recent date). In all cases, it is the ministry that obtains the authorization for borrowing and debt management from the parliament, gives instructions to the agency, and supervises its operations. This model requires not only resources for the debt office but also a certain number of treasury staff who are familiar with the problems of government debt and with financial markets and can interact with the debt agency—particularly since the central bank may be less able or willing to give support to the government debt manager.

There are advantages as well as drawbacks in having borrowing and debt management handled by a separate, identifiable agency of the government with a certain degree of autonomy, that is, a government debt office. A debt office can be the embodiment of the government's ambition to achieve cost minimization in debt management through professional operations in the market, within the limits set by the policy function (at the ministry). Its distinct role will set it apart from the more widespread and manifold tasks of the ministry. By creating a separate agency, the government will also make clear that debt management is not to be regarded as identical with or a part of monetary management, for which the central bank carries sole responsibility. For example, in the Netherlands, the agency of the ministry of finance handling debt is located in Amsterdam together with most of the banking community, rather than in The Hague with the ministry, although of course its debt management and borrowing activities are related to the budget process (and there are daily contacts between the ministry and the agency). But its responsibilities are entirely separate from those of the central bank—all coordination between debt management and monetary policy takes place between the ministry and the bank at the top management level.

Another advantage of a separate debt office is that staffing may be easier because it should be able to set salaries more freely than a ministry is usually able to do and provide more focused training. Given a certain size, the debt office could then offer an attractive career not only for regular treasury staff but also for people with a financial or managerial background in the private sector. Low turnover of staff will raise the level of competence of the debt office and thus its effectiveness as the government's market agent. High professional qualifications and standards are necessary for an agency that is involved in such high-risk activities as liability management and whose staff must be able to stand their ground in dealing with representatives of banks and major investors. Most important, a debt office can adopt an attitude and a work ethic that are more closely related to other commercial activities of the public sector than to the policymaking and control functions of the central bank and the ministry of finance. This should make for efficiency gains that will more than compensate for higher salary costs.

By contrast, in countries where both debt and money markets are still undeveloped and capital markets are rudimentary, a separate debt office may complicate rather than assist the coordinated development of the various functions enumerated above and particularly the twinning of debt and monetary management, which may be desirable at that stage. Keeping debt management within the ministry of finance, working in close collaboration with the central bank (to the point that the bank is virtually the operational agent of the ministry), is then likely to be the best arrangement. From this stage, evolution will come naturally as the volume of debt grows and markets become more sophisticated. In any event, wherever the functions of domestic debt management are located, it is vital to establish clear and transparent rules and procedures for taking and implementing decisions on government debt operations. Related responsibilities, lines of command, and accountability should be clarified and organized accordingly, and specific instructions adopted and made public so that there is no doubt, within the government itself or among the domestic and foreign players in the financial markets, about "who does what."

Coordination of Debt Management and Monetary Management

The previous sections demonstrate that the need for coordination between the policies and practices of the government debt manager on the one hand, and the central banker on the other, depends on the scope of activities under each of the enumerated functions and how the functions are distributed among agencies. Again, national practice varies and can change dramatically within a country following deregulation and market development.

The most obvious area of potential conflict between debt management and monetary policy is in the establishment of interest rate levels. The central bank, charged with the delicate task of managing the banking system so as to achieve central political goals such as low inflation, is anxious to avoid counterproductive influences from the debt manager's issuing or secondary market activities. The danger from this source appears to be the greatest in the intermediate stage of financial market development: in the early years, government issuing activities (mainly in the form of treasury bills sold to the banks and a few institutional investors) are very much a joint treasury–central bank activity designed both to finance the budget deficit and to provide instruments for monetary management. In the fully developed market, on the other hand, the ministry of finance will sell medium- and long-term bonds to the institutions through a network of dealers, trying to be cost-effective at whatever interest rates are dictated by the market as a result of central bank monetary policy, and will provide households with a variety of specialized nonnegotiable instruments, while the central bank will be equipped with an ample supply of treasury bills (and perhaps also its own very short-term instruments) with which to operate in the secondary market in order to influence bank liquidity and to send signals about the interest levels that it wants to see.

In the intermediate stage of financial market development, however, the ministry and the bank may find themselves in conflict over which goal is the more important: low cost of government borrowing, as advocated by the ministry, or monetary and price stability through an appropriate interest rate structure, as judged by the bank. The two players (or three, if there is an independent debt office) will need to share information about economic and financial trends, market developments, borrowing and hedging instruments, and so forth in order to arrive at a common platform for decisions. Moreover, it is at this stage that a formal body (e.g., an interagency committee chaired by a senior official of the ministry or a deputy governor of the bank) will be most desirable to sort out differences of views and arrive at a joint decision and coordinated action. The committee should meet regularly—once a month or at least once a quarter—

to consider government borrowing requirements, to monitor liquidity developments in various sectors, and to discuss the strategy through which the goals of debt and monetary management can both be met. Such an arrangement has been in force in a number of OECD countries during the past decade, with varying intensity and efficiency. The tendency is for the committees to be most active in the early stages of their existence, when members learn about each others' objectives and operating procedures and hammer out a consensus on how debt and monetary management should be conducted in reasonable harmony—for the long-run benefit of both. Later, when committee members know each other and have demarcated their formal positions, they tend to conduct much of the business of coordination by phone between meetings, which tend to be held less frequently; but it is important that the committee remains operational and can resume its activities if and when required.

Bibliography

Bröker, Günther, 1993, *Government Securities and Debt Management in the 1990s* (Paris: Organization for Economic Cooperation and Development).

Organization for Economic Cooperation and Development, 1993, *Emerging Bond Markets in the Dynamic Asian Economies* (Paris).

United Nations Conference on Trade and Development, 1989, *Effective Debt Management* (Geneva: United Nations).

□ 4 □

Survey of Public Debt Management Frameworks in Selected Countries

Montserrat Ferré Carracedo and Peter Dattels*

This chapter examines the key components that constitute a comprehensive framework for public debt management for a sample of 14 countries.[1] Strategies for achieving debt management goals are discussed, and various institutional and operational arrangements supporting debt management operations are compared across countries.

The following components of a debt management framework are surveyed and set out in the country tables at the end of this chapter: (1) the legal and institutional framework for establishing the authority to borrow, the accountability for debt management, and the principal and other debt management agents; (2) debt management objectives, and policy choices and instruments used to achieve those objectives; (3) debt management planning; (4) debt program implementation; (5) operational arrangements for debt management; and (6) location and coordination of debt management functions.[2] The survey reveals considerable diversity in the formulation of objectives, in the implementation of debt management strategies, and in the institutional and operational arrangements of debt management. Nevertheless, there is a broad convergence of approaches in industrial countries as to the overall debt management strategy that a government borrower should follow to raise funds in an effective and efficient manner. Criteria for choosing the location of debt management functions are examined.

---

*Montserrat Ferré Carracedo was a summer intern at the IMF when this chapter was written. Peter Dattels is a Senior Economist at the Fund.

[1]The countries were selected for their relatively well-developed frameworks for public debt management and diversity of institutional and operational arrangements.

[2]Preparation of the country tables has benefited from the cooperation of the ministries of finance, debt management offices, and central banks of most of the countries included in the survey. Provided with the basic framework, they contributed the information in each category.

1. Government Borrowing: Legal Framework, Accountability, and Authority

Legal Authority to Borrow

According to Miller (Chapter 13), the legal and institutional framework underpinning public debt management should enable the debt managers to carry out their functions smoothly and efficiently. It should also provide investors with the utmost security by ensuring that the government's debt management objectives are pursued and instruments are issued under the due authority of the country's highest constitutional body. With these principles in mind, the authority to borrow should normally be established in a public law that determines who has the authority to borrow and elaborates provisions concerning the issuance of government debt. These laws and provisions eliminate any legal uncertainty that might undermine the confidence of investors as to the authority to issue and the obligation to service and repay government debt. They may also provide clear and consistent principles for when and for what reasons debt is issued; the institutional arrangements for debt management; and the aim of debt management policies.

The survey reveals that the legal authority is usually established as a general statute providing a government institution with the authority to borrow and the responsibilities for public debt policies. In several cases, a law with a sunset provision provides the authority to borrow—usually over one year, corresponding with the budgetary plan. In some countries, a *public debt act* may elaborate basic types of instruments, the forms that government securities may take (e.g., physical—bearer or registered—or dematerialized), selling techniques, and so on.

Accountability

To enhance the accountability of the debt management process, in many countries, supplementary laws establish limits to the size of debt financing. By providing checks and balances on the amounts of debt issued, such limits establish an "accountability link" between debt issuance, budget performance, and fiscal sustainability. This is especially important in the absence of interim budget reviews (e.g., reviews may occur only during the formulation of the next budget). When debt issuance approaches the statutory limit or ceiling, the debt management authority must approach parliament for supplementary borrowing authority, thereby forcing debate on the reasons for borrowing in excess of that previewed in the budget and established by law.

In practice, such a ceiling does run the risk of "politicizing" debt management and may trigger a confidence crisis if market participants think that the government may default on its debt or in the event that the situ-

---

Box 1. Statutory Debt Limits

The survey reveals that many countries establish a ceiling on the amount of net new debt to be issued (or a ceiling on the outstanding stock of debt as, for example, in the United States). Of the 14 countries in the survey, 8 countries impose a debt ceiling, while of the 6 without a global debt limit, 2 establish limits for foreign currency borrowing. Usually, global limits are set in the context of the budget whose financing circumscribes the size of (net) borrowing in each year and therefore the ceiling. This ceiling may be established in a Budget Law (as in Argentina, Brazil, Japan, and Spain) or separately as a Borrowing Authority (as in Canada, Italy, and the United States).

Some variations on the above formulation occur. In Japan, debt creation is linked to public welfare considerations. To avoid placing an unfair debt-service burden on future generations from the debt financing of current government consumption, the issuance of government bonds is restricted to government works projects.[1] Therefore, special legislation must be passed every year for the bond financing of shortfalls of tax revenues covering current expenditures. In the context of encouraging prudent fiscal policies and sustainable debt management policies, rather than specifying an absolute amount of debt, the setting of a target path for the evolution of the ratio of the outstanding stock of debt to GDP has been introduced in New Zealand under the Fiscal Responsibility Act

---

[1]The Public Finance Act, which is the basic law concerning the Japanese fiscal and budgetary system, stipulates that budgetary expenditure should, in principle, be financed by tax revenues, and that government debt can only be allowed to finance public works expenditure. Because public works will help future generations, they too may contribute to the servicing of government debt.

---

ation is not resolved. However, it effectively forces public debate calling for actions to correct the budgetary cause of the situation. (The 1995 U.S. situation was a case in point, where congressional passage of an increase in the debt ceiling was being directly linked to the administration's support for achieving a balanced budget in seven years.)

In sum, debt limits as part of the framework for debt management can enhance accountability. The size of the debt limit should be closely linked to fiscal policy and the budget process, and in the long term, to the sustainability of debt financing. As global limits are part of overall fiscal management, they should be set by the highest constitutional authority. Box 1 highlights practices in the countries included in the survey.

Debt Management Authority and Agents

Because the rationale for borrowing is to finance the budget, the legal authority to borrow is normally given to the institution that formulates the budget and is accountable to the parliament. Generally, this is the ministry of finance (or the treasury) or the Minister of Finance, establishing the link between "budget making" and "budget financing."[3]

As the principal debt management authority, the ministry of finance has the responsibility for managing the public debt. However, the tasks and functions of debt management may be delegated by the ministry of finance to other institutions or to specialized departments or agencies of the ministry. As discussed in the preceding chapters and at the end of this chapter, the location of debt management functions may depend on comparative advantage (specialized knowledge) of institutions, on economies of scale in dealing with some functions of government debt (e.g., in combination with other activities such as the payment system functions of a central bank), on the stage of market development, or on whether debt issuance is a tool of monetary operations (see Chapter 9). Given the diversity and specialized nature of many debt management functions, it is efficient to delegate certain functions while ultimate responsibility for debt management rests with the principal debt management authority. The following debt management authorities and agents are identified in the debt management process:

- ministry of finance or treasury;
- central bank;
- debt management agency;
- retail debt agency;
- primary dealer group;
- stock exchange;
- central securities depository;
- securities commission; and
- debt consultation group.

Three possible institutional arrangements for the general conduct of debt management are highlighted in Box 2, involving the following authorities as key agents: (1) the ministry of finance or a special department of the ministry of finance (the treasury directorate); (2) the central bank; or (3) a special autonomous agency under governmental supervision (the debt office). Other debt management agents listed above perform specialized tasks.

---

[3]This is not always so. For example, the Swedish National Debt Office, which was founded in 1789 as an agency in charge of state borrowing, was initially subordinated directly to parliament. However, in 1989, the Debt Office was transformed from a parliamentary agency to an agency subordinate to the ministry of finance in order to improve the effectiveness of the implementation of debt management (see Chapter 11).

Box 2. Institutional Arrangements

Ministry of Finance as the Key Agent

In this classification, the ministry of finance is responsible for the tactical and strategic policy functions as well as many other debt management functions (e.g., in Argentina, Japan, and the United States). Debt management functions are usually undertaken by certain divisions within the ministry. In Japan, for instance, the ministry of finance comprises different bureaus. The Budget Bureau plans the total amount of new bonds to be issued, while the Financial Bureau determines the allocation of gross issuances according to maturities and determines the details and characteristics of each bond. Alternatively, a treasury directorate may be established within the ministry of finance, centralizing the management of financial resources and liabilities of the government and consolidating fiscal and debt management functions (Brazil, France, and Spain fall within this arrangement). Broadly speaking, in these arrangements, the central bank is responsible for only the more technical aspects of debt management, such as selling, banking, or settlement arrangements.

Central Bank as the Key Agent

In this classification, the central bank plays a role as an advisor in the formulation of debt management policy and may also, within well-specified parameters, be in charge of strategic policy and short-term management of the government's debt, as well as other functions supporting debt management operations. This provides some degree of policy and operational discretion to the central bank in debt management (as compared with the above arrangement) as is appropriate when debt management is integrated with monetary operations (e.g., in Pakistan, where treasury bills are used for monetary management purposes) or when the central bank is responsible for market development and functioning (e.g., debt program implementation is carried out by the central bank in Italy and in the United Kingdom).[1]

---

[1]In the United Kingdom, decisions on debt management are the formal responsibility of treasury ministers, who are accountable to Parliament. The relationship between treasury ministers, treasury officials, and the Bank of England is outlined in the Funding Remit (the first was issued in March 1994). In this document, the Chancellor of the Exchequer (head of the treasury) sets out the operations of the Bank of England in the gilt market and clarifies the division of responsibilities between the treasury and the bank. Debt management operations proposed by the Bank of England that fall within the terms of the "remit" are normally approved quickly by the treasury.

---

2. Debt Management Objectives, and Policy Choices and Instruments

Objectives

As discussed in the preceding chapter, debt management functions and institutions should begin with a statement about the objectives to be achieved.

Debt Office as the Key Agent

The establishment of a separate debt management office dealing with many debt management functions is a third type of institutional arrangement (e.g., in Ireland, New Zealand, and Sweden; see Chapters 10 and 11). This arrangement provides for greater institutional separation between fiscal, monetary, and debt management policies, though they generally operate within well-specified policies established by the ministry of finance. These offices are a fairly recent phenomenon, dating from the late 1980s, with the exception of Sweden, where the debt office was created in 1789 to borrow on behalf of the Kingdom of Sweden and manage the state debt. Parliament was responsible for the debt office until July 1, 1989, at which time it was transferred to the government. It is now an independent government agency subordinate to the ministry of finance. It is the sole institution that may borrow on behalf of the Kingdom of Sweden and is responsible for debt management.

Other Agents Involved in the Debt Management Process

Other debt management agents may be designated (or instituted) to support primary and secondary markets or both. For example, primary dealer groups are sometimes formed with specific obligations to facilitate the development, organization, and liquidity of efficient wholesale markets for government securities (e.g., in France, Mexico, Pakistan, Spain, Sweden, the United Kingdom, and the United States). Japan does not have a primary dealer system per se but relies on an underwriting syndicate for ten-year government bonds (the biggest Japanese bond issue). Over 800 firms are members of the syndicate, including banks, securities firms, and insurance companies. In the case of retail instruments that are sold to the general public, separate agencies are sometimes used to sell and service these specialized instruments—for example, the Central Directorate of National Savings Schemes in Pakistan; the United Kingdom uses the post offices as a distribution system for retail debt instruments. A securities commission may regulate and supervise government securities markets. The clearing and settlement functions may be supported by a central depository organization, either publicly or privately owned. Finally, special consultation groups are sometimes formed to assist in improving the design of debt management programs and to encourage the transparency of operations.

A clearly defined debt management objective is an important element of the debt management framework: (1) it facilitates the design of the debt management program in a manner consistent with the attainment of the debt management goals while avoiding conflicting objectives; (2) it enables the measurement of performance of the chosen debt management strategy; and (3) it harmonizes debt management policies with other policies.

Although the academic literature on public debt provides useful indications of what should be the long-term goals of government debt and welfare policies, it unfortunately offers little guidance in setting operational targets for debt management policy. Indeed, much of the academic literature (such as irrelevance theorems) stresses the impotency of debt management in achieving macroeconomic goals (prices, output, interest rates) or microeconomic goals of cost minimization. Relaxing the assumptions of perfect markets and information, and time-consistency assumptions, some literature supports the potency of debt management policy.[4]

Operational objectives are revealed in the survey. A basic objective is to cover the government's borrowing needs in the market: various primary and secondary objectives are highlighted in Table 1, along with a subjective ranking. Establishing an appropriate hierarchy of objectives is an important task of the authorities. This book suggests that the hierarchy of objectives depends in an important way on the stage of market and institutional development and will evolve over time with the government securities markets and the achievement of economic stabilization goals.

Countries with less-developed government securities and financial markets or a history of high inflation attach primary importance to monetary policy and market development considerations. For example, Mexico has, and until 1995 the United Kingdom had, as primary debt management objectives borrowing in a noninflationary way and support of monetary policy; in the United Kingdom, this was made operational through the so-called full fund policy, which seeks to exclude—in meeting the government borrowing requirements—all forms of financing that are deemed as "monetary financing"—such as funding from the central bank or (until recently) funding with very short-term treasury bills.[5]

With the development of financial and government securities markets, debt management objectives may evolve and the hierarchy of objectives

---

[4]For example, debt management policies might aim to enhance public confidence and reduce interest rate risk premiums by issuing index-linked debt (floating rate, inflation-indexed bonds, and foreign currency linked debt): by reducing incentives for the government to devalue, ex post, the real value of government debt through unexpected inflation, investor confidence may be enhanced (see Bank of England and H.M. Treasury, *Report on the Debt Management Review* (1995)). In addition, a foreign currency debt may play a hedging role against revenue shocks (where changes in taxes are distortionary) (see de Fontenay and others (1995) for a capsule review of the literature). When export enterprises are a large part of the economy, foreign currency debt would hedge falling revenues through offsetting declines in debt service in the event of an income shock due to a sharp currency appreciation.

[5]The full fund policy has changed over the years. Originally, the U.K. Government's policy covered maturing debt, the public sector borrowing requirement, and increases in foreign exchange reserves through sales of debt, all outside the commercial banking and building society sectors. Since fiscal year 1993/94, purchases of gilts by the monetary sector (commercial banks) are now included as funding. Between 1989 and 1996, treasury bill sales were not counted toward funding (treasury bills are used for liquidity management). From 1996, treasury bills were included in "full funding," bringing the United Kingdom in line with other industrial countries.

Box 3. Evolving Hierarchy of Debt Management Objectives

The United Kingdom provides a country example of how the hierarchy of debt management objectives has changed with the advancing state of development of financial markets and monetary instruments.[1]

Prior to 1995 review: "(1) to support and complement monetary policy; (2) subject to this, to avoid distorting financial markets; and (3) subject to this, to fund at least cost and risk."

After the 1995 review: "The objective of debt management policy is to minimize over the long term the cost of meeting the government's financing needs, taking account of risk, while ensuring that debt management policy is consistent with monetary policy."

---

[1]See Bank of England and H.M. Treasury, *Report on the Debt Management Review* (1995).

---

change (see Box 3). Reflecting the highly developed nature of markets and growing central bank independence of many of the countries in the survey, a common primary objective in industrial countries as shown in Table 1 is to minimize the (long-run) cost of debt at a given level of risk.

In countries with developed markets, a number of secondary, generally complementary, objectives are pursued in the management of debt; these are highlighted in Box 4.[6]

Because objectives broadly determine debt management policy and the evaluation of debt managers, their formulation should be a matter for the highest constitutional or executive authority and changes should be infrequent. In some cases, the objectives of debt management are inscribed in laws or decrees or made public in policy statements or publications by the debt management authority. In countries with a debt management office, the objectives are often contained in the law or ordinance that establishes the agency and its functions, paralleling the practice of central bank acts.[7] The survey tables provide a full listing of stated debt management objectives.

Monetary Policy Considerations

Debt management operations also impact on banking system liquidity. For this reason, debt management operations may need to be coordinated

---

[6]In some countries, these objectives might be considered primary objectives, for example, the development of secondary markets in the case of economies in transition.

[7]For example, in Sweden, the Government Ordinance setting the objective of the Swedish National Debt Office (No. 248, 1989) states: "the aim . . . shall be to minimize the costs of borrowings within the limits imposed by monetary policy."

Table 1. Ranking of Debt Management Objectives in Country Sample

Objective	Argentina	Brazil	Canada	France	Ireland	Italy	Japan	Mexico	New Zealand	Pakistan	Spain	Sweden	United Kingdom[1]	United Kingdom[2]	United States
Basic objective: cover financing needs	1	1			1	1	1	1			1		1	1	
Minimize borrowing cost			1	1	1	2	2	2	2	2	2	1	4	2	1
Minimize cost volatility			2										5		
Support monetary policy		3						3	1	1		2	2		
Develop domestic markets	2			3	3		3		3			4			
Avoid market disruption		2		2									3		2
Attract foreign investors						4									
Encourage savings of the public					2	6				3	4	5			
Diversify borrowing and broaden debt distribution	4			5		5				4	5				
Promote balanced maturity structure	3			4	3						3	3			3
Maintain creditworthiness									4						

Source: Subjective ranking of objectives based on country table survey.
[1] Prior to recent debt management reforms.
[2] Following debt management reforms.

Box 4. Secondary Debt Management Objectives

- To develop and improve the liquidity and efficiency of the domestic debt market. This goal was emphasized by most countries in the survey.
- To attract foreign investors by ensuring that government debt management practices are transparent, promote liquidity, and ensure the smooth operation of markets. These objectives are recognized in Canada, France, Ireland, New Zealand, Spain, and Sweden.
- To ensure government access to financial markets and diversify funding sources. This objective is recognized in Brazil, Italy, Pakistan, and Spain.
- To minimize financial market disruption of debt management operations. This objective is stated by France, the United Kingdom, and the United States.
- To encourage and mobilize savings from the household sector. This objective has sometimes been permitted to override the cost-effectiveness target (e.g., in Sweden up to 1989).

---

with monetary operations.[8] In some countries, this is achieved through joint coordination committees made up of high-level officials of the ministry of finance, the central bank, and the debt office (when applicable). Such committees exist in Mexico, Sweden, Pakistan, and Spain. Debt management operations are also coordinated informally through a continuous dialogue between the debt management agent (e.g., the central bank) and the principal debt management authority (e.g., the ministry of finance). This is found in Canada, Ireland (see Chapter 10), and the United States.

Formal coordination arrangements may be needed when debt management policy and monetary policy are separated along institutional lines—that is, between the central bank and debt office.[9] In Sweden, for example, the debt office is obliged by law to confer with the central bank on monetary policy matters and two policy coordination committees exist—one for domestic and one for foreign debt.

Policy Choices and Instruments

To make the objectives of domestic debt management operational, they must be translated into strategic and tactical policies. Broadly speaking,

---

[8]In Pakistan, the central bank has full discretion regarding the issuance and management of the treasury bill auction system for the purposes of conducting monetary management.

[9]Separate instruments may also be used for the conduct of debt management and monetary management (see Chapter 1); for example, in 1988, the Reserve Bank of New Zealand introduced central bank securities (reserve bank bills) for monetary management purposes, enhancing the separation of these policies.

strategic policies deal with the overall design and implementation of the debt management program including the design of instruments; the way primary issuance is designed and managed; how debt instruments are traded and liquidity provided; and the relationship between the issuer and the lender. In contrast, *tactical policies* deal with the management of the outstanding stock of debt and its composition (instrument mix and duration). Both policies affect the efficiency of debt operations, the cost and risk of debt management policy, and ultimately the fulfillment of debt management objectives.

As to strategic policies, the survey reveals a high degree of convergence in industrial countries in the broad debt management strategy to achieve primary and secondary objectives. This includes the following main elements:[10]

- adopting market-based methods for the primary issuance of government debt;
- improving market liquidity and the efficiency of the wholesale (institutional) secondary market for government securities;
- developing markets in related (derivative) instruments that contribute to market liquidity, including the repurchase agreement ("repo") market, strips market, and futures market;
- developing efficient clearing and settlement systems based on book-entry securities;
- providing predictability in the design, timing, and size of the debt program by publicizing the mix of instruments and maturity range, regularizing the calendar for debt issues, and preannouncing the size of issuance;
- developing an investor consultation and relations program to improve the design of the overall debt program by taking into consideration investors' needs and promoting transparency; and
- developing regular reporting to provide market-makers, investors, market analysts, and credit rating agencies up-to-date and accurate information on the fiscal situation as well as on the debt program.

The above broad strategy not only involves the design of instruments and the way they are sold and traded, but also the overall design and management of the debt program. *Developing such strategies should be a joint affair including the principal debt management authority (the ministry of finance) and the debt management agents in charge of the primary and secondary market functions (central bank, securities commission, and market intermediaries).* This reflects the fact that many of the measures will re-

---

[10]See also Chapter 13 and Bank of England and H.M. Treasury, *Report on the Debt Management Review* (1995).

quire coordinated efforts for policies to succeed as well as to advertise effectively and be understood by investors and the public. Precisely how these strategies are implemented differs from country to country and is revealed in the survey.

In many industrial countries characterized by large outstanding stocks of debt, the structure of the debt stock is an important determinant of debt-service costs, the volatility of debt-service costs, and the market value of the outstanding stock of debt (under varying interest rate and exchange rate environments). Thus, considerable resources are being spent to quantify *tactical policies* in managing the debt stock so as to minimize cost within acceptable margins of risk. In this regard, debt managers have been inspired by the finance literature and its application in financial markets.

The formulation of tactical policy varies from country to country, depending on the debt management objectives and the country's economic circumstances. Three approaches identified in the survey draw from risk-return analysis, portfolio management performance measurement, and asset and liability management, respectively; they are highlighted in Box 5.

In countries where the objectives of debt management are less well-defined or where markets are less well-developed or where cost minimization is secondary to other objectives such as minimizing refunding risk ("achieving a balanced maturity structure"), there is usually no specific method of measuring performance (e.g., in the United States and United Kingdom). Instead, countries seek to maintain a balanced maturity profile while satisfying investor demand at each term to maturity.

Finally, in economies with nascent government securities and financial markets, the above tactical approaches, which assume a wide range of possible instruments and maturities available to the debt manager, are not highly relevant. In these economies, tactical debt management policies should support economic stabilization and encourage market development. As some maturity lengthening becomes feasible, the risk-return trade-off approach may be usefully applied.

The *policy choices and instruments* to meet debt management objectives, both tactical and strategic, include:

- the design and use of debt instruments;
- the use of derivative instruments to manage (hedge) interest rate or currency risks;
- the term to maturity of issuance;
- the choice of currency of debt issued; and
- the target markets for debt.

Box 5. Three Tactical Approaches

Risk-Return Trade-Off

In Canada, tactical decisions are made on the basis of an identifiable cost-risk trade-off: the government's desire for *stabilization of debt-service charges*—achieved through the issuance of higher-cost fixed rate debt (i.e., treasury bonds)—versus *lower debt-service costs*—achieved through lower-cost floating rate debt issuance (i.e., treasury bills). Based on this trade-off, the government establishes a target for fixed versus floating rate debt. For example, the target mix of fixed versus floating rate debt in the outstanding stock of debt has been increased to 65 percent fixed rate and 35 percent floating rate (from the current position of about 55 percent floating and 45 percent fixed) to be achieved over a time frame of about ten years (see Chapter 13).[1]

Active Debt Management Policy

In Ireland and Sweden, debt managers aim to achieve cost savings within well-specified parameters through *active management of debt composition and issuance* (i.e., by taking views on interest rate and currency movements, or switching between different market segments—wholesale versus household). Debt management performance is measured against a hypothetical benchmark portfolio, representing a normal or passive pattern of debt issuance and debt composi-

---

[1]Many European OECD countries have about 70 percent to 90 percent fixed rate debt in the stock of debt.

Design and Use of Instruments

Three stratagems identified in the survey are: (1) promoting the liquidity and overall development of the domestic debt market; (2) tailoring the design of instruments to the needs of investors (thereby enhancing the demand for public debt); and (3) designing instruments that reduce risk premiums. In order to enhance secondary market liquidity, many countries in the survey are adopting the practice of building large "benchmark" stocks of debt that can be easily traded in the market. Reopening outstanding issues at the time of issuance builds the size of benchmark issues. Issued in this way, bonds become perfect substitutes in the secondary market, regardless of their date of issue. This procedure is being used in Canada, France, New Zealand, Spain, and Sweden. In some cases, treasury bill issues are reopened—for example, in Canada for the one-year treasury bill.

Selling instruments to small investors can be done either by wholesale market intermediaries—such as dealers, banks, mutual funds, and so on—or through the direct sales of specially designed instruments for the retail

tion.[2] In Sweden, a separate benchmark is designed for domestic and foreign debt. Risk tolerances are established within which the debt office exercises discretion.

Immunization Strategy

The New Zealand Debt Management Office's objectives are derived from modern portfolio management theory. Borrowing from techniques of asset and liability management in large financial institutions, the New Zealand debt manager's tactical policy is to achieve a debt maturity composition (optimal mix of short- and longer-term fixed rate debt) and currency composition (optimal mix of foreign-currency-denominated borrowings) that insulates or "immunizes" the government's net worth from changes in market interest rates and exchange rates. The primary objective of the Debt Office is twofold: (1) to identify a low-risk portfolio of net financial liabilities consistent with the Crown's aversion to risk, having regard for the cost of reducing risk;[3] and (2) to execute transactions in an efficient manner to achieve and maintain the desired portfolio. This objective is quantified in terms of the desired percentage of foreign currency debt and the duration of debt (domestic and foreign) measuring interest rate risk. Based on this analysis, New Zealand plans to reduce its foreign-exchange-denominated debt (currently about 40 percent) to zero (to eliminate currency risk) and to lengthen the duration of debt.

---

[2]In the case of Ireland, the benchmark portfolio is established by an outside service (J.P. Morgan, a U.S. investment bank).

[3]A low-risk portfolio of net financial liabilities is characterized by an immunized or duration-matched portfolio of assets and liabilities.

(household) market. More than half of the countries in the survey have specific programs designed for the retail investor; in many of these, encouraging household savings and diversifying funding sources are stated debt management objectives.

Unlike the institutional or wholesale market with its preference for a small number of large benchmark issues, research shows (see Chapter 13) that developing a successful retail program generally involves establishing a family of instruments. These instruments are generally nonmarketable, are sold on tap, and carry "put options" permitting the early redemption of principal.

Given the large administrative burden of dealing directly with many small savers and the specialized nature of the instrument and market, in many countries the management of retail debt is done by a debt management agency that can devote specialized resources to the task. For example, even in countries where marketable debt is managed by the ministry of finance or central bank, the administration of retail debt is done by an outside agency; this arrangement is used in the United Kingdom, Pakistan, and, more recently, Canada, where a separate retail debt agency is being formed.

A general case can be made for introducing new instruments that are cost-effective and broaden the market for fixed income securities. Furthermore, depending on the economic circumstances facing the country and on investor appetite, introducing index-linked or floating rate instruments can lead to cost savings to the government by reducing the inflation risk premium (the premium in yield that investors demand for covering, in addition to inflation expectations, the risk of volatile and higher-than-expected inflation) when stabilization programs are credible. In times of inflation or economic uncertainty, several governments have tended to rely on index-linked, variable (floating) rate instruments, or currency-linked instruments, as they may be the only cost-effective means of borrowing on longer maturities (see Chapter 8).

Many debt managers have introduced index-linked or floating rate instruments. Instruments used include inflation-indexed bonds with periodic returns adjusted (over and above the fixed real rate) for changes in the price index (e.g., Brazil, Canada, Mexico, New Zealand, and the United Kingdom); variable rate bonds whose return is tied to a short-term rate (in France, Ireland, Italy, and the United Kingdom); and currency-linked instruments (in Mexico and Pakistan). The use of these instruments should be carefully managed in the context of tactical policies so as to keep at manageable levels the volatility in debt-service cost that results from interest rate or currency changes.

Use of Derivatives

Derivatives are becoming a more widely used tool of risk and cost management.[11] Specifically, derivatives are being used to hedge interest rate risk, to hedge currency risk, and to reduce funding costs of floating rate (or fixed rate) debt.

In Ireland, in both domestic and foreign bond markets, interest rate swaps are used to adjust interest rate exposure while currency swaps are used to hedge foreign currency debt. Italy undertakes interest rate swaps with respect to issues placed in foreign markets; Argentina and Spain undertake currency swaps in foreign debt. In Canada, the government's comparative cost advantage (relative to enterprises) in raising long-term funds is captured by using a combination of long-term issues and interest rate swaps—fixed to floating—to create (synthetic) floating rate funds at a cost below that of treasury bills. New Zealand employs a wide spectrum of derivative instruments using foreign exchange forwards, interest rate and currency swaps, and futures in order to manage interest rate and currency exposure.

---

[11]For example, in France, section 56 of the 1991 Finance Act was adjusted and expanded to increase the debt management instruments available to the Minister of the Economy and authorizing the French Treasury Directorate to deal in interest rate swaps.

The use of derivatives should be guided by the overall tactical and strategic approach to debt management. Managing derivatives also requires establishing policies to control counterparty risk. Such policies should be made by the principal debt management authority who bears the risk. Furthermore, the debt manager should be well aware of market pricing of derivative products, especially in dealing in over-the-counter derivatives while mark-to-market positions of derivatives should be monitored. This argues for delegating the management of derivatives to a debt management agent that closely follows market developments such as a central bank or debt management office.

Maturities

The choice of maturity for new debt issuance is a management tool used for several purposes. First, lengthening or shortening the term to maturity adjusts the period of interest rate fixing, and therefore the volatility of debt-service charges and the market value of debt to changes in interest rates. Second, the term to maturity of new issuance—of either fixed or floating rate debt—can be used to balance the profile of maturing debt, thereby minimizing the risk that a bunching of maturities will disrupt refunding operations. Third, the choice of maturity can be used to exploit investor preferences, reducing the costs of debt issuance to the government.

Reflecting these varied purposes, the survey shows that some countries (such as Ireland and New Zealand) emphasize managing the maturity of new debt issuance with a goal of minimizing interest *costs*;[12] others emphasize minimizing the *variability* of cost as the main goal.[13] Interestingly, with the declines in long-term interest rates in the 1990s, there is a general trend toward increasing the proportion of longer-term fixed rate maturities (in Canada, France, Italy, New Zealand, Sweden, and the United Kingdom). Finally, in some countries, maturity choice is driven by the need of investors (the suppliers of funds) for a diversified structure of maturities (as is the case in Argentina, Brazil, Ireland, and Japan).

Currency

Modern portfolio theory suggests that borrowing in a variety of currencies and markets tends to diversify currency risk and reduce the interest cost of borrowing (just as investors can reduce risk and increase return by diversifying their bond portfolio across countries). Some empirical evidence of this is provided by de Fontenay and others (1995). Nevertheless,

---

[12]For example, in Ireland, the mix of maturities vis-à-vis the duration of the benchmark portfolio depends on the interest rate view of the Debt Office.

[13]Outstanding debt with a lower average term to maturity will require a larger annual volume of gross issues to refund maturing debt, increasing the possibility of more volatile debt-service costs.

as countries' revenues and assets are mainly in domestic currencies, foreign currency debt is often seen by debt managers as a large "risk" factor adding to cost volatility. As currencies have become more volatile, this view is gaining prevalence, especially in countries having substantial foreign currency debt. In addition, many developing countries aim to control external indebtedness by borrowing in local currency markets to which access by foreign investors can be restricted. In sum, while theory suggests that there are certain advantages both in terms of cost and risk in diversifying borrowing in foreign currencies, practices vary widely and many countries limit foreign currency issuance, as highlighted in Box 6.

Markets

Most countries develop strategies with respect to target markets in which to borrow. Markets may be classified into three categories: (1) domestic money and bond markets, (2) private markets (which includes households and other small investors), and (3) international capital markets.

Increasingly, countries are encouraging the development of deep and liquid *wholesale domestic debt markets* with the aim of reducing liquidity premiums and therefore interest costs. By enhancing transparency, liquidity,

---

Box 6. Use of Foreign Currency Debt

In Italy, the government was authorized in 1982 to issue securities denominated in ECUs (European currency units), and from 1984 it could borrow abroad in any foreign currency (in order to diversify borrowing, the Italian authorities issued U.S. dollar- and yen-denominated government securities). Other countries undertaking government borrowing in foreign currencies include Argentina, France, Ireland, and Spain. The French Treasury Directorate has been issuing securities denominated in ECUs since 1989, seeking to diversify its sources of funding and provide support for the monetary union. Another policy goal is to promote the development of an international capital market centered in Paris by establishing a liquid and structured market in ECU bonds. The French Treasury is the largest sovereign borrower in the long-term ECU market as well as the most regular borrower, with a fixed calendar of ECU issues.

Some countries do not undertake funding in foreign currency as a practical rule or because of a legal restriction. Countries in the sample borrowing only in domestic currency are Brazil, Canada, Japan, New Zealand, the United Kingdom, and the United States. In particular, Canada, New Zealand, and the United Kingdom use foreign currency issues for purposes of raising foreign exchange reserves. In the case of New Zealand, efforts are being made to reduce to zero the exposure to foreign currency debt refinancing, which stands at about 40 percent of the outstanding stock of debt.

and the smooth operation of the domestic debt markets, foreign participation in domestic markets is also encouraged. When foreigners participate in the domestic market, they assume the foreign exchange risk, which is an advantage to the government.

In theory, a fully integrated domestic market for government debt obviates the need to develop special instruments for the private market or to access the international market for domestic debt financing. Although there is a trend in this direction, in practice this singular approach may not fully meet debt management objectives, as evidenced by more than half of the countries in the survey that have designed specific programs for the *retail market* investor. As highlighted in the previous chapter, when borrowing needs are large, the government debt manager may need to tap all pockets of savings in the economy more or less at the same time. In addition, when boosting savings of the household sector is a specific debt management objective, then retail debt instruments offer an opportunity to target that sector directly.

In Canada and Pakistan, the private market is used to broaden the funding base and enhance the mobilization of savings from the household sector.[14] In some countries, the private market is used only to the extent that it is cost-effective compared with borrowing in the money and bond market (as in the United States and Sweden) or in comparison with external borrowing (as in Argentina). In some countries, market segmentation is discouraged, and the access of small investors to government markets is done mostly through the intermediation of financial institutions such as banks or mutual funds.

Finally, governments may also access *international capital markets* to diversify funding (by source and currency denomination) and minimize costs, as well as replenish foreign currency reserves. In some cases, borrowing in international markets permits term extension that is not possible (or too expensive) in the domestic market because of inflation or markets in maturity. Examples of countries accessing international markets include Argentina, with an extensive use of the international markets; France, with a structured calendar of ECU issues; Italy, with recent U.S. dollar and yen issues; and Sweden, where foreign currency borrowing expanded sharply in 1993.[15]

The three types of markets are sometimes reflected in the institutional approach to debt management organization. For example, the Swedish

---

[14]The promotion of household savings has often been considered an important objective of economic policy in order to fight inflationary pressures or to promote sources of investment.

[15]In autumn 1992, the Swedish National Debt Office borrowed in foreign currency on behalf of the Riksbank (central bank) in order to support the exchange rate (up to January 1993, these balances could not be used for budget financing). By fiscal year 1992/93, this support entailed an increase in foreign currency debt to 35.4 percent of total state debt.

National Debt Office is divided into three different departments along market lines: the Institutional Market Department borrows Swedish kronor (SKr) in the money and bond market; the Private Market Department borrows from households through four instruments specially created for borrowing in the private market—Lottery Bonds, Savings Certificates, the National Savings Account, and the National Debt Account; and the International Market Department borrows in foreign currencies, mainly through bonds issued in the Euromarket (and national markets) and through treasury bill programs in foreign currency.

3. Debt Management Planning

Debt management planning involves:

- forecasting fiscal requirements;
- determining the mix and pattern of debt issuance that incorporates tactical and strategic policies;
- providing the public with information on the debt program thereby lending transparency and predictability to the debt program; and
- reviewing past debt management operations.

Guidelines for issuing and administering government debt are decided—usually on an annual basis—by the principal debt management authority with inputs from the central bank and investor consultation groups; once formulated, this debt management program is normally approved by the highest political authority of the country (parliament or the council of ministers or both). The makeup of the program is then announced to the market. Debt management goals and the attainment of those goals is generally done in a backward-looking annual review.

Debt Management Program

Simply put, the debt management program consists of projections of government requirements (on at least a monthly frequency) and a program of debt issuance to meet those requirements. Generally the period for the debt program is yearly, corresponding with the horizon for the budget and formulated at the time of the budget. It is reviewed and updated during the year as circumstances necessitate.

The strategy for meeting budgetary requirements through the mix of instruments, maturities, currencies, and markets follows from the policy function. Thus, the policy and planning function go hand in hand because policy is achieved mainly at the time of refunding and new issuance rather than through secondary market transactions. For example, in the case of Canada (see Chapter 13), the tactical objective is to achieve a mix of

65 percent fixed and 35 percent floating rate of the outstanding *stock* of debt over a ten-year period, through a debt *issuance* mix of 70 percent fixed and 30 percent floating.

Transparency and Predictability

Economic theory suggests that reducing the uncertainty about the borrower's debt program is rewarded by lower yields. Increasingly, governments are making greater efforts to promote predictability and transparency of the debt program by providing information in varying degrees to the market about the size, pattern, and types of borrowings to be undertaken (see Chapter 14). Clearly, this requires a high level of accuracy about the government's own requirements and underscores the need for the treasury to predict requirements adequately. In the United Kingdom, for example, the treasury announces in each financial year an annual Debt Management Report that details (1) financing requirements (as well as the indicated sales split between gilts, National Savings, and other sources); (2) auction dates (calendar); and (3) the maturity structure of gilt issuance (approximate proportions of index-linked and short-, medium-, and long-term gilts).

In addition, it is becoming common practice in many countries to do an annual review analyzing market developments and the government's strategy for market development and providing information on outstanding stocks of debt and secondary market activity. This publication helps improve accountability of debt management by providing the equivalent of the annual report of a corporation. It also serves as an excellent advertisement of information to foreign investors that may be unfamiliar with the institutional framework and functioning of the secondary market (see, e.g., the annual report of the French Treasury).

4. Debt Program Implementation

Once debt management planning is set, its implementation consists of:

- the forecasting and management of cash balances;
- the management of primary issuance; and
- an information function.

Forecasting and Managing Cash Balances

Forecasting changes in cash balances concerns both the ministry of finance and central bank. Governments require positive cash balances from which to disburse while low levels indicate a need for issuing net new debt.[16] Errors in forecasting cash balances provide an early signal of possible budgetary overruns or revenue shortfalls.

Cash balances are a tool of debt management. They provide a bridge between net government disbursements—which are continuous operations with significant intramonth and intrayear seasonality—and debt management operations—which are discrete (periodic) operations. Cash balances also provide a cushion of issuance in the event of unexpected shortfalls in government receipts or increases in expenditures, or shortfalls in the market's appetite for government debt.

However, there is a cost of using this tool. Since interest income earned from holding positive cash balances is generally inferior to the cost of the underlying debt, such balances result in a net carrying cost to the government. Countries therefore attempt to maintain average cash balances at minimum levels.

Central banks also forecast cash balances. Changes in government cash balances affect banking system liquidity and monetary conditions and the stance of open market operations. Moreover, high levels (on the central bank's balance sheet) risk a rapid liquidity injection while consistent overdrafts may jeopardize the central bank's monetary stance and operational independence. When the central bank manages government debt issues, then the factors interesting to the ministry of finance are shared by the central bank as debt management agent.

In sum, the forecasting of cash balances and management of the level of cash balances are an important part of day-to-day debt management that concerns both the ministry of finance and the central bank. Thus, it is not surprising that the survey finds that both the central bank and the ministry of finance actively forecast and monitor cash balances in most countries.

Primary Issuance

The institutional responsibility for determining and executing primary issuance operations will largely depend on the goals of debt management and the state of market development. Townend (Chapter 9) builds a case for the central bank performing debt management operations in support of monetary management. By leaving the short-term management to the central bank, implementing debt management becomes a tool of monetary management. Pakistan and until recently the United Kingdom belonged to this category. When minimizing financial market disturbances is a debt management goal, central banks may have superior information on market conditions and the appetite for debt as a result of performing

---

[16]This is of the utmost importance for governments that cannot use temporary overdrafts or other forms of direct funding from the central bank.

other money market operations. Italy and until recently Canada fall into this category. When market response to interest rates (demand elasticity) is weak, market breadth narrow, and depth shallow, primary issuance will involve active management and tailoring of debt issues into the market (e.g., Brazil).

On the other hand, when markets are deep in relation to government requirements and the central bank has other monetary tools available, debt issuance may serve a more narrow purpose. In this case, the ministry of finance would generally take responsibility for the primary issuance function and active short-term debt management may be a tool for achieving cost-minimization objectives. This is the case in Canada, France, and the United States. In some countries, this responsibility is delegated to a separate debt office or agency (Ireland, Sweden, and New Zealand).

Information Function

Transparency and Predictability

Providing the market with advance information on debt program implementation provides transparency and predictability to the debt program. Disclosing information to market participants on day-to-day debt management operations and providing additional information on the borrowing calendar gives greater certainty to markets as to when and how the government borrows. Countries normally issue annual, semiannual, or quarterly calendars. For example, in the beginning of each calendar quarter, the Bank of England publishes maturity ranges for gilts to be sold at auction. While most countries publish forecasts of financing requirements so that the market is aware of the government's future borrowing needs at the time of the annual budget, some offer more frequent and up-to-date forecasts: Sweden, for instance, provides a monthly forecast; in the United Kingdom, the treasury is required by law to publish two forecasts a year.

The announcement of the characteristics and amount of securities to be issued is essential information for the market. While differences exist, the general practice among the countries in the sample is to announce the characteristics of an auction during the week before it takes place. The communications may be made by official decree, an official bulletin or press releases, and/or on electronic network services.

Announcements

All countries surveyed give considerable attention to publicizing issuance and pricing results shortly after auctions. This is increasingly done using electronic market information services to disseminate information rapidly and improve fairness through instantaneous access.

5. Operational Arrangements

Instruments

A summary of the range of debt instruments used across countries is found in the survey tables. The following trends in instrument use were identified:

- instrument design is becoming increasingly standardized across countries: this adds to simplicity and substitutability of instruments across countries, thereby attracting foreign investors and improving secondary market liquidity;
- a growing use of inflation-indexed bonds is found in industrialized countries;
- reliance on retail debt instruments, although important, has diminished with the growing importance of wholesale debt markets and improvements in liquidity; and
- because inflation is stabilizing at low levels in many industrialized countries, they are extending the term to maturity of their instruments and issuance to stabilize their debt-service costs and reduce refunding risk.

Selling Techniques

Among the countries surveyed, there is a general trend toward using auction systems and away from underwriting methods. The auction system now constitutes the main issuing technique in most of the countries in the survey. Underwriting syndicates are maintained for hard-to-sell or riskier instruments. For example, sales of ten-year bonds in Japan use an underwriting syndicate in combination with auction techniques.[17] In Canada, 30-year index-linked bonds (Canada Real Return Bonds) are sold through a syndicate system. Some countries use continuous sales methods, called tap issues, in which the price is set and flexibly adjusted in relation to secondary market conditions (in Ireland, 90 percent of sales are placed through the tap system; see also Chapter 15 for their use in Denmark). Nonetheless, there is a trend toward the use of periodic auctions and away from continuous auctions (tap sales). Typically, securities sold to the household sector are sold on tap; however, in this case, the price of the tap is usually fixed for the period of sale.

---

[17]Sixty percent of the total amount of monthly ten-year bond issues is auctioned; 40 percent of bonds are distributed to the syndicate members at the price determined by auction.

Timing of Issuance

The main consideration is between choosing a flexible versus fixed issuing calendar. As discussed, the arguments raised for favoring a fixed calendar are those of transparency, regularity, and predictability. Countries following a fixed calendar of issues include Argentina, Canada, France, Italy, Mexico, New Zealand, Spain, Sweden, the United Kingdom, and the United States. They believe, on the one hand, that regular and predictable offerings of government securities reduce the government's borrowing costs by lessening market uncertainty. On the other hand, some countries emphasize the need to have flexibility in their calendar in order to take advantage of opportune (bullish) market conditions (e.g., Ireland and the Netherlands).

Depository System

A centralized depository system offers economies of scale in the clearing and settlement of transactions. In many cases, the depository and book-entry system for government securities has been centralized in the central bank; however, private sector institutions also perform this function in some countries. Examples of countries with a centralized depository in the central bank include Ireland, Italy, Japan, Mexico, New Zealand, Pakistan, the United Kingdom, and the United States. Countries with a private-sector-owned depository institution include Canada (Canadian Depository for Securities) and Sweden (Swedish Securities Register Center, VPC AB); in Argentina, the government has an agreement with a private institution (Caja de Valores SA) to register public securities. In France, the central bank (Saturne System) is the depository institution for treasury bills and notes while for treasury bonds, a private company (Paris Bourse SICO-VAM clearinghouse) is the depository system operating a book-entry system.[18] There are plans, however, to merge the clearing and settlement of government securities into the same system.

In sum, the special interest of central banks in the systemic functioning and overall efficiency of clearing and settlement of government securities has led many of them to establish a central depository system for book-entry government securities. Where private sector institutions perform this role, their efforts are closely coordinated with the central bank to ensure utmost security and the development of delivery-versus-payment systems.

---

[18]SICOVAM is jointly owned by the Bank of France, the stock exchange, and more than 30 banks and professional associations.

Cash Balances

A general principle of treasury management is that there should be a single consolidated account through which government receipts and disbursements are made. This is a key element for effective treasury management. In all the countries surveyed, the consolidated fund is held with the central bank, which acts as the fiscal agent for the government.

However, banking arrangements are often developed with commercial banks also. This serves several purposes. First, by placing government deposits with the banking system, the government can earn competitive returns on its surplus balances. Second, as government cash balances draw funds away from the banking system, they may be recycled back into the banking system, facilitating the central bank's liquidity management. Third, deposit services are a commercial rather than central banking function.[19]

To maximize the interest earned, in Canada surplus cash balances are invested to the extent possible in higher-yielding term deposits (placed by auctions to commercial banks), as compared with demand deposits. In Sweden, the Debt Office manages its cash balances directly with the market through repos. In the United States, the treasury has interest-earning tax and loan accounts with commercial banks (fully collateralized by treasury securities).

Although the New Zealand Debt Management Office centralizes surplus cash funds, it decentralizes to government departments the responsibility for forecasting payments and other banking operations. In order to encourage departments to exercise good cash management and working capital control discipline, incentives are given to departments to forecast sources and uses of cash balances accurately (deviations from forecasted outturns—either surpluses or deficits—attract cost penalties).

Temporary borrowing from the central bank is allowed in some countries; however, the trend is to limit or eliminate recourse to central bank financing. For example, this prohibition is included in the Maastricht Treaty of the European Community.[20] Temporary shortages of funds are covered in some countries through the issuance of specific instruments, typically treasury bills with a very short term (one month or less)—for example, Canada (Cash Management Bills), Japan (Financing Bills), and the United States (Cash Management Bills).

---

[19]This requires, among other things, a well-developed and sound banking system (see Chapter 1).

[20]Article 104 of the treaty stipulates that "overdraft facilities or any other type of credit facility with the European Central Bank or with the central banks of the Member States in favor of Community institutions or bodies, central governments, regional, local or other public authorities shall be prohibited."

6. Location of Debt Management Functions and Division of Labor

There are numerous debt management functions, and various options exist for locating them. This section discusses the location of those functions, highlighting criteria for locating them.

The debt management policy function should rest with the ministry of finance, the principal debt management authority, which has the legal authority to borrow and is accountable to the parliament. Moreover, as chief economic manager, the ministry can effectively link fiscal policy with the budget-making process and its financing—debt management policy. Thus, for both accountability and economic reasons, the debt management policy function should be located with the finance ministry.

Nevertheless, the policy and planning function should also involve the central bank *as advisor* since the debt manager's pursuit of *tactical and strategic policies* indirectly affects monetary conditions and may pose risks to the central bank's monetary policies. To illustrate: (1) when the maturity profile is skewed to the short end, the risk of failed refunding operations increases; (2) the management of the outstanding debt stock changes the liquidity or money-like quality of assets held by the private sector; (3) the degree of risk of debt-service shocks increases with greater use of short-term debt, which could potentially limit the scope for tight monetary policy; and (4) the instrument mix of debt issuance affects the liquidity of markets in which the central bank operates for the purpose of monetary management. For these reasons, the central bank should have input into the debt management policy and planning decisions that are ultimately taken by the ministry and approved by the parliament. Insofar as there are conflicts between monetary objectives and budget and debt management targets, including central banks at this stage provides balance in setting policy targets.

While *implementation of the debt program* is a natural extension of treasury operations located in the ministry of finance, there are some reasons for locating this function elsewhere. When the implementation of the debt program is simultaneously used as a monetary tool, it makes sense to provide scope to the central bank for short-term management. This is also the case when a goal of debt management is to develop the government securities market, as often the central bank is more knowledgeable than the ministry about market conditions as a result of its monetary management responsibilities and is in a better position to manage market liquidity and foster liquid markets.

When the central bank has adequate tools and when government securities markets are sufficiently developed, the case for locating short-term management with the central bank weakens considerably. With developed markets, the hierarchy of debt management objectives is likely to change toward reduced emphasis on achieving monetary and market development goals, and greater emphasis on more narrow "micro" objectives of minimizing debt-service costs.

If the central bank performs both monetary and debt management functions in these circumstances, a policy conflict may arise. Wearing two hats, does the central bank tighten liquidity as called for by the monetary program or does it add liquidity to ensure the success of a large debt refunding? Furthermore, can the central bank be held accountable for debt-service cost-minimization objectives?[21] To illustrate, is debt service high because of tight money or because of bad debt management policies? Knowing the monetary policy stance, should the central bank adjust the term to maturity of debt issuance?

When markets are deep, the ministry of finance is well suited to undertake the role of debt management implementation. Using auction techniques, it need not be concerned with day-to-day market conditions and can plan its debt sales almost exclusively according to its funding needs.

Additional gains of enhanced accountability and improved public confidence may result in *placing debt program implementation in a separate agency*. First, with the establishment of such an agency, the parameters within which the implementation of debt management policy is conducted are more clearly established. This improves transparency and accountability. Second, a debt agency is an additional step removed from the political process; such distance may discourage the running of significant debt management risks. Because it is responsible and accountable for debt management policy only and not the budget process, an agency would be less likely to trade off long-term debt management policy goals (such as market stability and confidence) for short-term budget goals (such as attempting to offset budget overruns with low-cost but riskier short-term or currency-linked debt issuance). Locating debt management policy in a separate agency, therefore, may enhance public confidence in the government's debt program.

Selling arrangements are often placed either with the central bank or with a debt agency. This reflects the specialized nature of the function. Even though central banks may not play a role in debt management implementation, they often manage the selling arrangements: this is so because of economies of scale in having the central bank perform these functions and because no policy conflicts exist. The central bank can easily perform the role as an adjunct to its monetary operations; the infrastructure already exists—dealing systems, market contacts, and so forth.

---

[21]For example, it would not be desirable to include the objective of minimizing debt-service costs in a bank act.

Moreover, important *information externalities* may arise. By conducting auctions, the central bank gleans important information on market conditions, which it can use in formulating monetary management decisions.

Alternatively, managing selling arrangements may be considered an important tool for minimizing costs. In this case, the debt agency responsible for achieving the cost-minimization objective would also undertake the design and implementation of selling arrangements. This is especially the case for selling arrangements for retail debt, which tend to be administratively burdensome and expensive. Thus, by making the debt agency responsible for selling arrangements, the cost effectiveness of such arrangements can also be made accountable (as in Sweden).

Concluding Remarks

The scope of institutions and operating arrangements differ depending on country circumstances, the stage of market development, and efficiency considerations. Debt management functions under consideration can be passed through the criteria listed below, which serve as a guide for locating debt management functions. For each country, depending on the stage of market development and other circumstances, different institutional answers may present themselves for the appropriate execution and coordination of debt management functions.

- What is the objective of the debt management function? This guides the locating of each debt management function.
- Can accountability be established for the performance of the debt management function by the institution that is performing the function? This is an important tool for measuring the attainment of the objective.
- Are there overall efficiencies—economies of scale, comparative advantage, or information externalities—to be gained by an institution performing the function?
- Are public confidence and transparency enhanced by locating the debt management function within a particular institution?

Appendix
Public Debt Management Frameworks—Country Tables

	Argentina	Brazil
1. GOVERNMENT BORROWING: LEGAL FRAMEWORK, ACCOUNTABILITY, AND AUTHORITY		
Legal Framework		
Legal authority to borrow	Financial Management Law (Law No. 24.156)	The Federal Constitution (1988) establishes the National Congress as the competent authority in matters of debt management (with the approval of the President)
Who is authorized to borrow	Government; Ministry of Economy	National Treasury
Accountability		
Approval	Congress	Congress
Ceiling	Global limit established by the budget law	Based on the budget proposal submitted by the President to the Federal Senate; a global limit on the amount of consolidated debt of the center, states, districts, and municipalities is set
Debt Management Authority and Agents		
Principal debt management authority	Ministry of Economy	National Treasury
Debt management agents	Finance Undersecretariat. It issues treasury bills up to budgetary limits	Central Bank of Brazil
2. DEBT MANAGEMENT OBJECTIVES, AND POLICY CHOICES AND INSTRUMENTS		
Objectives		
Primary objective	To redeem debt, to finance public investment, and to cover temporary cash imbalances	To finance public debt requirements
• Horizon	Several years	As required to rollover debt
• Measurement of performance	Model in progress	To meet financing requirements
Secondary objectives		
• Monetary policy considerations	None; currency board type of arrangement	Public debt management takes into account monetary policy restrictions, and vice versa
• Others	To develop financial markets; to influence the shape of yield curve	To keep the market smoothly functioning in order to provide the Treasury with continuous funding at competitive costs

Public Debt Management Frameworks—Country Tables *(continued)*

	Argentina *(cont.)*	Brazil *(cont.)*
Policy Choices and Instruments		
Instruments	Designed for Euromarket and domestic wholesale market	Extensive use of index-linked instruments to reduce risk premiums and funding costs
Use of derivatives	Yes: currency swaps to hedge foreign borrowing and occasional use of interest rate swaps	No
Maturity	Aim for smooth distribution of maturities. Consider opportunities offered by market conditions	Normally ranges from three months to two years, depending on market demand
Currency	U.S. dollars, with diversification into yen- and DM-denominated securities	Generally issued in domestic currency to support monetary policy objectives
Markets		
• Domestic money and bond market	Attempt to develop market to lengthen maturities. Local costs are compared with that of external borrowing	Fairly well-developed domestic market for discount instruments
• Private market	No	No
• International capital markets	Main government debt market	No
3. DEBT MANAGEMENT PLANNING		
Debt Management Program		
Program and horizon	Ministry of Economy: Annual	National Treasury: debt program is incorporated in the Budgetary Directive Law, including provisions for debt issue once within a specified time frame
Transparency		
Publication and frequency	Annual Report of Ministry of Economy; Fiscal Bulletin quarterly	Multiannual plan and annual budget law
4. DEBT PROGRAM IMPLEMENTATION		
Day-to-Day Management		
Decisions	Finance Undersecretariat	Treasury, after consultation with the Central Bank of Brazil
Cash balance forecasting/ frequency	None	Treasury, monthly estimates, with intramonth updates
Transparency		
Borrowing calendar/ frequency	None	n.a.

Public Debt Management Frameworks—Country Tables *(continued)*

	Argentina *(cont.)*	Brazil *(cont.)*
Amounts of securities to be issued and other aspects	Finance Undersecretariat	Treasury
Announcements		
Publication of auction results	Public press releases. The Finance Undersecretariat communicates by electronic mail to the bidding entities	The Central Bank of Brazil discloses the results after the auction; they are officially published several days later
5. OPERATIONAL ARRANGEMENTS		
Instruments	• Treasury bills • Foreign-currency-denominated debt	• Treasury notes (index-linked instruments, linked to the U.S. dollar, to price indices, and to a rate of private securities) • T-bills (Letras do Tesouro National)
Selling techniques		
• Auction system	Yes	Yes
• Tap system	No	No
• Others	Private placements	No
Timing of issuance (Fixed/flexible)	Fixed/flexible	Flexible
Participants at auction	General public participation	Public participation, provided by financial institutions
Form of securities	Global registered certificates; only a few securities are in bearer form (dollar-denominated)	Book-entry
Central depository/ book-entry system	The government has an agreement with Caja de Valores SA (private entity) to register public securities. Caja de Valores SA has an agreement with CEDEL	Special Clearing and Depository System (Sistema Especial de Liquidacao e Custodia, SELIC), administered by the Open Market Operations Department of the Central Bank of Brazil
Cash balances	The Ministry of Economy administers national currency cash. The Central Bank of Argentina administers foreign currency cash	Maintains a large buffer of cash to avoid abrupt changes in issue size, which could negatively affect funding costs
Central bank credit to government	The Convertibility Law prohibits any direct credit from the Central Bank to the government, and limits Central Bank's total government holdings to 10 percent of international reserves	Yes. Can buy securities in the primary market for later sale in the secondary market

Public Debt Management Frameworks—Country Tables *(continued)*

	Argentina *(cont.)*	Brazil *(cont.)*
6. LOCATION OF DEBT MANAGEMENT FUNCTIONS		
Policy function		
• Strategic guidelines	Ministry of Economy	Treasury in consultation with Central Bank of Brazil
• Day-to-day operations	Finance Undersecretariat	Treasury in consultation with Central Bank of Brazil
Accounting function of outstanding debt	Ministry of Economy	Treasury and Central Bank of Brazil
Cash balance management	The Central Bank of Argentina administers foreign currency, and the Treasury directorate administers national currency cash balances	n.a.
Selling arrangement	Finance Undersecretariat	Treasury (selling agent: Central Bank of Brazil)
Debt maintenance		
• Issuance/settlement	Central Bank of Argentina/ Caja de Valores	Central Bank of Brazil
• Redemption	Ministry of Economy	Central Bank of Brazil
Secondary market intervention in government securities	None	Central Bank of Brazil

	Canada	France
1. GOVERNMENT BORROWING: LEGAL FRAMEWORK, ACCOUNTABILITY, AND AUTHORITY		
Legal Framework		
Legal authority to borrow	• Financial Administration Act R.S. cF-10, 1984; Borrowing Authority each fiscal year	Annual Finance Act, covering revenues and expenditures for the coming year, voted on by the parliament each December
Who is authorized to borrow	Government. After Parliament has authorized the issuance of securities, via the Borrowing Authority Act, the Governor in Council authorizes the Minister of the Department of Finance to determine terms and conditions of the issue and characteristics of the securities	The Finance Act authorizes the Minister of the Economy to borrow in French francs or ECUs to cover all treasury needs
Accountability		
Approval	Parliament and Governor in Council	The parliament examines the fiscal gap, reviews the execution of the budget, and verifies its compliance with Finance Act

Public Debt Management Frameworks—Country Tables *(continued)*

	Canada *(cont.)*	France *(cont.)*
Ceiling	Yes. A two-step process: (1) A ceiling is set by Parliament in the Borrowing Authority Act based on the requirements for new funds; (2) The Governor in Council approves the amounts to be raised for new bond offerings	None
Debt Management Authority and Agents		
Principal debt management authority	Department of Finance	Treasury Directorate
Debt management agents	• Central bank (Bank of Canada). Article 24 of the Bank of Canada Act R.S., cB-2, 1970, states that the Bank of Canada shall act as agent for the Government of Canada in respect of the management of the public debt of Canada • Primary dealers: Aid in the distribution and trading of debt	• Central bank (Bank of France) manages auctions on behalf of the Treasury Directorate • Primary dealers (Spécialistes en Valeurs du Trésor): Make two-way markets in all negotiable government securities under all market conditions. Purchase at auction a minimum of 2 percent of the annual volume of the securities issued (the average of the percentages for the three types of securities issued must be at least 3 percent). Perform other market supporting functions

2. DEBT MANAGEMENT OBJECTIVES, AND POLICY CHOICES AND INSTRUMENTS

Objectives

Primary objective	To raise the funds required by the government at the minimum long-term cost, while at the same time keeping variability in this cost at reasonable levels	To minimize the costs of borrowing over a long-term horizon
• Horizon	Several years	Several years
• Measurement of performance	Ad hoc reviews of debt management process	No systematic performance measurement. Control of general operations of the Treasury by the Cour des Comptes
Secondary objectives		
• Monetary policy considerations	Indirect: the Finance Department consults with the Bank of Canada on debt management decisions; sufficient surplus cash balances are kept in demand accounts	None

Public Debt Management Frameworks—Country Tables *(continued)*

	Canada *(cont.)*	France *(cont.)*
	with commercial banks to facilitate monetary management	
• Others	To improve the functioning of the market and its efficiency	To maintain the smooth functioning of the financial markets. Issuance policy of promoting the transparency, liquidity, and simplicity of the government securities market
Policy Choices and Instruments		
Instruments	The government's strategy for borrowing in fixed and float-ing rate form is based upon achieving a balance between cost minimization and cost stability. Looking out over the coming decade, the govern-ment's long-term strategy is to shift the balance toward more fixed rate debt (from 50 percent to 65 percent fixed rate)	Policy of reopening issues to maintain high liquidity. Short-term discount notes. Fixed rate, short-, medium-, and long-term notes and bonds. Floating rate notes
Use of derivatives	Since 1988, interest-rate swap program (C$7.8 billion stock in March 1993 with estimated savings of C$54.4 million per year)	The Treasury Directorate is authorized to engage in interest rate swaps
Maturity	Since 1990–91, the govern-ment has followed a practice, subject to market conditions, of issuing a higher proportion of longer-term debt to increase the average term to maturity	To limit its exposure to market risk when refinancing its debt, the government seeks to maintain a relatively high average maturity term on marketable securities
Currency	Funding is undertaken only in Canadian dollars. The govern-ment borrows in foreign cur-rency only for the purpose of raising foreign exchange reserves	Borrowing is undertaken in domestic currency and in foreign currency, in order to diversify the sources of funding. Since 1989, foreign borrowing has been concentrated in ECUs
Markets		
• Domestic money and bond market	The government has taken a number of initiatives to im-prove the efficiency of the markets with a view to increasing liquidity and lowering interest costs	The Treasury has taken many initiatives to promote deep and liquid domestic money and government securities markets to attract domestic and foreign investors
• Private market	The personal sector is directly targeted through issuance of Canada Saving Bonds	No

Public Debt Management Frameworks—Country Tables *(continued)*

	Canada *(cont.)*	France *(cont.)*
• International capital markets	Not used for domestic borrowing requirements	Euromarket for ECU borrowings

3. DEBT MANAGEMENT PLANNING

Debt Management Program

Program and horizon	Annual. The Finance Department prepares the annual debt management program, which is submitted to Parliament for its approval and signed by the Governor in Council. The financial requirements are stated in the Annual Budget for the upcoming fiscal year	• Annual. Treasury Directorate. The volume, timing, and terms of issue of long-term government debt instruments are agreed upon and approved by the Minister of the Economy at the beginning of each year • Volume, timing, and terms of short-term issues are determined solely by the Treasury

Transparency

Publication and frequency	Budget (annual) press release of Finance Department	• Ministry of Economy: Annual report/monthly information letter (includes details of auctions and an updated table of outstanding debt) • Forecast of financing requirements is published at the beginning of each year

4. DEBT PROGRAM IMPLEMENTATION
Day-to-Day Management

Decisions	Finance Department with the Bank of Canada as advisor	The Treasury Directorate determines every week the volume of treasury bill issues in view of the evolution of cash needs
Cash balance forecasting/ frequency	Finance Department (monthly) and Bank of Canada (daily)	Bank of France and Treasury Directorate forecast cash balances based on a historic pattern (daily)

Transparency

Borrowing calendar/ frequency	Finance Department (quarterly)	Treasury Directorate (annually published with the forecast of borrowing requirements)
Amounts of securities to be issued and other aspects	To improve the transparency of its debt operations, in 1992 the government adopted a bond-issuing calendar with regular quarterly 5- and 10-year bond issues, and announcements ahead of each quarter of dates for the remaining auctions scheduled for the quarter	Fixed calendar of auctions: weekly for bills, monthly for notes and bonds, every two months for ECU notes and bonds. The Treasury Directorate supplies information about the issuance and management of public debt through its monthly bulletin. The Treasury

Public Debt Management Frameworks—Country Tables *(continued)*

	Canada *(cont.)*	France *(cont.)*
		Directorate announces the securities to be put on sale together with the quantities proposed at least two working days before the auction
Announcements		
Publication of auction results	Finance Department or Bank of Canada (on behalf of the former): press releases	Bank of France: following auctions. Ministry of Economy: Official Journal, monthly
5. OPERATIONAL ARRANGEMENTS		
Instruments	Marketable instruments: • Cash management bills (maturities usually of 1–40 days) • Treasury bills (maturities of 3, 6, and 12 months) • Conventional fixed coupon bonds (maturities from 2 to 30 years). Average term of issuance is 8 years. • Index–Linked Bonds: "Canada Real Return Bonds" (with a maturity of 30 years). Since November 1991 Nonmarketable instruments: • Canada Savings Bonds (issues annually for a term of up to 12 years)	• Treasury bills (BTFs) (maturities of 13 weeks, 6 and 12 months) • Treasury notes (BTANs) (maturities of 2 and 5 years (FF and ECU)) • Fungible government bonds (OATs) (maturities of 7 to 30 years (FF, ECU)) • Floating rate OATs against long- (7-year) or short-dated (13-week) benchmark rates
Selling technique		
• Auction system	Yes	Yes
• Tap system	Yes for Canada Savings Bonds	No
• Others	Syndicate is used for index–linked bonds	Syndicated form (occasionally for foreign borrowing)
Timing of issuance (fixed/flexible)	Fixed for T-bills and some bond tranches; flexible for others	Fixed: pre-arranged calendar
Participants in auction	Primary distributors	Public participation
Form of securities	Bearer, fully registered, and book-entry (immobilized securities)	Book-entry system: "dematerialized securities"
Central depository book-entry system	Canadian Depository for Securities—for marketable securities (privately owned). Partial book-entry system (being developed toward a full book-entry system)	• SICOVAM clearing house (for bonds): Private company owned by the Bank of France, the stock exchange, and more than 30 banks and professional associations • Bank of France (Saturne System) for bills and notes
Cash balances	Bank of Canada and commercial banks	Bank of France

Public Debt Management Frameworks—Country Tables *(continued)*

	Canada *(cont.)*	France *(cont.)*
Central bank credit to government	Allowed	No. European Union obligations (Article 104 of the Maastricht Treaty) prohibit any borrowing from the central bank

6. LOCATION OF DEBT MANAGEMENT FUNCTIONS

Policy function

• Strategic guidelines	Finance Department with Bank of Canada as advisor	Ministry of Economy
• Day-to-day operations	Finance Department in consultation with Bank of Canada	Treasury Directorate
Accounting function of outstanding debt	Finance Department and Bank of Canada	Ministry of Economy
Cash balance management	Finance Department and Bank of Canada	Treasury Directorate
Selling arrangements	Bank of Canada, Financial Markets Department	Treasury with Bank of France's technical support

Debt maintenance

• Issuance/settlement	Bank of Canada, Public Debt Department/Banking Operations Department	For BTFs and BTANs: Bank of France Saturne System. For OATs: Relit system run by SICOVAM
• Redemption	Bank of Canada, Banking Operations Department	Bank of France on behalf of the Treasury
Secondary market intervention	Bank of Canada, Financial Markets Department on occasion for refunding operations	• Treasury: active debt management policy of intervening to improve technical position of the market (Fonds de Soutien des Rentes)

	Ireland	Italy

1. GOVERNMENT BORROWING: LEGAL FRAMEWORK, ACCOUNTABILITY, AND AUTHORITY

Legal Framework

Legal authority to borrow	Finance Acts	Financial Law (Law March 30, 1981, No. 119)
Who is authorized to borrow	Finance Ministry	The Treasury has the formal responsibility to borrow

Accountability

Approval	The National Treasury Management Agency (NTMA) operates under the general control of the Minister of Finance and is subject to whatever directions and guidelines he may give	Each year the parliament must approve (Budget Law) the upper limit for borrowing on domestic and foreign markets
Ceiling	• A limit may be imposed on foreign currency borrowing	Yes: for both domestic and foreign currency borrowing

Public Debt Management Frameworks—Country Tables *(continued)*

	Ireland *(cont.)*	Italy *(cont.)*
	• The amount of funding executed in any year on the domestic market is dictated by the need to refinance maturing debt, fund the government borrowing requirement, and have an adequate cash balance to carry forward into the next year	

Debt Management Authority and Agents

	Ireland *(cont.)*	Italy *(cont.)*
Principal debt management authority	Under the National Treasury Management Act 1990, the borrowing and debt management functions of the Finance Ministry and related operational responsibilities are delegated to a debt office, the NTMA	The Treasury determines the proportion of the public sector borrowing requirements ("PSBR") to be financed by new issues of securities on the domestic and foreign markets
Debt management agents	• Stockbrokers • Post Office for National Savings Schemes	• Central bank (Bank of Italy). Supports the Treasury, acting as a financial advisor, issuing manager, fiscal agent, and government banker • Primary dealers. Support primary auctions (underwriting commitment) and secondary market

2. DEBT MANAGEMENT OBJECTIVES, AND POLICY CHOICES AND INSTRUMENTS

Objectives

	Ireland *(cont.)*	Italy *(cont.)*
Primary objective	To manage Ireland's national debt and borrowing programs, in accordance with the general guidelines of the Minister of Finance, to (1) achieve specific budgetary savings and (2) outperform the benchmark portfolio	• To finance the PSBR in the market at minimum costs • To achieve a balanced average maturity of the outstanding debt in order to limit the size and frequency of refundings • To promote greater participation by foreign and domestic investors in public debt
• Horizon	Annual objective is set with regard to the position at the beginning of the year	The objective of full funding must be achieved over each financial year. Temporary under- or overfunding may occur
• Measurement of performance	The debt office (NTMA) seeks to meet an annual budget target in debt-service cost set by the Minister of Finance and at the same time outperform	Full funding of PSBR in market-related conditions

Public Debt Management Frameworks—Country Tables *(continued)*

	Ireland *(cont.)*	Italy *(cont.)*
	a benchmark that compares net present value of assets and liabilities of the actual versus the benchmark portfolio. The benchmark is reviewed every three years	
Secondary objectives	The Central Bank of Ireland is independently responsible for the formation and implementation of monetary policy	
• Monetary policy considerations	The debt office (NTMA) keeps the Central Bank fully informed of its transactions in order to ensure that the NTMA's day-to-day operations do not conflict with the Central Bank's day-to-day management of money market liquidity and of the foreign monetary reserves. In times of major currency crises, the NTMA and the Central Bank, together with the Finance Ministry, will coordinate their activities	Incorporated in the context of the Bank of Italy's debt management advisory role
• Others	The debt office (NTMA) seeks to improve the liquidity of its Irish marketable borrowing instruments	To diversify debt instruments in order to facilitate debt absorption and tailor instruments to market requirements
Policy Choices and Instruments		
Instruments	Irish pound bonds (fixed rate); Exchequer notes (discount notes); small savings instruments; and foreign currency funding instruments	In the domestic market, various types of financial instruments: short-term instruments; medium- and long-term instruments, with either fixed or variable rate coupons, in lira or ECUs. The offer of securities with a limited number of maturities by use of the reopening technique in tranches has increased the liquidity of outstanding issues
Use of derivatives	Interest rates swaps are used on the domestic bond market; interest rate and currency swaps are used in managing the foreign currency debt	Currency and interest rate swaps may be undertaken with respect to issues placed in foreign markets
Maturity	The maturity mix of funding depends partly on demand, but also on the interest rate view of the NTMA vis-à-vis	Since 1990, the Treasury has been financing the debt with more long-term securities (bonds with maturities of 10

Public Debt Management Frameworks—Country Tables *(continued)*

	Ireland *(cont.)*	Italy *(cont.)*
	the duration of the benchmark. Domestic bond issuance is in 5-, 10-, 15-, and 20-year benchmark stocks; Exchequer note out to 12 months maturity; and foreign borrowings of varying maturity	and 30 years) in order to limit the size of securities refunding
Currency	Net new funding is done in Irish pounds. The policy is not to increase foreign borrowing and, where possible, to reduce the amount outstanding. (Nevertheless the outstanding stock of foreign debt is sizable and actively managed)	Until 1982, the government could not borrow (directly) in foreign currencies. Since then, it has increasingly had recourse to the foreign market, adopting several borrowing procedures, different currencies, and a variety of financial instruments
Markets		
• Domestic money and bond market	• Short-term paper market: short-term paper is sold (over the counter) directly to corporates and banks. Surplus cash may be placed on deposit in the money market (with Central Bank agreement) • Bond market: the debt office (NTMA) is constantly seeking ways to improve the functioning of the domestic bond market	Extensive development of bond market to enhance liquidity: electronic and automated screen-based dealer market integrated with clearing and settlement system
• Private market	Tax-free national savings schemes are aimed primarily at private individuals	Household sector holds target amounts of treasury bills
• International capital markets	The objective in borrowing on international capital markets is to borrow at minimum cost and within the guidelines issued to the NTMA by the Minister of Finance so as to contribute to the primary objective	Euromarket for foreign currency financing

3. DEBT MANAGEMENT PLANNING

Debt Management Program

Program and horizon	Annual. The government decides on the annual borrowing requirement and the debt office (NTMA) is responsible for executing the borrowing and for managing the existing debt	Annual. The Treasury determines the volume of securities to be issued in order to cover the estimated budget deficit and the redemption of maturing securities on a monthly basis

Public Debt Management Frameworks—Country Tables *(continued)*

	Ireland *(cont.)*	Italy *(cont.)*
Transparency		
Publication and frequency	• The debt office (NTMA) publishes an annual report which is presented to the Minister of Finance and made available to the public • The Finance Ministry publishes monthly reports on the outturn net borrowing requirement • The Finance Ministry issues a quarterly statement commenting on the figures for the quarter and the expected outturn for the year	The Treasury publishes a quarterly program about the features and the minimum amount of new medium– and long-term securities to be issued. As regards timing, in the annual calendar, the Treasury communicates the auction dates of all types of issues. Among other sources, data is published on the Annual Report and Monthly Statistical Bulletin of the Central Bank

4. DEBT PROGRAM IMPLEMENTATION

Day-to-Day Management

Decisions	The debt office (NTMA) decides on all aspects of funding and national debt management, subject to guidelines issued to it by the Minister of Finance	The Treasury takes final decisions on debt management with the contribution of the Bank of Italy in an advisory role. On the basis of its contact with the market, the Bank of Italy advises the Treasury on the volume and maturity of securities to be issued
Cash balance forecasting/ frequency	The debt office (NTMA) monitors cash flow arising from the national debt, which it feeds into the Finance Ministry. The ministry monitors total cash flow of government expenditure and revenue; if problems are anticipated, funding plans are adjusted	Monthly. The Treasury establishes liquidity needs to cover the monthly PSBR; the Bank of Italy forecasts the liquidity required to set off the PSBR and the requirements of the banking system

Transparency

Borrowing calendar/ frequency	No calendar of borrowing is announced to the market	Treasury Ministry (annually)
Amounts of securities to be issued and other aspects	Issuance via taps. The size of the tap is announced to the markets 15 minutes prior to pricing. Two days' notice is given for auctions	Securities issued are announced by official decree. Dates of auctions are announced by the Treasury in official press releases. Debt issue announcements are published in all major domestic newspapers and financial on-screen networks

Public Debt Management Frameworks—Country Tables *(continued)*

	Ireland *(cont.)*	Italy *(cont.)*
Announcements		
Publication of auction results	Auction results are normally announced by the debt office (NTMA) on Reuters within 13 minutes	Auction results are released to the press by the Bank of Italy and published on the major financial on-screen networks
5. OPERATIONAL ARRANGEMENTS		
Instruments	Marketable instruments: • Treasury bills: Exchequer bills (maturities of 91 and 182 days); Exchequer notes (maturities of 7 days to 1 year) • Treasury notes (short-term government stocks), with fixed and variable interest rates (maturities of up to 5 years) • Medium-term fixed interest rate government bonds (maturities from 5 to 15 years) • Long-term fixed interest rate government bonds (maturities from 15 to 21 years) Nonmarketable instruments: • National Savings products (Savings Certificates, Savings Bonds, National Instalment Savings, Prize Bonds, Post Office Savings Banks Deposits)	Marketable instruments: • Treasury bills (Buoni Ordinari del Tesoro) (maturities of 3, 6, and 12 months) • Treasury bonds (Buoni del Tesoro Poliennali) (maturities of 3, 5, 10, and 30 years) • Floating rate treasury certificate (Certificati di Credito del Tesoro con Cedola Variabile) (maturity of 7 years) • ECU treasury certificates (Certificati di Credito del Tesoro) (maturity of 5 years) • Foreign-currency-denominated bonds (Republic of Italy) Nonmarketable instruments: • Post Office Savings Certificates (Buoni Postali Fruttiferi)
Selling technique	On the domestic bond market about 90 percent of bond funding is by tap with 10 percent by way of auctions. Commitment to hold one auction of bonds each quarter. Exchequer notes are sold on a daily basis over the phone by the debt office	The sole method for issuing government securities is the auction system: uniform-price auction for medium- and long-term instruments; discriminatory-price auction for short-term bills. Since February 1994, automated auctions have been introduced to place medium- and long-term government paper
• Auction system	Yes (10 percent)	Yes: for all treasury securities
• Tap system	Yes (90 percent)	Yes (for the Post Office Savings Certificates only)
• Others	Over the counter. Exchequer and National Savings	No
Timing of issuance (fixed/flexible)	Flexible: opportunistic; no regular calendar	Flexible for ECU treasury certificates; fixed (fortnightly) for the others

Public Debt Management Frameworks—Country Tables *(continued)*

	Ireland *(cont.)*	Italy *(cont.)*
Participants at auction	Public participation	Banks and investment companies (SIMS)
Central depository/ book-entry system	The Settlement Office run by the Central Bank of Ireland provides a book-entry clearing system for government bonds	Centralized Securities Accounts is an automated system managed by the Bank of Italy
Form of securities	Bonds are held in registered book-entry form available in physical form on request	Bearer or registered form
Cash balances	Central Bank of Ireland	Payments and receipts are debited and credited to a cash account that the Treasury has with the Bank of Italy. Since 1994, a negative account balance has been disallowed
Central bank credit to government	No. European Union obligations (Article 104 of the Maastricht Treaty) prohibit any borrowing from the central bank	No. European Union obligations (Article 104 of the Maastricht Treaty) prohibit any borrowing from the central bank

6. LOCATION OF DEBT MANAGEMENT FUNCTIONS

Policy function

	Ireland *(cont.)*	Italy *(cont.)*
• Strategic guidelines	Finance Ministry issues guidelines to the debt office	Treasury Ministry with Bank of Italy as advisor
• Day-to-day operations	Debt office (NTMA)	Bank of Italy
Accounting function of outstanding debt	Debt office (NTMA)	Treasury Ministry
Cash balance forecasting and management	Finance Ministry and debt office (NTMA)	Treasury Ministry
Selling arrangement	Debt office (NTMA); Post Office for National Savings products	Bank of Italy in its role of fiscal agent

Debt maintenance

	Ireland *(cont.)*	Italy *(cont.)*
• Settlement	Central Bank of Ireland and debt office (NTMA)	Bank of Italy in its role of manager of the payments system
• Issuance/redemption	Central Bank of Ireland and debt office (NTMA)	Bank of Italy
Secondary market intervention in government securities	Central Bank of Ireland	Bank of Italy

	Japan	Mexico

1. GOVERNMENT BORROWING: LEGAL FRAMEWORK, ACCOUNTABILITY, AND AUTHORITY

Legal Framework

	Japan	Mexico
Legal authority to borrow	The Public Finance Act (PFA) is the basic law concerning	The Constitution (Art. 74) and the Revenue Law provide the

Public Debt Management Frameworks—Country Tables *(continued)*

	Japan *(cont.)*	Mexico *(cont.)*
	the fiscal and budgetary system. In general, bonds can be issued only for public works/capital spending. Hence bonds issued for this purpose are called construction bonds. To cover deficit financing arising from others sources, a law to amend the PFA is enacted each year; debt instruments issued for this purpose are called deficit financing bonds	authority to borrow. The authority to issue government securities of different features and design is given through "Presidential Decree" (in the case of CETES) or "Congressional Decree" (in the case of Tesobonos)
Who is authorized to borrow	Minister of Finance	Finance Ministry's Secretariat of Finance and Public Credit (SHCP)
Accountability		
Approval	Diet (parliament)	Finance Ministry
Ceiling	Yes. Given by the Budget. In each of the annual budgets, the government has to specify the amount of revenue bonds to be issued that year and to obtain the approval of the Diet (parliament). If, during the year, additional borrowing needs arise, the Diet must approve a supplementary budget, including new debt issuance	None
Debt Management Authority and Agents		
Principal debt management authority	Minister of Finance: Under the Government Debt Act, the Minister of Finance is authorized to determine substantial matters concerning bond issues, such as coupon rates, issuing amount, maturity, auction, and issuing date	Finance Ministry
Debt management agents	• Central bank (Bank of Japan, BOJ). The Debt Act stipulates that the BOJ is the fiscal agent of the Minister of Finance with respect to specific procedures concerning issuing, redemption and interest payments • Underwriting syndicate for government bonds. Over 800 firms are members of the syndicate, including banks, securities firms, and insurance companies. They participate in auctions and are allocated 40 percent each new issue of 10-year bonds	• Central bank (Bank of Mexico). Acts as advisor and fiscal agent • Primary dealers: dealer agents (market-makers); brokerage firms

Public Debt Management Frameworks—Country Tables *(continued)*

	Japan *(cont.)*	Mexico *(cont.)*
2. DEBT MANAGEMENT OBJECTIVES, AND POLICY CHOICES AND INSTRUMENTS		
Objectives		
Primary objective	To secure the smooth and cost-effective issuance of government bonds covering the shortfall between receipts and expenditures and the refinancing of maturing debt	To finance the Federal government in a noninflationary manner and at low rates of return
• Horizon	Long-term	Strategy set and reviewed yearly
• Measurement of performance	No formal measurement	No formal measurement
Secondary objectives		
• Monetary policy considerations	No. There is no special committee or working group that coordinates government debt management policy and monetary policy	Yes. The Finance Ministry takes into consideration the advice of the Bank of Mexico on decisions where the debt management program affects monetary policy
• Others	Promote the liquidity, efficiency, and safety of government securities markets	None
Policy Choices and Instruments		
Instruments	Marketable instruments: discount instruments, medium- and long-term bonds, and cash management bills. To smooth redemption and maintain public confidence the Debt Consolidation Fund (sinking fund) is designated to repay debt with funds transferred from the general account of the government	A variety of instruments are used to attract investors and minimize funding costs: floating rate coupon, denominated in U.S. dollars but payable in pesos (domestic currency); instruments with returns indexed to the national CPI and foreign currency; short-term discount; and fixed-rate long term. Mix between domestic return (CETES) versus currency-linked (Tesobonos) is a policy decision
Use of derivatives	None	None
Maturity	In order to achieve the smooth issuance of bonds, a policy of diversification of maturities has been followed to meet the needs of investors	Mix between short-term (CETES) and longer-term (bonds) is a policy decision
Currency	No debt denominated in foreign currency. Funds are raised entirely in domestic currency	Foreign-currency-denominated debt is used

Public Debt Management Frameworks—Country Tables *(continued)*

	Japan *(cont.)*	Mexico *(cont.)*
Markets		
• Domestic money and bond market	In response to growing domestic and foreign demand, the amounts of treasury bill issues have been increased to further the development of an efficient and liquid short-term financial market	Debt operations are consolidated in the domestic market. Tesobonos are generally targeted and held by foreigners while CETES and bonds are generally held by resident financial institutions and individuals
• Private market	No	None
• International capital markets	No	To borrow at minimum cost under limits stated by the government

3. DEBT MANAGEMENT PLANNING

Debt Management Program

Program and horizon	Annual. The Budget Bureau of the Finance Ministry plans the total annual amount of new bonds. The Government Debt Division of the Ministry's Financial Bureau plans the allocation according to maturity. The Budget Bureau handles projections of government borrowing operations	Annual. Finance Ministry with Bank of Mexico as advisor

Transparency

Publication and frequency	Annual budget	The Finance Secretariat (SHCP) informs the Congress quarterly

4. DEBT PROGRAM IMPLEMENTATION

Day-to-Day Management

Decisions	The Minister of Finance • The Government Debt Division of the Finance Ministry determines the details of each bond issue: date, coupon, and amount per auction • The Treasury Division of the Ministry's Financial Bureau determines the issuance of financing bills in order to cover temporary shortfalls of funds	The Finance Secretariat (SHCP) with advice from the Bank of Mexico. Decisions on the amount of any security to be issued and its coupon are made by SHCP. Formal meetings are held weekly between the Bank and the SHCP to discuss projections of requirements and their financing
Cash balance forecasting/ frequency	Bank of Japan (daily)	The Finance Secretariat (SHCP) and the Bank of Mexico; informal meetings twice a week between officials

Public Debt Management Frameworks—Country Tables *(continued)*

	Japan *(cont.)*	Mexico *(cont.)*
Transparency		
Borrowing calendar/ frequency	None	Bank of Mexico (weekly)
Amounts of securities to be issued and other aspects	Bank of Japan: the morning of the auction, details are published. There is a weekly schedule for financing bills to be issued	The Bank of Mexico announces on the last day of the week the stocks and their maturity to be auctioned the following week
Announcements		
Publication of auction results	Finance Ministry	Bank of Mexico through the Mexican Stock Exchange and S.I.A.C. (Information system of the Bank)
5. OPERATIONAL ARRANGEMENTS		
Instruments	Marketable instruments: • Financing bills (maturity of 60 days) • Treasury bills (maturities of 3 and 6 months) • Medium-term interest-bearing government bonds (maturity of 2 years) • Medium-term discount government notes (maturity of 5 years) • Long-term interest-bearing government bonds (maturity of 10 years) • Super long-term interest-bearing government bonds (maturity of 20 years)	• Treasury bills (CETES), (maturities of 28, 91, 182, and 364 days). (About 30 percent) • Floating-rate treasury notes (Bondes) (maturity of 1–2 years). (About 30 percent) • Dollar-linked treasury bills (Tesobonos)(maturities of 28, 91, and 182 days). (About 10 percent) • Inflation-adjusted treasury notes (Ajusta-Bonos) (maturity of 3–5 years). (About 30 percent)
Selling technique		
• Auction system	Yes. All treasury bills, government notes, and 6- and 20-year bonds are issued in auctions	Yes
• Tap system	None	None
• Others	Underwriting by syndicate is used for sales of 10-year bonds	
Timing of issuance (fixed/flexible)	Flexible	Fixed
Participants at auction	Public participation through syndicate	Dealer agents (market-makers); broker firms; specialists
Form of securities	Three types of government securities: bearer form 2 percent, registered and book-entry forms 98 percent	"Dematerialized securities"

Public Debt Management Frameworks—Country Tables *(continued)*

	Japan *(cont.)*	Mexico *(cont.)*
Central depository/ book-entry system	A book-entry system is operated by the Bank of Japan. It is a multitiered automated system (since 1990), in which marketable bonds are issued, settled, serviced, maintained, and traded. The Bank maintains book-entry accounts for depository institutions and other entities including securities companies	Bank of Mexico: "dematerialized securities"
Cash balances	The Treasury Division of the Finance Ministry's Financial Bureau undertakes the daily administration of the Treasury	Ministry of Finance manages cash balances
Central bank credit to government	The Public Finance Act prohibits the underwriting or purchase of newly issued government bonds by the Bank of Japan. In the case of maturing debt, the government can sell new-issue government bonds directly to the Bank of Japan	None (since end of 1993)

6. LOCATION OF DEBT MANAGEMENT FUNCTIONS

Policy function		
• Strategic guidelines	Finance Ministry	Finance Secretariat (SHCP) and Bank of Mexico
• Day to day operations	Bank of Japan and Treasury Division of Finance Ministry	Bank of Mexico
Accounting function of outstanding debt	Government Debt Division handles statistical database on government debt	Finance Secretariat (SHCP) and Bank of Mexico
Cash balance management	Bank of Japan	Finance Secretariat (SHCP) and Bank of Mexico
Selling arrangements	The Bank of Japan is the fiscal agent of the Government Debt Division and is responsible for back office administration of issuance, redemption, interest payment, auction, registration, and so on	Bank of Mexico
Debt maintenance		
• Issuance/settlement	Bank of Japan	Bank of Mexico
• Redemption	Bank of Japan	Bank of Mexico
Secondary market intervention in government securities	Finance Ministry. In the bond market, both the Finance Ministry (through the National Debt Consolidated Fund) and the Bank of Japan purchase government bonds without any formal coordination	Bank of Mexico

Public Debt Management Frameworks—Country Tables *(continued)*

	New Zealand	Pakistan

1. GOVERNMENT BORROWING: LEGAL FRAMEWORK, ACCOUNTABILITY, AND AUTHORITY

Legal Framework

	New Zealand	Pakistan
Legal authority to borrow	The Public Finance Act 1989 provides the statutory authority for and control of the raising of loans, issuing of securities, and investment of funds	Public Debt Act
Who is authorized to borrow	The Public Finance Act is the enabling authority for the Minister of Finance to borrow in the name of the Crown including programs such as the issuance of domestic treasury bills, commercial paper, Euro-commercial paper, medium-term notes and Euro-medium-term notes	Finance Secretariat

Accountability

	New Zealand	Pakistan
Approval	Minister of Finance	Debt program is approved in the context of the budget
Ceiling	None	None

Debt Management Authority and Agents

	New Zealand	Pakistan
Principal debt management authority	Debt Office: The New Zealand Debt Management Office (NZDMO) is the branch of the Treasury responsible for managing the Crown's debt, all cash flows, and fixed-income assets within an appropriate risk management framework. NZDMO was formally established in July 1988	Finance Secretariat
Debt management agents	Central bank (Reserve Bank of New Zealand, RBNZ). Management of the Crown's domestic liquidity is delegated by the Debt Office (NZDMO) to the central bank through an Agency Agreement. The Agency Agreement sets out the framework and procedures for the daily domestic cash and liquidity	• Central bank (State Bank of Pakistan). The State Bank of Pakistan Act states in section 17 that the central bank will act as agent to the Federal Government in the management of public debt • Central Directorate for National Savings Schemes (government agency) • Primary dealers. They bid at management of the Crown auction on their own behalf or on behalf of clients and create a secondary market for the securities. The central bank has designated approximately 60 primary dealers, of which approximately 35 regularly submit bids

Public Debt Management Frameworks—Country Tables *(continued)*

	New Zealand *(cont.)*	Pakistan *(cont.)*

2. DEBT MANAGEMENT OBJECTIVES, AND POLICY CHOICES AND INSTRUMENTS

Objectives

Primary objective	The Debt Office (NZDMO) aims to (1) identify a low-risk portfolio of net financial liabilities consistent with the Crown's aversion to risk, having regard for the cost of reducing risk; (2) transact in an efficient manner to achieve and maintain that portfolio	To minimize the cost of borrowing and to raise noninflationary sources for government borrowing
• Horizon	The government aims to meet its annual financing requirements in a manner that preserves and increases the Crown's net worth	Long term
• Measurement of performance	Tactical debt management performance is measured against a benchmark (shadow) portfolio. This performance measurement system is currently being enhanced to provide a more comprehensive measure of the value added of strategic debt management operations	No formal measurement
Secondary objectives		
• Monetary policy considerations	The Reserve Bank Act 1988 established the independence of the central bank and separated monetary policy objectives from debt management objectives. Separate instruments are used for the conduct of debt management that reflect debt, not monetary policy, objectives	Yes, the State Bank of Pakistan manages the issuance of treasury bills for the purpose of controlling banking system liquidity and meeting monetary targets. A Debt and Monetary Management Committee, chaired by the governor of the central bank, meets on an ad hoc basis in order to coordinate debt and monetary management
• Others	• To develop the domestic debt market by ensuring the government transacts in a transparent manner, promotes liquidity in the market, and ensures the smooth operation of the domestic debt market • To contribute to the maintenance and enhancement of New Zealand's credit rating	• To mobilize savings from the household sector (nonbanks) • To mobilize savings from the informal sector

Policy Choices and Instruments

Instruments	Benchmark treasury bills and bonds are issued on a regular	Attempt to tap different market segments:

Public Debt Management Frameworks—Country Tables (continued)

	New Zealand (cont.)	Pakistan (cont.)
	basis to promote the liquidity and overall development of the domestic debt market. Short-dated cash management treasury bills are issued to meet short-term fluctuations in the government's expenditure/revenue flows	• Formal sector—Registered instruments: 6-month treasury bills; fixed-rate bonds (maturities up to 10 years) • Informal sector—Bearer securities (no name disclosure) • Household sector— Nonmarketable: savings schemes; prize bonds
Use of derivatives	The government has the ability to transact using forwards, swaps, and futures in order to fulfill its overall debt management objectives	None
Maturity	Ten-year benchmark bonds were established in the domestic market in 1991 to fulfill the government's objective of lengthening the duration of its domestic portfolio and further developing the domestic market	Introduced marketable long-term bonds in 1991 with a view to lengthening the average maturity structure of the debt
Currency	Since the adoption of a freely floating exchange rate regime in 1985, the government has borrowed externally only to rebuild the Crown's foreign exchange reserves and to refinance overseas debt, including that for which the government has assumed responsibility. Domestic borrowings are used to finance maturing domestic debt and the fiscal deficit excluding asset sale proceeds. In recent years, proceeds from an asset sales program have been used to repay foreign currency debt	Foreign currency and linked instruments used to raise foreign currency
Markets		
• Domestic money and bond market	The main aim is to develop the institutional (wholesale) market further by enhancing its liquidity and ensuring it functions smoothly and transparently	Strategy to develop liquid money and bond markets, to minimize interest costs
• Private market	The government meets demand from the small investor indirectly through the wholesale market and directly through retail debt issuance ("Kiwi" bonds)	Extensive distribution system for household savings instruments that compete with commercial bank deposits

Public Debt Management Frameworks—Country Tables *(continued)*

	New Zealand *(cont.)*	Pakistan *(cont.)*
• International capital market	The government transacts in most international capital markets using a wide range of instruments, including issuance under commercial paper or Euro-commercial paper and medium-term or Euro-medium-term note programs, to meet its overall debt management objectives	Use international capital market to raise foreign financing

3. DEBT MANAGEMENT PLANNING

Debt Management Program

Program and horizon	Annual. The yearly fiscal forecast and any updating is undertaken by the Treasury; NZDMO formulates the debt program	Annually. The debt management program is set in the context of the annual budget exercise. The Budget Wing of the Finance Ministry projects government requirements and, together with the target for cash balances, approves the debt management program

Transparency

Publication and frequency	The government domestic debt program is published at the same time the Annual Budget is presented	Annual release of budget documents by the Finance Ministry

4. DEBT MANAGEMENT IMPLEMENTATION

Day-to-Day Management

Decisions	Debt Office, advised by central bank. The central bank uses its network of financial market contacts to advise the NZDMO on market conditions and preferences	• Bond and other securities decisions are taken by the Finance Ministry with central bank advice • Central bank makes decisions on treasury bill auctions
Cash balance forecasting/ frequency	The annual fiscal forecast and any updating is undertaken by the Treasury. This is translated into daily cash requirements by the central bank	The government is developing a forecast of its monthly budgetary receipts and disbursements

Transparency

Borrowing calendar/ frequency	The annual domestic borrowing calendar is included in the announcement of the debt program at the same time as the Budget. Auctions are typically held every 3–4 weeks	None
Amounts of securities to be issued and other aspects	Details on the composition of the debt for auction are published by the Debt Office one week in advance of the auction date	Central bank. Tenders are announced one week before

Public Debt Management Frameworks—Country Tables *(continued)*

	New Zealand *(cont.)*	Pakistan *(cont.)*
Announcements		
Publication of auction results	Same day as auctions	Results of auctions are released by the central bank
5. OPERATIONAL ARRANGEMENTS		
Instruments	Marketable instruments: • Treasury bills (maturities of 3, 6, and 12 months) • Government bonds (maturities of 1 to 10 years) Nonmarketable instruments: • Kiwi bonds (maturities between 6 months and 4 years) • Inflation-adjusted Savings Bonds (minimum maturity of 5 years)	Marketable instruments: • Treasury bills (maturity of 6 months) • Federal Investment Bonds (FIBs) (maturities of 3, 5, and 10 years) • Foreign Exchange Bearer Certificates (FEBCs) • Foreign currency bonds Nonmarketable instruments: • National Savings Schemes • Prize bonds
Selling technique	Domestic government securities are issued using the discriminatory-price auction method to determine the price of securities on offer efficiently	The auction system was introduced in March 1991. It has helped develop the government market and stem the process of disintermediation that had begun because of the artificially low yields of government securities prior to then
• Auction system	Yes	Yes (initiated in March 1991)
• Tap system	None	Yes
• Others	None	Subscription
Timing of issuance (fixed/flexible)	Fixed: regular T-bills (each Tuesday) and government bonds (every 2–4 weeks) Flexible: cash management T-bills	Flexible
Participants at auction	Public participation	Public participation
Form of securities	Mostly electronic cash versus delivery. Physical delivery is possible. Settlement is normally through Austraclear. Government securities can also be settled through Euroclear and Cedel	T-bills and FIBs can be held as registered stock certificates or as "dematerialized" securities in the Subsidiary General Ledger of Accounts (SGLA) system
Central depository/ book-entry system	Central bank (RBNZ) Austraclear operated by the central bank is the system used for the settlement and clearance of securities. The RBNZ acts as the registry for all New Zealand Government	The central bank runs a (manual) book-based clearing and settlement system. The ownership of a government security is recorded in a book at the central bank (on the SGLA) maintained by the public

Public Debt Management Frameworks—Country Tables *(continued)*

	New Zealand *(cont.)*	Pakistan *(cont.)*
	domestic securities. A book-entry system has been in operation for over 50 years	Debt Department
Cash balances	The Debt Office is responsible for the banking arrangements that enable centralized cash management for all government departments. The government accounts are held with a commercial bank and the residual balance at the end of the day is swept back to the central bank	Budget Wing of Finance Ministry
Central bank credit to government	None	Limits placed on borrowing

6. LOCATION OF DEBT MANAGEMENT FUNCTIONS

Policy function

• Strategic guidelines	Minister of Finance and Debt Office	Finance Ministry
• Day-to-day operations	Central bank as agent for the Debt Office	Finance Ministry and central bank (T-bills)
Accounting function of outstanding debt	Debt Office	Central bank (Public Debt Department)
Cash balance management	Debt Office	Budget Wing of Finance Ministry
Selling arrangements	Central bank as agent for the Debt Office	Central bank (Securities Departments)

Debt maintenance

• Issuance/settlement	Central bank as agent for the Debt Office	Central bank (Public Debt/Accounting Department)
• Redemption	Central bank as Registrar	Central bank (Accounting Department)
Secondary market intervention in government securities	Central bank	Central bank (Securities Department)

	Spain	Sweden

1. GOVERNMENT BORROWING: LEGAL FRAMEWORK, ACCOUNTABILITY, AND AUTHORITY

Legal Framework

Legal authority to borrow	General Budget Law (as called for in the Constitution)	Act on State Borrowings 1988 (SFS 1988-1387)
Who is authorized to borrow	The Minister of Finance has delegated most of his powers to the head of the Treasury Directorate	The government in an Ordinance in 1989 instructed the Swedish National Debt Office to raise and manage funds on behalf of the State

Public Debt Management Frameworks—Country Tables *(continued)*

	Spain *(cont.)*	Sweden *(cont.)*
Accountability		
Approval	Parliament	Parliament
Ceiling	Yes. The net increase in outstanding debt (which includes the net indebtedness with the central bank) falls within the limit set by the annual budget law	There is no limit on domestic currency borrowing. The government, through consultation with the Riksbank (central bank) and the Debt Office, and under the parliament's guidelines, decides on a limit for foreign currency borrowing
Debt Management Authority and Agents		
Principal debt management authority	Treasury Directorate. Debt management is carried out under the direction of the Treasury	Swedish National Debt Office
Debt management agents	• Central bank (Bank of Spain). Advisor to the Treasury Directorate and provides operational support in debt management • Market-makers, authorized by the Treasury with the Bank of Spain's advice	Dealers in treasury bonds and T-bills. Authorized by the Swedish National Debt Office to bid for adequate amounts of government securities at auctions, maintain active and continuous two-way markets in these securities, and provide adequate market information within the financial community

2. DEBT MANAGEMENT OBJECTIVES, AND POLICY CHOICES AND INSTRUMENTS

Objectives		
Primary objective	To cover maturing debt and the public sector borrowing requirement at the lowest possible cost	To minimize the costs of borrowings within the limits imposed by monetary policy
• Horizon	The fiscal year with reviews every quarter	Several years
• Measurement of performance	No formal measurement	Benchmark portfolio
Secondary objectives		
• Monetary policy considerations	A debt issuance committee made up of three representatives of the Treasury and three representatives of the Bank of Spain plays a crucial role in the coordination of monetary and debt management policies	Yes. By legislation, the Debt Office must confer with the central bank. Coordination committee for both domestic and foreign currency debt has representatives of central bank's Debt Office and Finance Ministry
• Others	• Current policy is to lengthen the average maturity of outstanding debt	• Conservative degree of refunding risk

Public Debt Management Frameworks—Country Tables *(continued)*

	Spain *(cont.)*	Sweden *(cont.)*
	• To encourage the demand for government securities, both in the retail and institutional sector of the market	• Encourage transparency and predictability of debt operations
	• To improve market liquidity and transparency	
Policy Choices and Instruments		
Instruments	To increase market depth and liquidity, government securities have very few varieties. No attempt has been made to issue bonds with their principal indexed, so as not to encourage indexation in other markets	Policy of limited number of instruments with a view to increasing market liquidity
Use of derivatives	Not in domestic debt. There are currency swaps in foreign debt	Only for foreign currency debt
Maturity	The issue of government securities depends on interest rate expectations and yield curve. When long-term interest rates are high, new issues have been concentrated in short-end T-bills in periods of low or falling interest rates, the bulk of issues have been concentrated in medium- and long-term bonds	Since end-1992, debt has increasingly been financed on a more long-term basis compared with preceding years
Currency	The bulk of the borrowing requirement is raised in the national currency (pesetas)	For balance of payments support. A norm introduced in the mid-1980s precluded net foreign currency borrowing for the purpose of financing the central government budget deficit. This norm was rescinded in December 1992
Markets		
• Domestic money and bond market	The banking system plays an important role as final holder to maturity of government securities, although most of these are resold through "repos" to the public. Although insurance and pension institutions are not very developed in Spain, mutual funds have recently begun to play a greater role as holders of government securities. Nonresident demand for Spanish government securities was strongly encouraged by the	Develop and improve the functioning of the market

Public Debt Management Frameworks—Country Tables *(continued)*

	Spain *(cont.)*	Sweden *(cont.)*
	decision, in 1990, to exempt holdings from Spanish tax. Foreigners represent a significant portion of total demand	
• Private market	Small-saver holdings of government securities are concentrated in repo agreements with banks	This market is tapped to the extent that it is cost-effective compared with borrowing in the money and bond markets. Undertaken in a manner that ensures maximum savings
• International capital markets	Presence in international markets is maintained	For balance of payments support

3. DEBT MANAGEMENT PLANNING

Debt Management Program

Program and horizon	Annual: An annual government decree sets the broad lines under which the Minister of Finance will issue government debt. The Minister of Finance delegates to the Treasury Directorate most of his powers. The Treasury issues different by-laws, specifying an annual program of regular government debt issues and their conditions	Two-year plans (for foreign and domestic currency). The Treasury determines the volume of securities to be issued in order to cover the estimated budget deficit and the redemption of maturing securities on a monthly basis

Transparency

Publication and frequency	Annual (borrowing program is announced in January in each year) by the Treasury	Data are published in the Annual Report and Monthly Statistical Bulletin of the central bank, among other publications

4. DEBT PROGRAM IMPLEMENTATION

Day-to-Day Management

Decisions	Minister of Finance and the Treasury	Debt Office in consultation with the central bank
Cash balance forecasting/ frequency	Treasury and Bank of Spain (weekly)	Debt Office (daily)

Transparency

Borrowing calendar/ frequency	Treasury Directorate (annually)	Debt Office (semiannually)
Amounts of securities to be issued and other aspects	Treasury, in consultation with the Bank of Spain. The coupon and maturity date of bonds are announced some two weeks before auctions	Debt Office (biweekly)

Announcements

Publication of auction results	Treasury and Bank of Spain. The Bank publishes auction	Debt Office

Public Debt Management Frameworks—Country Tables *(continued)*

	Spain *(cont.)*	Sweden *(cont.)*
	results in Reuters, Telerate, etc., immediately after the auction takes place. Some days later, the Treasury publishes the results in the Official Bulletin (BOE)	

5. OPERATIONAL ARRANGEMENTS

	Spain *(cont.)*	Sweden *(cont.)*
Instruments	Marketable instruments: • Treasury bills (maturities of 3, 6, and 12 months) • Government bonds (maturities of 3, 5, 10, and 15 years) • ECU government bonds (maturity of 5 years) Nonmarketable instruments: • Special debt securities (maturity of 6 years) • Fixed rate loans (maturity of 3 years) • Floating rate loans (maturity of 3 years)	Marketable instruments: • Treasury bills (maturities of 3, 6, and 12 months) • Treasury bonds (maturity up to 15 years) • Lottery Bond Loans • Index-linked to price level (maturity of 18 years) Nonmarketable instruments: • National Savings System (savings bonds) • National Debt Account (savings account—choice of maturity; rate geared on pricing of outstanding securities)
Selling technique		
• Auction system	Yes	Yes
• Tap system	No	Yes, for household instruments
• Others	Underwriting by a syndicate of national and foreign banks is extensively used in foreign currency financing	
Timing of issuance (fixed/flexible)	Fixed	Fixed
Participants at auction	Public participation. Anyone can participate in the first round of auctions, but only market-makers are authorized to participate in the second round	Only authorized Swedish National Office Dealers are allowed to participate directly in the auctions
Form of securities	Book-entry form. Since 1987, all new issues of government debt take the form of book-entries	Book-entry system (introduced in 1993)
Central depository/ book-entry system	Central bank (Bank of Spain). Authorized agents keep the book-entries for any investor not allowed to hold its accounts directly with the Bank of Spain	The Swedish Securities Register Center (VPC AB). The Debt Office signed an agreement with VPC AB in the summer of 1993 regarding the registration of T-bills and T-bonds

Public Debt Management Frameworks—Country Tables *(continued)*

	Spain *(cont.)*	Sweden *(cont.)*
Cash balances	Bank of Spain	National currency, Debt Office; foreign currency, central bank
Central bank credit to government	Credit from the Bank of Spain has been disallowed since January 1994 (European Union obligations)	No borrowing from the central bank is allowed

6. LOCATION OF DEBT MANAGEMENT FUNCTIONS

Policy function

• Strategic guidelines	Finance Ministry and Treasury Directorate; Bank of Spain as advisor	Debt Office, after consultation with central bank
• Day-to-day operations	Treasury Directorate; Bank of Spain as advisor	Debt Office, after consultation with central bank
Accounting function of outstanding debt	Bank of Spain	Debt Office
Cash balance management	Finance Ministry	Debt Office
Selling arrangements	Treasury with Bank of Spain's technical support	Debt Office

Debt maintenance

• Issuance/settlement	Bank of Spain	Swedish Securities Register Center (VPC)
• Redemption	Treasury with Bank of Spain as paying agent	Debt Office
Secondary market intervention in government securities	Bank of Spain	Central bank

	United Kingdom	United States

1. GOVERNMENT BORROWING: LEGAL FRAMEWORK, ACCOUNTABILITY, AND AUTHORITY

Legal Framework

Legal authority to borrow	National Loans Act 1968; National Debt Act 1971; National Savings Bank Act 1972	United States Code Annotated (USCA), Chapter 31 of Title 31
Who is authorized to borrow	Decisions on debt management are the formal responsibility of the Treasury	Treasury Department. The Congress has delegated general responsibility for treasury debt management to the Secretary of the Treasury

Accountability

Approval	Parliament	See above
Ceiling	No	Yes. A ceiling on the outstanding stock of debt is set by the Congress

Public Debt Management Frameworks—Country Tables *(continued)*

	United Kingdom *(cont.)*	United States *(cont.)*
Debt Management Authority and Agents		
Principal debt management authority	The Treasury. The Chancellor sets an annual public Funding Remit (the first was issued in March 1995) for the Bank of England's (BOE) operations in the gilt market and provides broad guidelines for the operation of the remit by the BOE	Treasury Department
Debt management agents	• Central bank (Bank of England) (BOE). Any funding operation proposed by the BOE within the remit will normally be approved by Treasury officials	• Central bank (Federal Reserve System). The Federal Reserve acts as fiscal agent for the Treasury, handling many logistical operations in selling new treasury debt
	• Gilt-edged market-makers (GEMMs). To make, on demand and in any trading conditions, continuous and effective two-way prices at which they stand committed to deal	• Primary dealers. They are required to be active in both the primary and secondary markets for government securities

2. DEBT MANAGEMENT OBJECTIVES, AND POLICY CHOICES AND INSTRUMENTS

Objectives		
Primary objective	To minimize over the long term the cost of meeting the government's financing needs, taking account of risk, while ensuring that debt management policy is consistent with monetary policy	To raise cash at minimal cost to the U.S. taxpayer, while minimizing market disruption and maintaining a balanced maturity structure
• Horizon	To achieve full funding (see below) over each financial year as a whole. Within the financial year, temporary under- or overfunding may occur	Annual
• Measure of performance	No specific performance measurement	No specific performance standards
Secondary objectives		
• Monetary policy considerations	To finance borrowing in a noninflationary way. "Full Fund" policy: to cover the net total of maturing debt, the public sector borrowing requirement (PSBR) and any underlying increase in foreign reserves by sales of debt to the private sector	No. The Treasury is responsible for debt management policy. It is determined independently of monetary policy, which is the responsibility of the Federal Reserve System
• Others	To minimize market disruption	

Public Debt Management Frameworks—Country Tables *(continued)*

	United Kingdom *(cont.)*	United States *(cont.)*
Policy Choices and Instruments		
Instruments	Fixed-rate "gilt-edged" securities with maturities over 3 years. Treasury bills become eligible for funding in 1996. Inflation-indexed instruments are used to reduce inflation risk and lower funding costs. Greater emphasis has been given to building large benchmark issues, the development of a "strips" market (1996), and an open repo market	Marketable: Discount rates (short-term); notes (medium-term); bonds (long-term). Long-term notes and bonds may be stripped into their interest and principal components on the book-entry system maintained by the Federal Reserve. Once stripped, the securities may also be reconstituted into their original form on the book-entry system
	Nonmarketable: Savings schemes	Nonmarketable: Savings bonds
Use of derivatives	No	The Treasury does not engage in derivatives transactions to hedge market risk
Maturity	To ensure that the public sector does not create excess liquidity (money-like instruments), authorities ensure that funding is not concentrated in very short-term debt. Maturity may be adjusted according to investor demand, the shape and and slope of the yield curve, and the government's risk preference	A balanced maturity structure
Currency	Funding is undertaken entirely in sterling. Foreign issues are used for raising foreign exchange reserves and are not swapped into domestic currency for the purpose of funding	Conduct debt financing operations in domestic currency only
Markets		
• Domestic money and bond market	• Foster liquid gilt-edged market to attract domestic and foreign investors	• Largely institutional investors—U.S. and foreign
• Private market	• Savings schemes targeted for small saver	• Tap small savers through savings bonds
• International capital markets	• No	• No
3. DEBT MANAGEMENT PLANNING		
Debt Management Program		
Program and horizon	Annual Remit. The Treasury and Central Statistics Office are jointly responsible for the definition and measurement	Five years, which coincides with the U.S. Government budget horizon; the Treasury Department is responsible

Public Debt Management Frameworks—Country Tables *(continued)*

	United Kingdom *(cont.)*	United States *(cont.)*
	of the public sector borrowing requirement (PSBR). Schedule 5 of the 1975 Industry Act requires the Treasury to publish two forecasts a year. A formal consultation process will be introduced so that investors may provide inputs into strategic debt management decisions	

Transparency

Publication and frequency	Financial Statement and Budget Report (FSBR). Debt Management Report (to be introduced and published each financial year beginning in March 1996) will give financing requirements and indicate sales split between gilts, National Savings, and other sources; auction dates; and the maturity structure of gilt issuance (approximate proportions of index-linked, short-, medium-, and long-term gilts)	Treasury Department publications: Monthly Statement of the Public Debt—lists composition of outstanding public debt. Monthly Treasury Statement—lists receipts and outlays of the U.S. Government

4. DEBT PROGRAM IMPLEMENTATION

Day-to-Day Management

Decisions	Decisions on the amount of any stock to be created, and its coupon, are recommended by the Bank of England for formal approval by the Treasury. Any operation proposed by the Bank that falls within the terms of the Remit will normally be approved quickly	Treasury Department
Cash balance forecasting/ frequency	Treasury and Bank of England. Forecasts of both funding requirement and money market positions are made at least once a month, independently by both agents	Treasury Department. Cash balances are updated daily. Estimates of financing needs are prepared each month by examining expected cash balances, receipts, and outlays. Published in the Daily Treasury Statement, which lists cash and debt operations of the U.S. Treasury

Transparency

Borrowing calendar/ frequency	Bank of England (annually). The expected auction calendar is usually issued at the start of	Treasury Department (quarterly public communication)

Public Debt Management Frameworks—Country Tables *(continued)*

	United Kingdom *(cont.)*	United States *(cont.)*
	the financial year. Starting in 1996, the Bank of England, before the beginning of each quarter, will publish maturity ranges for gilts to be sold at auction in that quarter. The announcement will also give details of progress on the financing program and of any major changes to the financing requirement	
Amounts of securities to be issued and other aspects	Bank of England. In advance of each auction, two announcements are made: the first gives date and maturity range of the stock; the second, a few days later, gives full details; starting in 1996, the bank will announce the issue and size eight days before the auction	Treasury Department. Terms of Treasury securities and the method of sale are described in the Treasury offering circular. A separate announcement is made for each auction, providing the dates of the auction and settlement, amount, maturity, and other details. Transparency is enhanced by the availability of Treasury securities market quotes provided by various electronic network services
Announcements		
Publication of auction results	Bank of England	Treasury Department (Bureau of the Public Debt). Within an hour of the deadline for tenders
5. OPERATIONAL ARRANGEMENTS		
Instruments	Marketable instruments: • Treasury bills, for money market operations • For funding, four types of gilt-edged securities: straights or conventional gilts; convertibles; index-linked gilts; irredeemable gilts	Marketable instruments: • Cash management bills (no standard maturities) • Treasury bills (maturities of 13, 26, and 52 weeks) • Treasury notes (maturities of 2, 3, 5, 7, and 10 years) • Treasury bonds (maturity of 30 years)
	Nonmarketable instruments: • National Savings products (certificates, capital bonds, income bonds, yearly plan, investment account) and Premium Savings Bonds	Nonmarketable instruments: • U.S. Savings Bonds, series EE and HH
Selling technique	Auctions form the backbone of gilt-edged funding. The mixed range of issue techniques makes it possible to	Most Treasury securities are auctioned via the multiple-price, sealed-bid auction technique. Currently, 2- and 5-year

Public Debt Management Frameworks—Country Tables *(continued)*

	United Kingdom *(cont.)*	United States *(cont.)*
	respond flexibly to investor demand as it arises	notes are auctioned via uniform-price, sealed-bid method
• Auction system	Yes	Yes
• Tap system	Yes	No
• Others	Tenders (occasionally)	Fixed price public subscription
Timing of issuance (fixed/flexible)	Flexible	Fixed
Participants at auction	Public participation	Open to public participation
Form of securities	• Most gilts are available in registered form (registered with the BOE in the name of the investor) maintained in book-entry form • Partly paid stocks are in bearer form	Treasuries are issued in electronic form on a delivery-versus payment-basis either through the Federal Reserve's book-entry system or into Treasury Direct accounts, which are managed by the Bureau of Public Debt. Treasury Direct is designed to facilitate investment by smaller investors
Central depository/ book-entry system	• Central Gilts Office (CGO) of the BOE. Created in 1978 to provide a book-entry clearing system for gilt-edged securities • BOE Registrar's Department for non-CGO members • Central Moneymarkets Office (CMO) provides for investors in money market instruments (T-bills) a similar service to that of CGO for gilts • The BOE is developing a service broadly similar to CGO for securities denominated in ECUs	Depository institutions are entities described in section 19(b)(1)(A) of the Federal Reserve Act Book-entry system: • Commercial book-entry system, established, maintained, and operated by the Federal Reserve Banks • Treasury Direct: records on the Bureau of the Public Debt Department of the Treasury. Maintained by the Federal Reserve Bank of Philadelphia
Cash balances	Bank of England	Federal Reserve and commercial banks
Central bank credit to government	Bank of England may hold unsold bonds temporarily. However, European Union obligations (Article 104 of the Maastricht Treaty) prohibit the government from selling debt to the central bank	Not allowed. Federal Reserve may roll over holdings of maturing debt

6. LOCATION OF DEBT MANAGEMENT FUNCTIONS

Policy functions

• Strategic guidelines	Minister of Finance (Chancellor of the Exchequer) through the Remit	Treasury Department

Public Debt Management Frameworks—Country Tables *(concluded)*

	United Kingdom *(cont.)*	United States *(cont.)*
• Day-to-day operations	Bank of England	Treasury Department
Accounting function of outstanding debt	Treasury and Bank of England	Treasury Department (Bureau of Public Debt), with Federal Reserve acting as fiscal agent
Selling arrangement	Bank of England on behalf of the Treasury (Gilt-edged and Money Market Division)	Treasury Department (Bureau of Public Debt), with Federal Reserve acting as fiscal agent
Debt maintenance		
• Issuance/settlement	Bank of England: at the Registrar's Department for non-CGO members; at the Central Gilts Office (CGO) for CGO members	Federal Reserve book-entry system and Treasury Direct
• Redemption	Bank of England	Treasury Department (Bureau of Public Debt), with Federal Reserve acting as fiscal agent
Secondary market intervention in government securities	Bank of England (Gilt-edged and Money Market Division)	Central bank (Federal Reserve System)
Secondary market supervision	Bank of England (Wholesale Market Supervision Division)	Federal Reserve, Treasury Department, and Securities and Exchange Commission

Sources: Country ministries of finance, debt management offices, and central banks.

Bibliography

Bank of England, 1985, "The Future Structure of the Gilt-Edged Market: The Bank of England's Dealing and Supervisory Relationships with Certain Participants," Quarterly Bulletin, Bank of England, Vol. 25 (April), pp. 250–82.

_____,1989, *The Gilt-Edged Market Since Big Bang, Quarterly Bulletin*, Bank of England, Vol. 29 (February), pp. 49–58.

_____,1992, "Recent Developments in the Gilt-Edged Market," *Quarterly Bulletin*, Bank of England, Vol. 32 (February), pp. 76–81.

_____, 1993, *British Government Securities: The Market in Gilt-Edged Securities* (London, May).

_____, 1994, *Gilts and the Gilt Market: Review 1993/94* (March).

_____, 1994, "Operation of Monetary Policy: Annual Remit for the Bank's Operations in the Gilt Market," *Quarterly Bulletin*, Bank of England, Vol. 34 (May), pp. 112–13.

_____, and H.M. Treasury, 1995, *Report on the Debt Management Review* (July).

Boston, J., J. Martin, J. Pallot, and P. Walsh, eds., 1991, *Reshaping the State: New Zealand's Bureaucratic Revolution* (Auckland, New York: Oxford University Press).

Bröker, Günther, 1993, *Government Securities and Debt Management in the 1990s* (Paris: Organization for Economic Cooperation and Development).

Capomassi, L., 1992, "The Coordination of Public Debt Management and Monetary Management in Italy," paper prepared for the Second Informal Workshop on Government Securities and Debt Management in Central and Eastern European Economies, Budapest (June).

Cottarelli, Carlo, 1993, *Limiting Central Bank Credit to the Government: Theory and Practice*, Occasional Paper No. 110 (Washington, International Monetary Fund).

Dawson, Robert MacGregor, 1970, *The Government of Canada* (Toronto: University of Toronto Press, 5th ed.).

de Fontenay, Patrick, Gian Maria Milesi-Ferretti, and Huw Pill, 1995, "The Role of Foreign Currency Debt in Public Debt Management," IMF Working Paper 95/21 (Washington: International Monetary Fund).

Euromoney, 1993, *The 1993 Guide to World Domestic Bond Markets*, Euromoney Research Guides (London, September).

European Bond Commission, 1993, *The European Bond Markets: 5th Ed., An Overview and Analysis for Money Managers and Traders* (Chicago: Probus Publishing Company).

Fabozzi, F.J., and F.J. Jones, 1992, *The International Government Bond Markets* (Chicago: Probus Publishing Company).

France, Ministry of the Economy, 1993, *French Government Securities, 1993 Annual Report* (Paris: Ministry of the Economy).

Godron, Olivier, 1989, "Le Trésor et le Financement de l'État," in *Notes et Études Documentaires*, No. 4882, pp. 1–44.

Goldstein, Morris, and others, 1994, *International Capital Markets: Developments, Prospects, and Policy Issues*, World Economic and Financial Surveys (Washington: International Monetary Fund).

Leite, Sergio Pereira, 1992, "Coordinating Public Debt and Monetary Management During Financial Reforms," IMF Working Paper 92/84 (Washington: International Monetary Fund).

Quirós, Gabriel, 1994, *El Mercado Británico de Deuda Pública*, Documento de Trabajo No. 9404, Servicio de Estudios del Banco de España (Madrid).

Sargent, Thomas, and Neil Wallace, 1985, "Some Unpleasant Monetarist Arithmetic," *Federal Bank of Minneapolis Quarterly Review* (Fall).

Storkey, I., 1993, "Institutional Arrangements of Government Debt Management in New Zealand," paper presented in the OECD/IMF Workshop on Public Debt Management and Government Securities (Paris).

Sweden, National Debt Office, 1993, *A Guide to the Swedish Government Securities Market*.

———, *Annual Report Fiscal Year 1991/92, 1992/93*.

United Kingdom, Central Statistical Office, 1993, *Economic Trends*, No. 479 (London: September).

United Kingdom, H.M. Treasury, 1990, *Central Government Borrowing: A New Presentation*, Treasury Bulletin (London).

———, 1990, *The Treasury's Forecasting Performance* (London).

———, 1990/91, 1992/93, 1993/94, *Financial Statement and Budget Report* (London).

———, 1991/92, *Report—Annex: The Role of the Treasury* (London: Winter).

United States, Department of the Treasury, Securities and Exchange Commission, and the Board of Governors of the Federal Reserve System, 1992, *Joint Report on the Government Securities Market* (Washington: Government Printing Office).

Wormell, Jeremy, 1985, *The Gilt-Edged Market* (London: G. Allen and Unwin).

Zerah, Dov, 1993, "Le Système Financier Français: Dix Ans de Mutations," in *Notes et Études Documentaires*, No. 4980–81, pp. 1–294.

5

Government Versus Central Bank Securities in Developing Market-Based Monetary Operations

*Marc Quintyn**

Typically, in an indirect monetary policy framework, open market operations become the central bank's main instrument. One of the key issues, therefore, in designing technical arrangements that will lead to a successful transition to indirect monetary policy is the availability to the central bank of a financial instrument with which to develop and conduct open market operations. This chapter discusses the choice between central bank securities and government securities as a regular instrument to manage market liquidity, particularly in the initial stages of market development.

Unlike most of today's industrial countries, where financial markers were fairly mature before the introduction of indirect monetary policies, developing countries rarely have established government securities markets when their central banks start the transition to indirect instruments. Yet, it may not be feasible to wait for the full development of government securities markets to initiate open market operations. Existing (direct) instruments may be becoming increasingly ineffective, and there may be a need to absorb a liquidity overhang, built up during the period of direct controls. In such cases, a central bank can choose to start influencing monetary conditions and at the same time promote market development through so-called open market type operations, that is, the use of primary issues of assets or liabilities to influence liquidity conditions in the financial system.[1] In particular, the use of primary issues of securities will often

---

*Marc Quintyn is a Senior Economist at the International Monetary Fund.

[1]The term "open market type operations" is used to refer to the use of primary issues of securities through auctions ("primary market operations") or auctions of central bank credit or government deposits, and so forth, to achieve specific monetary objectives at the initiative of the central bank. "Open market operations" refers to transactions in secondary securities markets (outright or repurchase transactions). The term "market-based operations" will be used to cover both types of operations.

be the preferred technique until such time as the market for government securities has acquired some size and liquidity, so that more traditional open market operations in the secondary markets can start.

The use of primary issues of government securities for monetary interventions implies that fiscal and monetary authorities are required to operate in the same market with the same instrument for both debt and monetary management. This may lead to conflicts, for instance, when the central bank's planned volumes and features of primary issues of government securities are at odds with the treasury's goals. Such circumstances can affect the independence of the central bank's monetary policy. Therefore, appropriate delineation of responsibilities between fiscal and monetary authorities is needed to preserve the effectiveness of monetary policy.

Insofar as such coordination has proven difficult, several central banks have opted to conduct primary market interventions through their own securities. The use of central bank securities facilitates the achievement of operational autonomy for the central bank. However, the presence of both central bank and government securities risks segmenting the market, particularly when financial markets are thin, and poses problems for the coordination of the objectives and technical design of the two instruments.

This chapter, which is based on selected country experiences, focuses on the advantages and disadvantages of government securities versus central bank securities as the vehicle for market-based operations, with particular attention to the early stages of a typical transition. In passing, it discusses the possibility of using an alternative technique—auctions of deposits at the central bank—in those early stages.

The chapter is structured as follows. The opening section briefly recalls some relevant features of the early reform stage. The second section sets forth the criteria that should guide the selection of the financial instrument and briefly addresses whether the origin of the instrument matters, while section three delves deeper into the advantages and drawbacks of the respective instruments. The fourth section briefly discusses the issues that arise at later stages of reform. The concluding section describes the principles that should guide the selection of a financial instrument for open market operations. Finally, an appendix contains an overview of relevant country experiences with government securities and central bank securities.

Relevant Characteristics of the Early Stages of Financial Reform

Typically, financial markets are underdeveloped or nonexistent in most countries undertaking the transition to indirect monetary policy instruments as part of a comprehensive financial reform. Very often, these countries are also plagued by the persistence of excess liquidity, mostly as a result of the policies conducted during the period of direct monetary control. Thus, in the early stages of the reform, the central bank needs to develop instruments and techniques that enable it (1) to absorb this initial excess liquidity, (2) to manage the level of liquidity flexibly—both inject and absorb as needed—in the subsequent stages, and (3) to facilitate the development of money markets in parallel with the adoption of indirect monetary policy instruments.

For these purposes, the central bank may auction either government securities or central bank securities, or even more simply central bank deposits (deposits of commercial banks at the central bank). The selected country experiences analyzed in the Appendix reveal no clear-cut preference for either type of security in those early stages of the transition to indirect instruments. The following sections attempt to establish some criteria by which a selection between instruments can be made and to set forth specific arguments in favor of and against the use of government and central bank securities and of deposits at the central bank.

Criteria for the Selection

Three main criteria can be singled out regarding the selection of a financial instrument for market-based operations. All three are related to the nature of indirect monetary policy. The instrument should (1) ensure a fair degree of operational independence for the central bank, (2) assist in developing liquid markets, and (3) ensure that the transmission of monetary impulses to the real sector is effective and takes place smoothly.

When moving to a system of indirect instruments of monetary policy, a central bank needs a significant degree of operational independence, that is, the ability to control the growth of its balance sheet, enabling it to achieve its policy goals effectively and neutralize any movements that may interfere with their pursuance. Although this operational independence is usually not threatened when a central bank conducts open market operations in secondary markets for securities, it may be threatened if the central bank has to use primary issues of government securities for monetary policy purposes, since monetary and fiscal authorities are using the same instrument in the same market, typically to pursue separate (and sometimes conflicting) goals. So, the use of primary market interventions requires arrangements to safeguard the central bank's operational autonomy.

To facilitate (and expedite) the transition to indirect instruments of monetary policy, the central bank has a special interest in assisting in the *development of financial markets in general*. To that end, the central bank must have a combination of instruments that allows it to absorb and inject liquidity in a flexible way and, at the same time, support financial market development. The importance of the latter for financial reform cannot be overemphasized. Well-functioning financial markets give central banks the opportunity to absorb liquidity without draining the market altogether or without causing additional sharp and undesirable liquidity fluctuations. In turn, open market interventions themselves support financial market development as they provide liquidity to the particular market of intervention. Therefore, particularly in the early stages of financial liberalization, financial market development and the development of indirect instruments are two narrowly intertwined goals of the monetary authorities, and the design and operation of indirect instruments can, by themselves, play a major role in financial market development.

The third criterion relates to the extent to which instrument choice facilitates the *transmission* of monetary actions to the real sector. If central bank intervention takes place in an isolated money market segment (e.g., one with rigid and inflexible interest rates, with a limited number of participants, or with captive features), the central bank's actions are unlikely to be transmitted effectively to the rest of the financial markets and to the real sector of the economy.

In light of these three criteria, a first legitimate question to be addressed is whether, in general, the *origin* of the instrument used for open market intervention matters. In theory, the origin of the financial instrument used for market development and policy intervention is irrelevant. What matters are the *characteristics* of the instrument. Irrespective of origin, the instrument should be designed in such a way that it fosters the development of a free, well-functioning market in the instrument that, in turn, would facilitate the development of money markets in general and market-based monetary policy operations in particular.[2]

Insofar as these features can be adopted by both government and central bank paper, the choice between instruments is not of consequence in principle. The next question therefore is whether there are arguments in favor of or against either of the two in practice, and in particular during the early stages of financial reform.

---

[2]There are several important ingredients to this end: (1) interest rates should be freely determined by the market; in particular, captive markets should be avoided and the selling techniques and market organization should facilitate competitive and efficient determination of interest rates; (2) holdership should be defined as broadly as possible to stimulate competition and the volume and features of securities should enable a widening of the range of holders; broad holdership will also facilitate the transmission of monetary policy impulses; (3) the maturities and other technical features of the paper should be such that they stimulate secondary trading; (4) the transfer of ownership of the instrument and the settlement of payments for the instrument must be easy; (5) taxation should be simple and transparent; and (6) proper rules for rediscounting the financial instrument should be established.

Specific Advantages and Disadvantages

The country experiences discussed in the Appendix and in Quintyn (1994) indicate some advantages and drawbacks associated with the use of government securities and central bank securities in market-based operations. The discussion in this section reflects these experiences and concludes that it is difficult to express in the abstract an absolute preference for either one. From a market development point of view, there is a slight advantage with government securities, but their use as monetary instruments requires tight coordinating arrangements between central bank and fiscal authorities, which cannot always be honored. If such arrangements cannot be made, or are bound to fail, so that monetary policy independence cannot be assured, central bank securities offer a viable and reliable alternative. However, their use raises the risk of fragmenting financial markets, if government securities also circulate simultaneously, and hence, requires close coordination of the technical design of the two instruments in order to avoid market segmentation and direct competition among nearly identical securities. Finally, in the very early stages of financial sector reform, the central bank may consider auctions of central bank deposits to absorb liquidity from the financial system, as an alternative to issuing securities. While such a technique facilitates operational autonomy for the central bank, its main drawback is that it does not assist in developing securities markets. Table 1 provides an overview of the main advantages and disadvantages associated with the use of the three abovementioned types of instruments.

Government Securities

Advantages

Two arguments favor the use of government securities as the underlying instrument in primary market operations. First, when government securities are already in circulation and financial markets are thin, using them for monetary policy purposes reduces the risk of market fragmentation and supports the role of government securities as a catalyst for financial market development in general. Of course, this advantage only holds if the same types of security are used for monetary and debt management purposes. Second, the use of government securities shifts the cost of monetary policy tightening directly to the government and makes it overt in the government budget.

Supports the development of a government securities market as a catalyst for financial market development. Although both central bank and government securities are free from credit risk and can potentially be attractive investment and liquidity management vehicles, serving as benchmarks to price

**Table 1. Advantages and Disadvantages of Key Financial Instruments for
Developing Open Market Operations**

Instrument	Advantages	Disadvantages
Government securities	• Use for primary market operations helps the development of a viable market, which in turn will stimulate financial markets in general and transmission of monetary policy. • Shift cost of monetary tightening to government and make it overt in the budget. May encourage fiscal discipline on the part of the government, if direct central bank financing is discontinued.	• Require high degree of coordination with treasury. • If not properly coordinated with treasury, central bank's operational autonomy may not be guaranteed and primary market interventions may not be effective.
Central bank securities	• Facilitate the central bank's operational independence (provided their issuance is coordinated with that of government securities). • Provide flexible instrument for liquidity management.	• May, under certain conditions, reduce central bank profits, or lead to central bank losses if issued in large amounts. • Require some degree of coordination with treasury to avoid segmented and small markets.
Auctions of central bank deposits	• Guarantee the central bank's operational independence and avoid competition with treasury securities.	• Do not assist in developing securities markets (unless they are negotiable, but then they are similar to central bank securities).

other, more risky securities, government securities have a potential advantage. This advantage lies in the potential of the government to issue larger amounts of different maturities, given its typically sizable debt funding needs. A fast-growing market in government securities allows the central bank to expedite the transition to secondary market operations, thereby circumventing the disadvantages associated with primary market operations through government securities.

In theory, a central bank could also issue paper of varying maturities, but the scope for building up and maintaining a substantial volume of central bank paper in the market could be limited, since it is not the normal business of a central bank to raise funds in the market (unless they are simultaneously re-lent as part of a quasi-fiscal operation). Thus, the monetary use of government securities could complement and reinforce the market development potential inherent in deficit financing.

Makes the cost of monetary tightening transparent in the government budget. Transparency of the costs involved in absorbing liquidity is particularly important when it is impossible to remove at the root the factors underlying central bank losses (e.g., quasi-fiscal operations) or when past government policies are the cause of the liquidity overhang. Interestingly, however, country experience reveals several cases in which the cost-to-the-government argument was used by the authorities to end their support of government securities for primary market operations.[3] Therefore, the cost-for-the-budget as an argument against government support of the use of government securities in primary market operations needs careful consideration.

Absorption of excess liquidity always involves a cost (interest paid on the instrument of sterilization) that ultimately needs to be borne by the government either directly on the budget or indirectly through the effects on the profit and loss account of the central bank. When government securities are used for absorption, the cost will be directly visible in the government budget. Under the typical institutional arrangement, whereby the larger part of the central bank's profits are transferred to the government, the budget will be affected because of lower profits when central bank securities are used. In the case of losses, budgetary effects will depend upon the specific institutional arrangements to recapitalize the central bank. Depending upon these arrangements, central bank losses by themselves will complicate monetary control. Thus, the two approaches may, in principle, be equivalent in terms of cost, but in practice could have different implications for monetary control and the transparency of budgetary effects.

The cost to the government resulting from the use of treasury bills for monetary management is *not* generally a valid argument against the use of this instrument. Insofar as the government is reluctant to accept a needed monetary tightening because of its fiscal implications, the issue is not a choice of instrument but central bank autonomy. For any given stance of

---

[3]In Mauritius, where large capital inflows forced the authorities to conduct massive absorption operations, the treasury discontinued its support for the use of government securities in monetary operations. Excess liquidity became an issue in Kenya also, and the treasury was not willing to increase the issue of treasury bills in sufficient amounts to absorb the excess liquidity.

monetary policy, the choice between treasury and central bank securities mainly affects who bears the initial cost of monetary operations. Even if the cost is ultimately borne by the government, the initial effects could constrain behavior. This is an empirical question. In any event, reliance on government securities for monetary operations will improve the transparency of the operations, making the cost of the exercise overt and putting pressure on the authorities to address the underlying cost factors, which often are related to excessive fiscal deficits.[4]

Disadvantages

The main disadvantage associated with the use of government securities for monetary policy and market development goals is that the government must be willing to design, and adhere to, a division of responsibilities between itself and the central bank with respect to issuance procedures that ensure the bank's operational independence. Without such supporting arrangements and their strict implementation, the effectiveness of monetary operations will certainly be impaired.

To ensure monetary control, the combined use of primary issues of government paper for both debt and monetary management should contain the following arrangements: (1) the government and the central bank should agree on selling procedures and technical characteristics of the instruments so as to ensure an appropriate range of investors and market-clearing prices; (2) the volume at each issue should incorporate the monetary management needs; and (3) an arrangement should be established to "sterilize" the proceeds, if any, from securities sold over and above the debt management needs and to determine the interest payments on these proceeds.

Country experiences indicate that it is difficult for central banks and fiscal authorities to arrive at viable coordinating arrangements and that such arrangements are often very short-lived. The country survey contains a number of examples, demonstrating good (or potentially good) arrangements as well as the problems that arise when arrangements are flawed. A common problem is that the volumes at issue were determined by the government without due regard for monetary management objectives, thereby impairing monetary policy effectiveness; another is that the interest rates at auction are not at market-clearing levels because of government interference (for country examples, see Quintyn (1994)).

---

[4]From the viewpoint of transparency, it could also be argued that the entire cost of monetary policy should be borne by the central bank. While this point of view is certainly defensible, the case discussed above mainly concerns costs from past policies, which are not necessarily costs associated with monetary policy.

In contrast, an arrangement established in the early 1990s in the Philippines—allowing for overfunding of the deficit—was potentially workable. This arrangement required a high degree of coordination between fiscal and monetary authorities since the government had to commit itself to not using these funds, which in times of emergency financing needs led to conflicts and, ultimately, to modifications of the arrangement.[5] The arrangement between the treasury and the Central Bank of the Philippines meets the requirements set forth above, but the experience is illustrative of the difficulties associated with implementing effective coordinating arrangements.

Central Bank Securities

Advantages

The main advantage of the central bank issuing its own debt instruments for primary market interventions is that monetary management will be largely separated from debt management, thereby giving the central bank operational flexibility in its monetary policy interventions.

Disadvantages

Country practice reveals two types of disadvantages with respect to the use of central bank paper. The first is the risk of central bank losses when relying solely on the issuance of central bank paper to absorb a large amount of excess liquidity. The second is the risk of market segmentation when government securities markets also exist, and the lack of spillover to foster money market development in general.

Risk of central bank losses. If central banks rely on bank paper to absorb large amounts of excess liquidity, these interventions may eventually affect the institution's profit and loss account. This outcome is all the more likely if the yield structure of the central bank balance sheet is biased, that is, if some assets (credit to the government, credit to the commercial banks) do not (yet) have market-determined yields. Cases in point are the Philippines, Ghana, and Chile, where the issuance of central bank paper contributed to losses, while in Indonesia and Korea, central bank bills have had a significant negative impact on the profit and loss account.

---

[5]Recently, the central bank has resorted to issues of its own securities to fine-tune the interventions through treasury bills, because the government had expressed reluctance to bring the volume of treasury bills at issue fully in line with monetary management requirements. Under the arrangement, the cost to the Philippine Central Bank was slightly lower than the cost it would have incurred if it had had to issue its own securities to supplement the issues of treasury bills, because the bank was not required to pay interest on the entire deposit.

Central bank losses lead to two major problems. First, they undermine the central bank's prestige and autonomy (both institutional and operational), and second, the interest payments due on the outstanding debt and, perhaps, the accompanying losses themselves may undermine monetary policy effectiveness. In other words, losses themselves produce an expansionary effect, offsetting, in part, the effects of issuing central bank securities. Thus, both the effects of monetary policy actions and the transmission channels could be weakened by central bank losses.

Admittedly, the issuance of central bank securities is just one of several factors that have an impact on the central bank's profit and loss account.[6] Also, if the authorities have agreed on an arrangement so that the government budget deficit is allowed to be overfunded to meet monetary management requirements, and the central bank pays a market-related interest rate on these government deposits, the effect on the central bank's profit and loss account will be similar to the case in which the central bank replaces this overfunding with its own debt instruments.

The risk for central bank losses resulting from the use of central bank securities is greatest in the initial stages of the transition to indirect monetary policies, because of the need to mop up large amounts of excess liquidity that have been building under the direct monetary control regime.

Risk for small and segmented money market. A second observed disadvantage—although not a necessary outcome—is that markets for central bank securities have often remained very thin, with implications for the flexible use of central bank bills for monetary policy intervention and for financial market development in general. Often, monetary authorities design central bank securities to serve their immediate monetary policy purposes (usually to absorb excess liquidity) while neglecting market development goals. The demand for the instrument is sometimes based on government regulation (eligibility for reserve requirements, liquid asset requirements)—a problem also shared by government paper—that distorts market development; in addition, holdings are often restricted to a small group, for example, banks. As a result, the market never widens, and secondary market activity never materializes.

The size of this problem depends on the circumstances under which central bank paper is used, and in particular whether government securities are in circulation. *When government securities are already in circulation* (and these securities have the proper market-stimulating features, as listed above), there is no real problem if a central bank bill market remains small by design, as long as it is integrated with the overall money market. Financial market development can be achieved by fostering government

---

[6]For a comprehensive overview, see Leone (1993), p. 24.

securities markets, and, in addition, the central bank can fully enjoy the benefits of a separation between debt and monetary management to gain operational independence.

Nonetheless, what can happen—particularly when the government securities market is still in its infant stages—is that the simultaneous use of central bank and government securities leads to unnecessary competition between them or to a segmentation of the market for liquid assets. Both factors would slow down financial market development. Careful technical design of the instruments and of sales and transfer procedures can minimize market segmentation and will play a crucial role for both monetary control and money market development.

One way to avoid these problems is to endow both securities with exactly the same features (interest rate determination, maturity, eligible holders) so that the instruments are identical to the purchasers and a homogeneous market is created. This is the preferred option when both markets, taken separately, are expected to remain thin for a long time, because it adds some volume to the markets. The arrangements in Ghana and Mauritius are along these lines. In Mauritius, for instance, the treasury and central bank alternate issuance dates, depending on the treasury's needs for fresh funds. However, success depends to a large extent on the market's perception of the instruments. In some countries, the government had to pay a higher risk premium than did the central bank on otherwise similar securities, which caused confusion in the market and led to segmentation.[7]

Should the establishment of a homogeneous market prove to be impossible, both authorities should seek to differentiate their instruments from one another clearly; this will greatly reduce direct competition during the issue process.[8] In such a situation, it is generally desirable to issue central bank securities frequently and at very short initial maturities (one month or less) and adjust the volume to influence money market liquidity. Central banks typically operate at the short end of the market to achieve the strongest feed-through to interest rates. At the same time, treasury securities will be issued in longer maturities (three months and longer) in standard amounts related to debt management objectives. To facilitate set-

---

[7]Such was the case in the Philippines in the early 1980s and Poland in 1990. In Nepal, the central bank has a tendency to pay higher interest rates on its bills than the treasury does on its paper (in side-by-side auctions). As a result of this practice, the markets remain segmented. The Central Bank of The Gambia recently began to issue central bank bills to fine-tune its monetary management. Although these securities are identical to treasury bills, they are trading at a higher premium than the treasury bills, leading to a segmented market.

[8]In response to problems such as those described above, the authorities of the Philippines and Poland agreed to discontinue the use of central bank paper and concentrate on treasury securities. As argued before, this is the preferred alternative.

tlement and liquidity planning, the timing and frequency of issues, settlement procedures, and rediscount and secondary market arrangements for these instruments have to be closely coordinated. As the secondary markets for treasury securities build up in volume and liquidity, the authorities can replace central bank bill operations with appropriate repurchase operations in treasury securities, and thus eliminate the regular use of central bank paper altogether.

When no government securities market exists and the scope for developing one is limited because of fiscal surpluses or balanced budget rules, the authorities must ensure that the design and operation of central bank securities will bring about a viable market for such securities, thereby facilitating efficient transmission of monetary policy signals. The speed of financial market development will ultimately have an influence on the pace of adoption of indirect instruments and their effectiveness and efficiency.[9]

It is worth emphasizing that these shortcomings should not be considered inherent flaws in the use of central bank bills but reflect country-specific circumstances. When no government securities markets exist, the proper design of central bank paper is a crucial element for the reform process to be successful; nonetheless, it may be difficult to develop the desired characteristics for particular classes of securities. This is an empirical issue on which no generalization is possible.

Auctions of Deposits at the Central Bank

An alternative technique that has some appeal in the early stages of financial reform is the auction of deposits at the central bank as a liquidity management tool. Auctions of central bank deposits are easier to organize than securities issues since they do not require the establishment of a market infrastructure. They are especially useful when the government has little or no credibility and its debt instruments would sell only at a high-risk premium—for example, in some of the "post-chaos economies." Under these circumstances, if absorption operations become necessary, the introduction of auctions of deposits at the central bank might be warranted.

Although the greatest advantage of auctions of central bank deposits lies in safeguarding the central bank's operational independence, one major disadvantage in the medium term is that this technique does not help—in fact, may delay—the development of financial markets. This is

---

[9]See Quintyn (1994) for a discussion of two cases—Korea and Indonesia—in which the central bank securities market has (yet) failed to develop and integrate with the rest of the money markets, mainly because the respective central bank securities did not bear the desirable features.

under the assumption that the deposits are not negotiable. So, while useful in the initial stages, these auctions should at a certain point be replaced or complemented by other market-based operations involving central bank securities.

The Choice in Later Stages

Once financial markets have reached a certain size and degree of liquidity, the organization of open market interventions becomes easier for the central bank. Even among countries with developed government securities markets, central banks have used central bank paper for both normal liquidity management operations and as a means of coping with more exceptional circumstances, such as large capital inflows—although it is generally recognized that such operations are not sustainable beyond the short term.

Although in most developed financial markets, government securities—treasury bills in particular—have traditionally been the favored instrument for monetary operations (both outright and repurchase transactions), recently, more and more central banks have resorted to the use of central bank bills also. For example, the central banks of Denmark, Spain, and Sweden conduct transactions in central bank bills to influence the liquidity in the market and often conduct repos on the basis of these securities. Indeed, New Zealand regularly uses central bank bills (Reserve Bank of New Zealand (RBNZ) bills) for monetary management. Specifically, the RBNZ resorts to a combination of primary issues of central bank bills, outright transactions in government and central bank securities, and repos on the basis of both securities. RBNZ bills are tendered for constant amounts to financial institutions, as a means of providing a targeted volume of rediscountable assets. At the same time, open market operations are conducted using new issue treasury bills; the RBNZ determines the volume and maturity of these treasury bills, under an arrangement with the treasury. The RBNZ and the Government of New Zealand also have an agreement stipulating that the latter will bear all costs the RBNZ incurs on account of the issuance of its own securities.

The RBNZ bill market, as part of an arsenal of instruments to implement monetary policy, is limited to providing a liquid asset in specified amounts to financial institutions. The clear separation between government and RBNZ securities and the clear definition of their purposes ensure that there is no confusion in the marketplace to hamper financial market development. The main difference between New Zealand and most of the other countries reviewed in the Appendix is that the latter often do not have established government securities markets. In the absence of such well-established markets, problems of coordination of central bank and government securities assume importance for monetary control and market development.

The arrangements in New Zealand contain some useful elements that can be adopted in developing markets. For one thing, there is a clear agreement that the government will bear all costs related to the issuance of securities for monetary policy purposes, not only of the treasury bills but also of the RBNZ bills. For another, the central bank uses a government security (seasonal treasury bill) that is not used by the government for domestic debt management. Its sole reason for existence is monetary management, but the cost is borne by the government. The use of a specially designed treasury bill is also part of the arrangements in Israel. The Bank of Israel uses a specific government debt instrument that is not used for debt-funding purposes. This arrangement bears a lot of resemblance to the use of central bank paper, because it separates monetary from debt management while at the same time ensuring that the government directly bears the cost related to the securities.

Conclusion: Defining Guidelines

Based on a combination of analysis and country survey, some general lessons can be drawn on the use of government versus central bank securities for the conduct of primary market operations. Assuming that monetary policy instruments should provide operational flexibility and at the same time facilitate market development and ensure effective transmission of monetary policy, this paper concludes that no real preference can be put forward for either government or central bank securities. Much depends on the specific circumstances in each country, including whether a government securities market already exists, whether the government's credibility is sufficient to allow the development of a government securities market, and how well developed the working relations between the government and the central bank are. In light of this, the following paragraphs try to outline some general guidelines that could be adopted in managing the transition to indirect instruments.

(1) When it does not seem feasible to establish either a government or central bank securities market in the short term, auctions of deposits at the central bank offer an alternative for the central bank to start market-based monetary operations. This technique offers the central bank a high degree of operational independence, but it *does not contribute to the development of securities markets*. Thus, the central bank should, over time, move toward other techniques that assist in money market development.

(2) The use of government securities for both monetary and debt management offers advantages. These securities have the potential to be widely held and can play a catalytic role in financial market development,

strengthening the transmission process of monetary policy and facilitating the transition from primary to secondary market intervention. Therefore, monetary use of government securities, by avoiding a separate instrument for monetary policy intervention, complements and supports their market development potential. In addition, budgetary costs of liquidity absorption operations become transparent with the use of government securities for liquidity management. Thus, government securities meet two of the three selection criteria established earlier—financial market development and monetary policy transmission—in a better way than central bank securities can.

(3) However, to meet the third selection criterion—operational independence—the use of government securities requires solid coordinating arrangements between monetary and fiscal authorities, particularly in the initial stages. Such supporting arrangements should (a) provide for coordination of the tender volume, to allow the central bank to issue more securities than is strictly necessary for debt management purposes, (b) provide a mechanism for sterilizing the overfunding of the government's budget, and (c) bear the interest cost on this overfunding.

(4) Country experiences indicate that agreement on and implementation of such coordination are often the weaker part of the use of government securities. Therefore, if it becomes clear that the necessary coordination between monetary and fiscal agents cannot be achieved and that the central bank's operational independence might be impaired, it seems better to introduce a separate instrument for monetary management, such as central bank securities. However, the introduction of central bank securities does not relieve the authorities of the need to coordinate their respective operations to achieve shared objectives.

(5) When central bank securities are chosen, arrangements should be made to overcome the disadvantages associated with their use, that is, the danger of central bank losses and of small and fragmented markets:

(a) The government should stand ready to cover any losses the central bank incurs on account of the use of central bank securities. Such an arrangement can cover only possible losses or it can be more encompassing, stipulating that the government will bear the entire cost related to the use of central bank securities. The arrangement can be codified in the central bank law or can be part of a separate protocol between agencies.

(b) To achieve a successful coexistence of government and central bank financial instruments, it is necessary to coordinate their issues and to avoid or minimize market segmentation in the early stages. Depending on the particular situation in each country, these conditions can be met through various arrangements. As discussed, market homogeneity can be preserved if central bank and government securities are endowed with exactly the same features (interest rate determination, maturity, eligible holders).

If, however, the establishment of a homogeneous market proves impossible, the authorities should seek to clearly differentiate their instruments from one another in terms of technical design and coordinate the selling procedures, settlement, and secondary trading arrangements.

(6) An alternative solution—elements of which are found in the arrangements designed in New Zealand and Israel—is for the government to allow the central bank to use a government security specifically designed for monetary purposes, one that is not used by the government for debt-funding purposes. While safeguarding the central bank's operational independence in the use of the instrument, such an arrangement also implies that the government bears any costs related to the use of the instrument, thereby overcoming the danger for central bank losses related to the issuance of its own securities.

(7) Sometimes central bank securities emerge as the only viable alternative. For instance, in a "post-chaos economy," it may take some time for a government to regain its credibility. If the central bank is the only institution with any credibility, the only feasible options may be either central bank deposits or central bank securities. These securities should be carefully designed and operated so that they can contribute to financial market development in general. Later, when a government securities market emerges, the central bank securities can be phased out.

A second instance when central bank bills might be preferable to government securities is in monetary unions or regional monetary arrangements close to monetary unions. In such cases, it could be difficult for the central bank of the union to conduct primary market operations in government securities. Particularly for developing countries, there is a risk that government securities of different member countries are not equally valued and that, consequently, trade can be conducted in securities only of some member countries, giving these countries certain benefits. If, confronted with these issues, the union central bank itself were to select government securities from one or two member countries, it would give signals to the market about its risk perception and give the governments of these countries certain advantages, among others, in terms of seigniorage.

Appendix

Selected Country Experiences with Intervention Instruments
for Primary Market Operations

This Appendix provides a nonexhaustive overview of a relevant range of approaches that have been attempted in selecting the intervention instrument for primary market operations and designing supporting arrangements.[1] These approaches have met with varying degrees of success and have evolved through periods of changes and adjustments along the way.

The typical approach to introducing open market interventions as part of indirect monetary management has been to use primary market operations, often supported by direct instruments in the early stages. Although the eventual aim is to conduct open market operations in secondary government securities markets, the speed of the transition has varied. The type of supporting arrangements between fiscal and monetary authorities for conducting debt management and monetary operations in the same market has also varied.

Country experiences can be divided into four main categories (see Table 2).

- The first group of countries are those whose central banks have consistently used government securities in the development of open market operations. The countries presented are Kenya, Pakistan, The Gambia, Israel, and Mexico.

- A second category consists of countries that have been experimenting with both central bank and government securities and where the latter are currently the preferred instrument, namely, the Philippines, Sri Lanka, Poland, and Nepal.

- Group three countries have also experimented with both types, but their central banks are at present mainly relying on central bank securities: Mauritius, Ghana, Chile, and New Zealand.

- Finally, the fourth category groups countries that, in practice, have resorted only to central bank securities: Costa Rica, Indonesia, and Korea.

The reader is referred to Quintyn (1994) for a detailed description of the experience of the selected countries. The following paragraphs summarize the most relevant observations.

Types of Financial Instruments

With respect to the type of financial instrument—government or central bank securities or a combination of both—there is a greater variety of approaches in the newly liberalizing countries than in the industrial countries. In the industrial

---

[1]This appendix is based on Quintyn (1994).

countries, analysts have witnessed a certain convergence in both instruments and techniques used for open market interventions during the 1980s. Newly liberalizing countries, on the contrary, have tested a variety of options under specific local and historical conditions, and central bank securities have been tested and are used more frequently than in financially advanced countries. Among the reasons for this difference are: (1) the lack of government securities markets at the onset of the transition, when the central bank urgently needed a financial instrument for its open market operations,[2] (2) unwillingness of the government to establish such markets or to continue its support for the central bank's use of government securities in monetary operations, (3) shortcomings in previous supporting arrangements that allowed the central bank to use government securities for its primary market operations, and (4) a deliberate choice by the authorities to separate monetary from debt management (as was the case in New Zealand and Fiji).

Types of Supporting Arrangements

There is also variety in the types of supporting arrangements between monetary and fiscal authorities, ranging from good arrangements to very weak or nonexistent arrangements. The overview indicates that, more than the type of intervention instrument, the quality of the supporting arrangement seems to have a bearing on the success and smoothness of the transition to indirect monetary policy. In several countries in the analyzed sample, full transition to indirect instruments has been delayed owing to the lack of good supporting arrangements. In some of them, direct instruments could not be abolished completely.

Development of Secondary Markets

Irrespective of the financial instrument used for open market operations and the supporting arrangement in place, the development of active secondary markets in the intervention instrument in general seems to be a slow process. Of the countries surveyed, only the Central Bank of Mexico has moved to genuine open market operations in the secondary market, while the Central Bank of Poland uses repos and reverse repos. In a few other countries, secondary market activities have begun to take place sporadically. A host of other factors that fall outside the scope of this paper are also responsible for this lack of development, but the quality of the initial coordinating arrangements definitely plays a part.

Development of Government Securities Markets

Finally, government securities market development is in general the least advanced in those countries where central bank securities play the leading role in

---

[2]Indonesia is a special case in this regard because there is no need for the government to issue its own domestic debt instruments.

the development of open market operations (with the exception of New Zealand). Quite often, the central bank is forced to introduce its own securities because underlying the government's unwillingness to allow the central bank the use of government securities is a reluctance to move to market-based debt management techniques, for fear of higher funding costs. But in other cases, in which the instruments coexist, the development of government securities markets seems to receive less attention when central bank securities are also present.

Table 2: Government Versus Central Bank Securities for Open Market Operations (OMO): Selected Country Experiences

Country	Start Date of Open Market Operations	Financial Instrument Used for Open Market Operations	Intervention Market for Open Market Operations	Specifics of Coordinating Arrangements	If Central Bank Bills Are Used, Do Government Securities Markets Exist?	Is Secondary Market in Intervention Instrument Developing?	Date Direct Instruments Discontinued	Remarks
Group I. Countries using only government securities								
Kenya	1990	Treasury bills	Primary	Central bank has great autonomy in the auction as the government's debt manager.	—	Slowly developing	Still used	Treasury tries to to influence primary market (particularly rates at issue).
Pakistan	1991	Treasury bills	Primary	Nongovernment sector decides autonomously on auction.	—	Some activity	Still used	Government interference in auctions influences secondary market activity.
Gambia, The	1990	Treasury bills	Primary	Central bank has full autonomy to adjust auctions in line with monetary requirements; proceeds of auctions go to account at central bank.	—	Still low activity	1990	Government budget close to balance.

Israel	Early 1970s	Special type of government security	Primary	Central bank has full autonomy over this instrument, which is not used to finance government deficit. Proceeds are deposited in special account at central bank.	—	Slowly developing	1985	
Group II. Countries experimenting with both central bank and government securities								
Philippines	1983	Central bank bills	Primary	No	Yes	—	1981	Complaints of authorities that rate on government securities had to be too high to compete with central bank bills.
	1985	Treasury bills	Primary	Coordinating committee decides on volumes.				Central bank had to fine-tune with central bank bills.
	1987	Treasury bills	Primary	The above, plus proceeds of excess sales of treasury bills or account of monetary policy, are to be placed in deposit at central bank.	—	Yes		Central bank sometimes still intervenes with own securities in small amounts.

Government Versus Central Bank Securities—Country Experiences *(continued)*

Country	Start Date of Open Market Operations	Financial Instrument Used for Open Market Operations	Intervention Market for Open Market Operations	Specifics of Coordinating Arrangements	If Central Bank Bills Are Used, Do Government Securities Markets Exist?	Is Secondary Market in Intervention Instrument Developing?	Date Direct Instruments Discontinued	Remarks
Sri Lanka	1984	Central bank bills	Primary	None	No	—	1987	Government was not interested in development of treasury bills at that time.
	1987	Treasury bills	Primary	Joint forecasting committee, but volumes mainly based on maturing volumes.	—	...		
	1992	Treasury bills	Primary	Volumes based on monetary program.	—	Slowly		
Nepal	1988	Treasury bills	Primary	None—deficit financing needs prevailed.	—	...	1989	
		Central bank bills	Primary	None	Yes	...		
		Treasury bills and central bank bills	Primary	Central bank bills and treasury bills have identical features, issued in side-by-side auctions. Central bank bills are used to adjust volumes at issue for monetary policy purposes.	Yes	...		Rates are not identical, which tends to hamper market development.

Group III. Countries using both types but with preference for treasury bills

Mauritius	1988	Treasury bills	Primary	—	—	...	Some direct controls are still used.	Massive intervention needed to sterilize capital inflows.
	1991	Central bank bills	Primary	First on tap; later auctions; amounts to be issued are decided in consultation between treasury and central bank.	Yes	...		Treasury no longer willing to issue treasury bills for monetary management; securities have same characteristics but are not issued in same auction.
Ghana	1988	Treasury bills and central bank bills	Primary	Characteristics of central bank bills are identical to those of government securities.	Yes	...	1989	Central bank bills issued in several maturities to facilitate transmission of monetary policy and stimulate financial market development.

Government Versus Central Bank Securities—Country Experiences (concluded)

Country	Start Date of Open Market Operations	Financial Instrument Used for Open Market Operations	Intervention Market for Open Market Operations	Specifics of Coordinating Arrangements	If Central Bank Bills Are Used, Do Government Securities Markets Exist?	Is Secondary Market in Intervention Instrument Developing?	Date Direct Instruments Discontinued	Remarks
Chile	1975	Treasury bills and central bank bills	Primary	None	Initially yes. In late 1980s, disappeared owing to favorable fiscal position.	...	1976 (reintroduced during banking crisis 1982–87)	Central bank bills also massively used to rescue financial sector in early 1980s.
New Zealand	1985	Treasury bills	Primary	...	...	Some activity	1985	Central bank (RBNZ) was not satisfied with degree of autonomy for monetary management. Both central bank and government wanted clear separation between monetary and debt management.
		Central bank bills	Primary (secondary)	Reserve Bank of New Zealand (RBNZ) bills are main intervention instrument for monetary policy. RBNZ has an active role as the government's debt manager. Special treasury bills are used to neutralize impact of government cash flows on reserve money.	Yes	Some activity		

Group IV. Countries using only central bank securities

Costa Rica	Since late 1970s	Central bank bills	Primary	No coordinating arrangements	Yes	—	1992	Authorities are competing and face problems placing desired amounts.
Indonesia	1983	Sertificat Bank Indonesia (SBI) (central bank bills)	Primary	No coordination necessary	No	Slowly	1988	SBI worked only in one direction (absorption of liquidity). Thus, Bank Indonesia introduced another instrument (SBPU) to inject liquidity. Because SBI market not substantially integrated in broader money market, transmission of monetary policy is difficult.
Korea	1961	Monetary stabilization bonds (MSBs) (central bank bills)	Primary	None	Yes	Limited activity	Still used	MSB issued mainly at below-market rates to captive markets.

Source: Based on Quintyn (1994).

Bibliography

Alexander, William, Tomás J.T. Baliño, and Charles Enoch, 1995, *The Adoption of Indirect Instruments of Monetary Policy*, IMF Occasional Paper No. 126 (Washington: International Monetary Fund).

Emery, Robert, 1991, *The Money Markets of Developing East Asia* (New York, Prager).

Harper, Ian, and Julian Pearce, 1990, "Implementing Monetary Policy in an Era of Budget Surpluses," *Australian Economic Review* (No. 90, 2nd Quarter), pp. 53–65.

Harrison, I., 1988, "Central Bank Bills," *Reserve Bank of New Zealand Bulletin*, Vol. 51 (September).

International Monetary Fund, 1995, Monetary and Exchange Affairs Department, "Treasury Bill Auctions," Operational Paper, MAE OP/95/2 (unpublished; Washington: IMF).

———, 1995, "Short-Term Absorption of Capital Inflows," Operational Paper, MAE OP/95/3 (unpublished; Washington: IMF).

Klein, David, 1994, "Financial Deregulation in Israel: Policy and Results," in *Frameworks for Monetary Stability*, ed. by Tomás J.T. Baliño and Carlo Cottarelli (Washington: International Monetary Fund).

Kneeshaw, J.T., and P. Van den Bergh, 1989, "Changes in Central Bank Money Market Operating Procedures in the 1980s," *BIS Economic Papers*, No. 23 (Basle: Bank for International Settlements, January).

Leone, Alfredo, 1993, "Institutional and Operational Aspects of Central Bank Losses," IMF Paper on Policy Analysis and Assessment 93/14 (Washington: International Monetary Fund).

MacArthur, A., 1990, "Monetary Operations, Financial Market Development, and Central Bank Independence," background paper prepared for the Seminar on Central Banking organized by the Central Banking Department, International Monetary Fund, Washington, November.

Meek, P., 1987, "Government Financing: The Role of the Central Bank," paper presented at the SEANZA Central Banking Seminar, Sydney, November.

———, 1989, Monetary Policy and Debt Management (unpublished; Washington: World Bank).

Quintyn, Marc, 1994, "Government Versus Central Bank Securities in Developing Open Market Operations," in *Frameworks for Monetary Stability: Policy Issues and Country Experiences*, ed. by Tomás J.T. Balino and Carlo Cottarelli (Washington: International Monetary Fund).

Reserve Bank of Fiji, 1990, Research Department, "Reserve Bank of Fiji Notes: A New Monetary Policy Instrument," *Pacific Economic Bulletin*, Vol. 5 (December), pp. 15–20.

San Jose, A., and C. Polvorosa, 1984, "CB Bills as Instrument of Open Market Operations," *CB Review, Central Bank of the Philippines*, Vol. 36 (June), pp. 4–5, 23.

Spencer, Grant H., 1992, "Monetary Policy and the New Zealand Financial System" (Wellington: Reserve Bank of New Zealand).

Sundararajan, V., C. McAuliffe, and M. Quintyn, 1991, "Institutional Issues in Coordination of Debt Management and Monetary Policy—A Survey," *Appendix to the Advisory Report on China*.

Sundararajan, V., Peter Dattels, Ian McCarthy, and Marta Castello-Branco, 1994, "The Coordination of Domestic Public Debt and Monetary Management in Economies in Transition—Issues and Lessons from Experience," IMF Working Paper 94/148 (Washington: International Monetary Fund); see Chapter 1 of this volume.

6

Treasury Bill Auctions: Issues in Design

*Carlo Cottarelli**

This chapter examines two related issues: (1) why and when treasury bills should be sold by auction, and (2) the desirable features of treasury bill auctions. Accordingly, the first section discusses the role of treasury bill auctions in light of the requirements of government debt and monetary policy management, and the second and third sections deal with auction design.[1] Finally, although the chapter focuses primarily on the case in which treasury bills, while remaining an important vehicle for central bank intervention, are issued primarily as an instrument of debt management, a brief discussion of "monetary" treasury bills (bills issued purely as a tool to control liquidity) is also included.[2]

Treasury Bill Auctions: Why and When?

There are basically four techniques for selling treasury bills in the primary market (OECD (1982) and Bröker (1993)): (1) predetermined-

*Carlo Cottarelli is Division Chief, Central European Division II, at the International Monetary Fund. At the time this chapter was written he was in the Monetary and Exchange Affairs Department. He would like to thank Mario I. Blejer, Peter Dattels, Carl-Johan Lindgren, and Elizabeth A. Milne, as well as other members of the Monetary and Exchange Affairs Department, for their helpful comments and suggestions.
[1]While the views expressed in this chapter refer mainly to auctions of treasury bills (defined as debt instruments issued by the government, typically at a discount, with a maturity of up to one year), most of them could easily be extended to auctions of government debt instruments with longer maturity. It is worth stressing that this chapter does not cover other important issues related to the treasury bill market (such as the overall treasury bill market organization, the secondary market structure, the existence of rediscounting facilities, the accounting procedures for treasury bill transactions, the maturity of the bills, etc.) unless they have a direct bearing on the auction process. Some of these issues are covered elsewhere in this book.

[2]Monetary treasury bills are akin to central bank securities, the only relevant difference being that in the latter case the central bank, rather than the treasury, is responsible for servicing the securities. A full treatment of auctions of central bank securities, and therefore of monetary treasury bills, goes beyond the scope of this chapter.

price public subscription, in which treasury bills are sold at a predetermined price for a relatively short subscription period (some days); (2) tap sales at a predetermined price, differing from (1) because the subscription period is unlimited (continuous sale);[3] (3) private placement techniques (sale to a consortium of specialized investors at negotiated terms); and (4) auctions.

The choice among these techniques—and the specific features of each technique—should reflect the authorities' objectives. In this respect, it is important to distinguish between cases in which the bills are issued primarily as an instrument of debt management and cases in which they are issued primarily as an instrument of monetary control.[4]

Treasury Bills as Instruments of Debt Management

It is here assumed that, in deciding on the procedure for selling treasury bills, the authorities aim at (1) minimizing the cost of borrowing for the government, and (2) minimizing the disturbances for monetary policy management arising from debt management.[5] Given these objectives, selling treasury bills through auctions is, in most cases, appropriate.[6]

As to minimizing the cost of borrowing, in most instances, auctions are likely to be superior to the other techniques. With predetermined-price sales, there is the risk that, at least temporarily, securities will be sold at a price lower than the one required to cover a certain borrowing requirement. Sales by way of a consortium, using either private placement or subscription techniques, force the government to negotiate with a single counterpart, which may result in high underwriting fees. Instead, if properly designed, auctions take advantage of the competition among investors in buying a limited supply of securities. However, if the number of potential market participants is limited—as, for example, in some extreme cases of financial underdevelopment in which only one or two financial inter-

---

[3]In tap sales, the price is revised periodically; in some cases, the revisions can be quite frequent and reflect secondary market conditions.

[4]Between these two polar cases, a number of intermediate possibilities exist. For example, in Zambia, as in other developing countries, the treasury issues bills not only to finance its deficit but also to mop up liquidity, based on recommendations of the central bank. The revenue from the sale of the bills issued to mop up liquidity is sterilized in an account at the central bank, as is typically done in other countries for "monetary" bills (see the section "Treasury Bills as Instruments of Monetary Control" in this chapter).

[5]This is obvious if the central bank has been granted formal independence. But even if a country's legislation does not recognize the principle of central bank independence, a de facto separation between debt and monetary management objectives should be supported.

[6]An additional objective is avoiding market distortions. This objective implies that securities be sold at equilibrium prices in the absence of constraints. While this principle rules out any form of investment requirement, it does not allow discrimination among the above four sale techniques, which all imply transactions at equilibrium prices.

mediaries operate, and auction participation by other agents is prevented by lack of infrastructure or information—there is not much point in introducing auctions. In these cases, while trying to remove the obstacles to competition, predetermined-price sales, or sales through private placement, would be temporarily preferable.[7]

As to minimizing the disturbances for monetary policy, there is a major difference between predetermined-price sales (techniques (1) and (2)), on one side, and auctions, on the other. In predetermined-price sales, at least in the short run, the quantity sold acts as the absorber of demand and supply shocks (unless there is an underwriting commitment).[8] Therefore, delays in adjusting sale conditions will result in sticky treasury bill rates, which may be detrimental to monetary policy. This is particularly true if the government has access to central bank credit, because the latter can be used to finance a demand shortfall for given interest rates.[9] In summary, the separation between debt and monetary management requires that interest rates, rather than quantities, adjust to clear the treasury bill market: auctions clearly satisfy this requirement.[10]

Given the above-stated objectives, in most cases, selling treasury bills by auction is preferable. At the same time, the auction design should be such as to exploit fully the auction advantages, namely, interest rate flexibility and competition among investors.[11] In this respect, it is important to recognize that there is not much point in adopting auctions if the government is unwilling to accept their implications for interest rate flexibility.[12] At the

---

[7]Trying to establish auctions prematurely may result in frequent rejection of bids (as the only protection against lack of competition), and in excessive interest rate volatility, which would discourage market participation and, eventually, raise the cost of borrowing for the government. Faced with these developments, governments could shift back to fixed-price sales, but backtracking may destroy confidence in the working of market mechanisms.

[8]Of course, if prices are revised frequently enough in line with secondary market conditions, the features of predetermined-price sales tend to converge to those of (continuous) auctions.

[9]Oversubscription may also be a problem: a sharp increase of government deposits at the central bank will cause a decrease in reserve money, necessitating offsetting actions by the central bank.

[10]In principle, private placements or sales through an underwriting syndicate for predetermined-price subscription also allow a flexible adjustment of interest rates, but, in practice, this may not be the case. In private placements or sales through underwriting syndicates, the government negotiates with a single counterpart, in which case acting as a pure quantity setter might prove excessively costly and the temptation to adjust supply rather than interest rates might be correspondingly stronger. Nevertheless, there are examples of countries (notably Germany) where the sale of government securities by private placement is not regarded as inconsistent with central bank independence.

[11]The auction design should, of course, be reflected in clearly defined rules to be enforced consistently across all market participants.

[12]In particular, the treasury should not abuse its power to reject low-price bids, because such an abuse could make sales by auctions virtually identical to fixed-price sales. (See the section "Quantity Announcement and Discretion in Accepting Bids" later in this chapter).

same time, the potential consequences for the fiscal balance of accepting interest rate flexibility should be adequately emphasized.

Treasury Bills as Instruments of Monetary Control

In some countries, treasury bills are issued as an instrument of monetary control, that is, as a substitute for central bank securities.[13] In these countries, the conditions under which the bills are issued are determined by the central bank, and the corresponding proceeds are frozen in a government deposit at the central bank (see "Auction Design: The Case of Monetary Treasury Bills" later in this chapter). In such a context, the choice that the central bank faces is basically whether the bills should be sold by auction or at predetermined prices and interest rates. (Other forms of sale (e.g., private placement) are uncommon for monetary instruments.)

This decision involves the consideration not only of some of the aspects already discussed—such as the need to minimize the cost of monetary intervention—but also of several issues that go much beyond the scope of this chapter, including the choice of an interest rate, rather than a quantity, as a central bank operating target; the existence of alternative tools (e.g., administered discount rates) through which interest rate signals can be sent to the market; and the importance, for the central bank, of gathering information on money market conditions (auctions convey more information than predetermined-price sales).

Auction Design

The following aspects of the auction design will be discussed: (1) auction participation (excluding central bank participation); (2) bid screening and the risk of noncompliance; (3) central bank participation; (4) competitive bids; (5) price determination and allocation mechanism for competitive bids; (6) noncompetitive bids and postauction sales; (7) quantity announcement and discretion in accepting bids; (8) auction schedule; and (9) publicity requirements.[14] In this section, these aspects will be discussed with reference to the use of treasury bills as a debt management instrument, while the following section focuses briefly on the use of treasury bills as an instrument of monetary policy.

---

[13]For a broader discussion of the use of treasury bills as a monetary instrument, see Johnston and Brekk (1989).

[14]For simplicity, in this section the term "treasury" is used to identify the issuer of government securities. This section includes several statements concerning available results of theoretical auction literature and prevailing practices; unless otherwise indicated, these statements are based on Bartolini and Cottarelli (1994).

Auction Participation

In many countries, auction participation is restricted to some categories of bidders (banks, financial intermediaries, legal persons, domestic residents).[15] Moreover, some of these bidders may be admitted to auctions only indirectly, typically through the intermediation of a bank. These restrictions may increase the risk of collusion among bidders and, with the exception indicated below, should be avoided.

In order to foster competition and avoid the emergence of rent positions, the principle in this area—a principle that finds application in a number of countries—should be that *direct participation* is admitted for all domestic and foreign residents, both individuals and legal entities, subject only to the requirements needed to screen bids.[16] Even if direct participation may, in practice, not be appealing to many investors, the removal of entry barriers is important to deter collusion.[17]

An important exception to the above principle is when exclusive right of participation in the auctions is given to a class of agents (usually referred to as "primary dealers") in exchange for services they provide in developing the treasury bill market. These services range from the commitment to bid for at least a given percentage of the bid amount, to the willingness to act as secondary market-makers (standing ready to buy and sell at posted conditions on the secondary market), to submitting bids on the account of agents not directly admitted to the auctions. Because of these potential services, the issue of whether participation should be restricted to a class of primary dealers has to be settled in light of the overall organization of the treasury bill market, an issue discussed in detail in Chapter 7. Nevertheless, at least two aspects should be considered before opting for granting primary dealers exclusive right of auction participation: first, whether enough competition would be present in the auctions if participation were restricted and, second, whether the services of primary dealers could be compensated by alternative privileges (i.e., other than by exclusive participation).[18]

---

[15]This section deals with participation at competitive terms, that is, by submitting bids for which a price-quantity pair is tendered. Participation at noncompetitive terms is discussed under that heading later in the chapter.

[16]About 30 percent of the 42 countries surveyed by Bartolini and Cottarelli (1994) allow all agents to participate in the auctions. This percentage rises to almost 40 percent with respect to all domestic agents.

[17]Participation rules for nonresidents may have to take into account the applicable exchange regulation and various practical problems related to the administrative arrangements for bidding and settlement; initially, nonresidents could be admitted only through intermediaries.

[18]In some countries, primary dealers have access to special forms of financing from the central bank, or have the exclusive right to purchase treasury bills at predetermined conditions (usually the average auction price) for some time after the auctions (see Chapter 7, Appendix 2, "Primary Dealer Systems in Selected Industrial Countries").

As to *indirect participation*, financial intermediaries should be allowed to submit bids on behalf of their customers, as logistic problems (such as limited access to the central bank window where bids are submitted) may discourage direct participation. But allowing indirect participation should not be seen as a replacement for direct participation. The former may be less conducive to competition among bidders because the intermediary would inevitably know the terms of the bids submitted on behalf of its clients.[19]

Auction participants sometimes receive from the issuer an administratively set commission in exchange for their participation. Such a commission is justified as a remuneration of the service provided in intermediating between primary and secondary treasury bill markets. A commission may also improve transparency because retail customers would all pay the auction price. However, the remuneration of such a service, rather than being set a priori, might best be market-determined, that is, it could emerge as a difference between secondary and primary market prices, as long as sufficient competition exists in secondary markets. In countries where competition on the secondary market is very limited (for example, when only a single large bank sells treasury bills at the retail level), it may be inevitable that the level of the remuneration is set administratively. Even in this case, it would be preferable to set the price spread at which the treasury bills could be sold on the market, rather than granting a commission to auction participants, because the latter would benefit also those not active on the secondary market.

Bid Screening and the Risk on Noncompliance

If liberal auction participation rules are accepted, some form of bid screening is necessary in order to avoid the participation of an excessively large number of bidders, which would make auction administration too costly, and the risk of noncompliance with the buying requirement. The participation of an excessively large number of bidders can be limited by accepting only bids above a certain minimum value (see "Competitive Bids" later in this chapter).

As to possible noncompliance with buying commitments, two solutions (or a combination of them) are possible. The first solution—aimed at *enforcing compliance*—involves the imposition of deposit requirements (possibly as high as 100 percent of the bid) on bidders that do not have accounts at the central bank—usually the agent managing treasury bill auctions. More specifically, those bidders should be requested to present documen-

---

[19]What matters is not the participation of nonfinancial agents in the auctions but, rather, the absence of barriers to entry in the auction process. Actual auction participation of nonfinancial agents is relatively less frequent, particularly in industrial countries.

tation—to be submitted together with the bid—guaranteeing that the funds, or part of the funds, are available for the purchase. The guarantee can take several forms. Bidders can be requested to create an escrow account at a commercial bank, or to present a bank guarantee or a certified check, stating the availability of funds. Documentation of ownership of treasury bills, or other government securities, expiring on the settlement day should also be acceptable. The second solution, aimed at *discouraging noncompliance*, involves the introduction of stiff penalties on noncomplying bidders. The penalties typically include the exclusion of noncomplying bidders from subsequent auctions, or the loss of the required deposits.[20]

The choice between forcing compliance and penalizing noncompliance involves a trade-off. Forcing compliance avoids the risk of persistent misconduct, which may continue despite the penalties, thus disrupting, at least temporarily, the auction process. On the other hand, a large escrow account deposit may discourage participation, and the use of certified checks may be impeded by lack of legal or institutional arrangements. (For example, in Albania, escrow accounts have been preferred, owing to the absence of a check-based payment system.)

Central Bank Participation

There are advantages and drawbacks to allowing the central bank to participate in the auctions (Cottarelli (1993)). Treasury bill rates perform a pivotal role in many financial systems, and it may be crucial for the central bank to be able to influence them directly. But, for the very same reason, the pressure from the government aimed at influencing central bank bids could be commensurately stronger, thus threatening its independence. Thus, in countries with developed financial systems, in which the central bank can affect the monetary system through different channels, there is merit in prohibiting central bank participation in the auctions (this is the principle accepted in the Maastricht Treaty). In other countries, the central bank could participate, provided the rules for its participation be such as to minimize the risk of political pressures.[21]

---

[20]If noncompliance is penalized by the loss of the deposit requirement, the coverage of the latter could be relatively small (say up to 5 percent of the bid). In order to facilitate the settlement process, bidders might also be requested to accompany their bid with a check (not necessarily a certified check) payable to the treasury (or to the agency issuing the bills) covering the full amount of the bid; the delivery of the bills would occur only after the availability of the funds has been ascertained.

[21]This position is in line with the prevailing practice in industrial and developing countries. In the sample considered by Bartolini and Cottarelli (1994), about 60 percent of the countries do not allow the central bank to participate in the auctions. However, among those countries, industrial countries are relatively overrepresented.

If the central bank is likely to be subject to coercion, it might be better to avoid its direct participation in the auction to ensure an orderly working of the auction process.

In the first place, the central bank should not participate as residual buyer, because such an arrangement would substantially weaken its control of base money. Second, any voluntary purchase should be at noncompetitive terms: the central bank would bid a quantity but its purchase would be settled at the average auction price. This arrangement would reduce, albeit not eliminate, the risk of pressures from the government aimed at lowering the treasury bill auction yield.[22]

As to the issue of whether the central bank bid should be subject to prorating—rather than being met prior to other bids—there are arguments on both sides. In order to allow better liquidity programming, the central bank's bid should not be subject to prorating (so that the effect on liquidity of its bid would be known in advance) and should therefore be satisfied prior to other bids. On the other hand, there is an issue of perception: in the absence of prorating, the authorities could be seen as crowding out legitimate private demand for risk-free assets, and such a behavior could ultimately discourage private participation.

Apart, possibly, from the provision on prorating, the central bank's participation should be regulated by all auction rules applicable to other participants. In particular, its bid should be submitted before other participants' bids are opened.[23]

Competitive Bids

Competitive bidding involves the commitment to buy a certain quantity at a certain price, yield, or discount rate. (For formulas relating to treasury bill price, discount, and yield, as well as for other formulas relevant for the auction process, see the Appendix at the end of this chapter.) Three features of competitive bidding are particularly important: the admitted number of bids per bidder, the ceilings on the maximum award per bidder, and the minimum admissible bid.

As to the number of bids, a liberal format is preferable, as unconstrained bidding improves bidders' flexibility and, hence, participation. There may be some concern for receiving, in the absence of constraints, unrealistically low bids that, occasionally, may turn out to be winning, and for increasing administrative costs if bids are too numerous. However, the risk of receiving unrealistically low bids could be combated by the use by the

---

[22]Further protection would be given by a ceiling on the overall amount of treasury bills held by the government. For a discussion of the conditions under which such a provision, as part of an overall constraint on central bank credit to the government, would be appropriate, see Cottarelli (1993).

[23]An exception would be represented by countries in which intervention in the primary treasury bill market is the main form of money market intervention. In these countries, there may be a case for allowing the central bank to bid only after reviewing the bids submitted by other bidders, in order to enhance its control over money market conditions.

treasury of its right to reject bids (see "Quantity Announcement and Discretion in Accepting Bids" later in this chapter). Moreover, the experience of many countries shows that, in practice, these concerns are not well founded: the excessive proliferation of bids is not a common phenomenon. As to administrative costs, they could be dramatically reduced by technical progress, including electronic bidding.

Ceilings on the maximum award per bidder have been advocated as anticollusion and anticornering devices. However, at the theoretical level, their usefulness is debated and, in practice, most countries do not apply them.[24] Moreover, they can be easily circumvented, even in cases when the resources invested in auction supervision are substantial (see United States, Department of the Treasury and others (1992)).

As to the minimum size of bids, a balance must be struck between avoiding an excessively low minimum (which would allow participation of too many bidders) and a prohibitively high minimum (which would reduce the number of independent bidders, thus damping competition). In balancing these factors, authorities may be tempted to look at other countries' experiences. However, in comparing different countries, consideration should be given to the economic environment. More specifically, the strength of the "entry barriers" implicit in a given minimum bid is affected by the country's per capita wealth or income. For example, a minimum bid of US$1 million may have limited impact on participation in a country like the United States, but might be prohibitively high for most bidders in low-income countries.[25]

Price Determination and Allocation Mechanism for Competitive Bids

A crucial aspect of auction design is the mechanism for determining the price paid by bidders and for allocating awards. In general, there are two alternatives: *multiple-price auctions*, in which bids are arrayed in ascending

---

[24]Ceilings may strengthen collusive rings, as they reduce the ring-members' incentives to abandon the cartel to try to corner the secondary market individually.

[25]A rough indication on the "appropriate" size of the minimum bid, based on international averages adjusted for income differences, can be derived from the following equation:

$$log(MIB) = 1.22 * Log(PCAP)$$

where *MIB* is the minimum bid in U.S. dollars and *PCAP* is the per capita income, also in U.S. dollars. The reported elasticity (1.22) was estimated for a sample of 38 countries, with reference to treasury bill auctions (Bartolini and Cottarelli (1994)). The above equation implies that, based on the average of countries with similar per capita income, the size of the minimum bid in countries with per capita income of US$2,000 and US$4,000 should be, respectively, around US$10,000–11,000, and US$24,000–25,000. These figures should be considered as a mere starting point to be revised in light of more specific information on potential bidders (including average size of interbank transactions, the denomination of similar financial assets, and so forth).

order, winning bids are the highest allowing full absorption of supply, and bidders pay the bid price;[26] and *uniform-price auctions*, in which bidders pay the price of the lowest winning bid. The relative advantages of these alternatives can be assessed by looking at their potential for revenue maximization; their effect on monetary conditions and financial sector development; and the "revealed preferences" of authorities in countries where auctions are used.

The debate on which auction format maximizes government revenues has so far been inconclusive. At the theoretical level, there is a presumption that uniform-price auctions are superior because, though they do not allow the exploitation of the consumer surplus, they reduce the cost of the "winner's curse."[27] However, this conclusion has been reached only under restrictive hypotheses—including absence of risk aversion, homogeneity among bidders, sale of single objects, absence of collusion—that cannot easily be extended to treasury bill auctions. At the empirical level, recent experiments performed in the United States with the two auction formats (see Chapter 14) were also inconclusive, although there were indications that uniform price auctions encouraged the *direct* participation of relatively less informed investors.

As to the effect on monetary conditions and financial sector development, multiple-price auctions give an incentive for secondary trading, and hence may spur the development of the secondary market. Moreover, they have the advantage of lowering the volatility of the average auction yield, often used as a reference for setting other interest rates, because the average would be based on several bids rather than on a single marginal bid, as in the case of a uniform-price auction. This factor is important because treasury bill rates play a pivotal role in many financial markets; it may become crucial in thin markets in which the marginal bid is more likely to include a strong random component. On the other hand, the winner's curse may also be stronger in thin markets, owing to the wider dispersion of bids.

As to revealed preferences, multiple-price auctions are more common than uniform-price auctions. Indeed, the bias toward multiple-price auctions is overwhelming for treasury bills, albeit less marked for longer-term securities. In a sample of 42 countries, at the end of 1993, over 90 percent sold treasury bills through multiple-price auctions. Moreover, there are

---

[26]Prorating may be needed to allocate awards among lowest winning bids.

[27]The "consumer surplus" is the difference between the maximum price that each bidder would be willing to pay for the awarded amount of treasury bills and the price actually paid. The "winner's curse" is the cost that auction winners suffer because, on average, they buy at prices higher than the average market price (including nonwinning bids). To avoid this cost, rational bidders would lower their bid price, thus lowering revenues. By letting winners buy at the lowest winning bid price, uniform-price auctions reduce the cost of the winner's curse.

no examples of permanent shifts from multiple- to uniform-price auctions, while there are examples of shifts in the opposite direction.

Noncompetitive Bids and Postauction Sales

Noncompetitive bids involve the commitment to buy a certain amount of treasury bills at the average auction price; they are awarded prior to competitive bids. Noncompetitive bidding is appealing to bidders that do not have specific views on expected auction prices, or that wish to avoid the risk of buying at above-average prices. Allowing this form of participation widens the scope of the treasury bill market and should be favored, provided two conditions are set in place.

First, in order to avoid determining the average auction price over a very narrow section of the market, the share of noncompetitive awards could be capped, and prorating could be used to allocate noncompetitive awards within the cap. On the basis of available country experience, the cap is normally set at about 25–30 percent, but somewhat higher or lower percentages are also found. Second, a cap on the maximum size of each noncompetitive bid is also normally set. Otherwise, noncompetitive bids, which often aim at attracting medium-size bidders, may be crowded out (owing to the prorating mechanism) by a large noncompetitive bid submitted by an institutional investor.

The aim of spurring primary market participation of uninformed investors can also be satisfied by allowing the purchase of treasury bills at the average auction price for some time after the auction. More specifically, postauction sales could meet the demand of investors who are unwilling to face the uncertainty regarding yield or quantity involved in the auction mechanism.[28] A retail secondary market can serve the same purpose, but its development or efficiency may be impeded by lack of financial intermediaries. On the other hand, a proliferation of forms of participation (competitive, noncompetitive, postauction) may stretch the primary market and should be avoided. Thus, postauction sales should be considered only as a temporary replacement for a missing secondary market, and under three conditions: first, the price charged should be above the average auction price in order to compensate for the lack of uncertainty related to this type of purchase;[29] second, the postauction subscription period could be limited to one to two days for administrative reasons

---

[28]For example, competitive bidding involves uncertainty about the quantity awarded. Noncompetitive bidding involves uncertainty about the price paid and, possibly, the quantity (if prorating is necessary). Instead, in postauction sales, investors are certain about both the price paid and the quantity purchased.

[29]A surcharge may not be necessary if the right to buy in postauction sales is granted in compensation for services provided by certain investors, such as primary dealers.

and to encourage the secondary market development; and third, in order to avoid the multiplication of bill issues in circulation, the original maturity date of the bills should be maintained (and the price should be adjusted correspondingly to reflect the shorter maturity).[30]

Quantity Announcement and Discretion in Accepting Bids

With the exception of the case in which treasury bills are used mainly for monetary purposes, the treasury is normally responsible for deciding the terms at which securities are auctioned, and should have some degree of flexibility in accepting and rejecting bids.[31]

The first decision that the treasury needs to make is on the amount of treasury bills that it intends to issue. In a framework in which the bills are used primarily as a debt management tool, such a decision should be influenced by the treasury's borrowing needs and by its overall debt management strategy. Given this decision, and assuming a separation between monetary and debt management, the central bank should decide on the amount of intervention in the primary or secondary market consistent with its monetary objectives. In practice, rather than reacting retroactively to the debt management decision, the central bank may have an important role in advising the treasury on the quantity of bills to be issued.

In most countries, the amount of treasury bills to be issued is typically announced to the market.[32] This practice helps the market in forming expectations on equilibrium prices and enhances transparency. At the same time, after the announcement is made, some degree of flexibility is needed as a protection against collusive behavior. An extreme form of protection is the announcement of a cutoff price below which the treasury would be unwilling to sell, but this solution has serious drawbacks. In unsophisticated markets, bids may cluster around the announced cutoff price, thus reducing competition. Moreover, the cutoff price may be moved by the treasury only slowly, which, in combination with the clustering of bids, would reduce the flexibility of auction rates, thus depriving the auction mechanism of its main advantage vis-à-vis other sale techniques.

---

[30]Postauction sales may involve some liquidity control problems for the central bank, because the amount of treasury bills sold in this way cannot be easily anticipated. However, this concern can be allayed if postauction sales are admitted only within the limits described in the text.

[31]The central bank, as government agent, normally provides advice on auction conditions, but the treasury, which is responsible for servicing the debt, usually makes the final decision on auction-related matters.

[32]In the 42-country sample considered by Bartolini and Cottarelli (1994), only 2 countries (Spain, and, for some treasury bill maturities, Hungary) do not announce the auction size. The French Treasury announces a minimum and maximum auction size.

A more appropriate solution consists of allowing the treasury to reject bids below a preset, but not announced, price. In practice, this solution is equivalent to maintaining downward flexibility on the size of the securities' issue, because the treasury would retain the right to reduce the amount actually issued until after the bids have been tendered.[33] Alternatively, a cutoff rule could be announced: for example, all bids below, say, one standard deviation from the average price would be automatically excluded.[34] The advantage of the latter solution is that it does not involve discretionary decisions: therefore, the treasury would not be tempted to abuse the possibility of rejecting bids to avoid paying the appropriate market interest rate.[35] On the other hand, a fixed rule might be ineffective in preventing extreme forms of collusive behavior.

Finally, it would also be preferable if the treasury did not have the possibility, admitted in some countries, of rejecting individual bids without providing reasons. This possibility, sometimes justified as a device against money laundering, may involve risks for the credibility of the auction process. However, the possibility of excluding specific bidders from the auctions should be retained as a penalty for breaking auction rules.

Auction Schedule

The key aspects of the auction schedule are: (1) the frequency and the timing of the auctions; (2) the lag between auction announcement and auction day; (3) the lag between the deadline for presenting bids and the announcement of auction results; and (4) the lag between auction date and settlement date.

The frequency and timing of the auctions are important for the working of the treasury bill market and, more generally, of the money market, and should be decided in light of several factors: first, the financing needs of the government;[36] second, other institutional arrangements affecting the money market, such as the regulation on reserve requirements, in order to foster the coordination between money management and debt

---

[33]When bills of different maturities are issued, the cutoff prices must be set consistently. The possibility of increasing the auction size after receiving bids could also be admitted, but only within tight quantitative limits, which should be clearly specified in auction regulations, in order to avoid uncertainty on the auction process.

[34]This system is used in Mexico. The reference mean could also be computed over the highest 50 percent of bids, thus excluding the influence of abnormally low bids; the deviation from the mean could also be specified in absolute terms—say 1–2 percentage points (this system is used in Italy).

[35]Repeated rejection of bids may lead to the disruption of the auction process and to the possible underfunding of budget needs.

[36]For example, if the supply of government paper is limited (reflecting low borrowing requirements or the thinness of the financial market), there is a need to avoid frequent auctions of insufficient size, resulting in excessive interest rate volatility.

management; third, the need to spur the development of the secondary treasury bill markets (which may be impeded by excessively frequent auctions) and contain administrative costs; and fourth, the need to roll over the existing stock of treasury bills (on this account, shorter-term treasury bills should be auctioned more frequently).

In practice, based on a range of country experience, treasury bill auctions usually take place monthly or fortnightly in thin financial markets. Weekly auctions are often adopted at a later stage of financial market development, particularly for the three- and six-month maturities. A frequency higher than weekly would seem to be inadvisable. As to longer-term securities, a frequency higher than monthly seems inappropriate in thin financial markets; fortnightly (or even weekly) auctions could be introduced at a later stage.

As to coordinating auctions of different maturities, clustering auctions for securities of comparatively similar maturity may be appropriate: if all treasury bill auctions (for, say, 3-, 6-, and 12-month maturities) are held on the same day, demand shifts across different maturities are smoother. Moreover, in order to smooth the rolling-over of outstanding debt, the settlement date for the issue of new treasury bills should coincide with the maturity date of bills of the same type, and the auction day should be set consistently.[37]

The lag between auction announcement and auction date should allow a sufficiently long reaction time for investors, without forcing the treasury to announce auction conditions prematurely. One solution would be to announce an auction calendar every 6 or 12 months. A more specific indication on the auctions (amount issued, maturities, possible cutoff prices or rules, and any other auction-specific conditions) could be announced between two and five working days before the auction.

The lag between the deadline for presenting bids and the announcement of auction results should be as short as possible in order to reduce uncertainty. In most countries, a two- to four-hour interval is sufficient.

As to the lag between auction day and settlement day, a long lag exposes investors to interest rate uncertainty. However, the lag, at a minimum, must be long enough to allow the processing of the information on auction results and the issue of treasury bills (which depends, among other things, on whether the bills are bearer or book certificates); more generally, it needs to be set taking into account the constraints arising from the general practice in securities transactions. An additional factor is the re-

---

[37]This requires that the treasury bill maturity be specified in days or weeks, rather than in months. The advantage of expressing the maturity in weeks is that, in this way, it would be possible to hold the auctions, and issue the bills, always on the same day of the week, thus minimizing the disturbance to the auction schedule arising from nonworking days.

quirements imposed by the "secondary" distribution of the securities. A longer lag allows primary investors to find secondary ("retail") investors before the settlement date, thus reducing their financial outlay on that date. In most countries, a two-day lag is considered appropriate, but shorter lags are also found.

Publicity Requirements

The auction mechanism should be as transparent as possible, which requires full disclosure of auction rules and conditions, and adequate publicity of auction results. Auction rules should be fully specified in official documents available to the public. The main auction rules may be included in framework laws or government decrees, which would refer the definition of the details of each auction to treasury decrees. The latter should be given adequate publicity in the media. As already mentioned, the early publication of an auction calendar is also recommended.

As to auction results, auction theory places considerable importance on spreading any information the treasury has on the value of the auctioned securities (including information on previous auction results), in order to mitigate the winner's curse. On the other hand, excessive information creates greater scope for enforcing cartels, as cartel members' behavior can be monitored more easily. The appropriate balance seems to be to provide summary statistics in as much detail as possible, subject to the constraint of avoiding the identification of individual bids. In deep markets, this implies that all information concerning the distribution of bids and bidders by relatively narrow bid price intervals can safely be spread. In thinner markets, however, only aggregate data (such as minimum, maximum, and average awarded price; amount issued; number of bids and bidders; and amount and number of noncompetitive bids) are usually provided.

Auction Design: The Case of Monetary Treasury Bills

The recommended treasury bill auction rules do not necessarily extend to the case of monetary treasury bills. Even if a full treatment of this subject goes beyond the scope of this chapter, it may be convenient to recall some areas where differences are likely to be found.[38]

A first difference concerns the responsibility for deciding on the treasury bill issue conditions. Although for nonmonetary treasury bills the central bank would normally play only an advisory role, monetary treasury

---

[38]In the case of "mixed" treasury bill issues (see footnote 4), the auction rules should obviously be the same for both components of the treasury bill issue. Whether the rules should be closer to those expounded in the preceding section or here depends on the relative importance of the two components.

bills should be issued, if not formally, at least practically, at the discretion of the central bank. The latter should also be responsible for any decision concerning the issue (amounts to be issued, auction announcement, and cutoff rates). Correspondingly, the central bank does not need to intervene in the auction.

Second, as for any other monetary intervention channel, auctions of monetary treasury bills must allow the central bank to operate in a timely fashion and at short notice. Thus, the procedures regulating those auctions are typically more simplified and flexible than those appropriate for nonmonetary treasury bills. This implies, for example, that auctions of monetary treasury bills are typically opened only to financial intermediaries with accounts at the central bank, thus guaranteeing settlement within a short period (often within the same day).

Third, because the central bank determines the issue conditions, the coordination problems between monetary and debt management are simplified. This implies that further elements of flexibility—such as frequent deviations of issues from announced auction size, or even the absence of an auction size announcement—could be more easily admissible. The timing and frequency of the auctions could also be more easily attuned to the monetary control framework of the central bank and to institutional features of the money market.

Appendix

Formulas for Treasury Bill Auctions

Treasury bills are normally issued as zero-coupon financial instruments with their yield determined by the difference between the par value of the security and the issue price. Bids are accepted in terms of yield, discount, or price (see Bartolini and Cottarelli (1994)) for information on the practice followed in various countries), but the conversion from one to another way of expressing the bid is a matter of simple algebra. Defining:

d = discount of a bill (decimal) with t days to maturity, on an annual basis

F = the face value of the bill

P = the price of the bill

n = the number of days in the standard year used for the computation,[1]

the discount on the bill is defined as

$$d = [(F - P)/F] * (n/t),$$

and the price of the bill in terms of the discount is

$$P = F * [1 - d * (t/n)].$$

The yield on a bill (i) is based on the purchase price of the bill and is always higher than the discount (that is, the difference between yield and discount is rising with t). The simple yield expressed on an annual basis (that is, the yield expressing the return of an investment in treasury bills for a total period of one year, but without taking into account the reinvestment of interest income during a year; see below) is defined as

$$i = [(F - P)/P] * (n/t),$$

and the price of the bill in terms of the yield is given by

$$P = F/[1 + i * (t/n)].$$

While in many countries auction yields are computed based on the above formulas, it is more meaningful, in order to compare the annual return on assets of different maturity and interest payment schedules, to use compounded annual yields, that is, yields expressing the return of an annual investment after allowing for the reinvestment of interest paid out on the security during the

---

[1]In some countries (Denmark, France, Sweden, and the United States), the standard year ("financial year") is conventionally set at 360 days, while other countries use the calendar year of 365 days (Canada, Italy, Belgium, Finland, Spain, and the United Kingdom). This will have to be taken into account by investors when computing the actual yield of their investment. For example, in an auction in which bidders are requested to bid "financial year" yields, a bid of 20 percent corresponds to a yield of 20.278 percent on a calendar-year basis.

year. Typically, it is assumed that interest collected during the year is reinvested at the initial interest rate.

The compounded yield (c) is related to price and face value by the following formula:

$$c = (F/P)^{n/t} - 1.$$

Because c takes into account the reinvestment of interest paid, it is always higher than i (as long as t is smaller than n; when t is equal to n, i and c are also equal), that is, the difference between c and i is declining with t.

· Bibliography

Bartolini, Leonardo, and Carlo Cottarelli, 1994, "Treasury Bill Auctions: Issues and Uses," IMF Working Paper 94/135 (Washington: International Monetary Fund).

Bröker, Günther, 1993, *Government Securities and Debt Management in the 1990s* (Paris: Organization for Economic Cooperation and Development).

Cottarelli, Carlo, 1993, *Limiting Central Bank Credit to the Government: Theory and Practice*, IMF Occasional Paper No. 110 (Washington: International Monetary Fund).

Johnston, Barry, and Odd Per Brekk, 1989, "Monetary Control Procedures and Financial Reform: Approaches, Issues, and Recent Experiences in Developing Countries," IMF Working Paper 89/48 (Washington: International Monetary Fund).

Organization for Economic Cooperation and Development, Committee on Financial Markets, Group of Experts on Government Debt Management, 1982, *Government Debt Management* (Paris).

United States, Department of the Treasury, Securities and Exchange Commission, and Board of Governors of the Federal Reserve System, 1992, *Joint Report on the Government Securities Market* (Washington: Government Printing Office, January).

7

Microstructure of Government Securities Markets

*Peter Dattels**

This chapter applies the literature on market microstructure to the specific features of government securities markets and draws implications for strategies to develop government securities markets.[1] It argues for an active role of the authorities in fostering the development of efficient market structures.

During the 1980s and 1990s, significant reforms to develop government securities markets have been undertaken in many countries—industrial, developing, and economies in transition. In many of those countries, the authorities have played an active role in fostering the development of the institutional structure of the market, acting on the premise that an appropriate structure is needed for the efficient functioning of markets. To illustrate, the National Treasury Management Agency of Ireland (NTMA) has written: "The structural market changes now proposed by the Agency are based on the premise, which is well supported by authoritative research on market mechanisms, that the structure of markets is not just a channel to an inevitable outcome but actually affects the trading price itself and therefore the cost at which the Agency raises funds in the bond market" (Ireland, NTMA (1994)).

The expression "authoritative research on market mechanisms" refers to the market microstructure literature, which is the study of the process as well as the results of exchanging assets under specified trading mechanisms. A central proposition of this literature is that the pricing of assets cannot be determined independently from the institutional structure of the market (particularly the organization and mechanics of trading). If the

*Peter Dattels is a Senior Economist at the International Monetary Fund.
[1]This chapter was originally issued as IMF Working Paper 95/117 (Washington: International Monetarty Fund, 1995).

209

structure of the government securities market affects prices (interest rates), by extension it affects the cost of the national debt.

The relationship between market structure and the goals of the authorities—the debt manager, the monetary authority, and the regulatory authority—is multifaceted:

- as agent of the taxpayer, debt managers have an obligation to assure that the government securities market is functioning smoothly and efficiently, generally characterized by liquid and deep markets, so as to minimize debt-service costs;
- as monetary policy authority, central banks try to promote efficient price discovery (interest rate determination) as an important element in the transmission mechanism of monetary policy. In addition, because central banks typically intervene through government securities markets, their organization is an important consideration in linking the use of monetary instruments with the achievement of operating targets;
- as regulator, the government or its agency (often the central bank) is responsible for the sound and fair functioning of government securities markets. Rule making influences key aspects of the market structure, including the class of intermediaries that operate in the market, their capitalization, the scope of their activities, the degree of investor protection, and so forth;
- as provider of infrastructure, the central bank can play an important role in supporting the market structure of government securities markets, which often includes forming a central depository; providing trade comparison or matching systems; and providing delivery-versus-payment systems; and
- as agents of the financial liberalization process, the central bank, regulatory authority, and fiscal authority share joint interests in the promotion of efficient government securities markets to best achieve macroeconomic stabilization, liberalization of interest rates, and the formation of capital markets.

Following from the above, the common goals shared by the authorities are efficient price discovery and liquid and deep government securities markets. Achieving those goals requires efficient market structures. Can the development of efficient market structures be left solely to the private sector? Not always. First, vested interests of intermediaries (or groups of intermediaries) may support less-than-efficient market structures. Because existing market structures tend to be self-perpetuating, given network externalities, actions may be needed to promote a change in market structure.[2]

---

[2]The larger the number of traders that use a trading system (network), the greater the benefits (i.e., liquidity) that system can provide to traders.

Second, certain elements of market structure (e.g., electronic trading networks, clearing and settlement systems, and information systems) may be overly costly for market participants to provide. Providing these elements may be viewed as a public good, benefiting taxpayers (through lower debt-service costs) and the financial sector as a whole (promoting safe and efficient channels for savings and investment).

Third, in the case of developing countries and economies in transition where financial markets are less developed, an active role of the authorities in encouraging efficient market organization and functioning can be a powerful catalyst in the development of government securities markets.

Fourth, as users of government securities markets, the authorities' objectives and preferences require consideration in the design of the market structure.[3]

This chapter discusses the factors to consider in fostering the development of efficient market structures, and provides detailed information on the organization of government securities markets. It is structured as follows: Section 1 presents the arguments for why market structure matters for the efficient functioning of markets, highlighting the main propositions of the market microstructure literature. Section 2 briefly presents the types of market structure and discusses the salient features and advantages and drawbacks of various market structures. Section 3 discusses the suitability and selection of various market structures with respect to the institutional makeup of the national market. Section 4 draws the implications for the strategy to develop government securities markets, discussing the measures and actions that can be taken by the authorities. Section 5 presents the conclusions.

A number of appendices follow. Appendix 1 details the organization of various market structures and the role of intermediaries in price discovery, liquidity, and price stabilization. Appendix 2 compares the major characteristics of primary dealer systems in selected countries. Appendix 3 discusses the organization of transitional and market-supporting arrangements sponsored by the authorities; in particular, a secondary market window, discount house, and brokerage system. Finally, Appendix 4 reviews suitability criteria and market structure.

1. Market Structure and Efficient Markets: The Main Propositions of the Market Microstructure Literature

Classical price models generally characterize markets by a Walrasian auction process in which the demand and supply of the universe of buyers

---

[3]Unlike in equity markets, where the issuer is restricted by a choice of exchange on which to list its securities, the government exercises considerable discretion as to the organization of the government securities market under its monopoly position as issuer.

and sellers is revealed to the auctioneer, who sets equilibrium prices. Many of the assumptions underlying asset-pricing models—such as the Capital Asset-Pricing Model (CAPM)—include zero trading costs, continuous participation in the market by all traders, and full information available to all traders having homogeneous and rational expectations. Taken together, these assumptions imply that the organization of the market is irrelevant for the determination of asset prices. The microstructure literature relaxes these assumptions and examines the implications for both asset pricing and the structure of the market.

A central proposition of the microstructure literature is that trading costs have an important influence on market efficiency; while this is no news to investors, most asset-pricing models assume transaction costs are unimportant. When trading costs are high, investors will trade less because trading costs will reduce portfolio returns. In turn, lower trading volume may reduce the efficiency of price discovery of the market. Importantly, trading costs—both explicit (the bid-ask spread, order-handling charges, commissions, taxes, etc.) and implicit (such as adverse price movements as a result of thin markets)—distort market prices from their equilibrium value. Trading costs, and in particular the bid-ask spread, are, among other things, a function of the market structure.

A second proposition of the microstructure literature is that traders are fragmented both spatially and temporally: it is impossible to represent the universe of traders in a single market, on a continuous basis. In such real world circumstances, orders arriving in the market will be sporadic and uneven and thus not fully representative of underlying supply and demand conditions. Addressing fragmentation of traders and order flow and its consequences is, therefore, an important issue in market design. For example, Demsetz (1968) was first to elucidate the role of intermediaries (dealers) in providing a bridge between orders arriving in the market at different times by offering immediacy for buyers or sellers at a cost (bid-ask spread). Various market structures tackle this problem in different ways as discussed in section 2 and in greater detail in Appendix 1.

A third key proposition of the microstructure literature is that market structure determines the way in which information becomes incorporated into prices. Information is costly to acquire—it does not pay every investor to be informed on all aspects important to a security's valuation. Hence, there exist two kinds of traders in the market—informed or informationally motivated traders and uninformed or liquidity traders (Bagehot (1971)). The interaction of these two types of traders is influenced by the market structure and affects price determination and the bid-ask spread. For example, the bid-ask spread might reflect compensation for possible losses due to trading with more informed traders (Glosten and Milgrom (1985)). This issue is discussed in the context of designing electronic dealer markets (see "Type of Trader" in section 3).

A fourth proposition of the market microstructure literature is that a security's price is "discovered" in the secondary market through the interaction of supply and demand, just as with other economic goods.[4] Otherwise, traders could rely on an accepted pricing model giving the fundamental value at which securities could be exchanged in the market.[5] Thus, price discovery is a major function of a market. Appendix 1 discusses in detail the trading mechanism for price discovery of various market structures.

A fifth proposition of the microstructure literature is that deviations of market prices from their underlying equilibrium values may be caused by such factors as the size of the trader, the thinness of the market, the timing of arrival of orders, and so on. In turn, their effects on price volatility are influenced by the market structure, including trading rules, disclosure of information, clearing frequency of the market, and the existence of intermediaries. Appropriate selection of market structure is, therefore, important for market efficiency, as discussed in detail in section 4.

In summary, the microstructure literature relaxes many of the assumptions of classical price models and examines the elements of the security trading process. This concerns "the arrival and dissemination of information; the generation and arrival of orders; and the market architecture which determines how orders are transformed into trades. The analysis also explicitly takes into account the behavior of specific types of market participants: nonprofessional investors, institutional investors, speculators, dealers, and specialists" (Cohen, Schwartz, Whitcomb (1986)). The central proposition of the market microstructure literature is that "the pricing function of the capital markets, which is of critical importance to the allocation of investment, cannot be separated from the institutional structure of the market itself" (Blume and Seigel (1992)). For a survey of market microstructure theory, see O'Hara (1995).

2. Features of Different Market Structures

This section provides a taxonomy of market structure and discusses the salient features of various market structures. These features are important in determining the suitability of different market structures for the national securities market discussed in section 3.

---

[4]In the case of government securities and in countries with undeveloped secondary markets, price discovery may occur in the primary market (for example, by primary auctions of securities).

[5]Traders may also have heterogeneous expectations (different valuation models).

Types of Market Structure

There is a wide range of possible structures for government securities markets. The taxonomy used in this chapter to classify different market structures is presented in Chart 1. The detailed organization and functioning of each of these structures are found in Appendix 1.

Features of Market Structures

This section discusses the salient features of different market structures at a broad level, examining in particular: (1) periodic versus continuous markets, (2) dealer markets versus auction-agency markets, and (3) electronic versus floor-based markets.

The market microstructure literature has examined the treatment of order flow by different market structures. Following Demsetz (1968), D_i and S_i in Chart 2 represent the (aggregate) demand and supply of buyers' and sellers' *trade flows per unit of time* for security X_i. Because of the intertemporal fragmentation of order flow (orders may not arrive to the market at the same time), at a point in time, a buyer may exist but no seller (or vice versa). Thus, trades at the equilibrium price E_i are generally not possible.

In *periodic markets*, as the name suggests, trading occurs at periodic (or discrete) intervals. Between trading intervals, buying and selling interest is allowed to build, increasing the number of traders present during each trading session (intertemporal consolidation of order flow), thereby improving liquidity and adding to market depth. The execution of trades (multilateral) at a uniform price (represented by E_i in Chart 2 in the special case where the underlying demand and supply curves are stable over time) reduces transaction costs (i.e., the bid-ask spread associated with continuous markets, discussed below, is eliminated), which is another important benefit of periodic markets (see Economides (1993a, 1993b)). By centralizing trading, periodic markets provide economies of scale in order handling. The single (uniform) price outcome gives the same execution to all traders (fair treatment) and simplifies the clearing and settling of transactions, reducing costs and the possibility of errors.

In *continuous markets*, as the name suggests, trading goes on without interruptions. Continuous trade execution permits more flexible trading strategies than periodic markets. The continuous price discovery process provides contemporaneous information on prices, transactions, and market conditions. There are two basic types of continuous markets—dealer markets and auction-agency markets.

In *dealer markets*, the random arrival of orders to the market is bridged by intermediaries—dealers—that maintain continuous market condi-

Chart 1. Market Structure Classification

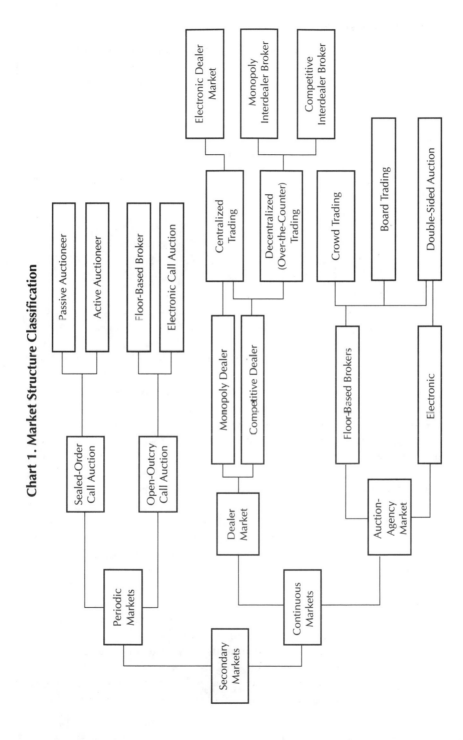

Chart 2. The Supply of Immediacy

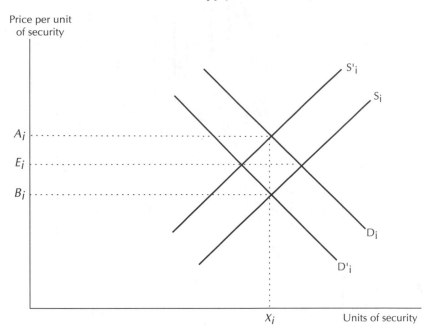

Price per unit
of security

A_i

E_i

B_i

S'_i

S_i

D_i

D'_i

X_i

Units of security

tions. Dealers provide two-way (bid and offer) quotations, supplying a high degree of immediacy to traders that may either buy or sell against those quotations.[6] Dealer markets are often described as "quote-driven" markets, underscoring the dealer's function in maintaining continuous markets. Covering the cost of providing "immediacy," an intermediary is willing to buy and sell against public orders at prices represented by the demand and supply curve D'_i and S'_i in Chart 2, which gives rise to the bid-ask spread (profits to dealers and transactions costs to traders) equal to the difference between A_i and B_i.

Auction-agency markets facilitate the interaction of buying and selling interest of public traders through a centralized auction and agency process (see Appendix 1). Reflecting this characteristic, they are often referred to as "order-matching" or "order-driven" markets. Cohen, Schwartz, and Whitcomb (1986) argue that Demsetz's analysis, discussed above, can be extended to auction-agency markets where public traders can compete as "suppliers of liquidity" by submitting limit orders, while those "demanders of liquidity" can execute immediately by

---

[6]In a pure dealer system, one public order does not have an opportunity to be exposed to another public order, which is the essence of auction-agency markets.

Chart 3. Order Imbalance and Price Volatility

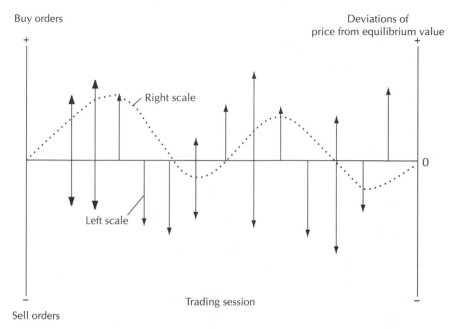

submitting market orders.[7] In this case, the demand and supply curves D'_i and S'_i in Chart 2 represent the limit order book (the consolidation of all limit orders) in an auction market. Importantly, auction-agency markets offer traders opportunities for price improvement, thereby lowering transaction costs—that is, the possibility of executing trades at a price somewhere in between A_i and B_i in Chart 2, inside the representative dealer's bid-ask spread.[8]

On the other hand, auction-agency markets rely on natural order flow to maintain continuous market trading: liquidity and market depth depend on the random arrival of orders from traders and speculators. If order flow is uneven, the market may become one-sided or imbalanced—illustrated in Chart 3 by arrows representing the size of buy and sell orders and their arrival during a trading session—and spurious price volatility (deviations of the market price from the underlying equilibrium value) may result—represented in Chart 3 by the dashed line. It follows that individual orders will be subject to execution risk as the size of that order in-

---

[7]A "limit order" is an order to buy or sell contingent on price. A "market order" is an order to execute a trade of a certain size at the best prices available in the market.

[8]The New York Stock Exchange (NYSE) publicizes "price improvement" as a feature of their market.

creases relative to the depth of the market. Therefore, the average price at which a large order is executed depends on the depth or elasticity of the order book at the time of trade execution.[9] In contrast, dealers insure traders against execution risk by setting quotes in advance.[10] Thus, Pagano and Röell (1991) distinguish between auction-agency and dealer markets by the absence of execution risk in the latter.

Electronic technology (computers, telecommunications, etc.) is rapidly changing all market structures. In general, it has improved the efficiency of markets by (1) replacing the mechanical aspects of trading functions—order routing, order ticket writing and processing, and so forth—thereby increasing the operational efficiency of markets; (2) providing instantaneous information dissemination (real-time information) on market prices and transactions, thereby improving the transparency of markets and increasing competition; and (3) creating new market structures offering automated trade execution, thereby replacing some traditional functions of intermediaries.

So-called *electronic market structures* are those in which trade execution is automated (see Domowitz (1992)). *Electronic call and auction-agency market structures* potentially enhance market deepening and liquidity. In floor-based auction-agency or call auction markets, very short-run trading in response to order flow (interactive price discovery) is generally confined to the traders on the floor of the exchange (typically called the "crowd"). By removing the spatial limitations of physical trading floor arrangements, electronic trading expands the potential size of the crowd, promoting deeper and more liquid markets with more efficient price discovery. Taking full advantage of this possibility, however, requires a sophisticated investor base that participates directly in the trading process. Some argue (e.g., Massimb and Phelps (1994)) that the access to order flow information by public traders and their ability to trade anonymously may discourage the active participation of intermediaries (the crowd) and therefore reduce overall liquidity in the market. Nevertheless, there is a distinct trend away from floor-based call auction and auction-agency markets and toward electronic markets for these market structures.

In *electronic dealer markets*, dealer quotations are centralized onto a screen-based network. Market orders are entered into the network and executed automatically against those quotations. Compared with decentralized over-the-counter (OTC) market structures, they offer several ad-

---

[9]Execution risk might be measured as the difference between the best limit price before the trade is executed and the actual average price at which the market order is filled.

[10]This does not mean that in a dealer market there is no price volatility, only that the execution price is known in advance. In general, dealers will provide this service efficiently if they are less risk-averse than traders or enjoy a comparative advantage in hedging risk.

vantages: (1) the transparency of price and transaction information is greater; (2) they provide price and time priorities to public traders—trades are executed on a first-in basis, against the best dealer price; (3) they eliminate the need for interdealer brokers (discussed in Appendix 1) whose "information" and "intermediary" functions are replaced by the centralized quotation system; and (4) they facilitate real-time auditing of transactions for market surveillance.

However, an electronic dealer market also changes the nature of traditional OTC dealer markets in a number of subtle ways. Centralized trading with transparent trade reporting reduces opportunities for dealers to compete for internalized (dealer-client) order flow and profit from that information (by transacting with other, less well-informed dealers). This may lower incentives for dealers to participate in the market, thereby reducing the supply of dealer services. In addition, dealers are unable to differentiate between uninformed and informed traders because trading is anonymous (impersonal). As a result, dealer quotations may be for smaller sizes and bid-ask spreads may be wider in an electronic market, so as to guard against being adversely selected by informed traders.

In summary, each market structure contributes to price discovery and liquidity in different ways (explored in detail in Appendix 1). Examining the features and advantages and drawbacks of each market structure does not lead to definitive conclusions about the general superiority of one market structure over another. Supporting this view is the variety of market structures in different countries, as highlighted in Table 1. It follows that the efficient market structure is a function of the institutional characteristics of the national market. This approach to determining the suitability of market structures is discussed in detail in the following section.

3. Suitability and Selection of Market Structure

This section identifies the institutional characteristics that bear an influence on the suitability of various market structures for the national market and discusses the selection of market structure based on those influences giving stylized country examples.

The following are the institutional characteristics identified as being important for selecting a suitable market structure:

- stage of market development;
- type of security;
- type of traders;
- degree of capitalization and competition;
- level and location of trading expertise; and
- objective function of the authorities.

Table 1. Market Structures in Selected Countries

Type of Market	Description and Country
1. Periodic Markets	**Sealed-order call auction** Kazakhstan (pre-1995, treasury bills)
	Open-outcry call auction Norway (bonds at open) Israel (treasury bills)
	Electronic call auction Italy (retail bonds) Israel (treasury bills and bonds)
2. Auction-Agency Markets	**Double-sided auction-agency** Ireland (bonds) Greece (bonds) Malta (bonds)
	Board trading Many developing countries
	Crowd trading United States (futures and options) United Kingdom (futures and options) United Kingdom (pre-1986, government bonds)
	Electronic order-matching Denmark Spain (retail) India (wholesale debt market)
3. Dealer Markets	**Single (monopoly) dealer** India (pre-1995, money market)
	Over-the-counter (OTC) Many developing countries' treasury bill markets
	OTC with interdealer brokers
	Competing **Monopoly** United Kingdom France United States Poland Spain Canada
	Electronic dealer Italy (bonds)

Stage of Market Development

Optimal Clearing Frequency

The optimal clearing frequency is an important consideration in market design. By lowering the clearing frequency, order flow arriving over

Chart 4. Optimal Clearing Frequency

Risk

Total risk

Risk of
spurious
price
volatility

*

Market risk

*
Optimal

Clearing frequency

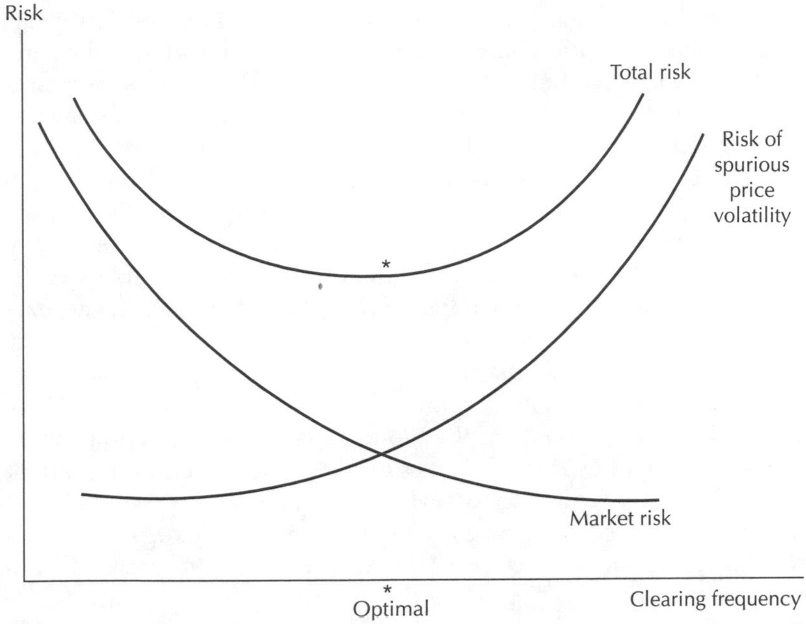

time to the market is consolidated, increasing the number of traders and deepening the volume and value of orders for each trading session.[11] This reduces the risk of spurious price volatility. However, lowering the clearing frequency lengthens the time interval between trading sessions, which increases the risk of equilibrium price changes occurring between trading sessions (i.e., market risk). Thus, the optimal clearing frequency of a market is that which minimizes total liquidity risk from these two sources, as illustrated in Chart 4.[12]

The optimal clearing frequency of markets will depend on the stage of development. A transition from low to high clearing frequency and from periodic to continuous market structures may be experienced by economies liberalizing their financial sector. Nascent financial markets are mostly thin and illiquid owing to the few participants. Execution risk is therefore high and periodic markets with low clearing frequency may be efficient. As markets develop with more participants and higher trading

---

[11]The analysis in this subsection follows Garbade and Silber (1979).

[12]Total liquidity risk equals the sum of (1) the variance of transient random differences between transaction prices and contemporaneous equilibrium values (spurious price volatility); and (2) the variance of equilibrium price changes between clearing intervals (market risk).

volumes, execution risk diminishes. At the same time, more liberalized interest rates, more open capital accounts, and greater integration of foreign exchange and money markets increase the number of factors that influence the equilibrium price. The market risk associated with periodic markets of low clearing frequency therefore rises. These factors suggest a transition in market structure to higher clearing frequencies, and from periodic to continuous markets at later stages of development.

Markets in many economies in transition, for example, the Baltics, Russia, and the other countries of the former Soviet Union, are in the early stages of development. Of those that are developing their secondary market, markets with low clearing frequency and periodic markets are in evidence at the outset, progressing to higher clearing frequencies as markets develop. For example, although the Moscow Interbank Currency Exchange (MICEX) in Russia has a continuous trading mechanism for treasury bills, it began trading on only two days of the week and for limited periods of time and could, therefore, be considered a periodic market. In the spring of 1995, trading sessions were increased to four days of the week.[13] Another example is Kazakhstan where, in 1994, the central bank initiated the secondary market for treasury bills by organizing several ad hoc call (periodic) auctions. Trading on a more frequent basis is beginning in the OTC market, while the exchanges are organizing themselves to compete as trading volumes increase.

Evidence of transition from periodic markets to continuous markets is provided by some of the seven major industrial countries. For many of them, the 1980s was a period of financial market liberalization, expanding debt stocks (Table 2), and growing participation of foreign investors (Table 3) in the domestic market. These factors contributed to more rapidly changing market conditions and a greater volume of trading, for instance, as shown by data for the French, the U.K., and the U.S. markets highlighted in Table 4. In response, trading offered in some European exchanges shifted from periodic to continuous markets. For example, government bonds ceased to be traded on a call auction market on the Paris Bourse after 1987, while the Frankfurt Stock Exchange introduced continuous trading in government bonds after 1988, although it still holds price-fixing sessions integrated with continuous markets.

Form of Market Organization

The stage of development may also influence the form of market organization. At an early stage, the need for sophisticated trading systems may be low (especially in small markets); the market may then evolve toward

---

[13]There is no secondary market trading on Wednesdays when primary auctions take place.

Table 2. Seven Major Industrial Countries: Government Debt Outstanding
(In billions of U.S. dollars)

	1980	Percent of GDP	1986	Percent of GDP	1990	Percent of GDP
United States	738	(27.2)	1,813	(42.5)	2,548	(46.1)
Japan	450	(37.5)	1,267	(54.1)	1,587	(50.5)
United Kingdom	254	(48.9)	298	(48.3)	345	(36.1)
Germany	120	(16.0)	217	(21.9)	401	(24.7)
France	93	(14.9)	185	(23.6)	348	(27.5)
Canada	73	(25.2)	177	(43.6)	269	(46.5)
Italy	229	(54.9)	566	(85.4)	1,147	(98.8)
Total	1,957		4,523		6,645	

Source: Goldstein and others (1994).

more sophisticated structures and systems. For instance, periodic markets might evolve from the simplest form of a sealed-order call auction to auctions with interactive price discovery. Floor-based or telephone-based markets might evolve to electronic market structures.

Often, nascent treasury bill markets begin as OTC markets (the simplest competing dealer market form). Initially, treasury bills tend to be held by a narrow group of institutions, mainly banks. That creates natural counterparts for trading, which reduces search costs and the need for elaborate and sophisticated trading systems. A relatively low level of transparency

Table 3. Seven Major Industrial Countries: Transaction Volume of Foreigners in Domestic Bond Markets
(Aggregate purchases and sales in billions of U.S. dollars)

	1980	1990	Compound Annual Growth Rate (percent)
European investors' transactions in U.S. bond market	60.7	1,578.2	38.5
Japanese investors' transactions in U.S. bond market	6.8	1,476.0	71.2
U.S. investors' transactions in European bond market	18.7	375.3	35.0
U.S. investors' transactions in Japanese bond market	4.0	80.2	35.0

Source: Abken (1991).

Table 4. Secondary Market Trading Volume
(Average daily volume in billions of U.S. dollars)

	1980	1986	1990
U.S. treasury securities	13.78	68.82	76.72
U.K. gilt-edged securities	1.39	2.46	6.75
French short- and medium-term securities	—	0.24	2.88

Source: Goldstein and others (1994).

may actually encourage dealers to seek arbitrage opportunities. Later, as the market develops, specialized intermediaries such as interdealer brokers are needed to improve transparency and trade execution (as highlighted in Appendix 1) and broaden participation in the market; alternatively, an electronic dealer market may be suitable (as was developed in Italy).

Type of Security

The characteristics of the type of government security—treasury bills, bonds, and futures—may influence the choice of market structure. Two of the most important characteristics are volatility and fragmentation.

Volatility

In accordance with the analysis under "Optimal Clearing Frequency" above, the higher the security's variance of equilibrium price change, the higher the optimal clearing frequency of the market in which it is traded. As a result of random fluctuations in the monetary base, external influences transmitted to money markets through foreign exchange channels, and active monetary policy operations, short-dated government securities (treasury bills) tend to be subject to greater yield volatility than longer-dated government securities (bonds). The optimal clearing frequency of markets for treasury bills may, therefore, be higher than for bonds.

Fragmentation

The degree of fragmentation may also influence the suitability of market structure for the various types of government security.[14] A unique feature of "cash" government securities in comparison with futures or equities is the fragmentation of outstandings into different issues, each with a

---

[14]The microstructure literature generally focuses on spatial and intertemporal fragmentation of traders, reflecting its almost exclusive concentration on equity markets.

unique maturity date. In particular, treasury bills tend to be highly frag-mented because they are normally issued with high frequency (weekly auctions) and across the maturity spectrum (for example, with original maturities of 3, 6, and 12 months).

In general, auction-agency markets, which rely on the consolidation of order flow to function efficiently, are less well suited than dealer markets to mitigate the negative effects on liquidity of security fragmentation. In contrast, dealers, as part of their market-making business, accommodate switches by public traders into and out of maturities of the same security, maintaining a so-called book of long and short positions of outstanding maturities.

Examining type-of-security criteria only, treasury bills, as compared with bonds, would tend to trade in markets with higher clearing frequen-cies (because of their higher degree of variance) and in dealer markets as opposed to auction-agency markets (because of their higher degree of se-curity fragmentation). These factors, among others, are at play in some European countries, such as Denmark and Germany, where bonds are successfully traded on exchanges (auction-agency markets), while treasury bills tend to trade in over-the-counter dealer markets. One reason that auction-agency markets are more common for government futures and options markets than for the cash market is the absence of security frag-mentation, which allows liquidity to be more easily concentrated.

Type of Trader

Traders can be classified into different types. The influence of these types on market structure is discussed below.

Patient Versus Impatient Traders

Patient traders—those willing to wait for the arrival of a counterparty—tend to prefer periodic markets over continuous markets, because periodic markets have lower transaction costs. In government securities markets, small retail or household investors, whose trading is motivated by rela-tively longer-term employment of funds or raising liquidity, are represen-tative of patient traders.

Impatient traders, on the other hand, tend to prefer continuous mar-kets: they willingly pay a higher intermediation (bid-ask) spread in return for immediate trade execution (see Harris (1993)). In government securi-ties markets, institutional traders are representative of impatient traders; they have relatively shorter investment horizons and trading strategies that are time-sensitive and information-sensitive—for example, dynamic hedging, market arbitrage, or spread trading strategies.

Block-Size Versus Small Traders

Block-size traders tend to prefer dealer markets, which provide insurance against execution risk. Small traders have less need for insurance and therefore tend to prefer auction-agency markets with their lower transaction costs.

Type-of-trader considerations may be factors in market structure selection. For instance, in Italy, where the retail (household) and wholesale (institutional) markets are formally segmented by the size of the trade, the former is supported by a periodic electronic call auction market (Rome Stock Exchange) while the latter is supported by a continuous electronic dealer market (Mercato Telematico Secondario).[15] In Germany, retail traders tend to participate in the fixing session (call market) for government securities, while wholesale traders tend to deal in the continuous auction-agency or OTC market.

Uninformed Versus Informed Traders

Uninformed or liquidity traders (those who transact to either raise or employ cash) prefer to disclose their identity, advertising that their orders carry no information about a security's valuation. In turn, market intermediaries supply liquidity to them more willingly and at fine spreads. Liquidity traders therefore tend to build direct relationships with dealers or to participate in auction markets on a limit-order basis to expose their orders to the market.

Informed traders (those who transact on the basis of superior information or understanding of a security's valuation in order to earn profits) may be disadvantaged if their identities are disclosed, resulting in poorer execution as prices adjust in response. Thus, they prefer market structures that allow them to remain anonymous.[16] In OTC dealer markets, informed traders attempt to keep their identities secret by working through agency brokers (in the case of public traders) or through interdealer brokers (in the case of dealers): nonetheless, their identities may be difficult to disguise. In contrast, electronic markets offer a high degree of anonymity to informed traders.

Efficient market selection and design may need to take into consideration the existence of informed and uninformed traders. For example, electronic call auction markets balance considerations of trader-type by offer-

---

[15]The minimum size of a wholesale transaction is Lit 5 billion.

[16]Large traders are sometimes taken for informed traders. This is one reason for the growth of so-called crossing networks in equity markets, which permit large institutions to transact blocks of stock with each other at prices established in the primary (auction) markets without exposing the order to that market. Informed traders sometimes attempt to masquerade as liquidity traders by, for example, breaking orders into small pieces.

ing a high degree of anonymity to all types of traders, with opportunities for order revision and disclosure of trial market-clearing prices, and same-price execution of all trades. Special consideration may need to be given to the choice for and design of electronic dealer markets when markets are dominated by informed traders. That structure, by preventing dealers from differentiating between informed and uninformed traders, may result in wider bid-offer spreads for a smaller transaction size compared with a decentralized dealer market. In part to address this finding, recent reforms (1994) to the Italian electronic dealer market include establishing a category of a small number of better capitalized market-makers (specialists) with greater obligations to maintain quotations on the screen-based market, for larger transaction size—for example, specialists must quote for a minimum size of Lit 25 billion compared with Lit 5 billion for primary dealers. The better-capitalized dealers should be less risk-averse in managing block-size trades from informed traders (see Stoll (1978b)), while their smaller number should permit specialists to more easily recoup losses from liquidity traders, also dealing in block size (see Glosten and Milgrom (1985)). Finally, these specialists are compensated by commensurate privileges in line with their market-making obligations (e.g., specialists have a line of credit with the Bank of Italy of Lit 100 billion, twice that of primary dealers).[17]

Degree of Capitalization and Competition

Issues of capitalization and competition may influence the appropriate selection and design of market structure. Specifically, whether a competing-dealer market structure is suitable will depend on preconditions of capitalization and the scope for competition in the market. When conditions of adequate capitalization and competition are not met, auction-agency market structures are more suitable.

Competing-dealer market structures require a network of institutions with strong capital positions to support market-making and the positioning of securities (market risk); to absorb counterparty risk (arising from failed or defaulted trades); and to create conditions for efficient interdealer trading (quote-driven trading and trading on an anonymous basis require well-capitalized counterparties). Adequate numbers of such well-capitalized dealers are needed to create competitive conditions leading to narrow bid-offer spreads, lowering the cost of providing immediacy to the public.

Auction-agency markets, on the other hand, inherently reduce the need for dealer capital—as orders cross between public traders directly—and

---

[17]See Appendix 2 for an overview of the Italian electronic dealer market.

for adequate numbers of dealers—these markets rely on competition among orders rather than competition among dealers. With respect to counterparty risk, exchange members or a clearinghouse provide trade guarantees, absorbing or pooling this risk.

There is some evidence suggesting that small countries (e.g., Cyprus, Malta, and Slovenia) that lack sufficient numbers of well-capitalized institutions to support competing-dealer markets tend to rely on auction-agency markets. In some cases, when there is insufficient volume of trade to support a competing-dealer market, countries have established discount houses to act as market-makers (discussed in section 4 under "Establishing Transitional and Supporting Arrangements").

When competition is low, opportunities for collusion among market participants increase, affecting the appropriate design of market structure. For example, such a situation may argue for sealed-order rather than open-outcry auctions or electronic markets that offer a greater degree of anonymity to traders. Those designs make enforcing collusive arrangements among participants more difficult. It may also argue for the authorities to participate directly in secondary market trading—for example, as an active auctioneer—to safeguard against price distortions caused by collusion.

Level and Location of Trading Expertise

Market structures with interactive price discovery and speculative stabilization of prices require highly developed trading expertise.[18] Insofar as trading expertise is not well developed, floor-based market structures may be more suitable than electronic market structures. Face-to-face (or telephone) trading can contribute to developing trading expertise and encourage dynamic trading as compared with electronic trading, which is impersonal. As expertise develops, electronic trading may be more readily adopted. This was a factor in the transition from floor-based to electronic market structures in Slovenia.

The location of trading expertise is an important determinant of efficient market structure. For example, in Pakistan, the trading expertise of the several stock exchange brokers—acting as interdealer brokers in the government securities market—played an important role in the development of an efficient dealer market. When trading expertise resides with sophisticated financial institutions (such as in Israel), then market structures that demand professional input into the trading process (such as an electronic call auction market) are possible.

---

[18]Note that the term "trading expertise" is distinguished from "portfolio management expertise." The latter reflects longer-term strategies based on asset mix, while the former reflects very short-term strategies based on market conditions.

Objective Function of the Authorities

As *users* of the government securities markets, the authorities—debt managers, monetary authorities, and regulators—have their own special needs, preferences, and objectives that influence the suitability of market structure.

Debt Managers—Primary Issuance

Debt managers that tend not to adjust the size (or timing) of their funding program in response to market conditions may be described as impatient traders with a high demand for immediacy. Those with large financing requirements also face execution risk (like block-size traders).

As market conditions vary, the market's absorptive capacity at a particular time may be tested—that is, by a shortfall in auction demand—placing upward pressure on interest rates and adding to debt-service costs. To insure against this possibility, many debt managers have built a commitment among a group of dealers—typically called a primary dealer group—to provide varying levels of underwriting support to primary (periodic) auctions of government securities (detailed in Appendix 2 for several countries). This commitment of capital resources by primary dealers has contributed to the debt manager's ability to auction large amounts of government securities at periodic auctions (e.g., primary dealers take down approximately 70 percent of U.S. treasury auctions),[19] with dealers providing pre-auction and postauction distribution of debt (intertemporal distribution of debt).

In contrast, debt managers that rely to a lesser extent on dealers and to a greater extent on auction-agency markets (such as in Ireland and Denmark) tend to manage primary issuance into the secondary market using *continuous* selling techniques. This technique allows the authorities to time and tailor issuance according to market demand conditions so as to minimize execution risk. These debt managers may be described as patient traders with a lower demand for immediacy. They believe that lower average funding costs result from minimizing market disruption and execution risk, from taking advantage of market conditions, and from avoiding costly primary dealer arrangements (see Chapter 15).

Debt Managers—Cash Management

Government cash balance management objectives tilt the choice of market architecture in favor of dealer markets and away from auction-agency markets. Like any corporate treasurer, the debt manager attempts to minimize the average level of treasury cash balances because the return on those balances is usually less than the cost of debt. The volatility of government net disbursements means that debt issuance must be actively

---

[19]See United States, Department of the Treasury and others (1992).

managed to maintain a broadly constant level of cash balances. This argues for greater use of a well-capitalized dealer network to support the active management of primary issuance. Even though dealer "transactions costs" result, savings from a lower average level of cash balances compensate.

Monetary Authority

As a *user* of the government market—central bank monetary operations are carried out using instruments closely linked with the market for government securities—the central bank is not indifferent as to its structure. Central banks tend to prefer continuous dealer markets for several reasons.

First, central banks prefer continuous markets because those markets provide real-time information about market liquidity and market expectations (the shape of the yield curve). In turn, this information is valuable input for designing the central bank's intervention strategy—for example, most central banks gather extensive information as the market opens and develops during the morning, which serves as an input into the intervention decision. In addition, continuous markets give the option to intervene at any time to react to sudden developments, and they make it easier to integrate the government securities market with the foreign exchange market (which is also continuous), improving the effectiveness of operations in government securities as a monetary instrument.

Second, central banks tend to prefer to conduct open market operations in a dealer market, which provides immediacy of execution and therefore a fast monetary effect.

Third, the central bank, unlike other informed traders, prefers well-advertised intervention to maximize the effect of its intervention. Dealers spread information and adjust market conditions rapidly by taking speculative (principal) positions in response to open market operations. Auction-agency markets, with fewer professional dealers, may be slower to adjust to central bank intervention. As well, central banks tend to build a close relationship with dealers that provide them information and useful insights into market developments.

Regulators

Regulators are primarily interested in promoting market integrity—fair markets that are mostly free of fraud. Markets that disadvantage traders or are susceptible to fraud tend to limit trader participation and may degenerate, causing serious problems for the government's access to market financing. Such was the case in India, where a US$1.4 billion securities scandal in April 1992 caused a virtual breakdown of the market.[20] So too was the in-

---

[20]This scandal involved fraud and unauthorized borrowing and lending through the repo market by some banks (domestic and foreign), financial institutions, and stock exchange members. Among other

tegrity of the U.S. government securities market threatened by the 1991 Salomon scandal (the submitting of fraudulent primary auction bids so as to amass tender winnings in sufficient size to create and profit from a "short squeeze" in the secondary market) and the Drysdale 1982 debacle[21] (involving fraudulent activity in the market for repurchase agreements). As a result, significant regulatory and infrastructure changes were made in both markets.[22]

The regulator's objective of enhancing the integrity of markets is achieved through (1) promotion of transparent markets with ample public disclosure of information on price and security transactions, empowering traders to self-police transactions; (2) the surveillance of market transactions; and (3) prudential regulation and supervision of market intermediaries.

Inherently, different market structures provide various degrees of transparency and difficulty in monitoring market activity. In general, centralized market structures offer a high degree of transparency, while electronic markets allow easy market surveillance, offering the capability of establishing real-time monitoring and electronic audit trails of all transactions. In contrast, the simple OTC market (without interdealer brokers) offers relatively poor transparency, while making it extremely difficult to establish audit trails.[23]

Thus, regulators prefer centralized and electronic market structures, especially in countries where institutions lack a track record or tradition of credibility and integrity, and where the regulator has limited ability to undertake prudential supervision. Many economies in transition and devel-

---

things, poorly developed systems for clearing and settlement made fraud possible by pledging collateral or promising to deliver securities that did not exist. Following an event leading to sizable declines in the value of equities, a number of banks found themselves with counterparties unable to repay, and holding nonexistent government and public sector undertaking bonds or promises to deliver.

[21]The firm Drysdale Government Securities—a newly created subsidiary of Drysdale Securities—took advantage of the lack of accounting for coupon payments in repurchase agreements using bond collateral. They "reversed in" bonds with high coupon rates and gave cash up to the value of the bond, then sold the bonds for the price plus accrued interest (high coupons carrying lots of interest), using the net proceeds for speculative investments. When the coupon date of these bonds arrived, Drysdale Government Securities was supposed to pay the owners of the bonds the coupon amounts, but it did not have sufficient funds. The firm, which lasted only three months, lost an estimated $250 million against $20 million in capital.

[22]For example, in the U.S. market, the passing of the Government Securities Act of 1986 and its extension in 1994 (providing the treasury with rule-making authority and closing gaps in regulation of market participants); improvements were made in market surveillance; changes were made in primary auction rules; and promulgation of sales practices rules are being considered. In India, an electronic book-entry system was introduced; regulations were tightened, and market surveillance enhanced; and measures were introduced to improve transparency.

[23]Following the Salomon scandal, the U.S. Securities and Exchange Commission (SEC) pressed for establishing audit trails for government securities transactions. In addition to difficulties in establishing the time of trade when dealing in a decentralized market, the costs of such reporting were estimated to be very high and would have, therefore, reduced liquidity and increased debt-service costs. The request was turned down by Congress.

oping countries fall into this category, and in response have encouraged the development of electronic market structures (e.g., Russia and China).

Selection of Market Structure

In any national market, the various criteria discussed above may give contradictory indications of the suitable market structure (see Table 5). Thus, the art of designing market architecture is to weigh the importance of each consideration. Those weights may vary depending on the tastes and preferences of the agents responsible for market structure—that is, banks, exchange members, securities commission, central bank, or ministry of finance. Chart 1 can serve as a decision tree, which, with the requisite weighting, could give a basis for selecting the appropriate market structure.

For example, in many European countries, considerations such as those outlined above have led to the development of wholesale continuous dealer markets for "cash" government securities. Increasing stocks of debt, liberalized financial markets, and growing participation of foreign investors (dealing across time zones) made for fertile ground for more continuous trading, and the market structure shifted accordingly. Also, with holdings of government debt concentrated in institutions with a high propensity to trade, the demand for immediacy for block-size trading was satisfied by dealers. Thus, market structure tended to migrate from auction-agency to dealer markets. In a number of countries, those trends were accelerated by the authorities, whose preferences and needs led them to establish special primary dealer arrangements supporting debt management and monetary operations.

Furthermore, a variety of market structures and different approaches to market architecture have emerged as government securities have diversified (cash, derivatives), trader types and tastes have multiplied, and technology has advanced. In some countries, *different market architecture serves different market segments*—for example, the wholesale and retail market. Some exchanges have targeted the retail segment of the "cash" market, providing low-cost intermediation for small-scale trade. For example, in Spain, the Madrid Stock Exchange introduced a CATS (Computer-Assisted Trading) system (electronic order-matching) to provide faster access and transparent trading for retail investors.[24] In Italy, the Rome Stock Exchange introduced an electronic call auction market in 1994, tailored to the more "patient" trading of the retail segment of the government securities market.[25] In some countries, *different market structures compete for*

---

[24]In conjunction with the Stock Exchange Interconexion system: a centralized communications network linking the four stock exchanges in Spain.

[25]This market also provides the basis by which the official prices are "fixed" and retail OTC trades are priced.

Table 5. Considerations in Market Selection

Institutional Characteristics	Market Structure Indication
Stage of market development	
Nascent	Periodic
Developed	Continuous: competing-dealer or auction-agency
Type of security	
Treasury bills	Continuous: dealer
Bonds	Periodic or continuous: dealer or auction-agency
Type of traders	
Patient	Periodic or auction-agency
Impatient	Continuous
Block	Dealer or call market
Small	Periodic or auction-agency
Informed	Electronic
Uninformed	OTC or floor-based
Capitalization and competition	
When insufficient	Auction-agency
Trading expertise	
When insufficient	Floor-based or OTC
Objective function of the authorities	
Debt manager:	
Impatient	Dealer
Patient	Auction-agency or call auction
Monetary authority	Continuous: dealer
Regulator	Electronic: auction-agency or call auction

trading in the same securities. For example, in Denmark, reflecting different traders' tastes, the Copenhagen Stock Exchange offers three trading systems to investors (see Chapter 15): the Match System, providing automated and continuous matching of orders (for large-scale trades); the Accept System, which is a semi-automated "electronic notice board" for posting bids and offers (for smaller-scale trades); and the Electro Broker System, with designated market-makers providing liquidity (for traders demanding immediacy and for trading on an anonymous basis). In turn, these trading systems offered by the exchange compete with the OTC telephone market (about 42 percent of bond trading between members of the exchange takes place via the trading systems, whereas 58 percent is traded by telephone and subsequently reported to the exchange). In Italy, the electronic dealer market competes with the OTC market for wholesale "cash" securities. In addition, *hybrid market structures* have been introduced capturing features of different market structures. For example, the Italian futures market combines features of electronic order-matching with competing market-makers. In Norway, bonds are traded through a continuous screen-based quotation system (dealer market), but the market opens with a call auction (see Bröker (1993)).

Conflicting indications and multiple possibilities for market structure notwithstanding, stylized country examples of suitable market structures are highlighted below.

- Countries in the nascent stage of development with thin markets are good candidates for periodic markets with low clearing frequency, which leads to market deepening and efficient price discovery.
- Small countries that lack sufficient numbers of well-capitalized financial institutions are likely to find call auction or auction-agency market structures more efficient than dealer markets.
- Countries where government securities are held and actively traded by the household sector are good candidates for auction-agency markets or call auction markets that provide low transaction costs and a high level of transparency.
- Countries where holdings of government securities are concentrated in institutions with large-scale portfolios and having a high demand for immediacy are good candidates for dealer markets.
- Countries where debt managers have sizable (and lumpy) government financing requirements and fixed borrowing calendars should foster dealer markets that support the underwriting of primary issuance and the distribution and trading of government debt.
- Countries where the monetary authorities are instituting indirect (market-based) monetary control should foster dealer market structures, because dealers are natural counterparties for the conduct of monetary operations and promote, over time, continuous markets with immediacy of execution to ensure the effective implementation of monetary policy.
- Countries with sophisticated public traders and sufficient trade volume should adopt electronic market structures for auction-agency or call markets, deriving the full benefits of technology for operational efficiency and market liquidity.
- Countries with limited supervisory capabilities and institutions that lack a track record of integrity are strong candidates for electronic market structures that promote transparency and self-regulation.
- Countries with "quote-driven" OTC markets whose authorities prefer centralized trading structures for transparency reasons and surveillance capabilities might encourage the development of electronic dealer markets.

4. Implications for the Development Strategy of Government Securities Markets

This section develops the main thesis of the chapter: authorities should seek to encourage the development of efficient market structures. Because one market structure may be more efficient than another, the authorities' strategy for the development of government securities markets consists of two parts: (1) selecting the appropriate market structure (discussed in the previous section); and (2) fostering the development of that market structure (discussed in this section).

Once selected, the authorities' actions aimed at fostering efficient market structures would include the following:

- establishing a regulatory framework supporting the market structure;
- organizing and possibly providing key elements of that market structure;
- establishing transitional and supporting arrangements aimed at promoting market development and the efficient functioning of markets; and
- adopting debt management strategies that promote the efficient functioning of the market structure.

In carrying out major reforms or development efforts, the authorities— the central bank, debt managers, ministry of finance, and regulators— might either take the general responsibility for matters of market structure (as does the Bank of England) or contribute an important voice on joint committees (as does the Market Committee in Italy; this decision-making body is made up of market participants, the Bank of Italy, and the Italian Finance Ministry).[26] In both cases, the authorities secure a vehicle to carry out a strategy for the development of efficient market structures.

Establishing a Regulatory Framework that Supports a Market Structure

The regulatory framework should support the development of efficient market structures by providing an appropriate balance between considerations of competition and market structure goals; promoting fair and efficient markets by enhancing transparency; building the framework within which the market functions; and enabling the authorities to pursue policies and use instruments to help ensure the efficient functioning of markets. Regulatory reform efforts are sometimes needed to create efficient

---

[26]The underpinning of such a general responsibility may come from one or more of the following sources: a public debt act, regulatory and prudential authority, or the role of issuer.

market structures by removing obstacles to competition. For example, in France, in order to establish a primary dealer system for government securities, the law providing the Paris Bourse with a monopoly on the trading of government securities was abrogated in 1987.

Conversely, regulation may seek to establish a type of market structure to achieve certain regulatory or market efficiency goals by limiting competition between market structures. In Poland, for instance, the securities act states that capital market instruments (which include government bonds) must be traded on a centralized exchange approved and registered with the securities commission to achieve the goal of "concentration of supply and demand for securities" (Poland, Securities Commission, Act on Public Trading (1991)). Over-the-counter trading is not permitted, thereby preventing a fragmentation of order flow from reducing overall market liquidity.

Information is an integral part of a trading system; it is also a product of the trading system. The availability of that information—transparency—is an important aspect of the efficient and fair functioning of markets. Increasingly, authorities are exerting efforts to improve transparency. To illustrate, in the United States, the regulators and lawmakers (through the threat of regulation) encouraged the introduction of a screen-based information system called GOVPX (owned by the primary dealers). This system displays quotation, transaction, and volume information passing through the major interdealer brokers on a real-time basis. It has greatly improved the transparency of the over-the-counter market for government securities, leading to savings for public traders (and reduced margins for intermediaries) and a fuller integration of the interdealer and dealer-client markets.

New market architecture and trading structures may require a new legal framework (separate from that supporting equity markets or over-the-counter markets for government securities). In Italy, the legal framework for the electronic screen-based dealer market and its functioning was established by several ministerial decrees. Another example is India, where ministry of finance directives established a national market system and the National Stock Exchange.

Finally, regulatory changes may be needed to support active debt management policies including, for example, the authority to engage in secondary market intervention. In France, for instance, Section 56 of the 1991 Finance Act was adjusted authorizing the Trésor to repurchase and swap loans in the secondary market.

Organizing and Providing Key Elements of Market Structure

An active role of the authorities in encouraging efficient market organization can be a powerful catalyst in the development of government securities markets in both less-developed and industrial countries. In the former, market participants may lack the resources to foster the emergence of efficient market structures. In such cases, the authorities might play an active role in organizing the market and providing resources to develop elements of the supporting infrastructure.

Even in industrial economies with adequate private sector resources, efficient market structures do not always emerge, especially when a group of market participants (e.g., members of an exchange) have the power to block change. Network externalities may pose a significant barrier to the emergence of a more efficient market structure because the new architecture needs to attract a critical mass of traders before benefits can be realized in switching trading. As these externalities are larger in more developed markets, radical changes in market structures in many industrial countries have typically involved active intervention by the authorities. Ireland is a case in point, where trading of government debt is being shifted from an auction to a dealer market structure by the authorities.

Finally, new electronic and highly integrated market structures, such as the electronic dealer market in Italy, tend to require a great deal of coordination between the authorities and market participants in achieving consensus on market organization, as well as an active role by the authorities in providing some of the supporting infrastructure.

Measures to organize the market may include all or some of the following elements: (1) defining the market structure; (2) defining the type of intermediaries and the role and obligations of intermediaries vis-à-vis the market and public; (3) selecting intermediaries; (4) designing, managing, and providing the trading system; and (5) providing the physical location of the market (if required).

In many countries, the authorities in fostering the development of government securities markets have organized the market around the architecture of *competing dealers*—typically called primary dealer systems—for the following reasons:

- By forming a specialized and recognized group of intermediaries, public confidence in the government securities markets is enhanced. In turn, order flow for securities transactions tends to increase and market-making as a business becomes more profitable and markets more continuous with greater liquidity. The resulting increase in competition with an expanding number of dealers, primary dealers, and other intermediaries tends to narrow secondary market spreads.
- Special facilities (such as lines of credit discussed in the next section) sometimes provided to primary dealers help to support continuous market-making and therefore improve secondary market liquidity and the development of the secondary market. In turn, government

securities enjoy greater liquidity and lower yields compared with nongovernment securities.
- In their capacity as market-makers, primary dealers facilitate the execution of open market operations and thereby improve the ability of the central bank to conduct monetary policy using indirect monetary instruments.
- Primary dealers, as agents of the central bank and treasury, provide valuable information about market conditions and investor preferences. This helps to improve the overall design of market-based debt management and monetary operations, thereby contributing to the smooth functioning of the market and increasing the depth and breadth of the government securities market.
- The formation of a primary dealer group facilitates the transition to market-based debt management operations by providing underwriting support (which is sometimes explicit in the agreement with the primary dealer) for primary auctions.

The Bank of England, for example, played a leading role in establishing a competitive group of market-makers called gilt-edged market-makers (see Bank of England (1985)). These market-makers have a positive obligation to support continuous market trading in gilts; they are selected by the bank and are under the direct supervision and regulation of the Bank of England. Appendix 2 provides an overview of the organization of primary dealer systems in France, Italy, Spain, the United Kingdom, and the United States.

With the goal of improving the transparency and efficiency of the government securities market, which was functioning as an unregulated OTC wholesale market, the Italian Ministry of Finance and the Bank of Italy, in conjunction with market participants, as noted earlier, introduced an electronic dealer market (see Chapter 8). This centralized, automated screen-based trading system for government securities—the Mercato Telematico Secondario—offers a highly integrated system by automating the trading system (typically called the front end) and integrating it with trade comparison or matching (typically called back-office functions), which is then electronically linked with the book-entry clearing and settlement system (see Appendix 2). The Bank of Italy carries out secondary market intervention (electronically) on the system.

In order to initiate the development of a nascent market for treasury bills, the National Bank of Kazakhstan organized a call (periodic) market on its premises, establishing trading rules and procedures for clearing and settlement. Similarly, the National Bank of Romania, in a joint effort with other authorities, is organizing an auction-agency market for government securities and equities. It will be located on the premises of the central bank.

Establishing Transitional and Supporting Arrangements

In the context of encouraging a transition from nascent to well-developed markets, the authorities may want to establish transitional and market-supporting arrangements aimed at promoting market development and the efficient functioning of markets, as well as a smooth transition to an efficient market structure. As markets develop and market structures evolve, some or all of these arrangements will be phased out. One indirect and several direct roles are possible:

- dealer—establishing one or more discount houses;
- market-maker—establishing a secondary market window;
- interdealer broker—establishing a simple brokerage system;
- price stabilizer—becoming an active auctioneer and market-maker of last resort; and
- provider of liquidity support—establishing credit lines.

Discount House

When trading volumes are insufficient to attract or support competing dealers, or sometimes when capitalization and competition are inadequate, the authorities may want to assist in developing a dealer market structure beginning with a single (monopoly) dealer or a limited number of dealers.[27] It is important to stress that the "monopoly" does not involve an exclusive legal right preventing other dealers from competing. Rather, in the context of a nascent market, with insufficient order flow and scarce capital resources, one (or a few) discount houses, whose role it is to provide liquidity to the secondary market through buying and selling of outstanding securities, are formed, sometimes by the pooling of capital of financial institutions (possibly including some capital ownership by the authorities) and generally supported by a line of credit from the central bank permitting them to function effectively as a market-maker and to inventory securities. Once established, the discount house, operating in the government securities market, attracts order flow in sufficient volumes to warrant the capital investment. Later, as the market develops, the discount house forms part of a broader arrangement—such as a primary dealer group—encouraging the emergence of competing dealers.

Country examples include Ghana, India, and Malaysia. In 1987, the Ghanian authorities decided that a specialist market-making institution

---

[27]It is important to note that the "model" discount house discussed here differs from that of the U.K. money market in that the model is designed to operate largely in the government securities market (as opposed to the interbank deposit market) and does not enjoy the privileges that tend to enlarge the role in intermediating interbank liquidity.

would be a useful way to help develop a money market, help break down the segmentation of the financial system, and facilitate the central bank's use of indirect methods of monetary control. The Consolidated Discount House was established, owned by several commercial banks and insurance companies. A second discount house was licensed in 1991 to encourage competition while the operating privileges of discount houses with the central bank were reduced.

In India, the Discount Finance House of India (DFHI) was formed to develop the money market by a pooling of capital from several financial institutions, including capital contributed by the Reserve Bank of India. In 1994, the Government Securities Trading Corporation (GSTC) was similarly established to develop the bond market. As trading volumes increased, the Reserve Bank of India established criteria (1995) for the development of a group of competing primary dealers. In this arrangement, the GSTC and the DFHI are two in a larger group of dealers that are under the same obligations and share equal access to the same facilities as other members of a primary dealer group.

In Malaysia, the authorities licensed a limited number of discount houses without central bank capital but with special privileges in order for them to operate efficiently in the money and government securities market. Later, as the market developed, special privileges were removed and the discount houses became part of a larger group of government securities dealers.

There are risks to the above strategy. Particularly important factors are the extent and nature of competition and the potential conflicts with policy goals of the central bank.

Licensing one or a limited number of discount houses may stifle competition. Thus, the establishment of discount houses should form part of an articulated strategy to develop efficient market structures. Even if there is only one discount house, other financial institutions should be permitted to trade in securities and be allowed to emerge as dealers over time, adding to competition (as in India). As the market develops and the demand for trading services increases, licensing should be expanded while privileges are reduced, encouraging the development of a market of competing dealers (as in Malaysia).

Moral hazards for the central bank may arise when it contributes capital to the discount house and provides arrangements supporting the discount house's operations. The profitable operations of the discount house become a direct responsibility of the central bank, a fact that may distract it from conducting monetary operations to achieve its primary goal of price stability. Thus, the participation of the central bank in the formation and operation of the discount house should be carefully considered.

Secondary Market Window

In nascent markets, the *liquidity risk* to dealers of accommodating customer trades to and from securities inventories is high because two-way markets are not yet fully developed. This lengthens the average time that a dealer holds a suboptimal portfolio of securities, lowering returns and increasing the exposure to changes in market conditions (see Stoll (1978a)).

In these circumstances and to foster the development of nascent competing dealer markets (OTC), market-making support is sometimes provided by the central bank through a so-called secondary market window, through which the central bank buys or sells securities from those dealers that are supporting secondary market trading, under certain conditions. This window tends to reduce liquidity risk, which encourages dealers to supply quotations to the public and maintain continuous market conditions. As markets become more developed and liquidity risk falls, the central bank withdraws from market-making activity, either by closing the secondary market window altogether, or by limiting its purpose to the conduct of open market operations or active debt management policies. This arrangement must be carefully designed so as not to unduly conflict with monetary policy objectives on the one hand (i.e., by carrying out operations that lead to unintended and large changes in base money) or discourage private sector market participants from emerging on the other hand (i.e., by becoming the counterparty to all trades in the market). The design and organization of secondary market windows is discussed in detail in Appendix 3.

Examples of countries that have instituted a secondary market window as a transitional arrangement to promote the development of a secondary market include Jamaica, Iceland, Thailand, Malaysia, and Nepal. A developed market example is provided by the Bank of England, which operates a secondary market window for gilt-edged index-linked instruments to encourage the market for that instrument.

Brokerage System

In the absence of real-time price information, a well-developed counterparty relationship between potential dealers, brokerage expertise, and clearing arrangements, the authorities might institute a brokerage/trading system, patterned after the market structure of monopoly interdealer brokers (Appendix 1).[28] Lending the authority's name and infrastructure to such facilities can promote confidence among major market participants and develop trading expertise. Moreover, these systems enhance the price

---

[28]Again, "monopoly" does not involve an exclusive legal right preventing other intermediaries from competing.

discovery process and provide transparency to developing markets. As the market develops, scope for private sector entrants increases and the need for such a facility may well diminish. Appendix 3 discusses the detailed organization of this possible role of the authorities. Country examples include Turkey, Thailand, and Poland.

In Poland, the National Bank of Poland (NBP) provided a screen-based interdealer brokerage system—called Telegazette—for central bank bills and treasury bills with supporting facilities to clear and settle government securities transactions. Dealers appointed by the NBP could telephone their buying and selling positions to the bank, and bank personnel would display bids and offers to the other dealers with the screen display system. After establishing a functioning market, the NBP has all but closed its facility; currently, there is one private sector interdealer broker functioning in the market.

Active Auctioneer and Market-Maker of Last Resort

As noted earlier, auction-agency markets and to a lesser extent call auction markets can be subject to execution risk and therefore spurious price volatility, particularly in lesser-developed markets. In such cases, the authorities can play a role as price stabilizer, participating directly in the auction-agency market as an active auctioneer or as a "market-maker of last resort." This encourages a broader range of participants in the secondary market and diminishes the liquidity premium on government debt. Care should be taken not to discourage the emergence of "speculative stabilization" by private sector intermediaries. Nor should the government influence price trends. Arrangements therefore have to be carefully designed so as not to conflict with market development or monetary or debt management objectives. As the market develops and deepens, the price stabilization role of the authorities should likewise diminish and ideally be eliminated. The role of the authority as an active auctioneer and price stabilizer is discussed in detail in Appendix 1.

In Germany, the Bundesbank, on behalf of the government, participates in the market on eight regional exchanges, buying and selling from time to time, as appropriate, to reduce price volatility and provide continuity and stability in secondary market trading. It also participates in the fixing session (call auction). In Ireland, the NTMA acts as a market-maker of last resort quoting prices on benchmark bonds listed on the exchange in order to help market confidence and stability (see Chapter 10). Malta is another country where the central bank performs this function.

Credit Lines

To foster a competing dealer market structure in the absence of well-developed funding markets (repo or call money markets), central banks often establish lines of credit with primary dealers. In less-developed markets, this encourages dealers to provide secondary market liquidity and cost-effective execution services. Such lines reduce financing risk, which may arise if, after taking an inventory position during the course of trading, a dealer discovers that funding is unavailable (or available only at exorbitant costs). For these reasons, many countries establish lines of credit to support primary dealers—for example, India, Italy, Canada, and the United Kingdom.[29] As efficient funding markets develop, the central bank can make support indirect through the conduct of open market operations (as in the United States and France) or can allow the size of such lines to diminish in importance (as in Canada) relative to the size of the market.

Adopting Debt Management Strategies for the Efficient Functioning of the Market Structure

Achieving the cost-minimization goal of public debt management generally includes the following broad policies: using market-based methods for the primary issuance of government debt; improving market liquidity and efficiency for government securities; developing markets in related (derivative) instruments that contribute to market liquidity, including the repo, strip, and futures market; developing new instruments that are cost-effective and deepen the market for fixed income securities; and promoting a broad distribution of government debt. To implement these policies, among other things, instrument design, selling techniques, and secondary market intervention arrangements should all be adapted to promote the efficient functioning of the market structure.

Instruments are successfully traded in the secondary market when their design is simple and easily understood, is standardized, and has features that enhance tradability. For this reason, the current trend in debt management is to provide few choices in the types of instruments, thereby enhancing standardization; importantly, they generally do not have redemption or call features so as to derive their liquidity from the existence of a secondary market and facilitate pricing. Illustrating this approach, the French Treasury describes its debt management strategy as one of "simplicity, transparency, and liquidity" (France, Economics Ministry, 1993).

In order to promote secondary market liquidity, the practice of establishing a limited number of benchmark bonds and reopening outstanding

---

[29]In this context, it is notable that the Bank of England has introduced initiatives to develop a repo market to improve secondary market functioning.

issues at consecutive auctions is becoming common in many countries. Especially when instruments are traded in auction-agency markets, the number of outstanding issues traded in the market should be small, minimizing the degree of security fragmentation. For example, in the case of treasury bills, this argues for making available as few original issue maturities (ideally only one of a long maturity) and reopening that issue for as long as possible. This technique would mimic the practice of futures markets of establishing a few standardized "contracts" that can be easily traded in an auction-agency market structure.

The type of *selling techniques* (primary market issuance) should also support the efficient functioning of the market structure. For example, in countries that rely on dealer markets, the authorities generally adopt *periodic* primary auctions of relatively low frequency. This encourages the dealer's role (and business) of maintaining continuous secondary market conditions and underwriting securities in the primary market by reducing competition from the primary market.[30]

In contrast, countries with auction-agency market structures (for example, Ireland and Denmark) often adopt continuous primary auctions, directly selling into the secondary market by joining, in a seamless manner, the double-sided auction (of buyers and sellers) at market prices.[31] In essence, this technique integrates the primary with the secondary market. The continuous sales technique reduces the execution risk and possible market disruption of selling a large block of securities at periodic intervals into an auction-agency market. It also permits the authorities to modulate the supply of securities on a continuous basis to take advantage of favorable market conditions and reduce the risk of selling large amounts into weak market environments.

Secondary market intervention is an important tool of active debt management policy in fostering efficient secondary market trading by improving the technical position of the market. For example, the Bank of England and the French Treasury entertain switches from dealers looking to trade into more liquid, currently traded outstanding issues, reducing problems related to the fragmentation of issues.[32] In addition, the authorities might intervene to purchase maturing stocks of bonds (before the maturity date) and sell new issue bonds, reducing the risk of market disruption of refunding operations.

---

[30]New primary issuance provides the offered side of the market, while maturing securities provides the bid side (at par) of the market.

[31]This technique is sometimes called tap issuance (see Bröker (1993)), but should not be confused with "fixed price" tap sales that are often used for over-the-counter sales of retail debt instruments.

[32]See France, Economics Ministry, 1993, for examples of active debt management policies.

5. Conclusions and Summary

This chapter argues that the authorities—debt manager, central bank, and regulatory authority—should play an active role in fostering the development of efficient market structures for government securities markets. In the case of developing countries and economies in transition, where financial markets are less developed, an active role of the authorities in encouraging efficient market organization can be a powerful catalyst in the development of government securities markets. In turn, these markets help support debt management, monetary policy, and financial market reforms.

Efficient price discovery and liquid and deep government securities markets are common goals shared by the authorities. Achieving these goals depends on the existence of efficient market structures, according to the microstructure literature and supported by empirical evidence. Various market structures exist and a taxonomy has been provided and their features discussed (see also Appendices 1 and 2). Advances in technology have led to continuous improvements in market functioning and to new electronic market structures with automated trading. A trend away from floor-based and toward electronic auction-agency and electronic call auctions is in evidence. Electronic dealer markets have been developed that compete effectively with over-the-counter dealer markets.

Examining the features of those market structures does not lead to definitive conclusions about the general superiority of one market structure over another, but the existence of various market structures across countries suggests that suitability depends on the institutional characteristics of the national market. The institutional characteristics identified as being important for market suitability are: (1) the stage of market development; (2) the type of security; (3) the type of trader; (4) the degree of capitalization and competition; (5) the level and location of trading expertise; and (6) the objectives and needs of the authorities. Implications of these suitability criteria for market structure, discussed in the text, are summarized in Appendix 4.

Applied to any one country or market, these criteria will likely lead to contradictory indications of suitable market structure. Weighing the importance of each consideration is the art of designing market architecture. Those weights will vary according to the tastes and preferences of the agents responsible for market structure—market participants, the central bank, the ministry of finance, or regulatory authorities.

For example, in many European countries, the above considerations have led to the development of wholesale continuous dealer markets for "cash" government securities. Increasing stocks of debt, liberalized financial markets, and growing participation of foreign investors (dealing across time zones) led to a shift from periodic to continuous markets in some countries. Also, with holdings of government debt concentrating in institutions with a high propensity to trade, market structure tended to migrate from auction-agency to dealer markets. In a number of countries, those trends were accelerated by the authorities, whose preferences and needs led them to establish special primary dealer arrangements to support debt management and monetary operations. Furthermore, a variety of market architecture and different approaches to market architecture have emerged with the diversity of government securities (cash and derivatives), different trader types and tastes, and advances in technology. In some countries, different market architecture serves different market segments—for example, the wholesale and retail market. In others, different market structures compete for trading in the same securities. Finally, hybrid market structures have been introduced that attempt to capture features of different market structures.

Notwithstanding the possibilities of conflicting indications and multiple market structures, the authorities' strategy for market development consists of two parts: selecting the efficient market structure(s) (stylized country examples appear above under "Selection of Market Structure"), then fostering its development. Measures aimed at fostering efficient market structures may include: (1) establishing a regulatory framework supporting the market structure; (2) organizing and possibly providing key elements of that market structure; (3) establishing transitional and supporting arrangements aimed at promoting market development and the efficient functioning of markets; and (4) adopting debt management strategies that promote the efficient functioning of the market structure.

The regulatory framework should support the development of efficient market structure by providing an appropriate balance between considerations of competition and market structure goals; promoting fair and efficient markets by enhancing transparency; building the framework within which the market functions; and enabling the authorities to pursue policies and use instruments to help ensure the efficient functioning of markets.

Regulatory reform measures are sometimes needed to create efficient market structures by removing regulatory obstacles to competition; conversely, regulation may seek to establish a type of market structure to achieve certain regulatory or efficiency goals by limiting competition between market structures. The regulatory authorities may need to exert pressure on intermediaries or introduce regulatory measures to assure an adequate degree of transparency for fair and efficient market functioning. New legal frameworks may be required to support new market architecture and trading structures. Finally, regulatory changes may be needed to support active debt management policies including secondary market intervention.

In economies in transition and developing economies, market participants may lack the resources to foster the emergence of efficient market structures—either its organization or the supporting infrastructure. Moreover, new electronic and highly integrated market structures tend to involve a great deal of coordination between the authorities and market participants, as well as an active role by the authorities in providing some of the supporting infrastructure. Measures to *organize the market* may include: (1) defining the market structure; (2) defining the type of intermediaries and the role and obligations of intermediaries vis-à-vis the market and public; (3) selecting intermediaries; (4) designing, managing, and providing the trading system; and (5) providing the physical location of the market (if required).

In the context of fostering efficient market structures, the authorities of countries in the early stages of development might develop dealer markets when (1) the monetary authorities are instituting market-based monetary control, using dealers as natural counterparties for the conduct of monetary operations, thereby promoting, over time, continuous markets with immediacy of execution to ensure effective implementation of monetary policy; and (2) the debt managers are instituting market-based issuing techniques, such as auctions, using dealers for underwriting and distribution support, thereby enhancing the depth of the primary market. In addition, by forming a specialized and recognized group of intermediaries, public confidence in the government securities markets is enhanced. In turn, order flow for securities transactions tends to increase and market-making as a business becomes more profitable and markets more continuous with greater liquidity. Special facilities (such as lines of credit) can help to support continuous market-making and therefore improve secondary market liquidity and the development of the secondary market. The market organization of primary dealer systems in a selected number of countries is provided in Appendix 2.

In the context of encouraging a transition from nascent to well-developed markets, the authorities can establish *transitional and supporting arrangements* aimed at promoting market development and the efficient functioning of markets, as well as a smooth transition in market structure as markets develop. Arrangements would evolve as markets develop with a diminishing role for the authorities. They involve a direct role of the authorities in the market as: (1) dealer—establishing one or more discount houses, possibly as part owner; (2) market-maker—establishing a secondary market window for supporting secondary market liquidity; (3) interdealer broker—establishing a simple infrastructure for the brokering of transactions of market participants and the displaying and reporting of prices; (4) price stabilizer—participating in an auction-agency market as an active auctioneer or as a market-maker of last resort; and (5) overview

Table 6. Transitional and Market-Supporting Arrangements

Market-Supporting Arrangements	Country Example
1. Discount house	Ghana, India, Malaysia
2. Secondary market window	United Kingdom (for index-linked gilts), Nepal, Jamaica, Malaysia, Iceland, Botswana
3. Brokerage operations	Turkey, Poland, Thailand
4. Price stabilization	Germany, Ireland (as market-maker of last resort), Malta
5. Lines of credit to dealers	Canada, United Kingdom, Italy, Pakistan

of indirect supporting arrangements for market-making—establishing lines of credit with market-makers to support efficient market-making by dealers and supporting inventory financing. Table 6 lists these types of arrangements and their use by countries. So as not to conflict with monetary policy objectives or discourage the participation of the private sector in market arrangements and market development, the above arrangements need to be carefully designed; this is discussed in Appendix 3.

Debt management strategies should support the efficient functioning of the market structure. This calls for the appropriate design of instruments, the choice and use of selling techniques, and appropriate secondary market intervention. Making instruments easily understood and easily traded in secondary markets is an objective in designing instruments. Improving liquidity by issuing only a few benchmark instruments and reopening outstanding issues to improve fungibility reduces the effect of security fragmentation on liquidity. In selecting selling techniques—periodic versus continuous auctions—the authorities should consider market structure: the former is appropriate for efficient functioning dealer markets and the latter for auction-agency markets. Finally, secondary market intervention can be designed to improve the technical position of the market and ease refunding risk, improving the functioning of the secondary market.

Appendix 1

Taxonomy and Organization of Market Structure and the Role of Intermediaries

This Appendix provides a taxonomy of market structure (see Chart 1 in the text) and describes how each market organization functions, summarizing the role of intermediaries in contributing to price discovery, market depth, and liquidity. There exists a diverse makeup of market structures that may be adopted for government securities markets. However, the various market structures can be classified as:

I. **Periodic markets**, or

II. **Continuous markets**.

In turn, continuous markets can be classified as:

IIA. **Auction-agency markets**, or

IIB. **Dealer markets**.

Various types of market design fall within the above classes and are discussed in detail below.

I. PERIODIC MARKETS

In periodic markets, trading occurs at periodic (discrete) intervals. At the specified time of the call auction, accumulated orders are executed in a multilateral transaction (batch) at a uniform (single) price that balances demand with supply.

All periodic markets share a number of properties:

- Traders benefit from an intertemporal consolidation of trading interest—the depth of the market is enhanced by increasing the number of traders present at a single trading session, which tends to stabilize the price and enhance liquidity.
- Transaction costs are low as a result of no "intermediation" costs (i.e., no bid-ask spread) and economies of scale in order handling of a centralized market structure.
- The single (uniform) price outcome simplifies clearing and settling of transactions, reducing costs and the possibility of errors.
- There is a high degree of transparency: all market participants receive the same treatment; all orders are executed at the same price, enhancing market integrity.

The various types of periodic markets shown in Chart 1 are discussed below. They differ in three respects—the price discovery mechanism, how price stabilization is achieved, and the role of intermediaries.

A. Sealed-Order Call Auction

1. With Passive Auctioneer

The price discovery mechanism of the sealed-order call auction market mimics that of the Walrasian auctioneer. The auctioneer in this market combines the orders of public traders to find the market-clearing price (see Table 7; the trading mecha-

Table 7. Illustration of a Double-Sided Auction

Buy Quantity 1	Cumulative Buy 2	Price 3	Sell Quantity 4	Cumulative Sell 5	Excess Demand (−) or Supply (+) 6	Total Possible Trade 7
—	0	101.00	10,000	93,000	+ 93,000	0
—	0	100.90	3,000	83,000	+ 83,000	0
—	0	100.80	15,000	80,000	+ 80,000	0
—	0	100.70	1,000	65,000	+ 65,000	0
13,000	13,000	100.60	5,000	64,000	+ 51,000	13,000
15,000	28,000	100.50	15,000	59,000	+ 31,000	28,000
11,000	**39,000**	**100.40**	**20,000**	**44,000**	**+ 5,000**	**39,000**
10,000	49,000	100.30	9,000	24,000	− 25,000	24,000
1,000	50,000	100.20	5,000	15,000	− 35,000	15,000
500	50,500	100.10	10,000	10,000	− 40,500	10,000
10,000	60,500	100.00	—	0	− 60,500	0
20,000	80,500	99.90	—	0	− 80,500	0

Box 1. Sealed-Order Call Auction Trading Mechanism

The trading mechanism works as follows:

(1) a date and time is set for the receipt of orders (e.g., the frequency of periodic auctions could be weekly, biweekly, daily, or bidaily or sporadic);

(2) traders submit, buy, and sell orders (price and quantity pairs);

(3) the auctioneer tabulates the buys and the sells arranged in two separate columns (see Table 7, columns (1) and (4)) in a double-sided auction—descending price in terms of buys and ascending price in terms of sales;

(4) the equilibrium price (100.40, Table 7, column (3), price in bold) is set which maximizes the total value of possible trades (39,000, see Table 7, column (7), or (equivalently) minimizes excess supply or demand (+5000, see Table 7, column (6));

(5) the share of unsatisfied orders at the market-clearing price among participants would be distributed according to some rule, such as a pro rata distribution;

(6) traders are informed of the market-clearing price and any unsatisfied orders; and

(7) the auction is cleared in a multilateral transaction at the uniform market-clearing price for buy (sell) orders that are equal to or above (below) the clearing price— all other orders are left unexecuted.

---

nism is detailed in Box 1). However, as traders have no knowledge (until after the auction) of the prices and intentions of the other participants, the price discovery process is a "black box." When an imbalance in orders occurs, price volatility (from one call session to the next) may result without any change in fundamental aspects of the security's valuation, reducing efficiency. To address this problem, exchanges using this system typically institute a maximum and minimum permissible price change at a single session as a mechanism to stabilize prices. An advantage of the sealed-order call auction is that it is simple to organize. Also, the sealed-order format reduces the risk of collusive arrangements forming among market participants by making it more difficult for ring members to enforce arrangements.

2. With Active Auctioneer

In this call market structure, price stabilization and price discovery are facilitated by an active auctioneer. The active auctioneer is not indifferent as to the price outcome of the auction, participating directly in the auction to influence its outcome (see Box 2). In the context of government securities markets, the active auctioneer could be the central bank, ministry of finance, or a designated specialized intermediary. (In the case in which the auctioneer is a designated intermediary, the auctioneer has full information about the order book. His role therefore cannot always be that of a "profit maximizer" but rather as a "market stabilizer," for example, the specialist on the New York Stock Exchange (NYSE) plays such a role at the market opening.) The objective function of the central bank may primarily reflect monetary policy considerations (which may or may not be compatible with price stabilization). In the case that the ministry of finance or the debt agency is the active auctioneer, the objective function is more likely to be that of price stabilization.

Box 2. Call Auction with Active Auctioneer Trading Mechanism

The trading mechanism involves an additional step to those described in Box 1:
After viewing the initial (undisclosed) price outcome of the call auction (Box 1, step 4), the auctioneer submits an additional order to stabilize prices or to achieve a particular price objective.

This form of market structure has the advantage of reduced risks of unwarranted price volatility, through the discretionary price stabilization of the active auctioneer, and provides a convenient framework for the central bank to conduct open market operations. (In the case that the active auctioneer is a private sector agent, his or her trading must be monitored given that agent's privileged access to information and position as active auctioneer. For this reason specialists on the New York Stock Exchange have a positive obligation for market smoothing and are required to buy on downticks and sell on upticks in prices.)

B. Open-Outcry Call Auction

1. Floor-Based

Price discovery is interactive in this call market structure. Traders (floor-based) are able to react to the submission of orders and the formation of "trial prices" by submitting new orders, before the market price is set: no bids or offers are binding until auction participants agree on the final price configuration (see Box 3). The technical term for this trading mechanism is a "recontracting auction." With respect to the theoretical literature, this outcome approximates a Nash equilibrium where each trader has bid optimally given the reaction of other traders (see Blume and Siegel (1992)). This transforms the call markets discussed above from a "black box" to an "interactive" market of price discovery.

In this market structure, the price stabilization role of the active auctioneer (monopolist) is replaced by floor-based intermediaries (competing). If members of the "crowd"—those traders that are members of the exchange and physically present on the floor—find the price diverging from their expectations, they may submit additional orders in order to profit from spurious price movements, thereby stabilizing prices and adding to market depth.

With interactive price discovery and "speculative stabilization," this market structure is likely to result in prices that are closer to their equilibrium values. In addition, the central bank or the ministry of finance may also participate in the call auction as part of the crowd, to achieve monetary or debt management objectives (as an active auctioneer). (As opposed to the previous call market structure, the actions of the active auctioneer are visible to the crowd, which may react in response.) Even though the price discovery process can lead to efficiency and market depth, these call auctions are administratively more complex to organize.[1] For this reason, they would generally be used for securities where there are suffi-

---

[1]It is for this reason that primary auctions of government securities are almost always sealed-bid. Of note, the U.S. authorities did examine the desirability of introducing "open outcry" or "recontracting" primary auctions following the Salomon scandal, but because of their complexity, the idea was rejected.

Box 3. Open-Outcry Call Auction Trading Mechanism

The trading mechanism works as follows:

(1) the auctioneer begins the auction process with an opening price (e.g., the price of the previous auction);

(2) the floor brokers submit customer and own orders and the resulting net excess demand or supply is revealed to the crowd;

(3) the auctioneer adjusts the price in response to a net excess demand (by raising the price) or supply (by lowering the price);

(4) floor traders are permitted to submit new orders (and in some cases revisions of old orders) in response to the contemporaneous developments in price and order demand; and

(5) the auction stops at the point where demand and supply are equilibrated—when there are no further orders to buy or sell.

Rules for beginning trading and arriving at the market clearing price vary from system to system. For a study on the effects and efficiency of such trading rules, see McCabe, Rassenti, and Smith (1993).

---

cient trading interest and market expertise to support the interactive process. Because of the close time frame within which the auction occurs and the physical limitations of voice/visual trading, direct participants in the auction are limited to the crowd. From one perspective, traders in the crowd act as intermediaries for public traders, providing a service of enhanced price discovery and price stabilization. From another perspective, traders in the crowd have certain advantages over public traders in terms of information on the formation of prices and in their ability to submit orders in response to that information.

2. Electronic Call Auction

In the preceding call auction, participation in the interactive price discovery process is limited to the crowd. By using instantaneous communication and trade execution systems, the electronic call auction market removes the physical barriers of the exchange floor. This permits public traders to participate on an equal footing with the crowd in terms of (1) the access to information on the formation of prices and order flow; and (2) the capability of submitting new orders on the basis of that information. Thus, the "crowd" may be enlarged significantly, potentially creating a deeper and more liquid market and leading to more efficient price discovery. To realize fully the possibilities of electronic call auctions, however, a sophisticated investor base that is interested in participating directly in the trading process is needed.

In 1994, the Tel Aviv Stock Exchange began operation of an electronic call auction market (called the Computerized Call Market) for government bonds. Also in 1994, the Rome Stock Exchange introduced an electronic call auction for the trading of retail bonds.

Box 4. Double-Sided Continuous Auction Trading Mechanism

The trading mechanism works as follows:

(1) the consolidated order book, maintained by an exchange, records buying and selling interest expressed as limit orders;

(2) a trade occurs either when limit orders cross (buy price exceeds or equals the sell price), or when an incoming market order (an order to sell or buy a particular quantity at the "best" price) is crossed against a limit order(s) in the order book; and

(3) the transaction is reported to the market.

II. Continuous Markets

As the name suggests, continuous market structures permit continuous trading. They share the following properties:

- Continuous price discovery with real-time information on prices, transactions, and market conditions;
- Immediate trade execution possibilities; and
- Flexible management of trading strategies.

There are two basic types of continuous markets: (IIA) auction-agency markets; and (IIB) dealer markets. The various types of these market structures are discussed below.

A. Auction-Agency Markets

Auction-agency markets are centralized to facilitate the interaction of orders (buying and selling interest of public traders). Reflecting this characteristic, they are often referred to as "order-matching" markets. The various types of auction-agency markets discussed in detail below differ in respect to the order-matching process and the role of intermediaries in the market. As classified in Chart 1, auction-agency markets are subdivided between floor-based and electronic markets. Floor-based markets are further subdivided into double-sided auction, board trading, and crowd trading systems.

1. Floor-Based

(a) **Double-Sided Auction Market (with Single-Capacity Broker).** At the center of this market structure is the "consolidated order book" where orders are stored and executed. There are two general types of orders—limit orders and market orders. Limit orders are contingent on a certain minimum price (in the case of a sell limit order) or maximum price (in the case of a buy limit order). Market orders do not specify a price, only the quantity to be executed at the best price(s) available. Limit orders may be thought of as a means for public traders to advertise their buying or selling interest to other public traders, thereby supplying liquidity to the market, while market orders permit public traders to buy and sell immediately, demanding liquidity of the market. The order book provides traders with a hierarchy of trade priorities: this includes "price priority"—the best price (highest buy or lowest sell) is executed before other prices; and "time priority"—in the case of two orders with the same price, the order submit-

---

Box 5. Board Trading Mechanism

The trading mechanism works as follows:

(1) floor members place bids and offers on the board, generally for the best and second best buy and sell prices for a standard "board lot" size;

(2) floor members are permitted to improve the bid or offer, thereby removing the previous (and inferior) bid or offer from the board; and

(3) any member can "lift" (buy) the offer or "hit" (sell) the bid on the board.

Board trading is done in a predetermined standard size termed a "board lot" in order to simplify trading and concentrate liquidity.

---

ted the earliest (i.e., that has been on the consolidated order book the longest) will receive priority of execution. The trading mechanism is described in Box 4.

Single-capacity brokers are so termed because they provide access to the exchange and manage public orders but are prohibited from submitting their own orders (orders for which the broker acts as principal). The management of orders in the best interest of public traders is a service provided by them: as public orders may arrive sporadically or unevenly, delegating the management to a broker of the timing of submission of orders into the auction can potentially reduce transaction costs.

Greece, Malta, and Ireland provide examples of a pure auction market for government securities, although the Irish market structure is in the process of changing into a dealer system (see Introduction).

(b) Board Trading. In markets characterized by "board trading," a central board replaces the consolidated order book, displaying only the most attractive prices. However, time priority is generally maintained for only the first and second prices listed. The advantage of board trading is its simplicity. The board might be a regular chalk board or an electronic board. Board trading is typical of stock exchanges in many developing countries. The trading mechanism is highlighted in Box 5. Board trading systems are compatible with hybrid dealer/agency market systems in which, for example, floor traders may be required to maintain a certain spread.

(c) Crowd Trading (with Dual-Capacity Brokers). In this market structure, floor-based intermediaries (called locals) are dual-capacity brokers—they act on behalf of their clients and on their own behalf as principal. As with all auction-agency markets, trading is centralized, occurring on the floor of the exchange in a particular location (sometimes called a trading pit or post) for each security. Crowd trading is characterized by bilateral trading between floor traders (there is no consolidated order book) using verbal/sign communication (see Box 6).

Locals expose public orders to the market (other locals) for execution. Locals may also trade on their own account as principals (hence the term dual-capacity). This permits them to provide liquidity actively in the market as compared with single-capacity brokers. For example, in the case of an arrival of a large order to the market, several locals may participate on the other side, thereby effectively breaking up the size of the order into smaller pieces, adding to the market depth.

Box 6. Crowd Trading Mechanism

The trading mechanism works as follows:
(1) public orders are routed to floor traders, "locals," gathered at a trading post;
(2) locals actively bid and offer into the crowd for both own-account and public trader interest; and
(3) a trade occurs when any two locals agree on a bilateral transaction.

Locals also play an active role in price stabilization. They react continuously to order flow arriving onto the exchange, following closely such factors as market momentum, size of orders, and the origination of orders. They tend to trade actively on an intraday basis, while closing positions by the end of the day. Highlighting their importance in providing liquidity, the locals on the Chicago Board of Options Trade contribute to about 60 percent of total trading volume (see Massimb and Phelps (1994)).

In the context of government securities markets, crowd trading is often used for government securities futures and options markets—for example, London's LIFFE and the Chicago Mercantile Exchange.

2. Electronic Order-Matching Systems

As in the case of electronic call auctions, electronic order-matching systems potentially expand the crowd by removing the limitations posed by physical trading floor arrangements, opening access to the market through electronic communications and trading facilities.

In electronic auction markets, public traders have access to order flow information and can trade on an anonymous basis in response. It is argued by some (for example, Massimb and Phelps (1994)) that this may discourage the active participation of locals and therefore reduce the overall liquidity in the market. Despite these concerns, there is a distinct trend toward electronic order-matching systems and away from floor-based auction-agency markets. Depending on market size and the required level of computer sophistication, electronic markets may be very cost-effective because they avoid having to maintain a physical trading floor.

Electronic order-matching systems are being used in Italy and Ireland for the futures (government securities) market, in India for some government securities on the Wholesale Debt Market, and in Spain where the Madrid Stock Exchange offers a CATS (Computer Assisted Trading System) for retail bonds.

B. Dealer Markets

In this market structure, the random arrival of orders to the market is bridged by intermediaries—dealers—that maintain continuous market conditions. Dealers supply two-way (bid and offer) quotations to public traders, which, in turn, may either buy or sell against those quotations. For this reason, dealer markets are often described as "quote-driven" markets, underscoring the dealer's function of maintaining continuous markets. Moreover, as opposed to auction/agency markets, in a pure dealer system, one public order does not have an opportunity to be exposed to another public order.

Box 7. OTC Trading Mechanism

The trading mechanism usually involves the telephone system and works as follows:

(1) dealer A telephones dealer B and requests a "run of quotes" on the most liquid benchmark issues of government securities;

(2) dealer B gives firm two-sided quotations (bid and offer) for the requested securities and states the size for which the quotations are good;

(3) dealer A will then either (1) "hit a bid" or "lift an offer" for any size up to the stated maximum, (2) ask whether a particular bid or offer is good for more, and after having the size confirmed return to (1) above, or (3) "pass" on the quotations (i.e., decline any trading business); and

(4) in the event that a trade is done, both traders enter the trade onto their trading blotter and the trade is later confirmed by the back office and prepared for clearing and settlement.

Two basic types of dealer markets are discussed below—competing and monopoly. Competing dealer markets are subdivided into decentralized and centralized (electronic) markets.

1. Competing Dealer Markets

Dealers provide continuous quotations in competition with other dealers thereby earning the spread between bid-offer quotations.

(a) Decentralized Over-the-Counter Market. The simplest form of dealer market—the over-the-counter market—is characterized by direct dealing (bilateral trading) between dealers (see Box 7), and between dealers and public traders (clients).

Nascent markets often begin as OTC markets. This is typical of treasury bill markets, for example. As treasury bills tend initially to be held by a narrow group of institutions, namely banks, the holders of treasury bills are known to each other, creating natural counterparts for trading and reducing search costs. Clients undertake a search among dealers to find the most competitive dealer quote (highest bid for a sale and lowest offer for a purchase). In markets in which the distribution of securities has broadened to nonbanks, single-capacity brokers may emerge to facilitate this search.

In the basic OTC market, trading and information are entirely decentralized, therefore, real-time information on prices tends to be limited. Inefficiencies may result as trades occur at different prices at the same time. Moreover, without price and transaction information, public traders may find it difficult to judge the quality of execution offered by intermediaries.

(i) Over-the-counter markets with competing interdealer brokers. For efficient price discovery, the OTC market discussed above will need to develop further. This is facilitated by interdealer brokers. The importance of the interdealer market and the role of interdealer brokers are discussed below.

An efficient interdealer market is essential to price discovery in decentralized OTC markets. In the first instance of trading, internal order flow (dealer-client trades) is accommodated into and from dealer inventories. As the cost of hold-

**Table 8. Composition of Dealer Market in Government Bond Trading
in Selected Countries**

(In percent of total value)

	United States	Canada	Spain	United Kingdom
Dealer-to-dealer	60	45	44	44
Dealer-to-client	40	55	56	56
Total	100	100	100	100

Source: Based on estimates of respective central banks.

ing a suboptimal portfolio rises the longer it is held (see Stoll 1978(a)), a dealer will attempt to adjust his or her inventory position quickly against other dealers supplying quotations. If competing dealers are experiencing net demand (supply) conditions, prices will quickly adjust upward (downward) in the interdealer market, contributing to price discovery. Table 8 highlights the importance of dealer-to-dealer trade, in this regard, in a few government securities markets.

Interdealer brokers are specialized intermediaries offering trade execution services (typically the essential communication network, the "hotline" telephonic connections and screen systems) to dealers that improve the efficiency of the interdealer market in the following ways.

First, Garbade (1978) identifies the economic role of interdealer brokers (in the U.S. Treasury market) in improving market efficiency by providing information on quotations and transactions that reduces search costs;[2] and improves competition among dealers, leading to a narrowing in the dispersion of market quotations.

Second, Harris (1993) highlights the interdealer broker's role in negotiating trades between dealers (illustrated by the trading mechanism in Box 8). Importantly, an interdealer broker system provides anonymity to dealers ("blind broker" system). This service is crucial in a market with informed traders, or dominated by large dealers.

Finally, unlike dealers, interdealer brokers are paid strictly on commission (as opposed to the bid-offer spread). Thus, interdealer brokers help to increase trading volumes by educating dealers as to possible trade and arbitrage opportunities. In a sense, trading is "commission-driven." This can be an important factor in promoting underdeveloped markets.

The importance and role of interdealer brokers in facilitating interdealer trade in well-developed government securities markets is highlighted in Table 9 for a selected number of countries.

Interdealer brokers compete with each other for trading business from dealers. In general, the market can support only a limited number of interdealer brokers as the benefit of consolidating market information (competing dealer quotations)

---

[2]As markets develop, search costs rise with (1) increasing numbers of market-makers; (2) increasing numbers of securities traded; and (3) market volatility, increasing the risk of holding a suboptimal portfolio.

Box 8. Interdealer Broker Trading Mechanism

The trading mechanism works as follows:

(1) a dealer telephones an interdealer broker to place a two-part trade with the broker—the first part consists of a firm quote (either buy, sell, or both) and the second consists of potential further amounts that could be made available, if interest is expressed;

(2) the interdealer broker publicizes the quotation (first part) either by telephone or screen to other dealers;

(3) an interested dealer telephones the broker and either (1) trades against the firm quotation or (2) negotiates with the broker for a larger size or possibly price improvement;

(4) the trade is reported to the rest of the market (either by telephone or screen);

(5) the interdealer broker earns a commission from one or both counterparties; and

(6) the trade is cleared and settled through the interdealer broker such that the parties to the transaction remain anonymous (blind brokers).

---

declines with the number of interdealer brokers, and as total commission income is spread over an increasing number of brokers. In practice, there must be fewer interdealer brokers than dealers. The number of dealers versus interdealer brokers in a selected number of countries is highlighted in Table 10.

(ii) **Over-the-counter market with a monopoly interdealer broker.** In some countries, such as France, there exists a single interdealer broker. In France, the interdealer broker Prominofi is owned by the primary dealers. A monopoly interdealer broker offers a full consolidation of quotation information onto a single system. However, it may not provide the same degree of competition as competing interdealer brokers. Nonetheless, in markets where there is insufficient trade to support competing interdealer brokers, such an architecture may suggest itself as a transitional arrangement (see the section "Brokerage Systems" under "Implications for the Development Strategy of Government Securities Markets" in the text). For example, the authorities in Poland instituted a interdealer system (owned by the

Table 9. Composition of Interdealer Trade in Government Bond Markets in Selected Countries

(In percent)

Trade	United States	Canada	Spain	United Kingdom
Interdealer brokers	99	65	37	96
Dealer-direct	1	35	63	4
Total interdealer trade	100	100	100	100

Source: Based on estimates of respective central banks.

**Table 10. Dealers Versus Interdealer Brokers in
Government Bond Markets in Selected Countries**
(In percent)

	United States	United Kingdom	Spain	France
Primary dealers	39	22	33	18
Interdealer brokers	7	3	4	1

Source: Respective central banks.

central bank) in order to develop their market and improve transparency (see Appendix 3).

(b) Centralized Dealer Market—Electronic Dealer Market. In an electronic dealer market, dealer quotations are centralized (consolidated) onto a screen-based network. Public trading interest is routed electronically onto the system and executed automatically against the best dealer quotations displayed on the screen-based system (see Box 9).

Centralized electronic (automated) trading offers certain advantages over OTC markets: (1) price and transaction information are more transparent; (2) price and time priorities are provided as customer orders are executed on a first-in basis, against the best market price; (3) interdealer intermediaries are not required—the centralized quotation system provides for the "information" and "intermediary" functions of the interdealer broker; and (4) real-time auditing of transactions for the purpose of conducting market surveillance is facilitated.

As discussed in the text, however, centralized automated trading changes the nature of OTC dealer markets in a number of subtle ways. Centralized trading with transparent trade reporting reduces opportunities for dealers to compete for internalized (dealer-client) order flow, and profit from that information (by trans-acting with other, less well-informed dealers) reducing dealer services supplied. In addition, the market-maker is unable to differentiate between liquidity traders

---

Box 9. Electronic Dealer Market Trading Mechanism

The trading mechanism works as follows:
(1) designated market-makers enter onto the system firm price quotations (bid and offer), along with the size for which the quotation is good;
(2) the electronic system displays the best bid and offer for each security that is listed on the system;
(3) agency brokers access the system and route client buy and sell orders (market orders only) electronically through the system;
(4) client orders are executed against the best quotation available on the system; and
(5) the transaction is flashed across the system and the price quote is restored by the dealer or a competing dealer.

(uninformed) and information (informed) traders as trading is impersonal (there is no relationship between the market-maker and the client). As a result, quotations provided by dealers may be for smaller size and bid-ask spreads may be wider, in order to guard against adverse selection by informed traders.

Italy provides an example of an electronic dealer market, introduced in 1988 as a reform of the OTC market. It was reformed further in 1994, as trading began to migrate back to the OTC market and abroad. The recent reforms addressed these design issues by adding a small number of well-capitalized market-makers with greater obligations to quote in larger size (discussed in the text); by providing more flexibility in managing trades (introducing interdealer brokers); and by locating electronic access points abroad, providing greater access to the system to attract foreign dealers.

2. Monopoly Dealer

A competing dealer market may not always emerge for reasons of economies of scale, presence of informed traders, and insufficient trading volumes.

Economies of scale in market-making may lead to a monopoly supply of dealer services. ("Monopoly" as used here does not necessarily involve an exclusive legal right that prevents other dealers from competing.) Evidence suggests that while economies of scale in market-making are apparent, they are not normally so large as to result in a monopoly dealer structure.

Glosten and Milgrom (1985) suggest that when dealers are adversely selected by "informed traders," only a monopoly dealer can maintain markets by recouping losses from liquidity traders. As compared with equity markets, trading in government securities is generally characterized by a high portion of liquidity versus information traders. Nonetheless, as discussed above, this has been a factor in the Italian electronic dealer market. However, evidence suggests it is not so significant a factor as to lead to a monopoly dealer market, even in fully electronic and anonymous systems.

In nascent markets, there may be insufficient trading volumes to attract and support competing dealers. For example, in India, as a transitional arrangement, the money market was supported by a "single dealer" (discount house) (see Appendix 3).

Appendix 2
Primary Dealer Systems in Selected Industrial Countries

This Appendix describes the major characteristics of primary dealer systems in France, Italy, Spain, the United Kingdom, and the United States.

FRANCE: PRIMARY DEALER SYSTEM

Market Structure Description	• Primary dealer system established in November 1986 as part of government securities market reforms (primary dealers were chosen in February 1987)
	• Quote-driven, over-the-counter wholesale market for government securities
Dealers	• 18 primary dealers (Spécialistes en Valeurs du Trésor (SVTs))
	• Reporting dealers (Correspondents en Valeurs du Trésor (CVTs)): none at this time
	• Dealers: stock exchange brokers, banks, securities houses, etc.
	• One interdealer broker (IDB) (Prominofi—owned by the SVTs)
Trading System	• The interbroker dealers provide: trading systems (screen/telephone) on an anonymous basis and compete for quotations from SVTs; securities lending and borrowing brokerage; and repo brokerage
Clearing and Settlement	• Intra-SVT clearing system; Bank of France (BOF) Saturne system (book-entry) for short- and medium-term government paper; long bonds are held in SICOVAM, the French central securities depository
Primary Market	• Auctions: eligible to all participants including individuals, banks, stockbrokers, financial companies—by electronic access or written tender
	• Securities: BTFs (short-term discount treasury bills), BTANs (annual, interest-bearing treasury bonds, typically 2- and 5-year maturities), and OATs (long-term bonds, in FF and ECU, typically 10 and 30 years); reopened (fungible) regularly
Primary Dealers Eligibility	• Eligible institutions: credit institutions, *caisse des dépôts,* banks, securities houses (institutions governed by Article 99 of the Banking Act); primary dealers will reflect the diversity of institutions active in market, including foreign institutions
Minimum Requirements	• Minimum capital requirement: F 300 million

Appendix 2 *(continued)*

	• Probationary period as a CVT
	• Willingness to meet obligations of a primary dealer and performance standards
	• SVTs and CVTs are selected annually
Obligations	• Primary auction underwriting: regular and significant participation; at minimum must win an average of 3 percent over the three types of securities in FF; and 2 percent in each issue over a one-year period
	• Secondary market making: must trade a minimum of 3 per-cent of total secondary market volume in each franc-denominated security, and 2 percent for securities in ECUs
	• Quote two-way markets on principal issues common to all primary dealers (list is established jointly by the treasury and the primary dealers)
	• Must promote sales domestically and abroad to clients (i.e., nonprimary and reporting dealers) and provide information (weekly) on distribution
Incentives	• Line of credit: none
	• Rights: exclusive access to the interbroker dealer
	• Other: only SVTs may submit noncompetitive bids; up to 10 percent of the proposed amount (midpoint of fourchette) at the auction, and up to 15 percent after the auction (up to midday the day after the auction), allocated on the basis of the average tender performance of each SVT of previous three auctions; only SVTs can strip and reconstitute OATs
Implementation	• "Cahier des charges des SVTs" (primary dealer agreement)—from time to time, the treasury issues broad guidelines and specific performance criteria for SVTs
	• Before becoming an SVT, an institution first demonstrates its ability to fulfill all the conditions listed above, during a probationary period, in which it serves as a CVT
	• SVT status is subject to performance standards reviewed annually (see above)
Open Market Operations	• Treasury conducts active debt management operations with SVTs
	• Bank of France (BOF) executes open market operations (in BTFs and BTANs only) through a group of 26 interbank market agents—selected separately by the BOF
Regulation	• Comité de la Réglementation Bancaire—rule making authority for lending institutions

---

Appendix 2 *(continued)*

	• Commission Bancaire—responsibility for ensuring compliance by lending institutions
	• Commission des Opérations de Bourse—supervises the operation of securities markets of listed financial instruments
Other Characteristics	• Well-developed repo market and future markets
	• Established benchmark securities
	• OATs bid/offer spread is about 5–15 centimes; blocks of F 50 million to F 200 million trade

ITALY: CENTRALIZED SCREEN-BASED AUTOMATED SYSTEM "MERCATO TITOLI DI STATO" (MTS)

Market Structure Description	• MTS was established in May 1988 (and revised Feb. 1994) by the Bank of Italy (BOI) and the treasury to enhance the transparency and efficiency of the government securities market
	• MTS is a wholesale debt market characterized as (1) a centralized quote-driven dealer market, with (2) automated screen-based trading, and (3) computerized electronic communication links with market centers and the clearing and settlement system of the BOI
Dealers—Participants	• Three-tier dealer system: 10 specialists, 31 primary dealers, and 173 dealers
	• Eligible participants as dealer include BOI, banks (including foreign banks operating abroad), stockbrokers, insurance companies, investment fund companies, securities firms (SIMs), and securities firms registered in the EU, all with net capital of at least Lit 10 billion
Trading System	• MTS—two-tier, screen-based trading system automated with book-entry and settlement system
	• First tier—specialists and primary dealers display firm two-way quotes on screen
	• Second tier—dealers access the MTS to execute (electronically) own and customer orders against those quotes
	• A special agreement "Convention" signed by all dealers establishes the organization and operational framework of MTS
Clearing and Settlement	• Involves clearinghouse, cash account, and centralized deposit systems
	• Clearinghouse: run by the BOI; located in 7 main cities electronically connected; cleared on a multilateral netting basis

Appendix 2 *(continued)*

	• Cash account: centralized accounts of banks and nonbanks are held at BOI for settlement
	• Centralized deposit: BOI runs the system and sets conditions for membership; automated link with clearinghouse system
Primary Market	• Auctions: bond auctions are uniform price; limited to banks and securities firms (which include primary dealers and specialists)
	• Commission is paid on auctioned bonds (ranges from 35 to 65 cents on long bonds)
Primary Dealers Eligibility	• Only securities firms and banks (including foreign— with a branch established in Italy) are eligible to be primary dealers and specialists
Minimum Requirements	• Primary dealers: minimum capital requirement of Lit 50 billion; and selling contracts in the previous year of at least Lit 10 trillion in government bonds
	• Specialists: status as primary dealer with at least Lit 75 billion in capital
Obligations	• Primary dealers: secondary market-making— (1) must have yearly trading volumes on MTS of at least 1 percent for each category of security; (2) must quote two-way market on minimum of 10 issues for minimum size of Lit 5 billion; and (3) must replace quote on screen within five minutes of trade (must be at least 2 dealers for each issue)
	• Specialists: primary auction underwriting—must have average annual share of at least 3 percent across all security categories issued by auction, and 1 percent for each security category; secondary market-making— (1) must commit to trade a volume of 3 percent of total market turnover on MTS and 1 percent for each security category; and (2) must quote for size of Lit 25 billion on benchmark stocks
Incentives	• Line of credit: specialists and primary dealers access at their initiative a special repo and reverse repo facility for up to a limit of Lit 100 billion and Lit 50 billion, respectively, for a period of up to 7 days, on a "carry-neutral" basis (repo rate set at the 2-week interbank rate, and the reverse repo rate is set at the yield of the securities); and specialists and primary dealers are sole market-makers on the first tier of MTS (screen)

Appendix 2 *(continued)*

	• Rights: specialists have exclusive access to supplementary reopenings offered at the discretion of the treasury (up to 10 percent of quantity issued at auction, awarded at the marginal price on a prorate basis as a percentage of their successful bids at the last three auctions)
	• Other: specialists can propose security transactions to BOI
Implementation	• Membership in screen-based system is controlled by the Management Committee composed of the BOI (gives final approval) and market participants
	• Dealers must sign "special convention" for trading obligations and rules
	• Specialists and primary dealers that no longer meet minimum requirements over a one-year period lose their status
Open Market Operations	• BOI conducts open market operations in repos off screen, with banks and some securities firms for monetary management
	• BOI conducts reverse auctions in T-bills only with primary dealers and specialists
	• BOI buys bonds (sometimes sells) on screen with primary dealers and specialists
Regulation	• Rules of MTS contained in ministerial decree of February 24, 1994
	• Management Committee of MTS is a self-regulatory organization; Italian Treasury and Commission for Stock Exchanges and Joint Stock Companies (CONSOB), and BOI participate in meetings of the committee
	• Dealers are signatories of the Convention
Other Characteristics	• Daily turnover of about Lit 15 trillion ($9.6 billion) (in September 1994)
	• Average spread (bid-offer) of about 2–3 basis points on liquid benchmark issues
	• Total of 114 different issues quoted

SPAIN: GOVERNMENT DEBT MARKET AND BOOK-ENTRY SYSTEM

Market Structure Description	• Book-entry system established in 1987 as a decentralized dealer market by the Bank of Spain (BOS) as part of reforms to improve secondary market efficiency
	• Quote-driven over-the-counter market
Dealer Market Participants	• Three-tier dealer system: 99 full-capacity registered dealers, of which 11 are Creados de Mercado (market-makers—all banks); and 22 aspiring market-makers Negociantes de Deuda

Appendix 2 *(continued)*

	• Wholesale market includes registered dealers and account holder entities (see clearing and settlement)
	• Client market: consists mainly of repo operations between registered dealers and investors
Trading System	• Wholesale trading takes place over the telephone— either direct or through brokers
	• Interdealer brokers (screen-based/telephone) provide anonymous quotations (blind broker system) for primary dealers; accounts for about 37 percent of interdealer trade
	• Stock exchange recently introduced an electronic small-order execution system for client market
Clearing and Settlement	• BOS owns and operates Central Book-Entry Office (CBO), which clears and settles all transactions among market members
	• Market members include: (1) account holder entities—can trade in their own name only and hold accounts (in their name only) at the CBO; and (2) registered dealers—can hold third-party accounts (clients) in government securities
	• Third-party nonaccount holders access CBO through registered dealers
Primary Market	• Auction committee: made up of 2 BOS and 2 ministry of finance members
	• Two types of auctions: (1) placement amount is not preannounced and stop-out rate is chosen by auction committee; and (2) placement amount is preannounced (infrequently used)
	• Auctions are open to residents and nonresidents— bid prices higher than the weighted average pay the weighted average price while bids below the average price pay the bid price (limited noncompetitive bids are also accepted)
	• If the placement target is not reached (auction type 2), the finance ministry may call a second round auction, for market-makers only, at freed prices, provided the amount accepted in the first round is equal to or greater than 70 percent of amount offered. Each market-maker is obliged to submit bids for an amount no less than its prorated share of the remaining portion
	• Following any auction type 1, or any thoroughly covered type 2, an automatic second round occurs, for market-makers only. Market-makers can bid at their option, but at

Appendix 2 *(continued)*

	interest rates no higher than the average yield resulting in the first auction. The Italian Finance Ministry must award a minimum of 10 percent of the accepted bids when bids accepted in the first round are greater than or equal to 50 percent of total bids received, or a minimum of 20 percent of accepted bids when bids accepted in the first round are less than 50 percent of total bids received
Market-Makers Eligibility	• Market-makers can include commercial banks, savings banks, or securities firms
Minimum Requirements	• (1) Must have a minimum capital of Pta 750 million, to be increased to Pta 1,000 million within two years' time; and (2) be under BOS's supervision and control
Obligations	• Primary auction underwriting: must participate in auctions and are obligated to bid for coverage of second round auction (see primary market above) • Secondary market-making: must maintain an active and continuous two-way secondary market with specified minimum and maximum spreads; and provide BOS with market information
Incentives	• Line of credit: none • Rights: market-makers and aspiring market-makers have exclusive access to interdealer broker system; market-makers have exclusive access to second round auctions; and market-makers have exclusive access to some categories of open market operations
Implementation	• Requirements for aspiring and qualified market-makers are revised from time to time by the BOS • Selection of aspiring and qualified market-makers made by the BOS based upon activity in primary and secondary markets, customer base, and quality of human and technical resources • Aspiring market-makers are ranked annually according to a weighted index of quantitative indicators of activity in primary and secondary markets: only the 12 best placed qualify for becoming market-makers for the coming year
Open Market Operations	• Though the bulk of open market operations are conducted through repo auctions in which banks participate, overnight repos and direct interventions are conducted only with market-makers
Regulation	• BOS, in coordination with the Spanish Ministry of Economy and Finance, is entrusted with the responsibility for the organization and management of both the primary

Appendix 2 *(continued)*

and secondary markets for government securities—supervision is shared between the BOS and the capital market authorities

Other Characteristics

- Average trade size for bonds is between Pta 500 million and Pta 1,000 million

- Average daily turnover of Pta 156 trillion of government securities and Pta 1,441 billion in repo for 1991

- Average bid-offer spread on liquid bond issues is about 5 to 10 basis points

UNITED KINGDOM: GILT-EDGED MARKET-MAKERS (GEMMS)

Market Structure
Description

- New structure of gilts was inaugurated October 27, 1986 (Big Bang)—trading moved off-floor

- Continuous improvements in book-entry system

Dealers

- 22 GEMMs (14 of which owned by foreign parents from the United States, Japan, and Europe)
- 3 interdealer brokers (IDBs)
- 8 stock exchange money brokers (SEMBs)

Trading System

- Over-the-counter, screen-based quotes
- IDBs act as "blind brokers" (anonymous quotes) for GEMMs

- GEMMs, IDBs, and SEMBs are all members of the London Stock Exchange

Clearing and
Settlement

- Bank of England's (BOE) Central Gilts Office (CGO)

  provides book-entry holdings of stock and a computerized stock transfer and payment system for its members

- Members (total of 175 direct) include GEMMs, banks, specialized financial institutions, insurance companies, and pension funds; and nominee companies (indirect members)

Primary Market

- Auctions: broad outline of financing (the Remit) is announced each March, followed by more detailed information prior to auction

- All types of investors are permitted to submit bids for auctions

- Tap issues: following auction or tenders, or from direct placement with the BOE, the BOE sells stock, typically in rising market conditions, to GEMMs, generally by way of a "mini tender"

Primary Dealers
Eligibility

- Must be a member of London Stock Exchange

Appendix 2 (continued)

Minimum Requirements	• Must be separately capitalized entities with dedicated capital held in the European Economic Area
	• No minimum capital requirement
	• Must comply with BOE's capital adequacy standards based on ratio of risk exposure to capital
Obligations	• Primary market underwriting: no fixed arrangements between BOE and GEMMs for primary issuance underwriting
	• Secondary market-making: must make, on demand and in all trading conditions, continuous and effective two-way prices in appropriate size in the full list of gilt maturities
	• Must meet capital adequacy standards at all times
Incentives	• Line of credit: access to a secured lending facility at the BOE (in relation to capital)
	• Rights: only GEMMs may borrow stock from SEMBs (and discount houses in stocks up to 7-year maturity); and only GEMMs are permitted access to interdealer brokers
	• Other: certain tax arrangements facilitating market-making; a direct dealing relationship with the BOE; and GEMMs may submit bids for auctions by telephone up to the auction deadline; other participants (that bid directly) must bid by "written tenders" the day before the auction
Implementation	• Memorandum of understanding—relationship between BOE and GEMMs is outlined in 1985 document "The Future of the Gilt-Edged Market: The BOE's Dealing and Supervisory Relationship with Certain Participants" and in 1986 "Operational Market Notice"
	• Prospective firm applies for GEMM status; the application is discussed with the BOE; guidelines as to expected market participation and size of quotations are discussed and drawn up in a letter to the prospective GEMM; firms have two weeks to confirm acceptance; BOE publishes a list of GEMMs
	• Market is conducted according to the rules and regulations of the exchange
Open Market Operations	• BOE occasionally purchases gilts with a maturity of less than one year
	• BOE receives bids for stock from GEMMs just before the market opening; BOE deals at its discretion
	• Money market operations conducted with discount houses

Appendix 2 *(continued)*

Regulation	• GEMMs are subject to regulation and prudential supervision of the BOE
	• BOE oversees protection of investors on behalf of the Securities and Futures Association
	• The London Stock Exchange monitors trade from the point of conduct of business
Other Characteristics	• Typical spreads are ½₂ for short-dated and up to ⅛ for longer-dated off-the-run issues
	• Turnover averaged about £6.3 billion a day in 1993
	• Total capitalization of GEMMs (1993) is £733 million

UNITED STATES: PRIMARY DEALER SYSTEM

Market Structure Description	• Quote-driven, over-the-counter (OTC) market
	• Treasury notes and bonds are listed on the New York Stock Exchange but trading volume is minuscule compared with the OTC market
Dealers and Market Participants	• 39 primary dealers; 1,700 broker/dealers; and 7 interdealer brokers
	• Largely a wholesale market in which institutional investors such as banks, thrifts, dealers, pension funds, insurance companies, mutual funds, and state and local governments operate
Trading System	• Interdealer brokers, screen-based/telephone, provide anonymous quotations (blind broker system)
	• Three interbroker dealers allow access to primary dealers only; another three allow access to Government Securities Clearing Corporation (GSCC) members; and one permits its own list of creditworthy customers to trade
	• GOVPX owned and operated by the primary dealers provides real-time price information and trading volume information on government securities
Clearing and Settlement	• Federal Reserve System owns and operates a book-entry system for title registry whose members are clearing banks, which in turn act as subdepositories for other market participants
	• Private sector GSCC provides automated trade comparison, and clearing and netting services for members (more than 60 of the most active banks, dealers, and interdealer brokers)

Appendix 2 *(continued)*

	• Final settlement for securities transactions occurs on the Fedwire
	• Treasury Direct book-entry system is offered primarily for retail investors that intend to hold securities to maturity; no custodial or transaction fees are charged
Primary Market	• Auctions: all types of investors are permitted to submit bids
	• Only depository institutions, government securities brokers, and dealers registered with the Securities Exchange Commission (SEC) are permitted to bid on behalf of customers
	• In 1991, primary dealers bidding accounted for about 72 percent of auction winnings, of which the top 10 primary dealers accounted for 50 percent
Primary Dealers Eligibility	• Commercial banking organizations subject to supervision by U.S. federal bank supervisors or broker/dealers registered with the SEC
Minimum Requirements	• Commercial banks must meet minimum capital standards under the Basle Capital Accord, and have at least $100 million of tier I capital; registered broker/dealers must have at least $50 million in regulatory capital and net free capital above regulatory warning levels
Obligations	• Primary auction underwriting: must participate in a meaningful way in treasury auctions
	• Secondary market: must make reasonably good markets in their trading relationship with the Fed's trading desk; and provide the desk with useful market information and analysis
Incentives	• Line of credit: none
	• Rights: exclusive access to open market operations
	• Other: permitted to submit bids on behalf of customers
Implementation	• Guidelines for primary dealers developed by the Federal Reserve Bank of New York (FRBNY)
	• Following the Salomon scandal, the primary dealer system is being adjusted to provide for a more equitable access to primary and secondary markets, for example:
	— administration of primary auctions was partially automated to provide easier access by investors
	— progress has been made in creating wider access to the interdealer broker systems

Appendix 2 *(concluded)*

	— FRBNY is automating its open market operations, thereby removing a technical constraint on the size of the primary dealer group
	— FRBNY has broadened its mandate, away from "dealer surveillance," which had conveyed the impression that it had the supervisory oversight of primary dealers, to "market surveillance"
Open Market Operations	• Open market operations are conducted by FRBNY through primary dealers
Regulation	• Treasury has rule making authority (Government Securities Act, revised 1993)
	• Enforcement by the SEC, bank supervisors, and federal financial institution regulatory authority
	• FRBNY heads an interagency working group on market surveillance consisting of the treasury, Federal Reserve, SEC, and the Commodity Futures Trading Commission
	• NASD (National Association of Securities Dealers): a self-regulating organization has (drafted) sales practice rules for government securities
Other Characteristics	• Average daily trading volume (to Sept. 1994) was between $150 billion and $250 billion
	• Average size of repo outstanding with dealers to Sept. 1994 was $800 billion
	• Bid-offer spreads are razor thin on benchmark issues: about $1/32$ on long-term treasury bonds (more narrow on shorter-term benchmark issues)

Appendix 3

Organization of Transitional and Market-Supporting Structures

Secondary Market Window

In the initial stages of market development, when two-way markets are yet to develop with sufficient numbers of market-makers to provide secondary market liquidity, central banks have often established a secondary market window standing ready to buy and sell government securities as a market-maker. As discussed in the text, the goal of this arrangement is to promote a more liquid secondary market through promoting more continuous market-making on the part of dealers by reducing the liquidity risk they face in holding inventories of government securities. This facility needs to be carefully designed so as not to conflict with monetary or market development objectives, as discussed below.

Two general approaches to establishing the functioning of the window are: (1) fixing buy and sell prices—either on an ad hoc basis or automatically against a reference price—and then announcing them to the market; or (2) flexibly managing prices and transactions and responding on a dynamic basis to market developments.

In the fixed case, with ad hoc adjustment, prices are generally set for a particular time period, say for several days or a week and adjusted as necessary with market-determined benchmark rates. Alternatively, prices can automatically adjust using a reference benchmark price plus or minus a percentage margin for buys and sells, respectively. Typically, in this case, the benchmark used is the interest rate established at the last treasury bill auction, especially in the absence of established secondary market benchmarks. In both cases, buy and sell margins should be set sufficiently wide to encourage direct trading.

In contrast, using the *dynamic* approach, secondary market window pricing by the central bank mimics a dealer by continuously adjusting price in response to market movements. Dynamic pricing usefully encourages the emergence of a continuous market; however, care should be taken that the secondary market window operation *facilitate* market adjustment as opposed to the central bank *becoming the market*. Rather than providing quotes to the market, and possibly stifling price discovery, the central bank should respond to quotes from market participants. In practice, this is generally implemented by the central bank by responding to market quotes from the participants (dealers) by either "doing the proposed deal" or simply "passing" on the proposed transaction. Participants are thereby encouraged to trade with one another rather than with the central bank.

In order to conduct dynamic secondary market window operations, the central bank trader needs to be in regular contact with market participants to determine how the market is being quoted and to find out volumes of trade occurring in the secondary market. Armed with this information, the central bank can better assess the appropriateness, given market circumstances, of conducting a secondary window trade.[1] As a rule, any participant approaching the central bank for a secondary window trade should normally have attempted to do the trade in the market before approaching the window.

Secondary market window transactions must strike a balance between the central bank's objectives for monetary policy and those for secondary market development. For example, it would be inappropriate for open market operations to drain liquidity from the system to tighten money market conditions, while, through the secondary window, purchasing large amounts of securities from the market, thereby injecting liquidity.

To avoid contradictory activities, operating rules should be established. For example, the secondary market window could be operated on such a basis that net purchases or sales are kept within a set daily margin. The operation of the window would seek to accommodate the market, where appropriate, while maintaining its book within set operating limits. In addition, in contrast to open market operations, which are for same-day settlement, secondary window transactions could be for next-day settlement. This would provide an opportunity to neutralize the liquidity effect of window operations the following day through open market operations.

Table 11 highlights examples of countries using these general approaches. Central banks may go through a transition from fixed to dynamic pricing as the market develops and becomes more continuous, while the role of the central bank in setting pricing and providing liquidity is reduced.

Discount Houses

In some countries, the authorities have encouraged the development of the market by establishing one or more discount houses—sometimes jointly owned by financial institutions, including possibly the central bank. Generally, a line of credit from the central bank is extended to the discount house to help provide financing for inventory arising from its market-making activity.

The discount house should at all times provide two-way quotes on selected benchmark securities under all market conditions. It will constantly adjust its buy and sell quotations (level and spread) according to market conditions to keep inventories of securities at manageable positions and to realize sufficient earnings from bid-offer spreads to make operations profitable. Care should be taken that the discount house does not discourage the emergence of market-makers in the private sector or unduly discourage direct interbank trading in securities. In this context, the profit motive is key; operating margins for market-making must attract other dealers if the market is to develop. Arrangements with the central bank would need to be carefully considered so as not to interfere with monetary operations (discussed in the text).

---

[1]Only if the central bank is informed of market conditions can it assess whether the participant has "done his homework." Importantly, the market intelligence will prevent the central bank from being arbitraged by the market—that is, it will prevent participants from buying from the market and selling the security simultaneously to the central bank at a higher price (lower yield).

Table 11. Structure of Secondary Market Window Operations

Structure	Country	Description
Fixed		
Ad hoc	India (up to 1992)	Central bank sets buy and sell price list and announces to market
Automatic	Botswana	Sets a price as a margin from the last primary auction of treasury bills
Dynamic	United Kingdom, Nepal	Central bank responds to dealers' quotes according to market conditions

Brokerage Systems

Some central banks (Poland, Turkey, and Thailand) have also encouraged the development of secondary markets by providing a brokerage or trading system, including facilities to clear and settle government securities transactions. Such a system can be very effective in nascent markets by providing transparency of price information and making the clearing and settlement of securities simple and effective. Importantly, the system can reduce resistance to establishing trading counterparties in the over-the-counter market when a lack of standardized trading practices and confidence in counterparties creates risks in securities dealing. In addition, such systems can be very simple to install, using existing technology, and require a small number of people to operate.

The National Bank of Poland, for example, operated a brokerage system with considerable success in initiating a secondary market in treasury bills. The simple screen-based broker system—called the Telegazette—worked as follows: (1) participants (selected dealers) telephoned their buying and selling positions and accompanying quotations into the central bank; (2) the central bank entered the quotations, which could then be seen on-screen by all other participants; (3) buyers and sellers telephoned the central bank, which displayed transactions against the quotations on the screen; (4) the central bank confirmed the trades by fax; and (5) the central bank cleared the trades through the banking department.

In situations where there are few, or several large, market players it is particularly important that quotations are on a "blind" basis—that is, participants' names should not be revealed, and each side of the trade should be done through the central bank so that traders remain anonymous. An example of "blind broking" is provided by the Bank of Turkey, which acts as the counterparty to each trade (fully backed by collateral in the event of a default).

Appendix 4

Suitability Criteria and Market Structure

Stage of Development

Nascent markets are unlikely to exhibit sufficient trading volumes to either sustain continuous auction-agency markets or attract sufficient competing dealers, resulting in a high degree of spurious price volatility and execution risk. Such markets are good candidates for commencing as periodic markets that lead to market deepening and efficient price discovery. As the number of participants grows and financial markets are liberalized, scope increases for more continuous trading and market structures such as auction-agency or competing dealer markets.

Type of Security

Different government securities might be traded in different market structures, reflecting type-of-security characteristics. For instance, treasury bills as compared with bonds: (1) have greater yield volatility, arguing for a market structure with a higher clearing frequency and more continuous trading than bonds; (2) have a higher degree of security fragmentation, arguing for dealer markets over auction-agency markets; and (3) are generally held by a narrower group of institutions, facilitating direct trading on an OTC basis.

Type of Trader

Trader types and their tastes may influence market structure. When securities are widely held (dispersed) by the household sector—characterized as small, patient traders—auction-agency and call markets, which provide for price improvement and low transaction costs, are appropriate. When holdings are concentrated with institutional traders—characterized as impatient, block-size traders—dealer markets, which provide a high degree of immediacy and accommodation of block-size trading, may develop.

Capitalization and Competition

Competing-dealer market structures require adequate numbers of well-capitalized dealers to create competitive conditions and support "quote-driven" trading. When preconditions of capitalization and competition are not met, as in small countries, auction-agency or call markets, which rely on competition among orders rather than dealers, are appropriate.

Trading Expertise

Electronic trading systems tend to be impersonal. By contrast, floor-based or over-the-telephone trading may be more effective in developing trading expertise and encouraging dynamic trading. As expertise develops, electronic trading systems may be more readily adopted deriving the full benefit of those features. The location of trading expertise is also an important determinant of efficient market structure.

Objectives of the Authorities

Debt managers with sizable financing requirements and rigid issuance calendars, characterized as impatient traders with a high demand for immediacy, prefer dealer markets, which facilitate the underwriting of primary issuance, reducing execution risk.

Appendix 4 *(concluded)*

Central banks generally prefer continuous dealer markets because dealers are natural counterparties for open market operations, providing "immediacy" of execution and supporting continuous market trading for effective monetary policy implementation.

Regulators generally prefer centralized and electronic markets that are highly transparent and lend themselves easily to market surveillance and establishing audit trails. This is particularly the case in some developing countries and economies in transition where institutions may lack a track record or tradition of credibility and integrity, and where the regulatory body has a limited ability to undertake thorough prudential supervision.

Bibliography

Abken, Peter A., 1991, "Globalization of Stock, Futures, and Options Markets," *Federal Reserve of Atlanta Economic Review*, Vol. 76, No. 4 (July/August), pp. 1–22.

Bagehot, Walter, 1971, "The Only Game in Town," *Financial Analysts Journal* (March–April), pp. 12–14 and 22.

Bank of England, 1985, "The Future Structure of the Gilt-Edged Market: The Bank of England's Dealing and Supervisory Relationships with Certain Participants," *Quarterly Bulletin*, Vol. 25 (April), pp. 250–82.

Benston, George J., and Robert L. Hagerman, 1974, "Determinants of Bid-Asked Spreads in the Over-the-Counter Market," *Journal of Financial Economics*, Vol. 1 (December), pp. 353–64.

Blume, Marshall E., and Jeremy J. Siegel, 1992, "The Theory of Security Pricing and Market Structure," *Financial Markets, Institutions, and Instruments* (July).

Bröker, Günther, 1993, *Government Securities and Debt Management in the 1990s* (Paris: Organization for Economic Cooperation and Development).

Cohen, Kalman J., and others, 1978, "The Returns Generation Process, Returns Variance, and the Effect of Thinness in Securities Markets," *Journal of Finance*, Vol. 33, No. 1 (March), pp. 149–67.

Cohen, Kalman J., S. R. Schwartz, and D. Whitcomb, 1986, *The Microstructure of Securities Markets* (Englewood Cliffs, N.J.: Prentice Hall).

Demsetz, Harold, 1968, "The Cost of Transacting," *Quarterly Journal of Economics*, Vol. 82 (February), pp. 33–53.

Domowitz, Ian, 1992, "A Taxonomy of Automated Trade Execution Systems," IMF Working Paper 92/76 (Washington: International Monetary Fund).

Economides, Nicholas, 1993a, "Proposal to the Bank of Greece on the Organization of the Secondary Market for Greek State Bills, Notes, and Bonds," New York University, Stern School of Business, Department of Economics Working Paper No. EC–93–18 (September), pp. 1–31.

————, 1993b, "Electronic Call Market Trading," New York University, Stern School of Business, Department of Economics Working Paper No. EC-93-19 (September), pp. 1–22.

Euromoney, 1992, *The 1992 Guide to Selected Domestic Bond Markets*, Euromoney Research Guides (London, January).

————, 1992, *The 1992 Guide to European Domestic Money Markets*, Euromoney Research Guides (London, September).

France, Economics Ministry, 1993, *French Government Securities: 1993 Annual Report* (Paris).

Garbade, Kenneth D., 1978, "The Effect of Interdealer Brokerage on the Transactional Characteristics of Dealer Markets," *Journal of Business*, Vol. 51 (July), pp. 477–98.

————, 1978, "Technology, Communication, and the Performance of Financial Markets: 1840–1975," *Journal of Finance*, Vol. 33 (June), pp. 819–32.

————, and William L. Silber, 1979, "Structural Organization of Secondary Markets: Clearing Frequency, Dealer Activity, and Liquidity Risk," *Journal of Finance*, Vol. 34 (June), pp. 577–93.

Glosten, Lawrence R., and Lawrence E. Harris, 1988, "Estimating the Components of the Bid Ask Spreads," *Journal of Financial Economics*, Vol. 21 (May), pp. 123–42.

————, and Paul R. Milgrom, 1985, "Bid, Ask and Transaction Prices in a Specialist Market with Heterogeneously Informed Traders," *Journal of Financial Economics*, Vol. 14, No. 1 (March), pp. 71–100.

Goldstein, Morris, David Folkerts-Landau, and others, 1994, *International Capital Markets: Developments, Prospects, and Policy Issues*, World Economic and Financial Surveys (Washington: International Monetary Fund).

Grossman, Sandford J., 1976, "On the Efficiency of Competitive Stock Markets Where Trades Have Diverse Information," *Journal of Finance*, Vol. 31, No. 2 (May), pp. 573–85.

————, 1992, "Informational Role of Upstairs and Downstairs Trading," *Journal of Business*, Vol. 65 (October), pp. 509–28.

————, and Merton H. Miller, 1988, "Liquidity and Market Structure," *Journal of Finance*, Vol. 43 (July), pp. 617–37.

————, and Joseph E. Stiglitz, 1980, "On the Impossibility of Informationally Efficient Markets," *American Economic Review*, Vol. 70 (June), pp. 393–408.

Hamon, Jacques, and others, 1993, "Market Structure and the Supply of Liquidity," of the New York University Salomon Center's Conference, "Global Equity Markets: Technological, Competitive and Regulatory Challenges" (October).

Harris, Lawrence, 1993, "Consolidation, Fragmentation, Segmentation, and Regulation" (unpublished), School of Business Administration, University of Southern California (May).

Ho, Thomas S.Y., and Hans R. Stoll, 1981, "Optimal Dealer Pricing Under Transactions and Return Uncertainty," *Journal of Financial Economics*, Vol. 9 (March), pp. 47–73.

————, 1983, "The Dynamics of Dealer Markets Under Competition," *Journal of Finance*, Vol. 38, No. 4 (September), pp. 1053–74.

International Organization of Securities Commissions, *Transparency on Secondary Markets—A Synthesis of the IOSCO Debate* (Milan, 1993).

Ireland, National Treasury Management Agency, 1994, *Proposals for Development of a Market Making System in Government Bonds* (June).

Jones, Frank J., and Frank J. Fabozzi, 1993, "The International Government Bond Markets," *A Probus Guide to World Markets* (Chicago: Probus Publishing Company).

Kamara, Avraham, 1988, "Market Trading Structures and Asset Pricing: Evidence from the Treasury-Bill Markets," *Review of Financial Studies*, Vol. 1 (October), pp. 357–75.

Massimb, Marcel N., and Bruce D. Phelps, 1994, "Electronic Trading, Market Structure and Liquidity," *Financial Analysts Journal*, Vol. 50 (January), No. 1 (Virginia, Association for Investment Management and Research), pp. 39–50.

McCabe, Kevin, Stephen Rassenti, and Vernon Smith, 1993, "Institutional Design for Electronic Trading," Paper presented at the New York University Saloman Center's Conference "Global Equity Markets: Technological, Competitive, and Regulatory Challenges" (October).

Neal, Robert, 1992, "Comparison of Transaction Costs Between Competitive Market Maker and Specialist Market Structures," *Journal of Business*, Vol. 65 (July), pp. 317–34.

O'Hara, Maureen, 1995, *Market Microstructure Theory* (Cambridge, Massachusetts: Blackwell).

Pagano, Marco, and Ailsa Röell, 1990, "Trading Systems in European Stock Exchanges: Current Performance and Policy Options," *Economic Policy: A European Forum*, Vol. 5 (April), pp. 65–115.

————, 1991, "Auction and Dealership Markets: What Is the Difference?" Financial Markets Group Discussion Paper No. 125 (September).

Poland Securities Commission, "Act of 22 March 1991 on Public Trading in Securities and Trust Funds (in force as of 14 February 1994)" (Warsaw: 1994).

Röell, Ailsa, 1990, "Dual-Capacity Trading and the Quality of the Market," *Journal of Financial Intermediation*, Vol. 2 (June), pp. 105–24.

Ross, Stanley, 1990, "Market-Making—A Price Too Far (III): The March of Technology," *Market-Making—A Price Too Far*, IFR (Autumn).

Scarlata, Jodi G., 1992, "Institutional Developments in the Globalization of Securities and Futures Markets," *Federal Reserve Bank of St. Louis Review*, Vol. 74 (January/February), pp. 17–30.

Schwartz, Robert O., 1991, "Reshaping the Equity Markets—A Guide for the 1990s" (New York: Harper Business).

Stoll, Hans R., 1978a, "The Supply of Dealer Services in Securities Markets," *Journal of Finance*, Vol. 33 (September), No. 4, pp. 1133–51.

————, 1978b, "The Pricing of Security Dealer Services: An Empirical Study of NASDAQ Stocks," *Journal of Finance*, Vol. 33 (September), pp. 1153–72.

————, 1985, "Alternative Views of Market Making," in *Market Making and the Changing Structure of the Securities Industry*, ed. by Amihud, Ho, and Schwartz (Lexington), pp. 67–91.

————, 1992, "Principles of Trading Market Structure," *Journal of Financial Services Research*, Vol. 6, No. 1 (May), pp. 75–106.

————, 1993, Microstructure of World Trading Markets: A Special Issue of the *Journal of Financial Services Research*, Vol. 6, No. 4 (Kluwer Academic Publishers).

Tinic, Seha M., 1972, "The Economics of Liquidity Services," *Quarterly Journal of Economics*, Vol. 86, No. 1 (February), pp. 79–93.

————, 1972, "Competition and the Pricing of Dealer Service in the Over-the-Counter Stock Market," *Journal of Financial and Quantitative Analysis*, Vol. 7 (June), pp. 1707–27.

————, 1974, "Marketability of Common Stocks in Canada and the U.S.A.: A Comparison of Agent Versus Dealer Dominated Markets," *Journal of Finance*, Vol. 29, No. 3 (June), pp. 729–46.

United States, Department of the Treasury, Securities and Exchange Commission, and Board of Governors of the Federal Reserve System, 1992, *Joint Report on the Government Securities Market*, January (Washington: Government Printing Office).

————, Securities and Exchange Commission, 1994, *Market 2000: An Examination of Current Equity Market Developments* (Washington: Government Printing Office).

Wagner, Wayne H., 1988, "The Taxonomy of Trading Strategies," *Trading Strategies and Execution Costs* (Institute of Chartered Financial Analysts), pp. 426–43.

——, and Mark Edwards, 1993, "Best Execution," *Financial Analyst Journal* (January–February), pp. 65–71.

Case Studies of
Selected Country Experiences

8

Italy: Public Debt Management and Monetary Control

*Carlo Santini**

This chapter describes the problems of monetary control faced by a country such as Italy, with long-standing, large government budget deficits and mounting public debt. It also recounts the innovations of the last few years in public debt management and traces their main consequences for monetary management and for the financial structure. It does not, however, treat what remains the crucial problem for Italian economic policy, namely, curbing the deficit itself.

Budget Deficits and Public Debt

The financing of public works and services and the development of a generous social security system in the past two decades have resulted in budget deficits that have been large both in absolute terms and in proportion to GDP. In 1980, the public sector deficit amounted to 8.6 percent of Italy's GDP (Table 1); by 1985, it had increased to 12.6 percent, the highest ratio among the major industrial countries; it has remained appreciably higher since then.

The succession of large budget deficits has resulted in the rapid growth of public debt; treasury issues have been subscribed mainly by households and nonfinancial firms. The public debt has increased from 59 percent of GDP in 1980 to 84 percent in 1985, and 123 percent at the end of 1994 (Table 2).

The budgetary measures enacted since the mid-1980s have only managed to diminish the deficit somewhat in relation to GDP. In 1992 and

---

*Carlo Santini is an Executive Director with the Bank of Italy. The views expressed here are the author's and not necessarily those of the Bank of Italy.

**Table 1. Seven Major Industrial Countries:
General Government Financial Balances**
(Surplus (+) or deficit (−) as percentage of nominal GDP)

	1980	1985	1990	1991	1992	1993	1994
United States[1]	−1.3	−3.1	−2.5	−3.2	−4.3	−3.4	−2.0
Japan	−4.4	−0.8	2.9	3.0	1.5	−1.4	−3.5
Germany	−2.9	−1.2	−2.1	−3.3	−2.9	−3.3	−2.5
France	0.0	−2.9	−1.6	−2.2	−4.0	−6.1	−6.0
Italy	−8.6	−12.6	−10.9	−10.2	−9.5	−9.6	−9.0
United Kingdom	−3.4	−2.8	−1.2	−2.6	−6.1	−7.9	−6.5
Canada	−2.8	−6.8	−4.1	−6.6	−7.1	−7.1	−5.3

Source: Based on Organization for Economic Cooperation and Development (OECD) data.
[1]Excludes deposit insurance outlays.

1993, structural reforms were enacted for the medium-term adjustment of the finances of the health care system, the social security system, and the local authorities, which have traditionally run substantial deficits that have had to be financed out of the central government budget. The measures first led to the elimination of the primary budget deficit (i.e., net of interest payments) and subsequently generated a primary surplus, so that the borrowing requirement is now lower than interest payments. In 1994, the government drew up a program for the restoration of sound public finances that envisages a reduction in the treasury's borrowing requirement to 5.6 percent of GDP in 1997 and a decline in the ratio of public debt to GDP beginning in 1996.

Since the 1970s, the mounting budget deficits have presented monetary authorities with a dilemma between monetary financing of the deficit and raising interest rates sufficiently to attract the required investment in government securities. Covering the treasury's borrowing requirement with money created by the central bank entails large and probably increasing costs for macroeconomic performance. Particularly with free capital movement and a high degree of international financial integration, monetary growth significantly outpacing an economy's capacity to supply goods and services has repercussions on the balance of payments, on the exchange rate, and above all on prices. Through its impact on the expectations and behavior of economic agents, it may result in an uncontrolled inflationary spiral.

In a pathological situation, the state could use its sovereign monetary powers to reduce the real value of its debt to the private sector; for as prices rise, the real value of nominal credits throughout the economy diminishes, impoverishing investors who have subscribed government securities. This "inflation tax" is incompatible with the maintenance of free capital markets; more important, it is arguably inconsistent with democ-

Table 2. Seven Major Industrial Countries:
General Government Gross Financial Liabilities[1]
(As percentage of nominal GDP)

	1980	1985	1990	1991	1992	1993	1994
United States	37.7	48.1	55.6	59.3	62.5	64.3	63.2
Japan	52.0	68.7	69.8	67.7	71.2	75.1	81.7
Germany	32.8	42.5	43.4	42.7	47.3	51.8	54.6
France	30.9	38.6	40.1	41.1	45.6	52.9	56.8
Italy	59.0	84.3	100.5	103.9	111.4	120.2	122.6
United Kingdom	54.1	53.4	35.0	35.5	41.4	47.4	51.6
Canada	44.3	64.7	73.1	73.1	88.2	94.0	94.6

Source: Based on OECD data.

[1] Refers to general government debt. It should be noted that the definition of debt applied under the Maastricht Treaty differs from the National Account definitions used by the OECD.

ratic principles, because it has not been enacted by any law, and is inequitable in the extreme. These aspects underscore the importance of defending the monetary yardstick, especially in modern economies characterized by very substantial financial wealth.[1]

As discussed in more detail below, in recent years Italy has relied increasingly on private saving to fund the borrowing requirement through securities issues. Since the start of the 1980s, the share of the state sector borrowing requirement covered by securities issues and other forms of private domestic saving has never been less than 70 percent and has risen steadily (Table 3). Conversely, monetary financing by the Bank of Italy was modest and declining, especially from the mid-1980s until 1990, when it ceased altogether.

Move Toward Independence in the Conduct of Monetary Policy

Since the mid-1970s, the need to control the monetary aggregates, given the expansionary fiscal policy stance, has prompted the monetary authorities to take long-term action to enhance the independence of the central bank and improve Italy's financial structure through institutional and organizational reform. Of these, one of the most important institutional measures was the so-called divorce between the treasury and the Bank of Italy in 1981. This step ended the automatic subscription by the central bank of any government securities not taken up by the public on issue. The Bank of Italy had begun to act as residual purchaser of

---

[1]On the inflation tax in Italy, see Masera (1984).

Table 3. Italy: Financing of the State Sector Borrowing Requirement
(Percentage composition)

		1980	1985	1990	1991	1992	1993	1994
Borrowing requirement of the state sector		100.00	100.00	100.00	100.00	100.00	100.00	100.00
Market subscription of government securities	(a)	-18.01	66.16	78.48	90.98	89.90	84.79	115.14
Other forms of private domestic saving	(b)	7.66	10.22	21.54	15.34	11.81	17.34	19.86
Of which:								
Post office funds		5.93	7.39	8.82	7.77	6.96	8.57	15.36
Other[1]		-0.40	0.43	2.38	3.93	4.74	1.15	-1.61
Foreign loans		2.13	2.40	10.34	3.64	0.11	7.62	6.11
Government securities and private saving (a + b)		-10.35	76.38	101.02	106.32	101.71	102.13	135.00
Net purchases of government								
Securities at issue by Bank of Italy	(c)	82.71	20.61	-2.97	-7.96	-6.04	19.22	36.28
Other borrowing from Bank of Italy	(d)	27.65	3.01	1.95	1.64	4.33	-21.25	-71.28
Monetary base (c + d)		110.36	23.62	-1.02	-6.32	-1.71	-2.13	-35.00

Source: Bank of Italy, *Relazione Annuale*, various years.
[1]Mainly lending by banks.

treasury bills in 1975 with the reform of treasury bill auctions. Bank and nonbank purchasers were allowed to participate together with the Bank of Italy. This was a first step toward allowing a crucial interest rate to be determined by market forces. However, the reform was initially subject to two major limitations: the central bank's function as residual purchaser and the treasury's setting of a floor price. These limitations put a ceiling on interest rates, thus weakening the Bank of Italy's most powerful instrument of monetary control (Caranza and Fazio (1983); Goodman (1992), pp. 169ff; Padoa-Schioppa (1987); Passacantando (1994)).

The divorce overcame only one of these limitations, and the treasury continued to set a floor price at treasury bill auctions until 1989 (Salvemini (1983)). If the price fixed by the treasury differed from that resulting from the free play of supply and demand, the Bank of Italy was obliged to choose between monetizing the debt and refusing to finance the treasury, with possibly serious consequences. Monetization was made partly automatic by the law then in force, which required the Bank of Italy to provide financing to the treasury through a special current account overdraft facility; overdrafts were limited to 14 percent of budgeted spending for the year, and only when the limit had been reached was the central bank required to suspend payments made on behalf of the treasury.[2] This actually did happen at the end of 1982; the problem was quickly solved with parliament's passage of a law requiring the Bank of Italy to grant the treasury an extraordinary advance of Lit 8 trillion for one year. This episode underscored the precariousness of the Bank's monetary control in the presence of large deficits and financial markets that were not efficient enough to meet the treasury's needs without generating excessive interest rate volatility (Eizenga (1993), pp. 16ff).

To overcome these difficulties, the monetary authorities undertook a far-reaching reform of the structure of the monetary and financial markets, essential to the achievement of the "monetary constitution" called for by Governor Carlo Azeglio Ciampi in 1981. The fundamental feature of this constitution was to be the complete independence of the monetary authority "from the agents that determine expenditures" (Bank of Italy, *Annual Report for 1980*, p. 181).

---

[2]The dilemma that the Bank of Italy might have faced was vividly described in 1974 by the Governor, Guido Carli, in the bank's *Annual Report* for 1973: "We asked ourselves then, and continue to do so, whether the Banca d'Italia could have refused, or could still refuse, to finance the public sector's deficit. . . Refusal would make it impossible for the Government to pay salaries. . . and pensions. . . It would give the appearance of being a monetary policy act; in substance it would be a seditious act, which would be followed by a paralysis of the public administration" (p. 189). In the circumstances of the time, such a declaration amounted to an appeal for the use of all economic policy instruments, first and foremost those of fiscal and budgetary policy, rather than a declaration of surrender by the central bank in the face of spiraling public deficits.

The 1980s and early 1990s saw important changes in the monetary control techniques adopted by the Bank of Italy. With the end in 1983 of a long period of administrative controls on the expansion of bank credit, greater use was made of indirect instruments, whose effectiveness depended on increasing the efficiency of the monetary and financial markets. Since 1984, the Bank of Italy has set a yearly target range for the growth of M2 as an intermediate monetary policy objective. From 1981 on, Italy's participation in the European exchange rate mechanism (ERM) implied an increasing importance of the position of the lira within the European Monetary System (EMS) fluctuation band as an indicator for monetary policy; the exchange rate discipline was not fully binding as long as exchange controls remained in place, but the constraint became tight in 1990 with the complete liberalization of capital movements and the passage of the lira from the 6 percent fluctuation band into the 2.25 percent band. The exit of the lira from the ERM in September 1992 did not alter the basic stance of monetary policy, which is still aimed at controlling inflation, but did cause a change in intermediate objectives and policy indicators. Among the latter, M2 continues to play an important role, together with the volume of credit and the exchange rate.

It was not until the start of the 1990s that conditions were appropriate for granting the Bank of Italy full control over the instruments of monetary policy. Of decisive importance was Italy's participation in the project for European economic and monetary union embodied in the Maastricht Treaty. The treaty provides for the establishment of a European system of central banks in the final stage (composed of a European central bank, which has yet to be created, and the central banks of the member states), makes price stability its primary objective, and grants it complete independence, while expressly prohibiting the monetary financing of budget deficits. Recent Italian legislation is based on the central bank model envisaged in the Maastricht Treaty.[3]

Other pivotal changes include a 1992 law establishing that the official discount rate and the rate on central bank advances shall be set independently by the Governor of the Bank of Italy; previously, the governor only proposed changes in the rates to the minister of the treasury. In addition, parliament in November 1993 replaced the treasury's current account by a new "payments account" with the Bank of Italy, accompanied by a ban on advances of any kind to the treasury. By the same law, compulsory reserve requirements were recognized as a monetary policy instrument falling under the responsibility of the Bank of Italy, within broad limits.

---

[3]See Temperton (1993), especially the essays in Parts II and III; and Padoa-Schioppa (1994).

Table 4. Italy: Composition of Government Securities

	1980	1985	1990	1991	1992	1993	1994
	(Percentage composition of outstanding stock)						
Treasury bills	53.1	34.6	32.1	29.7	29.9	27.1	25.5
Floating rate treasury credit certificates	20.3	52.5	41.3	37.5	38.2	34.9	33.7
Treasury bonds	12.4	7.2	20.1	27.4	27.5	32.2	35.6
ECU treasury credit certificates	0.0	1.6	3.7	3.5	3.6	3.4	3.4
Others	14.2	4.1	2.8	1.9	0.8	2.5	1.8
Total	100.0	100.0	100.0	100.0	100.0	100.0	100.0
	(Percentage composition of net issues)						
Treasury bills	104.6	12.4	38.8	10.9	32.6	4.8	12.8
Floating rate treasury credit certificates	11.0	73.9	47.1	7.2	43.7	7.9	25.1
Treasury bonds	−7.0	3.7	21.6	85.0	27.3	82.6	67.5
ECU treasury credit certificates	0.0	3.4	6.2	1.3	0.2	−0.5	1.8
Others	−8.7	6.6	−3.7	−4.4	−3.9	5.2	−7.1
Total	100.0	100.0	100.0	100.0	100.0	100.0	100.0

Source: Bank of Italy, *Relazione Annuale,* various years.

Previously, most changes in the reserve requirement called for a decision by the Interministerial Committee for Credit and Savings.

The abolition of the current account enabled the Bank of Italy to reform the compulsory reserve system. In the 1980s, compulsory reserves had acted as an instrument for the automatic absorption of monetary base created by the treasury outside the central bank's control through the discretionary use of its overdraft facility (Bank of Italy, *Economic Bulletin* (1994)). In May 1994, the Bank of Italy reduced the reserve coefficients with the aim of reducing the implicit cost of reserves for the banking system.

Reform of the Monetary and Financial Markets

The steady improvement in the treasury's ability to finance its borrowing requirement through recourse to private sector savings would not have been possible if the monetary authorities had not undertaken a radical restructuring and modernization of the monetary and financial markets. Specifically, organizational measures in the sphere of public debt management have modified the kinds of instruments offered and the arrangements in both the primary and secondary markets.

For many years, the most commonly held type of government paper was represented by floating rate treasury credit certificates, which now account for about 34 percent of total outstanding government securities (Table 4).

These were first issued in 1977, at a time when high and variable inflation discouraged subscriptions of fixed rate paper. Offering a coupon equal to the rate on 12-month treasury bills plus a spread, the certificates enabled households to invest in a financial asset sheltered against inflation and short-term real interest rate variations. While lengthening the average maturity of the public debt, the treasury could finance the deficit at a cost that would diminish with the reduction in inflation and the lowering of interest rates. In the first half of the 1980s, the certificates were by far the most widely held security issued by the treasury (Table 4). However, the large share of debt indexed to short-term interest rates—plus the large volume of treasury bills with maturities of 3, 6, and 12 months—set constraints on central bank action. Under such conditions, rises in short-term rates—as part of anti-inflationary policy—will have virtually immediate repercussions on the cost of servicing the public debt, exacerbating the conflict between the goal of price stability and that of containing the burden of interest payments.

In the medium term, resolution of this potential conflict demands measures to curb the borrowing requirement and to establish the conditions for sustainability of the public debt and long-term price stability. Only then, in fact, can there be large-scale, continuing reliance on the most appropriate instrument for financing the borrowing requirement, namely, long-term, fixed rate treasury bonds. These securities, which have been issued at a variety of maturities since the turn of the century, suffered severe capital losses during the 1970s with the rise in prices and in interest rates. From the mid-1970s onward, accordingly, their share in total net issues declined in favor of short-term and floating rate instruments. Since 1986, disinflation and the powerful emergence of institutional investors have made it possible to increase bond issues with longer maturities. Issues of treasury bonds were still negligible in 1985 but have since expanded significantly, in line with the moderation of inflation and the decline in interest rates. In 1991, for the first time in 40 years, fixed rate 10-year bonds were issued; in 1993, for the first time ever, 30-year bonds were launched, with success.

At the turn of the 1980s, in order to reduce servicing costs and lengthen the maturity of the debt, the range of securities offered to the market was further diversified. The launching of treasury certificates with variable coupons in 1977 was followed in 1982 by a second significant innovation, namely, the issue of certificates denominated in ECUs, fixed rate instruments with maturities between three and eight years. In 1987, these were joined by 12-month treasury bills in ECUs. For a time, these issues provided a reduction on interest expenditure, since their corresponding yields, even corrected for exchange rate changes, were lower than rates on lira-denominated instruments. These favorable conditions have clearly been altered by the foreign exchange crisis of 1992.

As a result of these innovations, the composition of the public debt was profoundly modified toward longer maturities. The average residual maturity on government securities rose from about a year in 1980 to three years in 1992, but it is still too short, requiring gross monthly issues equivalent to between 4 percent of GDP and 5 percent of GDP.

Monetary policy must, therefore, make sure that the interest rate structure is compatible with the placement of this large volume of securities, on penalty of losing control of the monetary aggregates, and possibly very quickly indeed. Monetary control in the short term, which the Bank of Italy accomplishes mainly through repurchase agreements and currency swaps, primarily influences the overnight rate in the interbank market. Since 1990, this rate has served as an indicator of the monetary policy stance and consequently as a reference rate for both individual and professional investors participating in auctions in the primary market for government securities (Angeloni (1994)).

Important innovations were also introduced in issuing techniques. Since 1988, medium- and long-term government securities have no longer been sold at a fixed price but by uniform-price (or Dutch) auction, in which all securities are awarded at the lowest bid accepted. Since 1990, treasury bonds have been issued in tranches at regular intervals, with the aim of enhancing their liquidity. Finally, in 1992 the auction floor price was replaced by a stop-out mechanism that excludes outlier bids while avoiding undue rigidities in the auction mechanism. The tender method for treasury bills is the competitive bid auction, with each successful bidder paying his bid price (Buttiglione and Drudi (1994)).

Orders for treasury securities from domestic and foreign savers and investors are mainly channeled through banks and securities firms, which participate directly in the auctions; tender prices are normally in line with those on the secondary market. Since mid-1994, treasury bond auctions have been run by an automated system, which has improved reliability and speed of communication. With a view to stabilizing market expectations, in 1994 the treasury began to make quarterly announcements of the intended issue volume of all the main types of securities. The financial characteristics of the principal government securities and the auction methods by which they are issued are detailed in Table 5.

One necessary condition for regularly placing large amounts of securities is an efficient and liquid secondary market. The chief organizational measure in this regard was the creation of the screen-based wholesale market for government securities in 1988. The wholesale market flanks the stock exchange, where small-lot trading continues, and enables institutional investors to effect large transactions in government securities, improving the efficiency of trading and portfolio management.

Table 5. Italy: Issuing Conditions of Government Securities

Type of Issue	Treasury Bills	Zero-Coupon Treasury Certificates	Treasury Bonds	Treasury Credit Certificates	ECU Treasury Certificates
Currency of denomination	Lira	Lira	Lira	Lira	ECU
Initial maturity	3, 6, 12 months	2 years	3, 5, 10, 30 years	7 years	3, 5 years
Coupon frequency	No coupon	No coupon	Semiannual	Semiannual	Annual
Coupon type	Zero coupon	Zero coupon	Fixed	Indexed to 12-month treasury bill + spread (0.30%)	Fixed
Issue method	Competitive bid auction	Uniform-price auction	Uniform-price auction	Uniform-price auction	Uniform-price auction
Type of bid	On price	On price	On price	On price	On price
Commission fee paid by treasury	No	0.25%	0.35% (3 yrs) 0.60% (5–10–30 yrs)	0.60%	0.35%
Date of issue	Middle and end of month	Middle and end of month	Beginning and middle of month	Beginning and middle of month	Variable
Form	Bearer	Bearer	Bearer or registered	Bearer	Bearer or registered
Withholding tax	12.50% on interest (in advance)	12.50% on premium at maturity	12.50% on coupon and on premium at maturity	12.50% on coupon and on premium at maturity	12.50% on coupon and on premium at maturity
Minimum amount	Lit 5,000,000	Lit 5,000,000	Lit 5,000,000	Lit 5,000,000	ECU 5,000
Listing:					
Stock exchange	No	Yes	Yes	Yes	Yes
Screen-based market	Yes	Yes	Yes	Yes	Yes
Over the counter	Yes	Yes	Yes	Yes	Yes

Source: Bank of Italy.

At the beginning of 1995, the screen-based market counted 319 Italian and foreign participants, including 30 primary dealers who are committed to quote continuous firm bid and offer prices on an assigned range of securities. The 99 securities listed are mostly treasury certificates and treasury bonds. Daily turnover amounted to over Lit 15 trillion (about $9 billion) in the second half of 1994.

To improve liquidity and efficiency, a major overhaul of the secondary market for treasury bonds was undertaken in the early part of 1994. This included the remote access of nonresident participants and the creation of a new category of market participants called "specialists." The specialists are market-makers who undertake to effect transactions equivalent to a minimum share of the primary and secondary market; they are, at the same time, the only market participants that have access to the reopening of treasury bond auctions.[4] At the beginning of 1995, there were 12 specialists.

The diffusion of fixed rate paper among Italian and foreign investors has been facilitated by the introduction of futures contracts on five- and ten-year treasury bonds, first on the London International Financial Futures Exchange (LIFFE, 1991) and subsequently (1992) on the Italian financial futures market (MIF). The futures market permits professional portfolio managers to hedge interest rate risks and consequently enhances the depth and liquidity of the cash market. Unlike LIFFE, MIF uses a screen-based system and has primary dealers who continuously quote prices and guarantee liquidity. The market for treasury securities was completed in 1994 with the introduction of trading in options on futures contracts. Trading in futures contracts on treasury bonds has greatly benefited the cash market, with a growth in volume, a narrowing of the bid-offer spread, and an appreciable reduction in price volatility.

Italy's Financial Structure

The public sector deficit has powerfully affected the Italian financial structure. Without attempting to offer a comprehensive explanation for the evolution of the financial flows between households, firms, intermediaries, and the public sector in recent years, we can safely say that the saving rate of the Italian household sector, which although declining remains one of the highest in the industrial world (Table 6), has attenuated the adverse repercussions of the expansion of the public debt on economic growth.[5] Nonetheless, the destruction of savings by the public sector

---

[4]The treasury reopens each issue, for a maximum amount of 10 percent, at a fixed price equal to the one resulting from the auction.

[5]On Italy's high saving rate and on the interrelations between the saving rate and government deficit in Italy, see the essays by L. Guiso, T. Jappelli, and D. Terlizzese, and by N. Rossi and I. Visco, in Ando, Guiso, and Visco (1994).

Table 6. Major Industrial Countries: Household Saving Rates
(Percentage of disposable household income)

	1980	1985	1990	1991	1992	1993	1994
United States	8.1	6.6	4.3	5.1	5.2	5.2	4.2
Japan	17.9	15.6	14.1	15.1	14.3	15.0	14.9
Germany	12.8	11.4	13.8	12.7	12.9	12.9	11.0
France	17.6	14.0	12.5	13.2	13.9	13.7	13.5
Italy	23.0	18.9	18.2	18.2	17.4	15.7	15.0
United Kingdom	13.4	10.7	8.4	10.5	12.8	11.7	10.4
Canada	13.6	13.3	9.7	9.6	9.8	9.2	7.6

Source: Based on OECD data.

deficit has reduced the amount of private investment that could be financed without generating unsustainable balance of payment deficits. After several years of moderate but steady deficits, a surplus in the current account of the balance of payments reappeared only in 1993 and 1994, following the depreciation of the lira and a severe economic recession.

The most important change in Italy's financial structure in the last decade was the growth in the share of government securities held by households. At the beginning of the 1980s, households held 34.5 percent of the outstanding stock of government securities, while the banking system held 42 percent and the Bank of Italy, 18 percent (Table 7). In 1990, the household sector's share had risen to 67 percent, those of the banks and the Bank of Italy having fallen to 15 percent and 6 percent, respectively.

A considerable portion of households' savings is invested in treasury bills. Given their liquidity, these short-term instruments represent the closest substitute for bank deposits, whose share in households' financial assets fell from about 60 percent to 32 percent between 1980 and 1990. This shift was due to a yield differential in favor of treasury bills, as well as to the introduction of new public debt instruments, as mentioned above. In recent years, households have also become major holders of long-term securities.

A further characteristic of Italy's financial structure in recent years has been the growing volume of international capital movements. This development is rooted in important institutional and market factors. The chief institutional event was the foreign exchange liberalization that Italy initiated in the second half of the 1980s and completed in 1990, which gave rise to growing Italian investment abroad but also strengthened capital inflows. Another institutional factor contributing to the inflow of foreign capital—and to the financing of the borrowing requirement—was the treasury's introduction of Euromarket issues in the second half of the 1980s.

Table 7. Holders of Italian Government Securities
(Percentage composition of outstanding stocks)

	1980	1985	1990	1991	1992	1993	1994
Bank of Italy	18.12	11.43	6.35	5.60	6.30	6.47	11.70
Banks	43.54	31.51	15.58	18.47	20.47	19.68	19.54
Household	32.73	51.31	67.24	63.53	59.56	54.54	50.49
Nonresidents	3.00	1.37	4.03	4.83	5.83	10.90	9.95
Investment funds	0.00	2.23	2.30	2.66	2.54	3.29	3.21
Others	2.61	2.16	4.51	4.91	5.31	5.12	5.11
Total	100.00	100.00	100.00	100.00	100.00	100.00	100.00

Source: Bank of Italy, *Relazione Annuale,* various years.

In the mid-1980s, the share of issues of Italian government securities held abroad was less than 1 percent (Table 7). By 1991, the choices available to foreign investors had broadened markedly, thanks to the new types of instruments offered and the opening up of the financial market. In 1991, nonresidents held about 4.5 percent of the total volume of Italian government securities, and by the end of 1993, the share had grown to 11 percent, with a preference for treasury bonds and ECU-denominated securities.

The liberalization of capital movements and the consequent opening of the Italian financial market have heightened the importance of the international dimension of monetary control. Although Italy has had no formal exchange rate commitments since the autumn of 1992, owing to their influence on inflation, the exchange rate retains an important role among monetary policy indicators; this implies a link between monetary policy in Italy and that in other leading countries.

Exchange liberalization and its consequences have increased the need for market supervision measures that, within the framework of growing international coordination, ensure the transmission of monetary policy impulses and the stability of the system. The capital base of intermediaries has been strengthened; prudential supervision has been extended to nonbank intermediaries, for which minimum capital ratios have been set; and initiatives have been undertaken to improve the efficiency and security of the payment system (Majnoni, Rebecchini, and Santini (1992)).

In a broader perspective, the growing external openness of the Italian financial market and its international integration make it all the more imperative to bring the budget deficit under control and to pursue a monetary policy of stability, in line with that of Italy's principal partners. In other words, it is necessary to strengthen the conditions of stability and confidence that can foster the formation of saving and enable Italy to share the gains in efficiency associated with the free movement not only of goods and services but also of capital.

Table 8. Yield Differentials Between Italian and German Long-Term Government Securities[1]

	Italian Yield	German Yield	Differential
1989	13.82	7.05	6.77
1990	14.53	8.82	5.71
1991	13.17	8.55	4.62
1992	13.28	7.86	5.42
1993			
Average	11.29	6.44	4.85
Dec. 93	8.84	5.70	3.14
1994			
Average	10.55	6.98	3.57
Dec. 94	12.25	7.68	4.57

Sources: Bank of Italy; Bank for International Settlements.
[1]As of December 13.

In effect, in the three years from 1989 to 1991, which were marked by foreign exchange stability and strong expectations of Italian economic adjustment, foreign purchases of Italian securities were accompanied by a narrowing of the yield differential between Italian and German long-term government paper from about 6.7 percentage points to 4.6 percentage points (Table 8). With the inflation rate holding steady at about 6 percent, this reflected a decline in the real yield demanded by the market for Italian government securities, which fell to below 5 percent, and substantial alignment with the real rates on French and German bonds. This trend was interrupted in 1992 by the rise in interest rates needed to counter foreign exchange tensions, and again in the second half of 1994 when political uncertainties translated into a higher risk premium on Italian government securities.

Conclusions

Several lessons are to be drawn from Italy's experience in financing the budget deficit and managing the public debt. First, the course of events demonstrates the usefulness of developing efficient money and financial markets in which professional investors operate, subject to supervision to ensure stability and transparency. It also shows the desirability of offering a range of financial instruments capable of satisfying the different needs and preferences of savers and institutional investors. The soundness of intermediaries, the efficiency of markets, and the diversification of financial instruments facilitate the flow of private savings to the treasury, and the integration of the domestic market with those abroad reduce the cost of financing and assist monetary policy in achieving its stability objectives.

Nonetheless, persistent budget deficits and increasing debt create mounting difficulties for monetary control. In these circumstances, a rate of money creation compatible with price stability requires higher interest rates, which tend to penalize productive investment, curtail the growth of income and employment, and aggravate the public deficit itself because of the increasing burden of interest payments. On the other hand, lowering interest rates to alleviate the burden of debt would lead to excessive money creation, depreciation of the currency, and inflation.

This conflict cannot be overcome without action to restore sound public finances, first stabilizing and then reducing the ratio of public debt to GDP.

Bibliography

Ando, Albert, Luigi Guiso, and Ignacio Visco, eds., 1994, *Saving and the Accumulation of Wealth: Essays on Italian Household and Government Saving Behavior* (Cambridge, England: Cambridge University Press).

Angeloni, Ignazio, 1994, "The Bank of Italy Monthly Money Market Model: Structure and Applications," *Economic Modelling*, Vol. 11 (October), pp. 387–412.

Bank of Italy, *Annual Report for 1973* (Rome).

———, *Annual Report for 1980*, abridged version in English (Rome).

———, 1994, "The Recent Reform of the Reserve Requirement," in *Economic Bulletin*, No. 19 (October).

Buttiglione, L., and F. Drudi, 1994, "The Auction Mechanism for the Settlement of Medium and Long-Term Securities of the Italian Treasury," in *Bond Markets, Treasury, and Debt Management: The Italian Case*, ed. by V. Conti, R. Hamani, and H.M. Scobie (London: Chapman & Hall).

Caranza, Cesare, and Antonio Fazio, 1983, "Methods of Monetary Control in Italy, 1974–1983," in *The Political Economy of Monetary Policy: National and International Aspects*, Conference Series No. 26, ed. by Donald R. Hodgman (Boston: Federal Reserve Bank of Boston, July).

Eizenga, W., 1993, "The Banca d'Italia and Monetary Policy," SUERF Papers on Monetary Policy and Financial System, No. 15 (Tilburg).

Goodman, John B., 1992, *Monetary Sovereignty: The Politics of Central Banking in Western Europe* (Ithaca: Cornell University Press).

Majnoni, G., S. Rebecchini, and C. Santini, 1992, "Monetary Integration versus Financial Market Integration," in *The New European Financial Market Place*, compiled by Alfred Steinherr (London; New York: Longman).

Masera, Rainer S., 1984, "Monetary Policy and Budget Policy: Blend or Dichotomy?" in *Europe's Money: Problems of European Monetary Coordination and Integration*, ed. by Rainer S. Masera and Robert Triffin (Oxford; New York: Oxford University Press, Clarendon Press).

Padoa-Schioppa, Tommaso, 1987, "Reshaping Monetary Policy," in *Macroeconomics and Finance: Essays in Honor of Franco Modigliani*, ed. by Rudiger Dornbusch and Stanley Fischer (Cambridge, Massachusetts: MIT Press).

———, 1994, *The Road to Monetary Union in Europe: The Emperor, the Kings, and the Genies* (Oxford: Clarendon Press).

Passacantando, Franco, 1994, "Monetary Reforms and Monetary Policy in Italy from 1979 to 1994," in *Proceedings of the Conference on the Quest for Monetary Stability*, Fundacao Getulio Vargas, Rio de Janeiro (September).

Salvemini, Maria-Teresa, 1983, "The Treasury and the Money Market: The New Responsibilities After the Divorce," *Review of Economic Conditions in Italy*, No. 1 (February), pp. 33–54.

Temperton, P., ed., 1993, *The European Currency Crisis: What Chance Now for a Single European Currency?* (Chicago: Probus Publishing Company).

9

United Kingdom: Coordination Between Public Debt Management and Monetary Policy

*John Townend**

The countries of the Organization for Economic Cooperation and Development (OECD) do not all manage their public debt and monetary policy in the same way but rather follow a range of models, each with advantages and disadvantages. This chapter discusses the general case for coordination between monetary policy and debt management, focusing in particular on the theory and practice governing the design and implementation of these policies and on how the institutional arrangements in the United Kingdom facilitate quick and effective coordination.

The following fundamental objectives may be ascribed to debt management policy:

- To meet the government's need for finance in the most cost-effective way.
- To support the government's monetary policy. This is not an explicit objective in every OECD member country. However, debt management policy has implications for monetary conditions. A strong case can be made that integrating strategic decisions in these two areas improves macroeconomic management.
- To avoid disruption to the financial markets. This objective will, in practice and in the long term, contribute to the fulfillment of the first objective: cost-effective funding will generally be promoted by stable market conditions. It is, however, an important consideration in its own right. Financial markets are closely interlinked; a disturbance in

---

*The author is Deputy Director of the Bank of England.

one market may lead to rapid price movements or systemic distur-bances in another market. In order to reduce the risk that debt oper-ations may cause disruption in other markets, continuous and effec-tive day-to-day, tactical coordination is required between those official agencies operating in all the markets in which the authorities are active.

Monetary Policy and Funding Policy: Theory and U.K. Experience

Let us begin by considering the fundamental link between the govern-ment deficit (broadly defined to include all public sector activities, i.e., those of the central government plus state-owned corporations and local authorities) and monetary conditions. Any excess of public sector expen-diture over revenue implies ex ante an equivalent addition to private sec-tor liquidity. The final economic impact will depend on how the deficit is financed, and in particular whether the financing method offsets the in-crease in private sector liquidity.

The public sector borrowing requirement in any given period, plus any outstanding public debt maturing in that period, may be financed by:

- net sales of *marketable* government debt[1] to the private sector (to nonbanks or to banks);
- net sales of *nonmarketable* government debt to the private sector (in the United Kingdom, this chiefly takes the form of "National Savings," comprising various nonnegotiable instruments sold to the public and savings accounts held by them);
- borrowing from the commercial banks;
- selling foreign currency reserves and using the domestic currency proceeds; and
- borrowing from the central bank, which implies an increase in *high-powered money*—either additional currency in the hands of the public, or an increase in commercial bank balances at the central bank.

This last possibility, that a public sector deficit may result in an increase in the monetary base, is of grave importance. Monetary theory teaches that increased currency in the hands of the public will lead to an increase in nominal demand until real balances have returned to their equilibrium level. If it is assumed that real output is fixed, this will occur by means of a rise in the price level. Similarly, if the reserve balances of commercial banks at the central bank increase above the level that the banks require, or wish, to

---

[1]Naturally, sales of debt of local authorities or state enterprises, and bank borrowing by these institu-tions, are included within these definitions.

hold, an ex ante increase in commercial bank lending may result, producing a further increase in private sector liquidity, and a further expansion of nominal demand. This process is likely to have serious potential consequences for inflation. For this reason, central bank financing of the public sector is outlawed for European Union countries under the Maastricht Treaty.

If the public sector deficit is fixed in the short term, how is central bank financing, with its inflationary risks, to be avoided? First of all, the quantity of maturing debt is also outside the government's control in the short term. (In the medium term, it will depend in part on the *maturity* of previous government borrowing: heavy reliance on short-term debt entails a more rapid rollover of debt and, hence, a higher total financing requirement in succeeding periods.) The extent to which the public sector deficit can be financed by selling foreign currency reserves is limited: the reserves will eventually be depleted; and the government may have a target for the reserves, for example, where an International Monetary Fund program is in place. Governments, therefore, face a choice between borrowing from the commercial banks and selling marketable or nonmarketable debt to the nonbank private sector. In the United Kingdom, the government issues special forms for nonmarketable debt, called National Savings, designed to attract household investors. They make a useful contribution to meeting the funding requirement, but the bulk of the funding to be done is accomplished through sales of marketable debt—"gilts" or "gilt-edged securities" in U.K. terminology. This instrument is more flexible than National Savings, on which changes to the terms of investment to attract larger or smaller flows of funds are made only infrequently.

Borrowing from commercial banks, whether through selling debt instruments to them or by using overdraft facilities, represents an increase in bank assets. This, in turn, represents a counterpart to broad money.[2] Other things being equal, this represents an increase in liquidity in the economy, and hence a possible source of pressure on nominal demand and potentially on inflation. From 1976 onward, counterinflationary policy in the United Kingdom placed explicit emphasis on controlling growth in broad money. Under the Medium-Term Financial Strategy (MTFS), first introduced in 1980, debt management policy assisted the pursuit of the broad money target; at times, more debt was sold outside the banking sector than was required to finance the pubic sector deficit, taking account of changes in the foreign exchange reserves. Such "overfunding" had the effect of reducing the commercial banks' claims on the government.

---

[2]The broad money aggregate, M4, which is monitored in the United Kingdom, is conventionally measured in terms of commercial bank and building society *liabilities*. Assets and liabilities will, over the medium term, tend to rise or fall in parallel; the counterparts to M4, which represent lending by banks and building societies, are also closely monitored by the authorities.

By the mid-1980s, inflation had fallen from the high levels observed in the 1970s, even though the broad money targets set in the MTFS had frequently been overshot, while the relationship between broad money and nominal GDP appeared to have broken down. Broad money ceased to be the intermediate policy target, although the government continued—and continues—to monitor developments in broad money. Moreover, the overfunding that had taken place drained liquidity from the banking system and necessitated a high level of central bank refinancing. This led to distortions in the market for commercial bills—the instruments predominantly used in our money market operations.

Funding policy ceased to be directed toward influencing broad money growth. Instead, a so-called Full Fund policy was adopted, by which the public sector borrowing requirement (PSBR), plus maturing debt and any net increase in the foreign exchange reserves, were to be offset by debt sales to nonbanks. (This meant that the government's financial transactions had *no* net effect on the commercial banks' balance sheets.) By deducting the contribution of National Savings, a target figure for sales of marketable debt to nonbanks was derived. This ensured that the government's debt management policy did not interfere with monetary policy; no net increase in the liquidity of the nonbank private sector should therefore result from the financial activities of the government.

There is some room for debate as to whether the sector—bank or nonbank private sector—to which government debt is sold is ultimately of importance. Net commercial bank purchases of government debt represent a rise in the counterparts to broad money. It is not absolutely clear that a proportional rise in liquidity in the economy will occur; for example, commercial banks may scale back their lending to the private sector to buy government debt (put another way, banks may be most inclined to buy government debt when alternative lending propositions are scarce). Government debt is, in general, a highly liquid asset, and banks may sell their holdings to enhance their reserves or to increase their ability to lend. However, when they sell debt to the private sector, this naturally drains private sector liquidity and so works to offset the effect of nominal demand on any additional lending they undertake. In 1993, the United Kingdom adjusted the Full Fund policy so as not to exclude purchases of government debt by banks and building societies from counting as funding. Provided that there is no long-term trend in holdings of government debt by banks and building societies, this will not affect the total amount of funding, but it will probably help to smooth the pattern of liquidity growth through the economic cycle by reducing the amount of funding undertaken in recessions, when banks are most likely to buy government debt in preference to lending to the private sector, and increasing the amount of funding when the economy is more buoyant.

Implementation of Debt Management Policy: The Links with Monetary Policy

A sale of government debt into the private sector entails a transfer of funds from the private sector into government accounts when the deal is settled. Other things being equal, this creates a shortage in the money market on the day of settlement, which needs to be offset by the central bank's operations. The period in which the additional refinancing would have to be provided depends on money market arrangements; in the United Kingdom, refinancing needs to be provided on the day a deal in government securities is settled; in systems in which bank reserves are averaged, it is sufficient for the central bank to provide refinancing within the same reserve maintenance period. As the government spends the funds raised via the sale of debt, the stock of refinancing provided by the central bank can be run down.

It is desirable to try to minimize the strain caused by issues of government securities on monetary operations, in the interests of maintaining stable short-term interest rates in the money market. This, in turn, enables investors buying government debt to finance their purchases with confidence. Careful coordination can contribute to smooth handling of the money market consequences of debt management operations in various ways.

Debt Issue Techniques

In the United Kingdom, government debt has, on occasion, been issued partly paid, that is, only part of the price is paid at issue with a further payment, or payments, to be made to the government at a subsequent date or dates. The strain on the money market posed by a large debt issue, for example an auction, is thereby spread across two or more individual days, which will usually be at least one month apart. And although the United Kingdom uses a program of auctions to sell large blocks of stock into the market, it also makes full use of the flexibility afforded by "tap" sales, whereby smaller blocks of one or more stocks held in official portfolios are sold into the market in response to demand. Of course, the main objective of this method is to secure a good price for the government while promoting market stability. But the technique also tends to spread the creation of money market shortages over several days.

Timing of Gilt-Edged and Money Market Operations

Although the U.K. authorities do not have a fixed timetable of debt auctions, they have—and they convey to the market—a broad idea of the frequency and size of auctions in each financial year, depending naturally on the overall size of the funding requirement. At the same time, several other factors affecting money market conditions are known in advance or can be predetermined. For example, days on which large tax payments are due, and days on which calls from previous auctions are due, are known in advance. The influence of the daily fluctuations of banknotes in circulation is known; this has the effect of tightening monetary conditions on the last working day of each week and easing conditions on the first working day. Finance provided by the Bank of England to the money market frequently takes the form of sale and repurchase (repo) agreements over a fixed period of two or more weeks, so that the dates on which such assistance matures are known well in advance.[3]

All this information enables the Bank of England to plan debt and money market operations so as to even out the pattern of shortages from day to day to some extent, and so to help reduce the volatility of very short-term interest rates. For example, calls on government debt are not usually made on a Friday, when the market is likely to be short. Bill repo maturity dates may be chosen so as not to clash with auction settlement or call dates. When responsibility for debt management and monetary operations is combined in one unit, this planning is easily accomplished.

Debt Management and Monetary Policy Signals

One important function of monetary operations is the signal that is given to the market and hence to other agents in the economy. Operations in government debt, and in particular the maturity mix of the stocks to be brought to the market, should be executed bearing in mind the effect that they may have in supporting or contradicting the monetary policy signal. For example, if the yield curve in government securities is upward sloping, there is an implication that the market expects interest rates to rise in future years.[4] A government with a strong commitment to a low inflation target would expect interest rates in the medium- and long-term to fall. It might, therefore, seem inconsistent with a cost-effective debt issue strategy to issue long-term debt in such circumstances. Either short-term debt

---

[3]In its daily operations, the bank may offer bill repo finance over a period of two to three weeks; and twice a month, its Repo Facility offers gilt repo finance for periods of two to three and four to five weeks (at the option of the borrower).

[4]In some circumstances, the upward slope may reflect a risk premium. It is generally the case that the price of longer-term fixed coupon bonds is more volatile than that of shorter-dated or floating rate bonds, and investors will expect a higher yield in return for the higher price risk. It is not clear that this has a strong empirical justification nowadays in countries where the main investors are institutions with very long-term obligations, but may well still apply where investment in government debt is primarily undertaken by individuals.

should be issued, in the expectation of rolling over the debt at lower yields in later years, or index-linked debt may be sold. In practice, there are counterarguments: first, heavy reliance on the issue of short-term debt may lead the market to believe that the government will be reluctant to raise short-term interest rates, because of the debt-service implications, and this may undermine the credibility of the counterinflationary policy; second, large-scale issuance of short-term debt may create difficulties in later periods when a large volume of maturing debt produces a larger financing requirement; and third, and in particular if the initial financing requirement is relatively large, there may be advantages in issuing a balanced range of stocks so as to capture demand from investors with different maturity preferences. All these arguments need to be weighed in the balance in debt management strategy, and they should not be considered in isolation from the monetary policy implications.

Influence of Monetary Policy on Debt Management

The influence of government debt operations on money market conditions is self-evident, given the size of debt auctions in many industrial countries relative to the day-to-day surpluses and shortages that may arise in the money markets for other reasons. It is equally clear that money market conditions may affect the success of debt management operations. Market-makers and investors alike sacrifice the chance to lend money, or incur the need to borrow it, when holding government bonds. Monetary policy changes involving a change in short-term interest rates affect rates further along the yield curve. But so also may day-to-day conditions in markets. Both should be taken into account when considering the timing of auctions and the choice of stock to be brought there.

It is important to recognize that cost-effective debt management depends on the long-run experience of participants in the government bond market. No doubt individual issues of stock could be sold more cheaply by manipulating monetary policy immediately before the issue. In the medium term, this would not be a successful practice. A key element in successful debt management is to provide, so far as is consistent with the aims of monetary policy, stable and predictable conditions for debt issuance. This may entail trying to avoid violent movement in interest rates immediately before or after large stock issues. To change rates immediately after an issue may leave the market with the impression of having been deceived. Changes before an issue avoid that risk and may in certain circumstances be necessary, but are likely to distribute windfall gains and losses among those holding long and short positions in advance of the issue, even though, in London at least, there are excellent opportunities to hedge exposures in the cash markets by taking appropriate positions in derivatives markets.

These considerations relate to large, planned issues of government debt and should be distinguished from those that apply to U.K. tap issues. If economic indicators or a change in money market conditions— including policy-induced interest rate changes—bring about an increase in demand for government debt, whether at one maturity or across the curve, it is entirely appropriate to bring debt for sale if that is consistent with the overall funding strategy. The market is able to predict stock issuance of this kind, and the issues contribute to the stability and liquidity of the market, in turn virtues that contribute to the long-term attractiveness of government debt and hence the cost-effectiveness of debt management.

Institutional Arrangements

Ultimate responsibility for public debt management in the United Kingdom rests with the treasury, which has discretion with regard to the timing and method of debt issue and the choice of stocks issued. The Bank of England advises the treasury on these issues and conducts operations in the market for government securities on behalf of the treasury. Within the bank, the Gilt-Edged and Money Markets Division conducts these operations. Since March 1994, these operations have been conducted under the terms of an annual, published Remit set by the Chancellor of the Exchequer.

As its title suggests, the Gilt-Edged and Money Markets Division also has the responsibility for day-to-day implementation of monetary policy. This division, together with the Foreign Exchange Division and the Wholesale Markets Supervision Division, which is responsible for prudential supervision of the main players in the gilt market and the discount houses (the specialized intermediaries in the money market), and certain other firms active in the wholesale money markets, ultimately report to one Executive Director of the bank.

Experience shows this to be a highly advantageous arrangement, both in terms of the smooth coordination of policy and the most efficient deployment of staff resources. Many international and domestic economic, financial, and political developments affect all the markets in which the bank is active—government debt, foreign exchange, and money markets. Analytical work carried out elsewhere in the bank may similarly have a bearing on all three markets. It is, therefore, economical and efficient to have one closely integrated group of staff responsible for the operations in each market. When confronted with an external shock, or with an unexpected development in one of the markets, the staff is able to consider all the implications simultaneously and to discuss the situation as necessary with one single set of counterparties at the treasury. Similarly, the division and its directors conduct a continuous dialogue with the main participants in the government debt and money markets, so enabling it to convey the objectives of policy to the marketplace and also ensuring that the views of the markets and an understanding of their workings can be taken into account in policy implementation when appropriate. There are close linkages between the markets in monetary instruments and negotiable government debt instruments, and the division's interlocutors expect the dialogue regarding issues in either market to be fully informed regarding the other.

Conclusion

This description of the interlinkages in policy implementation between debt management and monetary operations will be familiar to many, especially in theory. The fundamental point to be stressed is that this coordination is accomplished easily when both functions are performed by the same group of people, responding in each market to the same external events. It would be far more difficult, more time-consuming, and more resource-intensive if continuous liaison between separate debt management and monetary teams were necessary.

* * *

Editors' Note

John C. Townend's chapter, "United Kingdom: Coordination Between Public Debt Management and Monetary Policy," was written in July 1993. In 1994, a major review of debt management practices in the United Kingdom was begun and in July 1995, Her Majesty's Treasury and the Bank of England published jointly a Report on the Debt Management Review. The review resulted in new policy objectives, institutional arrangements, and initiatives to improve the efficiency and liquidity of the gilt-edged securities market.

Mr. Townend's paper continues to provide the basic rationale for and a good example of close coordination of debt management policy with monetary policy and for locating debt management functions within the central bank. Moreover, the institutional framework for coordinating monetary and public debt management has, de facto, remained unchanged. On the other hand, the review has resulted in a number of important policy changes and changes in operating arrangements. These changes are, to a large extent, a response to developments in the United Kingdom and international capital markets. The main changes and initiatives are summarized and highlighted in this note.

Restatement of the Objectives of Debt Management

Prior to the review, a formal statement of the U.K. Government's objectives for debt management policy was set out in the Financial Statement and Budget Report for 1990–91: "(1) to support and complement monetary policy; (2) subject to (1), to avoid distorting financial markets; and (3) subject to (1) and (2), to fund at least cost and risks." To reflect current practices and policy objectives, the review restates the debt management objectives, changing the hierarchy as follows: *"The objective of debt management policy is to minimize over the longer term the cost of meeting the Government's financing needs, taking into account risk, while ensuring that debt management policy is consistent with monetary policy."*

This restatement reduces the priority of and emphasis on monetary policy and market stability considerations, although the goal of ensuring consistency between debt management and monetary policy is explicitly mentioned. In addition, beginning in 1996/97, the government's "Full Funding" policy will include short-term securities—the issuance of treasury bills and gilts of less than three years to maturity—providing greater flexibility in meeting debt management objectives using these instruments (as discussed in the chapter, they had been excluded from Full Funding so as to limit holdings of highly liquid money-like assets—a monetary policy consideration—and to encourage conservative funding practices).

Greater Emphasis on Predictability and Transparency of Debt Issuance

- Each financial year (beginning in March 1996), the government will release an annual *Debt Management Report* that will detail financing requirements (as well as the indicated sales split between gilts, National Savings, and other sources) and a calendar of auction dates and the maturity structure of gilt issuance (approximate proportions of index-linked and short-, medium-, and long-term gilts).
- At the beginning of each calendar quarter, the Bank of England will publish maturity ranges for gilts to be sold at auction to be held in that quarter, as well as any changes to the financing requirements.
- A more stable calendar of debt issuance will improve predictability of the debt program along with the increased reliance on auctions over tap sales.
- A formal consultation process will be introduced so that investors' input into strategic debt management decisions may be garnered by the treasury and the bank in a regular and transparent manner.

Instrument and Market Development

Greater liquidity and efficiency in the gilts markets are expected to result from the development of an open and competitive repo market (beginning January 1996) and a new facility (in the second half of 1996) permitting the efficient stripping of gilt-edged securities.

Several initiatives are being considered to promote the demand for index-linked gilts, including improving their secondary market liquidity by establishing market-makers for index-linked gilts.

Tax Reform

By treating the taxation of interest income and capital gains on gilt-edged securities and repo transactions in a more uniform manner, the emergence of a repo market will be encouraged and tax-induced pricing anomalies reduced. In addition, by exempting "strippable gilts" from withholding taxes, the development of that market will be encouraged.

10

Ireland: Institutional Arrangements for Monetary and Debt Management Policy and Their Coordination

*Michael Horgan**

Several legislative provisions govern the Central Bank of Ireland, the National Treasury Management Agency, and exchange rate policy. The central bank is an independent body, by statute, required by Section 6 of the 1942 Act to take "such steps as the Board may from time to time deem appropriate and advise toward safeguarding the integrity of the currency and ensuring that, in what pertains to the control of credit, the constant and predominant aim shall be the welfare of the people as a whole." The Minister for Finance has the power under the 1942 Act to request the governor or the board "to consult and advise him" on the central bank's performance of its general functions and monetary policy in particular, and the board is required to comply with such a request. At the time of the writing, this power had never been exercised by the minister. The central bank is independent in the carrying out of its functions, including the formation and implementation of monetary policy.

The National Treasury Management Agency was established as a statutory body under the National Treasury Management Agency Act of 1990. Under the act, the agency is statutorily responsible for the management of the national debt subject to "the control and general superintendence of the Minister." In this regard, the minister issues annually to the agency broad guidelines within which borrowing and debt management in that particular year are conducted. Within these guidelines, the agency carries

*The author is Deputy Director—Domestic Debt in the National Treasury Management Agency of Ireland and Chairman of the OECD Group of Experts on Government Debt Management. The views expressed in this paper are his personal responsibility and are not necessarily the official views of the National Treasury Management Agency or of the Central Bank of Ireland.

on its functions day to day independently of the department of finance and the central bank.

Finally, Section 24(2) of the Central Bank Act of 1989 provides that exchange rate policy is determined by the government. The section states:

> The minister for finance may, whenever he considers it necessary after consultation with the Bank, do either or both of the following, that is to say
>
> (a) vary the general exchange rate arrangements for the time being for the Irish pound in respect of any or all other monetary units.
> (b) make specific exchange rate adjustments consistent with those arrangements.

It is a matter for the central bank to operate exchange rate policy on a day-to-day basis by using the available instruments, namely, exchange rate movements within the European exchange rate mechanism (ERM) band, changes in interest rates, and interventions in the foreign exchange market.

Central Bank Operational Functions Carried Out on Behalf of the Agency

The Central Bank of Ireland acts as the government's banker. This involves centralizing in one account—the "Exchequer Account"—the custody and movement of all government funds, including those managed by the National Treasury Management Agency. The central bank also acts as the agency's fiscal agent, by handling the register of government bonds, servicing outstanding issues, and redeeming maturing issues. In addition, the central bank also provides a settlement system to secure contemporaneous payment for and delivery of government bond transactions.

Monetary Policy's Daily Interface with Markets

An end-of-day shortage or excess of money market liquidity is either supplied via the Short-Term Facility (STF) (quota-based) or absorbed through the Overnight Deposit Facility (ODF) (unlimited). It is a prerequisite that any institutions applying for these facilities must have an Irish pound settlement account with the central bank. Once granted, the use of the facilities is at the discretion of the institution. The rate applied to the Short-Term Facility, currently 7¼ percent, normally sets an upper limit on short-term wholesale money market interest rates, while the rate applied to the Overnight Deposit Facility, currently 4 percent, normally sets a floor.

In addition to the standing facilities (STF and ODF), the central bank regulates the underlying amount of liquidity available in the wholesale money market through the use of two principal instruments. When the central bank wishes to add liquidity, the main instruments used are repurchase agreement ("repo") operations. When the central bank wishes to absorb liquidity, the main instruments used are fixed-term deposit operations. Repo and fixed-term deposit operations are normally advertised for tender on Reuters page "CBIX" and are normally conducted at prevailing market rates. However, the central bank may conduct these operations bilaterally or at rates slightly above or below prevailing market rates. Foreign exchange swaps may occasionally be used to supplement the repo or fixed-term deposit operations. Most of the central bank's operations are confined to overnight or one-week terms. However, the central bank occasionally conducts one-month transactions or transactions for other appropriate terms. The central bank is normally regarded as having influence on the level of short-term (overnight to one-week) wholesale money market rates.

Changes in the official external reserves (OERs) may not directly affect domestic liquidity. In the absence of foreign exchange intervention by the central bank, changes in the OERs are reflected in changes in government balances with the central bank, and the impact on liquidity occurs when these balances are spent in the domestic economy.

Open Market Operations by the Central Bank

Outright purchases or sales by the central bank of government securities have not been used to date in Ireland for the purposes of increasing or decreasing the banks' short-term position vis-à-vis the central bank. Instead, the central bank uses the techniques described above. The central bank gave priority in the 1980s to the foreign exchange and money markets in order to minimize the threats to monetary stability posed by the financing requirements of the large government budget deficits that existed before the late 1980s. It was appropriate for the Central Bank of Ireland, as it was gaining experience in the European Monetary System (EMS), to rely primarily on money market instruments for intervention purposes. Such instruments could be used discreetly as external reserves fell or rose temporarily. On the other hand, outright market purchases or sales of bonds in a thin bond market that was being overfed with new issues by the government would not have readily accommodated flexible interventions. It was easier to conduct the interventions in the interbank money market, where they could be "unwound" relatively easily as the official external reserves reverted to what was regarded as an appropriate level. There was another limitation to the purchasing and selling of government securities for managing the banks' short-term position vis-à-vis the central bank: it would have had the potential to run counter to public debt management policy in the relatively small, illiquid market that existed at that time, although the situation today is different to the extent that the turnover in the bond market is relatively large and liquid.

It should be noted, however, that the provisions of the Maastricht Treaty concerning monetary financing (Articles 104 and 104b(i)) prohibit central bank financing of the public sector. The enabling regulations prohibit direct purchase by the (future) European central bank of public sector debt instruments. Member states are required to ensure that secondary market purchases by central banks are not used to circumvent that prohibition.

Day-to-Day Coordination of Monetary Policy and Debt Management Policy

A primary objective of national debt policy is to minimize the long-term costs of servicing the debt: this is essentially why the National Treasury Management Agency was established. In carrying out this function, the agency at all times keeps the central bank fully informed, through a formal process, of its daily transactions in order to ensure that with knowledge of the agency's day-to-day operations, the central bank can decide, in turn, on its day-to-day management of money market liquidity and of the official foreign reserves. In normal circumstances, a temporary increase in the government's receipts from the private sector can be accommodated by the central bank by, for example, the use of additional repos, and vice versa if the government's balance declines because of payments to the private sector.

To help the central bank in its management of day-to-day liquidity in the money market, the agency supplies the money desk in the central bank, on a daily basis, with the net movements on agency's sales and purchases of both short-term paper and bonds; this information allows the central bank to anticipate as precisely as possible the net amount to be settled between itself and the banks at the close of business each day. On a monthly basis, the agency provides figures for the outstanding amount of short-term paper, and it also provides the central bank with a quarterly statement of any deposits held abroad.

When the agency sells government securities, the proceeds add to the agency's deposit balance in the government account at the central bank. Since the agency's deposit balance at the central bank tends to be maintained over time around an average level, the central bank will not necessarily intervene to supply liquidity as a result of bond sales except to meet, temporarily, a situation of exceptionally high deposit balances by the agency, that is, in order to smooth out temporary liquidity imbalances that occur as a result of the activity in the bond market. However, an exact offset by the central bank will not necessarily occur at any particular time because the central bank is involved also in managing liquidity imbalances arising from sources other than agency operations, such as inflows of foreign funds. The proceeds of foreign currency transactions by the agency are in the main exchanged for Irish pounds with the central bank. The agency does not take a position against the currency in the foreign exchange markets.

Interaction between debt management and money market management can prove to be particularly sharp at the short end of the yield curve or, specifically, where the agency attempts funding in bills or notes. The rate of interest paid thereon, together with the amount of funding done in bills or notes, can bear on the financial market's perception of the short-term interest rate stance of the authorities. The approach of the central bank is that managing the residual liquidity of the money market lies solely in its domain. Thus, the central bank will intervene in the money market as it sees fit to adjust for the effect on liquidity of, for example, action by the agency, such as the sale of bills or notes. If the volume and price paid for short-dated funding by the agency were to nudge interest rates above prevailing levels, the central bank would, as it sees fit, intervene to nudge them back down. Accordingly, the agency will tend to fund at prevailing market rates only.

Coordination of Strategic Monetary Policy and Debt Management Policy

Over and above the normal day-to-day contacts between the agency and the central bank—which are essentially an information flow—there can be, exceptionally, a need for close policy coordination. This need arises most obviously in times of currency crisis.

The ERM turmoil in 1992–93 was a case in point. During this crisis, there were meetings on a regular basis at the highest level of the department of finance, the central bank, and the agency to coordinate and to decide on policy. With a massive outflow of funds from Ireland during that period, the agency was obliged to make a fundamental change in its funding strategy. This change was implemented in close consultation with the minister for finance and the central bank, and was driven by the priority of the national interest rather than by pure debt management considerations. The agency's withdrawal from the domestic market was dictated by the need for foreign currency borrowing to replace some of the outflow of funds; by the very high level of Irish interest rates, which was already causing major problems for other borrowers; and by the inevitability that domestic borrowing by the agency would have driven interest rates to even higher levels with devastating budgetary and economic consequences. Continuing recourse to foreign borrowing was undertaken in agreement with the minister for finance and the central bank; a primary objective of this was to bolster the official reserves held by the central bank.

To help underpin the stability and liquidity of the bond market, the agency also maintained firm bid prices in its benchmark bonds and in bonds maturing within one year. Despite heavy selling of Irish government bonds by nonresidents, the bond market remained relatively orderly and liquid because of, in large measure, buying back by the agency as well as the capacity of the secondary market to absorb stock.

Conclusion

In summary, the decision during the 1992–93 ERM currency crisis not to fund in the domestic market, combined with the sale of Irish bonds by nonresidents, necessitated foreign borrowing by the agency for government funding reasons; and, in addition, this foreign borrowing by the agency was required to replenish the monetary reserves of the central bank, which had become depleted during the currency crisis. Exceptionally, during this crisis there existed coordination at the highest level of national debt management policy and of monetary policy, with the predominate requirement being exchange rate policy. Outside times of crisis, the central bank and the agency pursue in the normal course their separate statutory functions, so that monetary policy and debt management policy are carried out independently of each other but subject to a real-time flow of information from the agency to the central bank about the agency transactions, data that allows the central bank to manage monetary policy.

11

Sweden: Separating Public Debt Management from Monetary Policy

*Staffan Crona**

The Swedish National Debt Office is a government agency responsible for issuing loans on behalf of the Swedish state and managing the state debt. The objective is to fulfill this target as cost-effectively as possible. The debt office borrows in three markets—the domestic money and bond market; the private market; and the Euromarket and foreign capital market.

In the domestic money and bond market, the debt office borrows in Swedish kronor through treasury bills and treasury bonds. The treasury bills are issued in original maturities of 3, 6, and 12 months. In the bond market, the debt office has concentrated its issues into a few benchmark loans—at present, seven loans with maturities of between 2 and 15 years—in order to promote a high degree of liquidity. The borrowing is made in a standardized and highly predictable manner, also with the purpose of promoting a liquid and efficient market. The issues are conducted through a network of dealers, approved by the debt office, who also maintain a secondary market in those issues. The final investors are mainly major financial institutions, many of which invest in international markets. The short-term financing and liquidity management is handled through short-term repurchase ("repo") agreements, treasury bills, and short-term loans and deposits.

In the private market, the debt office borrows directly from households and small institutions. These borrowings are made in Swedish kronor through Lottery Bonds, the National Debt Account, and the National Savings Account. The National Debt Account is a zero-coupon bond with a fixed or floating interest rate. The National Savings Account is a special form of bank account in which the deposits are transferred to the debt of-

---

*The author was formerly Director General of the Swedish National Debt Office.

fice. The private market comprises a large number of small lenders (about 2–3 million). Thus, operating in this market requires extensive administration and marketing of instruments. The borrowing is nonetheless cost-effective, since the interest rate is determined with a sufficient margin to alternative borrowings in the money and bond market.

Foreign currency borrowings are made in the Euromarket and in the foreign and domestic capital markets through bond issues, bank loans, and commercial paper programs. The debt office has an active debt management policy and employs swap agreements, forward contracts, and the like, to manage the debt stock in a cost-effective manner.

Other responsibilities of the debt office include acting as an internal bank of the state; issuing guarantees on behalf of the state; coordinating state guarantee operations and loans to industry and commerce and monitoring the related costs; and issuing forecasts covering state receipts and disbursements and ensuring that these transactions are managed as cost-effectively as possible.

Development and Composition of the Debt

There has been a dramatic rise in Swedish state debt since 1990, as shown in Chart 1. A major factor underlying this development was the recession in the Swedish economy at the beginning of the 1990s, which resulted in declining state tax receipts and rising expenditures for unemployment benefits. In addition, the costs to the state arising from the Swedish banking crisis significantly increased the borrowing requirements. In 1994/95, as a result of improving economic conditions and declining bank loan losses, the borrowing requirement began to turn down, as shown in Chart 2.

Chart 3 depicts the composition of the state debt. The bulk of the debt denominated in Swedish kronor consists of treasury bonds and treasury bills. Although the borrowing in the private market is substantial, over the past few years, it has ceased to increase in nominal terms; consequently, its share in the total debt has declined since the beginning of the 1990s. Over the same period, debt denominated in foreign currency has grown in significance, more than doubling its share of the total debt stock.

Historical Developments

The Swedish National Debt Office was founded in 1789 as an agency in charge of state borrowing, subordinated directly to parliament. The purpose was to strengthen parliamentary control of the state's expenditures. Concomitantly parliament, through the debt office, took full responsibility for the previous accumulation of state debt.

Chart 1. Sweden: Central Government Debt

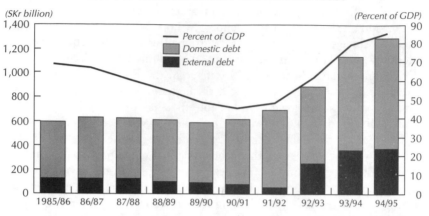

Source: Swedish National Debt Office.

Chart 2. Sweden: Borrowing Requirement
(In billions of Swedish kronor)

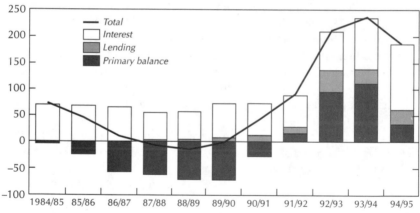

Source: Swedish National Debt Office.

Since its foundation, the relationship between the debt office and the central bank—the Riksbank—has evolved through stages. During almost the whole nineteenth century, the debt office and the Riksbank acted quite independently of each other. Although the Riksbank had the responsibility for foreign currency reserves, it had none of the other responsibilities typical of a central bank. When the debt office started to borrow heavily

Chart 3. Sweden: Composition of State Debt, February 1995

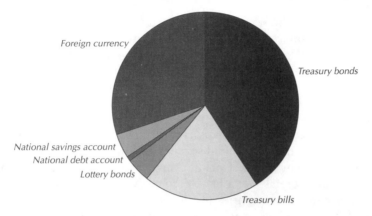

Source: Swedish National Debt Office.

in foreign currency at the end of the century to finance a national railway network, contacts with the Riksbank were strengthened. This relationship intensified when the Riksbank was made the central bank of Sweden in 1897. From the Second World War to the mid-1980s, the debt office's independence was limited. Debt management was, to a large degree, part of the monetary policy of the Riksbank and the economic policy of the government.

Integration of Debt Management with Monetary Policy and Stimulating Household Saving

The capital markets in Sweden were, in many areas, highly regulated between the Second World War and the mid-1980s. Banks and insurance companies were forced to invest a substantial part of their assets in bonds issued by priority sectors, that is, the state and the mortgage institutions. The interest rates on these loans were determined by the Riksbank at a level lower than that seen as the market price.

For a long period, therefore, the debt management policy aspects of state borrowing were of secondary importance: instead, the monetary aspects of state borrowing dominated. In practice, debt operations and more precisely the setting of interest rates on state bond loans were regarded as one of the most important tools in monetary policy. In this system, there was little scope for an independent debt management policy. Borrowing from the large domestic institutions formed a part of the priority credit system. Furthermore, currency regulation prevented foreigners from investing in krona-denominated bonds even if the yields had been attractive.

A large portion of the state debt was raised from households through instruments like Lottery Bonds and savings certificates. Lottery Bonds, for example, have a history going back to the beginning of the century in Sweden. The state began to issue savings certificates at the beginning of the 1960s. Until the mid-1980s, these loans were issued with the twofold purpose of financing the state budget deficit and stimulating household saving, thereby reducing the pressure on the current account. The yield on these instruments was typically tax-exempt. In the early 1980s, the promotion of household saving was considered so important that a new instrument, the National Savings Account, was introduced. This instrument operates like a bank account, with the holdings transferred to the state. The activities in this field were coordinated by the ministry of finance. Thus, even in this sector, the independence of the debt office was limited.

Deregulation and Start of an Independent Debt Management Policy

In the 1980s, the capital markets in Sweden were gradually deregulated. This process took more or less the entire decade. In 1982 and 1983, the debt office started to issue treasury bills and treasury bonds with the purpose of creating a market for state securities. In 1986, the priority credit system was abolished; from then on, the debt office had to borrow in the domestic markets without the support of favorable regulation. Currency regulations lasted for three more years before they, too, were finally abolished in 1989.

The deregulation of capital markets had a profound effect on state debt management. In the new borrowing situation, two basic institutional options presented themselves. The debt office could issue directly to investors (through a network of market-makers), or it could place its issues with the Riksbank and permit the Riksbank to sell the securities to the final investors. Because the Riksbank favored having only one agency operating in the market on behalf of the state, it preferred the second option. However, following a commission proposal and on further consideration, the government and parliament decided to allow the debt office to issue securities directly into the market. An important factor in this decision was that a rapidly developing market made it possible to issue state securities quickly and flexibly using auction techniques. The debt office could then decide on the volumes to issue, allowing the interest rate to be determined by the market instead of by the Riksbank. Using this technique, and in conjunction with more developed markets, it was evident that there was increased scope for a more independent debt management policy.

Even though the use of auction techniques solved many of the basic conflicts between debt management and monetary policy, problems remained, and various issues routinely presented themselves. Representatives from the debt office and the Riksbank discussed these matters in informal meetings—so-called joint advisory groups. Two groups existed: one for foreign currency borrowing and one for domestic borrowing. The Governor of the Riksbank was chairman of the foreign currency group, while the Undersecretary of State of the Ministry of Finance chaired the domestic borrowing group.

The Riksbank initially met many of its monetary policy requirements through domestic borrowing operations, mainly because of an interest-ladder-system implemented in 1985, through which the Riksbank determined short interest rates by controlling the availability of the banking sector's primary liquidity. This liquidity was, to a considerable degree, influenced by the state's borrowing requirements. The Riksbank wanted the borrowing operation to be conducted so as to offset fluctuations in banking system liquidity. In addition, the Riksbank also needed to build a large and liquid market for treasury bills that could be used for monetary policy purposes. In the late 1980s, when the state budget was in surplus, this objective sharply constrained debt management policy. For a few years, only limited volumes of bonds could be issued.

As the market continued to develop, the Riksbank gradually found it possible to control liquidity using monetary instruments of its own—for example, repos and loans. This meant that the Riksbank no longer needed to influence the debt office's borrowing plans for monetary purposes. The borrowing program could subsequently be held more in line with traditional debt management objectives and according to a more stable schedule. Subsequently, the joint advisory groups have, over the last years, played a more passive role, mainly serving as a forum for exchanging information. The institutions are now also represented by lower-ranking officials.

Reorganizing the Debt Office

As a consequence of these developments, the decisions regarding the borrowing program and the composition of the debt stock were increasingly taken within the debt office. A 1989 government commission investigating these matters concluded that the office's increased role in debt management called for its reorganization. In particular, the objective of the debt office was to be narrowly focused on the minimization of borrowing costs. Other, sometimes competing, objectives—such as increasing savings rates and so on—were eliminated: debt management was not regarded as a sufficiently powerful tool in achieving economic development goals.

The debt office was transformed from a parliamentary agency to an agency subordinate to the ministry of finance. This paved the way for the modernization of the debt office, a process driven by the increased importance of debt-service expenditures in the total state budget. The Board of Directors of the debt office was charged with determining the general guidelines for, and time frames of, borrowings. The Director General, who is also Chairman of the Board, was given the task of deciding on the terms for individual loans within these parameters.[1]

The debt office was also reorganized along product or market lines (as are many financial service companies) with different departments for institutional borrowing, foreign currency borrowing, and private market borrowing. A separate department was also set up for issuing guarantees on behalf of the state.

The law governing borrowing activities was also revised slightly, enabling the debt office to repurchase outstanding domestic debt. According to the Act on State Borrowing, the debt office may raise funds on behalf of the state for the purposes of:

(1) financing current deficits in the national budget and other expenditures incurred pursuant to resolutions by parliament;
(2) providing such credits and fulfilling such guarantees as have been resolved by parliament;
(3) effecting amortization and redemption of state borrowings and, in consultation with the Riksbank, repurchase of state debt; and
(4) meeting the requirements of the Riksbank in respect to the foreign currency reserve and of government securities for capital market operations.

The instructions for the debt office issued by the government explicitly articulated the objective of making state borrowing as cost-effective as possible within the limits imposed by monetary policy. The debt office was also directed to confer with the Riksbank on matters concerning the general direction of the debt office's activities, primarily significant monetary policy issues. The debt office's cost-minimization objective was given further quantification: since the reorganization, the government periodically provides in a letter to the debt office a cost of the borrowing target in reference to the cost of a benchmark, representative portfolio. The exact composition of the benchmark portfolio—currency composition and duration—is decided by the board.

---

[1]Previously, the debt office had a Board of Commissioners who decided the terms for each individual loan.

Recent Changes in Coordination with Monetary Policy

Disuse of the Credit Line Facility Within the Riksbank

A clear example of the interaction between debt management and monetary policy is the debt office's access to a credit line facility within the Riksbank. This credit line had been used to finance daily swings in borrowing requirements. As a consequence, budget payments and receipts strongly influenced the banking sector's liquidity. The Riksbank was forced to conduct monetary operations in order to maintain its target level for liquidity. Since July 1994, the debt office no longer uses the credit line with the Riksbank, although the underlying legislation has not so far been amended. Instead, short-term financing is handled in the market by short-term repurchase agreements, treasury bills, and short-term loans and deposits. This new policy has further separated debt management from monetary policy.

End of Riksbank Participation in the Primary Market

The Riksbank had regularly purchased small amounts of treasury bonds and treasury bills directly in the debt office's primary auctions. However, in March 1995, the Riksbank altered its policy. Since then, it has made all purchases of state securities in the secondary instead of in the primary market. Taken together with the disuse of the credit line facility, these changes now put Sweden in compliance with the Maastricht Treaty regulation that disallows financing of government expenditures by the central bank.

Requisitions of Treasury Bills by the Riksbank

Financial imbalances led to several periods of currency unrest during the early 1990s.[2] In response, the Riksbank intervened massively in the treasury bill market. To carry out such large-scale operations, the Riksbank had to requisition treasury bills directly from the debt office. The debt office decided that these amounts should not influence the regular program of debt issues, thus observing a distinction between monetary policy and debt management. However, the extra costs incurred by the debt office of issues to the Riksbank were borne by the state rather than by the Riksbank. According to a proposal from a state commission in 1993, these costs, if they reoccur, should be paid by the Riksbank. The commission also proposed that extraordinary issues to the Riksbank for monetary purposes should be decided by the government.

---

[2]Sweden maintained a fixed exchange rate policy until November 1992.

Present Coordination with Monetary Policy

Foreign Currency Borrowing

The present outstanding stock of foreign currency debt of the Swedish state dates back to the late 1970s, when the state borrowed abroad in order to finance current account deficits. By the mid-1980s, foreign currency debt amounted to approximately 20–25 percent of the total debt stock. In 1984, parliament adopted the so-called foreign currency borrowing norm, which directed that the state should not borrow net new funds in foreign currency. The purpose of the norm was to establish a mechanism whereby increased state borrowings would automatically impinge on domestic interest rates and thereby clearly indicate the need for an improved budgetary balance. In the late 1980s, this norm was defined more strictly: the state was required to pay back loans in foreign currency and reduce the outstanding stock of foreign currency debt.

This policy was pursued until September 1992 when, as a result of currency instability, the debt office, on request from the Riksbank, raised substantial amounts of foreign currency debt in order to replenish the foreign currency reserves. Later in 1992, the foreign currency norm was replaced by new guidelines from parliament, allowing foreign currency borrowing to be used to reduce the domestic financing requirements. According to these new guidelines, the bulk of state borrowing should be made in domestic currency, and the government will decide on the amount of borrowing in foreign currency after consultation with the Riksbank.

During 1992 and 1993, the foreign currency debt increased from 8 percent to 30 percent of the total state debt. In 1994, the net borrowing in foreign currency was more modest. For 1995, the government decided that the debt office should borrow SKr 30 billion in foreign currency. The debt office had the right to increase borrowings above this amount to a certain extent if good terms could be arranged.

Repurchases of Domestic Debt

As a result of the debt office's policy of issuing benchmark loans, the bond portfolio has been concentrated in a small number of large-scale loans. In order to reduce the associated refinancing risk, repurchases are made before maturity. The Act on State Borrowing directs that repurchases of state debt should be made in consultation with the Riksbank. Such coordination has resulted in a repurchase program under which the debt office decides which loans to repurchase and on what conditions, and the Riksbank, in turn, makes the necessary contacts in the market and carries out the repurchases on behalf of the debt office.

Other Matters of Coordination

The debt office is obliged (under its general instructions) to confer with the Riksbank on matters related to its debt program and operations. Such consultations primarily concern significant monetary policy issues. Representatives of the debt office regularly present the borrowing plans to representatives of the Riksbank and the ministry of finance. The general direction of the borrowing and the introduction of new instruments—for example, swaps—are examples of issues discussed in these meetings.

On a more operational level, the relationship between the debt office and the Riksbank continues in two other areas. First, the Riksbank is the state's bank. All government payments are executed through the state's checking account in the Riksbank. The debt office borrowing activities are, however, channeled through the debt office checking account in the Riksbank. Second, the debt office uses the Riksbank when exchanging foreign currency for domestic currency.

Conclusion

The deregulation and development of capital markets were prerequisites in Sweden for the separation of public debt management from monetary policy. During this process, the debt office has, within more or less the same legal framework, substantially increased its influence over the borrowing activities of the state. In order to develop a sound and balanced approach to debt management, establishing clear objectives and a clear organizational responsibility for the debt office were paramount.

As a consequence of those developments, practically all decisions regarding debt management matters, both formally and in practice, have been transferred to the debt office. At the same time, the need for formal coordination with monetary policy has subsequently been reduced with the development of the Riksbank's own monetary instruments. The composition of both domestic and foreign currency borrowing is now decided solely within the debt office. The volume of borrowing in foreign currency is, however, decided by the government after consultation with the Riksbank.

12

Spain: Monetary Control and Government Debt Management During Financial Sector Liberalization

Pedro Martínez Méndez *

This chapter describes the Spanish experience with liberalizing its financial system, reorienting its monetary and debt management policies toward the market, and developing deep and sophisticated money and government debt markets. It focuses on operational and institutional issues, in particular interrelations between monetary control and government debt management, with only passing references to policy objectives or general economic developments.

The primary force in the transition to the present situation was the advent of a market-oriented monetary policy in the early 1970s. At that time, a host of nonmarket features and inefficiencies existed: direct controls on bank credit; automatic bank refinancing mechanisms at the central bank; rules enjoining the banking system to comply with mandatory investments; controls on bank interest rates; foreign exchange controls; absence of market-oriented government financing; lack of a money market; absence of an efficient secondary market for government debt; and poor and untimely information on banks' balance sheets and on the evolution of financial conditions.

To reform this environment was no simple task. However, the Spanish case illustrates that the monetary authorities can start to control some target of their choice while many nonmarket features and inefficiencies persist in the system. It also shows that the adoption of a market approach to monetary policy will lead inevitably to its extension to wider areas of financial policy. Thus, the introduction of some market-based monetary instruments and the early attention to money market development helped to achieve

*Pedro Martínez Méndez was formerly Department Head of Monetary Studies on Statistics at the Bank of Spain.

control of the rate of monetary expansion. This laid the foundation for a gradual liberalization of bank interest rates, an increasing role for indirect monetary instruments, a growing participation of securities in government finance, and a rapid development of the market for government securities. Yet, the piecemeal and gradualist transition to a market-oriented monetary policy was also a source of significant transitory inefficiencies in the conduct of monetary policy and the working of financial markets. The long and sinuous path to fully market-oriented financial policy in Spain offers, as a result, a wide assortment of both good and bad lessons.

This chapter is organized as follows. The first section offers a summary view of the overall approach to monetary policy targets and monetary control. The second section briefly describes the sources of bank liquidity, focusing on the basic cost considerations that inhibited government market financing, as well as the adoption of market-oriented monetary instruments. The gradual acceptance of market interest rates and market instruments by both the ministry of finance and the Bank of Spain (BOS) is the basic theme of the next three sections, which examine the chronological development of (1) government debt management practices; (2) monetary intervention practices; and (3) the money market and the secondary market for government securities. The final two sections offer some concluding remarks on monetary and debt management coordination, and on general technical issues, respectively.

Monetary Policy Framework

In the early 1970s, the Bank of Spain started to abandon its longstanding approach to monetary policy based on ill-defined targets and non-market instruments. Required reserves were introduced in 1970, and direct controls on bank credit were totally abandoned in 1971. This paved the way for an indirect control of monetary developments, based in principle on BOS interventions—using market instruments—in the money market or the market for government securities. There were, however, no such markets or instruments; even a clear formulation of monetary policy targets was missing. Such a formulation, in 1973, became the leading factor in efforts to overcome the other basic deficiencies. The adoption, almost simultaneously, of a floating exchange rate regime became another important feature of the new framework. This section highlights the essential aspects of monetary targets and monetary control procedures that were to dominate the following years.

Monetary Policy Targets

In 1973, Spain became one of the first countries to adopt quantitative targets for the rate of growth of money (publicly preannounced since 1978).

On the verified assumption of a rather stable function for the demand for money, monetary policy was geared to the control of domestic nominal expenditure, relying, as an intermediate variable, on the control of the supply of money. The most reliable definition of "money" always proved to be a wide one, including all kinds of bank liabilities to nonbank residents. When, after 1982, nonbank holdings of short-term government securities and the repurchase agreements ("repos") on both short- and medium-term securities started to grow significantly (largely at the expense of bank deposits), econometric analysis confirmed that such holdings had to be brought into the definition of money, because the relation between this wider concept and nominal GDP was more stable than narrower ones. The development of a market for government securities had, thus, as a side effect that the government was creating "money" (about 25 percent of the total in the recent past), alongside the banking system. Nobody considered this a reason to somehow limit issues of such securities or repo trading. Instead, monetary control procedures were adjusted, as noted below.

The success of the new approach cannot be judged from the actual rate of monetary expansion, which was always fairly high, but on the basis of its closeness to the targets formulated in advance, and its fairly smooth evolution (Table 1, columns (4)–(7), and Chart 1). Lack of ambition in monetary targets may be attributed to a long tradition of low but steady inflation, as well as to high, abnormally persistent unemployment levels. Exceptional events, such as the two oil crises, political uncertainties in the transition from dictatorship to democracy (1975–82), and a protracted and deep solvency crisis in the banking system (1978–85), also contributed to the expansionary bias of monetary targets.

Quantitative targets for money were rather strictly pursued during the 1970s and the first half of the 1980s, accepting large fluctuations in short-term interest rates (Chart 1). After 1984, more emphasis was placed on the stability of interest rates, and, after 1986, on exchange rate objectives.[1] This also contributed to the expansionary bias of monetary growth targets, as well as, in the recent past, to failure in attaining them. In fact, conflicts with these competing objectives were always present.

Concern about the level and evolution of interest rates always strongly influenced the authorities. High nominal interest rates raised strong apprehensions involving the cost of government financing and the cost of monetary intervention by the BOS. Misgivings about their impact on private investment were ever present, even when real interest rates were neg-

---

[1]Following a new law on BOS autonomy, driven by European Union (EU) directives in 1994, the BOS shifted to explicit targets on the rate of inflation and has dropped the announcement of money growth targets. No further reference will be made to this change, which did not affect monetary control procedures.

ative or barely positive, more so when high before-tax real interest rates emerged. By contrast, the fact that after-tax real interest rates were never abnormally high was widely ignored. All this contributed to the lack of ambition of quantitative targets, the persistence of controls on bank interest rates, and the slow introduction of market-oriented intervention instruments. It also explains certain episodes of transient relaxation of monetary control in order to exert a downward pressure on interest rates.

The volatility of short-term interest rates was also a factor delaying the introduction of market-oriented borrowing techniques, or prompting their transitory abandonment, because of the ensuing uncertainty on the cost of intervention. Volatility was a direct outcome of the pursuit of quantitative targets. However, there were additional contributing factors: an unsteady approach to monetary control, with periods of relaxation followed by sudden tightening; the difficulty of transmitting BOS initiatives from the money market to the financial markets at large, owing to controls on bank interest rates and the absence of financial instruments providing a close link; the slow adjustment by banks to the novel need for flexible cash and lending management; and some initial limitations on the averaging of required reserve balances.[2]

As the new approach to monetary policy was introduced, the earlier fixed exchange rate policy was abandoned (mid-1973). However, continuous and sizable intervention in the foreign exchange market (Chart 2) attests to the significant weight attached to exchange rate targets. Several episodes (1973, 1976, 1978, and 1982) of onetime significant depreciation of the nominal and real exchange rates proved unsustainable. After the mid-1980s, market pressure for an additional appreciation of the exchange rate was strongly resisted. Exchange rate adjustments became even more problematic after Spain joined the EEC exchange rate mechanism (1989).

Control Mechanism

The explicit formulation of monetary targets was never abandoned; it was sufficient simply to state or pursue them more flexibly in order to cope with alternative circumstances. As a result, the mechanism for monetary control introduced in the early 1970s has remained basically unchanged to the present. Essentially the mechanism works as follows: a forecast of the evolution of those components of money not subject to

---

[2]Market volatility was rarely an autonomous phenomenon in the absence of BOS intervention, which could have been reduced by additional market-oriented intervention. As a rule, money market rates always closely mirrored the volatile BOS intervention rates. The presumably negative impact of volatility on market development is also difficult to ascertain, as both volatility and market development were highest in overnight loans, and were inversely related to maturity. The most obvious negative impact of volatile interest rates on market-oriented techniques was the one noted in the text.

Table 1. Spain: GDP, Money, Government Deficit, and Balance of Payments

	Gross Domestic Product (Actual Rates of Growth)			Money (Annual Average Rates of Growth)				Central Government Deficit (Percentages of GDP)			Balance of Payments (Percent of GDP)		
	Nominal	Real	Deflator	Target min.	Target max.	Actual	Deviation from target max.	Primary deficit	Interest payments	Total deficit	Current account	Capital net	Foreign reserves[1]
	1	2	3	4	5	6	7 = 6−5	8	9	10 = 8+9	11 = 12−13	12	13
1970	10.4	4.2	5.9			17.6		0.6	−0.5	0.1			
1971	12.9	4.6	7.8			19.2		−0.4	−0.5	−0.8	2.1	1.4	−3.6
1972	17.4	8.1	8.5			23.9		0.5	−0.5	0.0	1.2	1.6	−2.8
1973	20.6	7.8	11.8			24.7		1.5	−0.5	1.0	0.8	1.0	−1.8
1974	22.5	5.6	16.0	18.0	18.0	21.7	3.7	0.5	−0.4	0.1	−3.6	2.9	0.7
1975	17.4	0.5	16.8	19.0	19.0	18.8	−0.2	0.5	−0.4	0.1	−2.8	2.5	0.3
1976	20.3	3.3	16.5	19.0	19.0	18.7	−0.3	0.6	−0.3	0.3	−3.6	2.9	0.7
1977	26.9	2.8	23.4	17.0	17.0	19.4	2.4	0.1	−0.4	−0.3	−2.5	3.9	−1.4
1978	22.4	1.5	20.6	14.5	19.5	19.4	−0.1	−1.2	−0.4	−1.6	0.9	1.6	−2.5
1979	17.0	0.0	16.9	15.5	19.5	19.7	0.2	−0.7	−0.5	−1.2	−0.6	2.0	−1.4
1980	14.9	1.3	13.4	16.0	20.0	17.6	−2.4	−2.1	−0.5	−2.6	−3.0	2.6	0.4
1981	12.4	−0.2	12.6	14.5	18.5	16.3	−2.2	−2.3	−0.6	−2.9	−3.3	3.0	0.3
1982	15.7	1.6	13.9	15.0	19.0	18.4	−0.6	−5.1	−0.7	−5.8	−2.5	0.7	1.8
1983	14.2	2.2	11.8	14.0	18.0	16.4	−1.6	−3.9	−0.9	−4.8	−1.5	1.6	−0.1
1984	13.3	1.5	11.6	10.5	14.5	15.1	0.6	−3.9	−1.6	−5.5	1.4	1.7	−3.1

1985	10.5	2.6	7.7	11.5	14.5	14.6	0.1	-3.1	-3.0	-6.0	1.4	-2.8	1.4
1986	14.6	3.2	11.1	9.5	12.5	13.5	1.0	-1.7	-3.5	-5.2	1.7	-0.8	-0.9
1987	11.8	5.6	5.8	6.5	9.5	15.5	6.0	-0.6	-3.0	-3.5	0.2	4.2	-4.4
1988	11.1	5.2	5.7	8.0	11.0	13.4	2.4	-0.1	-2.9	-3.0	-0.9	3.3	-2.4
1989	12.2	4.7	7.1	6.5	9.5	15.5	6.0	0.8	-2.9	-2.2	-2.9	4.2	-1.3
1990	11.3	3.7	7.3	6.5	9.5	14.7	5.2	0.2	-2.9	-2.7	-3.4	4.8	-1.4
1991	9.5	2.2	7.1	7.0	11.0	12.1	1.1	0.9	-3.2	-2.3	-3.0	5.7	-2.7
1992	7.5	0.7	6.7	8.0	11.0	6.0	-8.0	0.9	-3.3	-2.4	-3.1	0.0	3.1
1993	3.2	-1.1	4.4	4.5	7.5	7.0	-0.5	-2.0	-3.8	-5.8	-0.9	0.0	0.9
1994	6.2	2.0	4.1			6.7	[2]						

Source: Bank of Spain.

[1] Increase −; decrease +.

[2] Following a new law on BOS autonomy, driven by European Union (EU) direct ves in 1994, the BOS shifted to explicit targets on the rate of inflation and has dropped the announcement of money growth targets. No further reference will be made to this change, which did not affect monetary control procedures.

Chart 1. Spain: Money, Interest Rates, and Prices
(In percent)

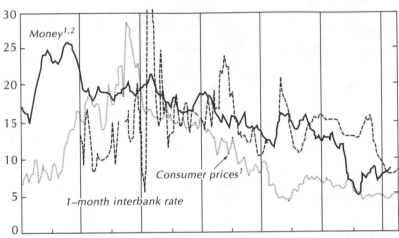

Source: Bank of Spain
[1]Centered rate of growth over 12 months.
[2]Money is defined very broadly, including all kinds of bank liabilities to nonbanks, plus nonbank holdings of short-term government securities and repos on government securities.

Chart 2. Spain: Effective Exchange Rates and Changes in Foreign Exchange Reserves[1]
(Quarterly data)

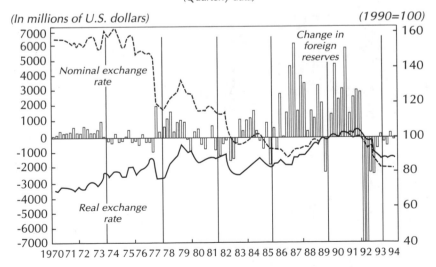

Source: Bank of Spain.
[1]Exchange rates are effective rates against the European Union. Real effective exchange rate is based on consumer prices.

reserve requirements (currency and short-term government debt holdings) is subtracted from the target for money, to obtain a target of bank liabilities subject to reserve requirements (basically coincident with bank liabilities integrated in the definition of money). This in turn is translated, using the required reserve ratio, into a target for banks' required reserves, all of them BOS liabilities. All such forecasts refer to monthly averages of daily figures, from which a daily path for banks' reservable liabilities and required reserves is obtained.

This mechanism sets the background for monetary control. In the BOS balance sheet, banks' reserves are affected by several factors escaping short-run control (currency, lending to government, foreign assets, etc.). However, the BOS is in a position to offset them through interventions affecting its relations with banks. As a result, a rather accurate control of the level of bank reserves and, indirectly, of the quantity of money can be attained.

Information Requirements

The approach described in the preceding section assumes that daily figures on actual bank reserves are known without significant delays, and that offsetting intervention by the BOS takes place daily in a market supplying reliable information on interest rate developments. It also implies a need for forecasts on the daily evolution of the main items in the BOS balance sheet. This approach is clearly infeasible without adequate information.

In the early 1970s, the only information available consisted of monthly bank balance sheets and three monthly (day 10, day 20, and end-of-month) BOS balance sheets, known with significant delays. Not a single market supplied information on its interest rates. Accordingly, early efforts were directed at plugging these basic information gaps. By mid-1973, the BOS was already in a position to know in just a few hours its main balance sheet items, in particular, deposits held by banks. The 1974 reform of reserve requirements (described under the next heading) provided daily data on bank liabilities. The early development of a money market also permitted interested parties to obtain, from 1974 on, essential information on short-term market rates. At a later stage, the development of book-entry facilities for government debt, managed by the BOS, provided daily information on nonbank outright and repo holdings of government securities.[3] So, the difficulty of forecasting the evolution of such

---

[3]See "First Stage," "Second Stage," and "Third Stage" below, under the subheading "Government Debt and Money Markets."

somewhat volatile components of money was overcome by revisions based on the knowledge, with a one-day lag, of their actual development.

Several other problematic forecasting issues had to be faced to facilitate flexible daily intervention by the BOS. Forecasts concerning BOS balance sheet items proved very reliable in the case of currency; BOS operations with banks; foreign assets (as a result of the usual one- or two-day settlement lag); and government financial transactions (since the BOS was acting as fiscal agent). Forecasting difficulties centered on the impact of non-financial budget execution on BOS net lending to government. Yet, cooperation between the BOS and the finance ministry to establish such forecasts was always limited to information on broad trends, major tax collection dates, and large special transactions. The BOS soon learned that the *averaging of daily bank reserves plus the utmost flexibility in intervention excluded the need for very precise forecasts*. Even under the most strict adherence to a bank's reserve target, averaging of daily bank reserves allowed for daily deviations from target in actual reserves, which could be offset by intervention on subsequent days. Big occasional errors were clearly signaled by abnormal developments in the money market and called forth immediate additional intervention.

Reserve Requirements

The initial definition of reserve requirements, introduced in 1970, was inadequate, and reforms were undertaken during the 1970s. First, starting from diversified reserve ratios, a gradual unification process led to a single required reserve ratio, common to all banking institutions and to all categories of liabilities. This feature, infrequent in international experience, has remained up to the present. Second, reserve requirements were initially based on only three dates of the month, following the available information sources. The collection of daily BOS data revealed that such a system was useless. This prompted the introduction of required reserves based on averages of daily liabilities over roughly ten-day reporting periods, adding up to one month. Eligible assets were averaged over similar ten-day periods but lagged by two days. As a result, the computation of reserve requirements was basically nonlagged. This system has also persisted to this day.[4]

Defining bank liabilities subject to reserve requirements exactly as they were integrated in the definition of money was a longtime aim. It also be-

---

[4]Initially, daily deficiencies equivalent to more than 1 percentage point below the required reserve ratio were forbidden, while daily holdings of eligible assets in excess of the required reserve ratio plus 1 percentage point were ignored in the calculation of average reserve holdings. The first restriction was discontinued in March 1980, and the second in January 1984.

came a demanding one, because new categories of bank liabilities frequently emerged in attempts to avoid controls on interest rates, required reserves, or taxes. The only eligible assets have always been currency (excluded, however, since 1988) and deposits with the BOS. All bank deposits with the BOS were eligible as required reserves, and always remained available for settlement purposes. Required reserves were not remunerated.

After an initial period of very frequent modifications in required reserve ratios, the authorities settled, by 1978, on a common ratio (5.75 percent), excluding as a matter of principle future changes for short-run control purposes. Several exceptional changes took place in later years, however. After 1990, required reserves were gradually brought down to the current low level (2 percent) (see the Appendix (item D.a)).

Main Issues in Control of Bank Liquidity

Given the framework just described, the basic problem was devising a set of market-oriented intervention instruments that would allow the BOS, on a daily basis, to control bank liquidity and to offset unwanted influences stemming from autonomous sources of liquidity creation. Lack of a secondary market for government securities excluded outright open market operations.[5] Instead, the chosen approach was to control the net financial position of banks with the BOS. To do so through market-oriented instruments became, however, a difficult task.

Chart 3 displays a summary BOS balance sheet, in which net foreign assets, net lending to government, net lending to banks, and a residual balance of other accounts appear as a percentage of currency in circulation (itself not represented in the chart).[6] It reveals that throughout the period under study, net lending to the government and net foreign assets were both very important sources of liquidity creation, in marked contrast to the more frequent international experience, when it is the first element that mainly counts.

The evolution of central government deficits and the ratio of government debt to GDP are shown in Table 1, columns (8)–(10), and Table 2,

---

[5]Such outright operations were not used for monetary control, even after the development of secondary markets. Over the years, the BOS bought and sold very small amounts of government securities in the secondary market, initially as a means to provide liquidity to the emerging markets, later for a number of special reasons. Such transactions were never geared to monetary control. As a result, the BOS portfolio of government securities has been treated in this chapter as part of lending to the government.

[6]This presentation tries to avoid the distortion that inflation imposes on absolute figures. Other magnitudes (bank reserves, the monetary base, bank deposits, or total money) might have been used as alternative denominators. However, currency has the advantage of simplicity, and has no major shortcoming in view of the descriptive aims pursued. (A 13-month centered moving average of currency is actually used, to avert its strong seasonality.) Charts 3 and 4 illustrate structural relations, but do not indicate anything as to the stance of monetary policy at each stage.

Chart 3. Bank of Spain Balance Sheet: Summary
(Percent of currency in circulation; end-of-quarter data)

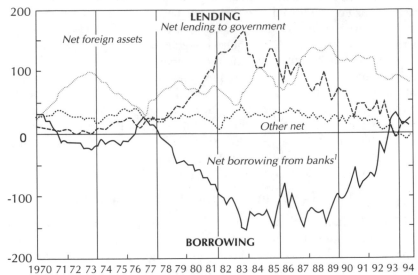

Source: Bank of Spain.
[1]See details in Chart 4.

Chart 4. Bank of Spain Balance Sheet: Detail of Net Borrowing from Banks[1]
(Percent of currency in circulation; end-of-quarter data)

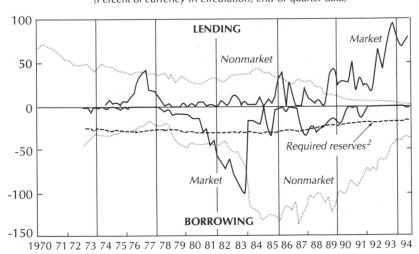

Source: Bank of Spain.
[1]Borrowing and lending instruments included in each category are explained in Table 4.
[2]Adjusted to a conventional minimum technical level (see text).

columns (1)–(8), respectively. Among other self-evident trends, only two will be stressed here, as most relevant for the coordination of monetary policy and government debt management. First, outstanding direct government borrowing from the BOS, historically low, increased to a maximum of 11 percent of GDP in 1982, becoming the main component of a growing total debt.[7] Fortunately, this development was later offset by increasing government reliance on domestic market borrowing, as detailed in later sections. As a result, while total debt still increased significantly, BOS credits declined to levels below 2 percent of GDP after 1990. Second, external borrowing by the government (Table 2, column (3)) never reached significant amounts. Other things being equal, foreign credits were bound to increase the stock of BOS foreign assets (high, even excessive, during most of the time), thus becoming tantamount to direct BOS credits to the government. That explains the infrequent recourse to this source of finance, and several episodes of decline in the outstanding stock.

Several factors, too complex to describe here, contributed to the formidable growth of BOS foreign assets. Contrary to past experience, the new approach to monetary policy coincided with transitory current surpluses and, in particular, with large capital inflows (Table 1, columns (11)–(13)). As already noted, the authorities resisted any important appreciation of the exchange rate and accepted instead large increases in foreign reserves (reaching a record level of $72 billion by mid-1992). The resulting monetary expansion was, thus, a major problem faced by the BOS during most of the last two decades. The 1992 crisis in the European Monetary System (EMS) put an end to this worry, with massive losses of reserves and a significant depreciation of the exchange rate.

Growth in net lending to government and net foreign assets, coupled with the aim of keeping monetary expansion under control, forced the BOS to become a large-scale net borrower from banks. This was a critical departure from the past, as monetary expansion had been based since the early 1940s on lending to banks (most of the time indirectly financing the government or government-sponsored activities, however). Not only did new instruments have to be devised, but also a deep change in traditional attitudes toward monetary control became necessary.

Chart 4 provides a breakdown of BOS net borrowing from banks into some conventionally defined major components, also expressed as a percentage of currency in circulation. Gross BOS borrowing and lending to banks have been split between market and nonmarket components. The

---

[7]Within very lax annual limits, the government overdrew on its single cash account with the BOS, through which the whole government budget was executed. No interest was paid on such balances. Occasional consolidation into long-term, low-interest credits took place. After 1990, the end-of-year overdraft balance was subject to an invariable limit, though intrayear balances could exceed it. In 1993, as a result of EU directives, new BOS lending to the government was totally forbidden.

Table 2. Spain: Government Debt
(Percentages of GDP)

	Outstanding Central Government Debt[1]								Government Securities Holdings[2,3]				
	Total	Bank of Spain[4]	Foreign credits	Marketable securities				Non-market debts	Banks	Banks (Net of repos)	Banks (Repo sales to nonbanks)	Nonbanks	Nonbanks (Net of repos)
				Total	TPNs	TBs	Bonds						
	1 = 2+3+4+8	2	3	4 = 5+6+7	5	6	7	8	9	10 = 9 − 11	11	12	13 = 11 + 12
1970	8.1	1.2	0.8	4.7			4.7	1.3	4.3	4.3		0.5	0.5
1971	8.3	1.1	0.8	4.8			4.8	1.6	4.2	4.2		0.6	0.6
1972	7.3	0.3	0.7	4.4			4.4	1.8	3.6	3.6		0.8	0.8
1973	6.3	0.6	0.6	3.6			3.6	1.5	3.0	3.0		0.6	0.6
1974	6.2	1.6	0.6	2.8			2.8	1.3	2.5	2.5		0.3	0.3
1975	6.3	2.3	0.6	2.2			2.2	1.2	2.1	2.1		0.1	0.1
1976	5.2	1.2	1.0	1.7			1.7	1.4	1.6	1.6		0.1	0.1
1977	6.2	1.6	2.1	1.4			1.4	1.1	0.4	0.4		1.0	1.0
1978	6.0	2.6	1.3	1.4			1.4	0.8	0.9	0.9		0.5	0.5
1979	6.9	3.4	1.0	1.6			1.6	0.9	0.6	0.6		1.1	1.1
1980	8.9	5.4	0.9	1.8			1.8	0.7	0.3	0.3		1.5	1.5
1981	11.9	7.7	1.3	2.3	0.2		2.1	0.7	0.3	0.3		2.0	2.0
1982	17.9	11.0	1.9	3.0	0.6		2.4	1.9	0.9	0.8		2.1	2.2
1983	23.8	10.3	2.8	8.2	5.8		2.4	2.5	1.2	1.2		7.0	7.0
1984	30.6	6.5	3.1	16.9	14.4		2.5	4.1	13.5	12.1	1.4	3.4	4.8

1985	35.5	7.5	2.6	21.3	18.1		3.2	4.1	16.8	11.3	5.5	4.6	10.0
1986	36.7	4.7	1.6	26.8	18.4		8.4	3.6	20.8	11.9	8.9	6.1	14.9
1987	38.0	3.4	1.3	30.2	14.8	7.0	8.5	3.0	20.9	8.5	12.4	9.3	21.7
1988	38.1	2.3	1.1	31.7	12.6	9.1	10.0	2.9	22.4	8.8	13.7	9.3	22.9
1989	37.4	2.6	1.0	31.5	10.1	12.0	9.4	2.3	22.2	5.9	16.3	9.3	25.6
1990	37.1	2.0	1.2	31.8	7.4	14.7	9.6	2.2	22.9	6.9	16.0	8.9	24.9
1991	37.3	1.9	1.5	31.4	4.8	14.0	12.5	2.5	17.1	3.0	14.1	14.3	28.5
1992	39.4	1.6	2.5	31.4	1.2	16.6	13.6	3.9	17.0	3.6	13.4	14.5	28.0
1993	46.5	-2.1	3.6	41.2		17.6	23.6	3.8	18.2	3.9	14.3	23.0	37.2
1994	50.4	0.1	4.0	42.5		18.1	24.3	3.6	22.9	8.1	14.8	19.5	34.3

Source: Bank of Spain.

Note: TBs = treasury bills (Letras del Tesoro); TPNs = treasury promissory notes (Pagares del Tesoro).

[1]Nominal values, except column 3, which was valued at current exchange rates.

[2]Details of column 4 (4 = 9 + 12 = 10 + 13). Columns 9, 10, and 11 are effective accounting values.

[3]"Banks" include all categories of financial institutions, except insurance companies, pension funds, and mutual funds.

[4]Net of government deposits.

main items in each category are detailed in the Appendix. Bank reserves, the control of which was the operational target of monetary policy, are separately identified. Bank reserves appear in Chart 4 as a rather stable percentage of currency, because they have been adjusted to a constant required reserve ratio.[8]

Without significant exceptions, the BOS has managed since the early 1970s to keep total required reserves (therefore, adjusted reserves) under its effective control. This is the main fact supporting the assertion that the new approach to monetary control was an effective one, whatever the vagaries in the monetary targets actually pursued at each point in time. As a result, the inverse correlation, in Chart 3, between net borrowing from banks and the remaining items (particularly net lending to government) is not only an accounting by-product, but also a genuine expression of an active monetary policy that counteracted developments in net foreign assets and lending to government.

Chart 4 also shows that the continuous presence of limited market-oriented lending and borrowing mechanisms, allowing an effective control on bank reserves, was critical for the success of the new approach to monetary control.

However, the coexisting large volumes of gross lending and borrowing (the former adding to the need for the latter), and the significant role, in both cases, of operations under nonmarket facilities attest to the hesitations in the transition to a market approach to monetary control. These can be traced back to concerns regarding interest costs, which, combined occasionally with other factors, constrained the speed of adoption of market-based instruments of monetary and debt management and contributed to the gradual approach to reform. Two contradictory strands of cost considerations impinged, however, on BOS lending and borrowing, respectively.

On the lending side, the presence of sizable nonmarket lending to banks is explained by two separate developments. In the 1970s, it was due to the permanence of three ancient nonmarket lending facilities, limited in volume, but sizable and fully used as a result of subsidized interest rates (a special rediscount instrument, Lombard credits on certain government securities, and an ordinary rediscount instrument; see the Appendix (A.a, b, and c)). Although phasing out the last two facilities would have strongly drained liquidity, the authorities delayed such decisions (until 1982 and 1983, respectively), fearing too big a disruption to

---

[8]The conventional limit for required reserves geared exclusively to monetary control purposes has been defined as 2 percent of eligible liabilities, plus currency in the hands of banks. The objective is to treat required reserves over this (or any alternative) conventional level as what they really are: a nonmarket BOS borrowing instrument (see the Appendix (C.a)).

traditional banking practices, and the likely impact on the bank's borrowing and lending rates. Starting in 1978, however, a large new source of lending had appeared, under the form of special bank-solvency credits (detailed in the Appendix (A.d)). Similar fears and political reasons led to subsidizing such loans through nonmarket interest rates. Because of such developments, and given an overall net need to borrow from the banking system, most of the time there was little scope to use any market lending instruments.

On the borrowing side, a critical aspect of the coordination between monetary policy and government debt management became obvious: the same cost considerations preventing the government from issuing its own securities under market conditions also hindered BOS borrowing from banks under market conditions. As a result, market BOS borrowing was difficult to introduce, and never persisted for more than some indispensable minimum. Instead, a large volume of nonmarket borrowing (through different forms of mandatory deposits, detailed in the Appendix (C)), emerged and played a critical role. Several facets of this conflict deserve examination.

Growth in BOS net lending to government proved the government's reluctance to finance its deficit by issuing securities. Any attempt by the BOS to offset it by borrowing from the banking system under market terms was equivalent to substituting BOS issues for government securities issues. However, lending to the government at zero interest and borrowing at market rates was a sure recipe for reducing BOS profits, which had always been fully transferred to the budget and were also under pressure because of large subsidized lending to banks. Any such BOS initiative was bound to have the same adverse effect on the government accounts as an increase in direct market placements of government securities. Therefore, the same considerations preventing the government from directly issuing securities led it to resist BOS initiatives to issue its own instruments under market conditions. The political embarrassment of any emerging BOS net loss, for which there was no historic precedent, added to the conflict, and also made the BOS more ready to accommodate the government's views.

In the case of an expansion of BOS net foreign assets, a more subtle but similar conflict between monetary control and cost to government existed. Foreign assets yielded a market interest rate. Although covered interest parity conditions were rarely fulfilled in the short run, the BOS could have financed a large stock of foreign assets by borrowing from banks under market conditions, without incurring over the medium term any significant loss or profit. However, traditional accounting conventions failed to show this result. Capital gains on foreign assets were recorded as BOS revenue only when realized, that is, normally when reserves declined. As reserves tended, on the contrary, to increase, financing foreign assets by issuing any domestic instrument under the high prevailing nominal interest rates imposed a heavy burden on BOS recorded profits and on the attendant government revenue.

This conflict led, in turn, to still another problem. Excessive growth in net foreign assets could have been offset by the government issuing more securities in the market. The government would not have incurred any net cost, because larger interest payments would have been offset by the positive impact on BOS profits of the attendant decline in BOS lending to government. Some moves in this direction took place at certain stages. However, although the government finally accepted financing its current deficit by issuing government securities in the market, it remained reluctant to reduce its net borrowing from the BOS, let alone to build a (nonremunerated) net asset position with the BOS.

The BOS needs to borrow from banks, and therefore the outlined conflicts were aggravated by the large outstanding volume of subsidized nonmarket lending to banks. It was also marginally intensified by a BOS preference, in common with other central banks, to be a lender to the banking system. Central banks tend to think that they have more leverage on the system if banks are indebted to them than otherwise. In the BOS case, the preference was actively to operate a market-oriented very short-term lending instrument, geared to day-to-day intervention.[9] However, facing a large required net borrowing position, this preference increased the necessary gross borrowing. It also fostered the need for nonmarket borrowing mechanisms, since, under a normal upward-sloping yield curve, any persistent medium-term borrowing to lend short term would lead to systematic BOS losses.[10] Preference for keeping leverage on the banking system through the lending side, and opposition to very short-term borrowing facilities, added other nonmarket twists. A significant and variable volume of short-term liabilities cannot be managed without accepting the need to pay a market interest rate. By contrast, a certain volume of lending can be managed either by requiring a market interest rate or by accepting lower-than-market rates. Softening the trade-off between prices and quantities is bound to be small and

---

[9]This also explains why the BOS never set up a regular mechanism for overnight borrowing from banks, and why market-oriented borrowing mechanisms have always operated in the range of one to three months.

[10]Chart 4 shows that, as a rule, market borrowing excluded market lending, and vice versa. Yet there are many minor exceptions, and a few more significant ones. They are largely owing to the relatively long maturity and intermittent issue of borrowing instruments, making the simultaneous use of offsetting overnight loans inevitable for fine-tuning bank liquidity. Such simultaneous use increased at times when the BOS delayed a reduction in borrowing on wrong expectations of future autonomous creation of bank liquidity, or when it wished to keep, even at a cost, its leverage on the lending side.

temporary, but some central banks feel that it may be relevant. Lending interest rates may tend as a result to lag behind market requirements, a risk repeatedly confirmed in the Spanish experience.

Finally, a general problem underlying all the preceding assertions merits attention. The gradualist approach to reforms adopted by the authorities was often justified with the argument that banks needed time to adapt to them. The argument had some merit but could also be used to cover the hesitations that the authorities themselves entertained concerning novel practices. Gradual reforms implied, in addition, a larger number of partial reforms, to which the same argument was often applied. Not only did long delays in attaining certain reforms ensue, but also an excessive number of minor changes in monetary control instruments and a lack of confidence in the longevity of any new solution.

All these issues are abundantly illustrated in the following sections, offering a chronological account of the most salient features in government debt management, monetary intervention, and development of the money and government securities markets. They refer to three distinct periods— 1973–81; 1982–87; and 1987–94—in the evolution of government debt management practices in Spain.

First Stage, 1973–81

Government Debt Management

The new approach to monetary policy after 1973 was not followed by any immediate change in government debt management. From 1959 on, medium-term government securities had been placed mainly with the banking system through mandatory investment ratios.[11] Government deficits remained moderate in the early 1970s, and the volume of securities thus placed was low (Table 1, column (10), and Table 2, column (7)). However, in 1977, the government accepted that all new bond issues

---

[11]The complex evolution of mandatory investment ratios in Spain can only be briefly outlined. With ancient precedents in some cases, they received a boost when automatic refinancing facilities at the BOS were limited or eliminated (1959 in the case of government securities, and 1971 in the case of certain categories of subsidized long-term credits). They included both government debt and certain eligible credits. Their relevance for government financing was minor in the early years of the period, and nil after 1977, as explained in the text. Afterwards, they included credits to the private sector (housing, exports, equipment goods), plus a special government paper (here excluded from government debt) fully earmarked to refinance certain official banking institutions, also financing the private sector. After 1977, gradual reductions in mandatory investments, with temporary setbacks, led to their complete elimination by March 1989. This excludes a separate special mandatory investment ratio in treasury promissory notes during 1984–93, discussed later in the text.

would no longer be eligible under mandatory investment ratios.[12] The implicit acceptance of market interest rates on all newly issued securities was a cornerstone for future government debt management, though its immediate practical relevance was minor. The government, facing a large increase in bond yields (Chart 5)—a result of overall financial trends, rather than the noted policy change—refrained from an active issuing policy.[13] Outstanding government securities increased up to 2.1 percent of GDP by end-1981, largely because of growing nonbank holdings (Table 2, columns (4), (9), and (12)). Such humble improvement contrasts with the growth during the same period in BOS lending to government, from 0.6 percent to 7.7 percent of GDP (Table 2, column (2)).

The finance ministry's persistent refusal to issue short-term securities was to become, as detailed in the following section, a source of trouble. Lack of historical precedent, an inadequate legal notion (short-term debt being conceived as purely transitory), and low borrowing needs had supported this attitude in the past. When growing deficits in a high-inflation context made the need for short-term securities compelling, the high and volatile interest rates prevailing in the money market offered new ground for objections. However, cost was not the only consideration. There was also a clear reluctance to issue securities that would directly compete with bank deposits. Overcoming an ingrained preference to shelter banks from competition was difficult, as shown by the continual enforcement of legal limits on bank deposit interest rates.[14]

In fact, the government accepted the need to issue, from 1973 on, small amounts of short-term treasury monetary bonds (TMBs), meant to facilitate monetary intervention by the BOS. However, the odd features of this instrument, described in the following section, only confirm the preceding assertions.

Monetary Intervention

Instruments adequate for controlling net lending to banks took shape only slowly. Resistance to phasing out the sizable older lending facilities

---

[12]There have been only five bond issues between 1970 and this moment. Two of them were not eligible for the mandatory investment ratio, and commanded a 6 percent issue yield, compared with 5 percent for the three remaining eligible issues.

[13]Securities were under paper form and had fairly long maturities. Offered on tap for a short while, at rates in line with market rates, they were subscribed by banks and, through them, by the public. Banks were paid commissions for their intermediation, while individual investors were lured by credits in their personal income tax.

[14]Very slow progress was made in eliminating them (deposits over three years were freed in 1969, over two years in August 1974, and over one year in July 1977). Plans (envisaged in 1977) for a rapid liberalization of the shorter maturities failed to materialize, largely because of fears stemming from the emerging bank solvency crisis.

Chart 5. Term Structure of Spanish Interest Rates
(In percent)

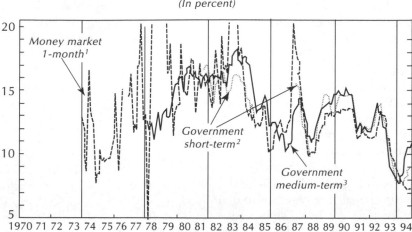

Source: Bank of Spain.
[1]Up to June 1987, interbank loans; after June 1987, interbank repos.
[2]Issue yield of 12- to 18-month treasury promissory notes
(Oct. 81–Aug. 85) and 12-month treasury bills (after June 1987).
[3]Secondary market yields: up to June 1987, stock market for two-year maturity and over;
after June 1987, OTC market for three-year maturity.

(Appendix (A.a, b, and c)) has already been noted. The ordinary rediscount facility became in fact an active instrument, as access limits and interest rates (always below market rates) were now more frequently revised. It was, however, totally inadequate for accurate control of bank liquidity. A policy, up to 1978, of frequent change in reserve requirements attests to the difficulties, and also contributed to delays, in setting up or using alternative intervention mechanisms.

Very early, a market-oriented BOS borrowing facility was introduced, for which there was no historical precedent. As noted above, the government accepted, from February 1973 on, the need to issue one-, two-, and three-month treasury monetary bonds. The BOS purchased them from the government and placed them in the market (see the Appendix (D.a)). However, government reluctance to engage in regular short-term issues was evident in the limited volumes available, the low and unvarying interest rates paid, and the restriction of holdings to financial intermediaries.[15] The use of this facility was, however, desultory during the early 1970s. When in 1978 the need to borrow became more pressing, significant outright placements of

---

[15] Thus, the TMB can be best conceived as a direct BOS issue, rather than a government security issue. This is the solution—validated by later developments—adopted in the statistics supporting this paper.

TMBs were made under strong BOS pressure on banks to subscribe. This was also the first instance of any security legally being traded over the counter, outside the costly and inefficient stock exchange procedures.

The move to period averaging of required reserves prompted the introduction (July 1974) of so-called money market loans, a market-oriented facility with features still akin to the old rediscount facility (see the Appendix (B.a)). At this stage, both the BOS and banks were generally reluctant to use any overnight or short-term lending mechanisms, and their attitude led to frequent premature consolidations of seven-day loans into longer-term loans of up to six months. It took three more years before the introduction (September 1977) of "short-term money market loans" (one- and seven-day), distributed through daily multiple-price auctions, as a general lending mechanism (see the Appendix (B.b)). As the basic need at this stage was to drain liquidity, balances under the new facility never reached a significant level during this period. However, the new facility implied the recognition by the BOS of the need for some overnight instrument to control bank liquidity accurately, and it was the first instance of use of the formal auctions to allocate any financial instrument regularly. This facility, with marginal subsequent reforms, would remain in regular use until the present.

As the need to borrow increased, a serious breach with the market-oriented approach to monetary control occurred. In January 1979, banks were required to place special deposits with the BOS, remunerated at below-market rates (see the Appendix (C.b)). Soon, their volume far exceeded TMB placements. In addition, a precedent was created that, under different guises, was to persist until the present.

Yet, almost simultaneously (February 1979), the BOS discontinued outright placements of TMBs, and started to borrow by means of 7- to 90-day repos on TMBs (see the Appendix (D.b)). This implied the reintroduction of repos in Spanish financial markets, from which they had been absent for many years. The government accepted significant, though still insufficient, increases in TMB issues. However, it also accepted (February 1980) that the BOS had started issuing its own certificates of deposit (BSCDs), with the same features as TMBs, to support its growing borrowing activity through repos (see the Appendix (D.c)). As a result of the bank's growing need to borrow, outstanding repos on TMBs and BSCDs exceeded again special deposits by end-1981. Although BOS short-term borrowing was replacing in point the government securities issues, it did not raise any special coordination issue, other than the negative impact, accepted by the government, on BOS profits.

In summary, the BOS sustained during the period an important volume of nonmarket lending to banks, despite the overall need to borrow. In addition, a large share of gross borrowing was also under nonmarket terms.

Still, there was sufficient room for significant marginal intervention through market-oriented instruments: short-term money market loans, and longer-term outright or repo placements of TMBs and BSCDs. As a result, the BOS generally maintained adequate control of daily levels of bank liquidity and money market conditions.

Government Debt and Money Markets

During 1973–81, government securities remained as thinly traded in the stock exchange as in earlier days (Table 3, column (4)), though yields increased very substantially, to levels comparable to bank lending rates (see Chart 5).

In a context of rigidly regulated bank intermediation, and the absence of a significant market for government securities, the early success in developing a free and active money market was critical. It increased the scope for BOS intervention using market mechanisms, became the first gear in the transmission of BOS initiatives to the financial system at large, and offered the only reliable information on market interest rates. It is also significant that the development of the money market was an autonomous process, without any direct inducement on the part of the authorities. However, it would have never taken place without certain policy initiatives.

First, interbank lending, contrary to other bank operations, had been exempt since 1969 from any control on interest rates and any other legal restrictions. Interbank operations were never subject to reserve requirements and were exempt from any withholding tax. Second, interbank lending became a necessity as soon as all facilities allowing banks automatic access to BOS credit became limited, and marginal discretionary BOS lending under market terms was introduced, in particular when combined with the presence of reserve requirements. Third, the introduction, in early 1974, of the averaging of daily reserves forced banks to manage their liquidity actively, and to rely increasingly on interbank lending.[16]

Interbank lending was carried out over the telephone, either directly or with the intervention of so-called money market brokers. These were not really brokers, but "finders," that is, agents providing information about potential borrowers and lenders, without any participation in the execution of transactions, though receiving in such cases a fee from both parties. They emerged spontaneously (from precedents in the foreign

---

[16] Limitations on averaging, noted above, were aimed at fostering interbank lending, and overcoming banks' traditional aversion to interbank borrowing and lending. Banks quickly surmounted, for obvious economic reasons, their aversion to interbank financing.

Table 3. Spain: Money and Government Debt Markets

	Money Market (Outstanding Interbank Balances)[1]			Secondary Markets for Government Securities (Annual Trading as a Percent of Average Outstanding Securities)[2]								
	Total	Loans settled through STMD	Repos on BOS or govt. paper	Stock exchange (bonds)	OTC stock exchange depository (TPNs)	Over-the-counter market (BOS depository)					Forward dealers market (bonds)[3]	Futures options market (bond futures)
						Total	Of which: Dealers market[3]	TPNs[4]	TBs	Bonds		
	1 = 2 + 3	2	3	4	5	6 = 8 + 9 + 10	7	8	9	10	11	12
1970				6.6								
1971				6.0								
1972				4.5								
1973				5.0								
1974												
1975				7.1								
1976		...	...	6.8								
1977	...	1.3	...	3.9								
1978	...	1.8	...	8.4								
1979	...	1.9	...	5.4								
1980	...	2.1	...	5.2								
1981	...	2.1	...	3.5			...	...				
1982	...	2.1	...	3.2	15.4		...	...				
1983	...	2.6	...	5.0	4.7	34.9	34.9	34.9				
1984	7.7	4.7	3.0	6.3	10.8	...	22.9	22.9				

1985	8.4	4.7	3.8	15.6	3.3	...	36.1	36.1				
1986	12.9	9.9	3.1	17.1	1.0	...	29.0	29.0				
1987	13.2	10.7	2.5	5.5	1.2	23.6	14.2	13.8	88.2	14.1		
1988	12.4	10.2	2.2	1.7	0.4	76.5	53.2	9.1	79.2	173.8	5.8	
1989	12.6	10.9	1.8	1.0	0.2	97.9	37.7	19.4	159.7	121.7	61.8	
1990	12.7	11.3	1.5	1.0		105.0	30.2	26.0	106.5	175.5	84.6	41.9
1991	13.9	11.9	2.0	0.5		234.9	78.3	56.4	195.4	382.8	142.2	88.0
1992	14.3	12.0	2.3	1.8		399.8	141.8	32.7	153.7	772.0	73.1	133.6
1993	18.7	14.6	4.0	5.3		847.8	258.7	22.3	184.0	1484.1	72.0	401.4
1994	16.3	12.3	4.0	23.5		921.8	283.2		139.4	1506.7	57.1	869.0

Source: Bank of Spain.

Note: TBs = treasury bills (Letras del Tesoro); TPNs = treasury promissory notes (Pagares del Tesoro); STMD = servicio telefonico del mercado de dinero.

[1] Annual averages of monthly figures, as a percentage of bank liabilities to domestic nonbanks. Significant interbank balances excluded from market trading (correspondent accounts, relations among affiliated banks, etc.) are ignored.

[2] Denominators are adjusted to each trading category.

[3] Trading in which both parties are dealers (most nondealer trading involves a dealer as one of the parties).

[4] Data on nondealers trading missing for 1984–86.

exchange market) and were not subject to any explicit regulation. "Finders" mediated a large share of all market-oriented interbank lending. Simultaneously, some banks became increasingly active in arbitrage dealings.

Personal interbank loans were initially traded under overnight and other very short maturities. Maturities from three months up to one year were offered after 1977. By 1981, outstanding interbank loans traded through the payments facility described below amounted to 2.1 percent of bank liabilities to domestic nonbanks (Table 3, column (2)). Interbank repo trading of TMBs and BSCDs developed after 1979.

Interbank lending was initially settled with checks, physically picked up at the paying bank and taken to the BOS for direct same-day settlement. A critical innovation took place in late 1976, when the BOS set up a small facility (the STMD, or "servicio telefonico del mercado de dinero") offering banks the possibility of communicating over the telephone interbank loans for same-day settlement. A peculiar feature of the system was that banks were required to communicate at the same time the date and amount of the reimbursement flow (including interest) at maturity, which was to be automatically carried out by the BOS on that date.[17]

Participation in the system was voluntary, but soon a significant volume of interbank lending was being settled through it. Convenience was a major reason, but banks also placed high value on the unintended role of the BOS as informal registrar. This compensated for the weak authentication procedures prevailing in interbank lending. The BOS also derived significant benefits: almost instant knowledge of money market developments; the ability to feed back daily information on average interest rates; and the possibility of monitoring, for supervision purposes, the net market position and rating of individual banks.

The linkage of the STMD with the general payments settlement process through the BOS also deserves comment. Payments clearing and settlement had always taken place at the end of the business day. Deposit balances held as required reserves were fully available for that purpose, subject to penalties in case of failure to comply with minimum requirements. General clearinghouse balances and the separate STMD balances were combined into provisional final balances to settle (at 15:00 hours). No overdrafts at the BOS were ever permitted, and no penal lending facility existed to face cash deficiencies. So, if necessary, banks were allowed to enter new interbank borrowing operations to cover any cash deficiency. No specific time limit was set for this final adjustment, which normally

---

[17]Both lender and borrower submitted, to separate telephone numbers, a standard communication of each operation. Only fully matching orders were processed by the BOS. A single written confirmation of all telephone orders had to be provided within the day.

took place quickly. This procedure has remained unchanged until the time of writing.

The telephone lines of the STMD were also used to collect and distribute information on BOS money market loans and repos on TMBs and BSCDs, and to carry the subsequent auctions of money market loans. Settlement of such transactions took place through the STMD. After 1979, TMBs and BSCDs were issued under book-entry form, and the STMD facility was in charge of keeping such records. It was also responsible for the settlement of interbank repo trading in such instruments, thus ensuring same-day settlement, as well as delivery versus payment. This was the starting point of what in later years would become the standard settlement procedure for over-the-counter wholesale trading in government securities. In the case of interbank repos, simultaneous orders for the spot and forward transactions were entered into the STMD, thus offering information on terms and interest rates.

Second Stage, 1982–87

Government Debt Management

A decisive innovation characterized this period: the overdue acceptance by the government (October 1981) of the need to issue a short-term discount paper—denominated "Pagares del Tesoro" or "treasury promissory notes" (TPNs)—initially addressed to financial institutions but soon made available to any investor (April 1982). The new securities were to be placed through fortnightly auctions, carried out by the BOS, and open to any investor. Initial multiple-price auctions were replaced by uniform-price auctions in 1983; volumes offered were never preannounced. In addition, there were crucial changes (detailed below under "Government Debt and Money Markets") related to the secondary market: the authorization of over-the-counter trading, the endorsement of repo trading by nonbanks, and the introduction of book entries for the public at large.

Yet old inhibitions had not entirely disappeared. Large TPN minimum denominations and maturities of 6 and 12 months were meant to minimize competition with bank deposits. In addition, 6-month issues disappeared in 1984, at the same time that 18-month issues were introduced; 12-month issues also disappeared in 1987. The reason was that, in the absence of rules requiring accrued recording of interest in the government accounts, such changes allowed interest payments to be shifted into subsequent budgets.

Willingness to pay market rates was critical for the success of this paper, yet it was not always the only relevant factor. Yields were always highly

Chart 6. Market Structure of Spanish One-Year Interest Rates
(In percent)

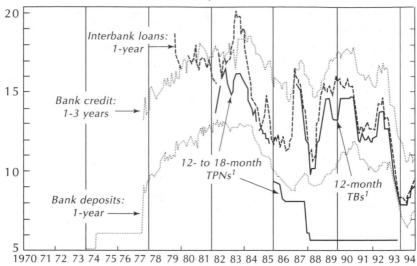

Note: TBs = treasury bills; TPNs = treasury promissory notes.
Source: Bank of Spain.
[1]Marginal issue yield.

competitive with bank deposit rates (Chart 6). However, nonbank investors were also attracted by the fact that, contrary to bank deposits, TPNs were not subject to a withholding tax and could be traded over-the-counter, offering more scope for tax evasion than alternative instruments. This factor became increasingly important in view of the parallel initiatives (fully operative by 1985) requiring banks and other intermediaries to provide information to the fiscal authorities on interest income paid on bank deposits and other sources of capital income. The endorsement of repo trading by nonbanks (January 1984) gave an immense impetus to their demand for TPNs, because, in the absence of shorter maturity issues, it provided the means to better reconcile yield and liquidity preferences.

The yields on TPNs were not initially attractive compared with interbank rates, particularly during a 1983 episode of monetary tightness (Chart 6). By late 1984, the situation had changed, and banks' demand started to increase, spurred by the ability to refinance TPN holdings through repos with nonbanks, for which a strong demand was developing. Thus, after a somewhat slow start, the TPN became a success story (Table 2, column (5)). By the end of 1984, the outstanding volume had reached 14.4 percent of GDP. However, the success was soon cut short by two misguided policy decisions.

A special mandatory investment ratio in TPNs was imposed on banks (12 percent of deposits in June 1984, reduced to 11 percent in February 1985 and 10 percent in October 1985). The level and subsequent reductions of the ratio reveal that it was just a precautionary move, due to fears prompted by the cost problems faced in 1983. In fact, the government continued to offer attractive yields, and banks significantly exceeded the required ratios. Nevertheless, the investment ratio became finally binding as a result of the second major development.

As part of ongoing efforts to fight tax evasion of capital income, a withholding tax on capital gains on fixed rate securities was introduced, as well as additional reporting requirements by financial intermediaries to the tax authorities (May 1985). However, in view of the large outstanding stock of TPNs, the government excluded them from these rules. By one stroke, the TPN became an official tax shelter for individuals and enterprises, though not for banks. The government was somewhat slow to draw the logical implication that interest paid on TPNs need not be as high as on instruments subject to tax, but by mid-1986, it had reduced the rate sufficiently to keep it attractive to the public, though unattractive to banks (Chart 6). From that moment on, the mandatory investment ratio became the only reason for banks to keep a portfolio of TPNs, while nonbanks were still eagerly buying them. Interest rate and secondary market developments hinged subsequently on these odd demand factors, with adverse consequences for monetary control. Anyway, by the end of 1986, the stock of TPNs reached its historical maximum (18.5 percent of GDP, about half total government debt).

Concerning medium-term securities, there were also some relevant reforms, and a more active issuing policy. The government introduced bonds with single redemption at final maturity and without any tax privilege (October 1982) and started placing them through multiple-price auctions open to any investor (September 1983). These were all major improvements over previous practices; otherwise, outdated features persisted.[18] Taking advantage of a marked downward trend in bond yields (Chart 5), the government issued a large volume of securities. Outstanding bonds reached, as a result, 8.4 percent of GDP in 1986 (Table 2, column (4)), a significant performance, though still far from the parallel growth in TPNs.

On the whole, between 1981 and 1986, outstanding marketable securities increased from 2.3 percent of GDP to 26.8 percent of GDP,

---

[18]Issues did not follow any regular calendar; securities were in paper form; and they were negotiable only in the stock exchange. In addition, old-style bonds with some tax privileges were issued on tap side by side. With a view to extending the average maturity of the government debt, rather costly ten-year bonds were issued, in addition to three-year bonds. All of them were fixed interest rate issues, and a single variable rate issue in 1986 has remained to this day the only Spanish experience with this instrument.

roughly in parallel with total government debt (Table 2, columns (1) and (4)). After 1984, a new pattern of government securities holdings started to emerge (Table 2, columns (9)–(13)). Banks tended to become the main outright holders of government securities, by far exceeding outright nonbank holdings. However, banks were increasingly financing their holdings by selling them to nonbanks under repo agreements. Taking into account both outright and repo holdings, the opposite picture emerged: nonbank holdings tended to exceed bank holdings. This pattern, which would become a permanent feature in later years, was already well established by 1986. In addition, a novel structure of interest rates had developed (see "Government Debt and Money Markets" below).

Monetary Intervention

The pressing need to drain liquidity led finally to the elimination of the old automatic Lombard credits on pre-1957 government securities (April 1982) and of the ordinary rediscount facility (May 1983). Short-term money market loans introduced in the previous period remained as a market-oriented lending mechanism, though developments did not allow for any substantial use.

On the borrowing side, the combination of special deposits plus repos on TMBs and BSCDs prevailed for a while. Special deposits and ordinary reserve requirements still experienced exceptional increases in 1982 and in 1983 (see the Appendix (C.a and c)), though from early 1982 on, repos exceeded the volume of special deposits. A new change in borrowing techniques took place, however. Repos on TMBs and BSCDs were discontinued (April 1982), to be replaced by direct placements of a new BOS short-term discount paper, so-called monetary certificates (BSMCs), with the novelty that they were placed through multiple-price auctions (see the Appendix (D.d)). The change was meant to be only a technical improvement on the earlier borrowing facility. This also explains why the BOS refused to use the newly issued TPN as a means of supporting its own borrowing activity: it was unclear at this stage whether the government would be ready to issue a large enough volume of TPNs, while the negative experience with TMBs called for caution. The volume of outstanding BSMCs was to experience very important increases, and the BOS drained the largest amounts ever reached under a market-oriented mechanism (Chart 4). Unfortunately, such increases, together with a 1983 episode of monetary tension, led to increasing government and BOS reluctance to accept their cost implications.

The situation ended in a radical change of the whole approach of draining liquidity (January 1984). Ordinary nonremunerated required reserves were reduced but were supplemented by special remunerated required reserves, much higher than the old special remunerated deposits, now phased out (see the Appendix (C.a and c)). BSMCs were eliminated, replaced largely by the newly required reserves. As a result, the bulk of the BOS's need to borrow was covered by this nonmarket mechanism, which experienced additional increases in 1987 (Chart 4). In addition, while the remuneration of the new mandatory deposits was initially close to interbank rates, successive reductions were introduced, and after mid-1986, the rate was to remain significantly below market levels.

Yet, room was left for a new market-oriented borrowing mechanism (also January 1984), now under the form of repos on TPNs, previously bought from the government (see the Appendix (D.e)). The government accepted the implicit substitution of TPNs for BOS loans at zero interest, and the BOS was able to issue a significant volume of such repos throughout 1984 and 1985. Fortunately, the need to drain liquidity diminished subsequently, because from mid-1986 on, market interest rates on TPNs were increasingly distorted by the anomalous factors noted above (Chart 6). It became increasingly difficult for the BOS to accomplish meaningful interventions in such a market, and the early 1987 increases in remunerated required reserves, mentioned in the preceding paragraph, mirror this state of affairs.

On balance, this period showed for the first time an intense interaction between monetary control and government debt management. The experience was very positive in many respects (detailed in the next section) and became a strong basis for developments in the coming years. However, against a background of monetary tensions, events also proved how the unwillingness of both the government and the BOS to accept fully cost implications led to disastrous consequences and to the need to start again almost from scratch. Nonmarket lending and borrowing remained important during this period, though as in earlier days, marginal market-oriented mechanisms for the control of bank liquidity still allowed the BOS to exert the desired leverage on monetary expansion and market conditions.

Government Debt and Money Markets

The trading of government bonds in the stock exchange was significantly stimulated by the new issuing policy noted above but remained thin. By contrast, an active over-the-counter secondary market for TPNs developed.

Over-the-counter trading of TPNs, by both banks and nonbanks, was legally authorized; and to facilitate it all, the TPN could be issued under book-entry form. This was the first antecedent of any security held by nonbanks that could be traded over the counter and be maintained under book-entry form. Initially, only TPNs held by banks were under book entries maintained by the BOS. Nonbanks could keep them under a special depository service at the stock exchange, as well as in paper form (this became the exception). However, banks could act as agents for the stock exchange depository, and trade the deposited TPNs over the counter. Two separate though closely linked over-the-counter markets developed: a wholesale one supported by the BOS depository, and a clients' market supported by the stock exchange depository (Table 3, columns (5) and (8)).

In January 1984, nonbanks were given access to the BOS book-entry depository, by allowing a limited number of banks to act as subdepositories of the BOS. This system (subject to loose controls and limited reporting requirements) was the precedent on which, in coming years, a formal and tightly controlled BOS book-entry depository for all government securities would be built. Simultaneously, repo trading by nonbanks was allowed and regulated, and this proved a far-reaching innovation. In fact, it turned out to be more important than intended, because interest rates on short-term bank deposits were still subject to legal control, and they were far exceeded by rates on short-term repos. From then on, there were two separate, though linked, clients' markets: a fast-growing one, supported by the BOS depository and its subdepository agents (on which, unfortunately, no information was ever gathered), and a declining one, supported by the stock exchange depository. In both markets, repo trading (not reported in Table 3) immediately far exceeded outright trading.

An effective dealer system started to emerge, despite the fact that no direct inducement was offered to banks to play any specific role in the market for TPNs. TPNs, particularly when sold on a repo basis, became strong competitors with bank deposits, and this was a powerful reason for banks to refrain from mediating in their sale to the public. However, such an intermediation offered attractive business opportunities, and banks that abstained from it risked losing deposits without any counterpart. Preference for repos, instead of outright placement, was encouraged not only by the absence of really short-term issues and by controls on deposit interest rates, but also by convenience to banks. Under accounting rules that are still in force, securities sold on a repo basis remained in the banks' portfolio, and repos appeared as a liability, exempt of reserve requirements. Banks could, as a result, show as a change in the composition of their balance sheet what would otherwise be a reduction in its size. As a result of these factors, all large banks soon ended playing an active role as dealers in government securities, as noticed earlier from a different perspective (Table 2). On the other hand, repos on TPNs were also actively traded in the interbank market. Initially, they were a mere substitute for interbank loans, like the preceding repos on TMBs, BSCDs, and BSMCs. However, the wholesale market for TPNs took on a life of its own, as interactions with the parallel nonbank market became important. Active placement of TPNs with the public forced banks, in turn, into a more active role in the primary market for TPNs. Consequently, TPNs provided the training ground for the subsequent development of an over-the-counter secondary market for all government securities, in which banks would play the role of dealers as much as it suited their preferences.

The TPN also became the first instrument actively traded in the money market and by the public at large, thus providing a strong transmission mechanism between BOS monetary control initiatives, money market developments, and general financial conditions. An important change in the structure of interest rates ensued (Charts 5 and 6). TPN yields gradually moved from initial levels close to bank lending rates to levels closer to bank deposit rates, pulling down both government bond yields and interbank rates. Interbank rates, which until 1983 had been clearly associated with bank lending rates, now became strongly coupled to government securities yields. Both would move from then onward somewhere in between bank lending and deposit rates, approaching one or the other only at times of significant change, because of the sluggish adaptation of bank lending and deposit rates to such changes. This provided retroactive confirmation that earlier market-oriented intervention had been indeed quite costly, not (as it was often claimed) because it was based on BOS borrowing instruments, but owing to the absence of any financial instrument providing an adequate bridge between the money market and the market for bank deposits.

As to the money market, the only additional relevant change was the removal (January 1984) of the remaining restrictions on averaging required reserves. This increased the scope for a more flexible management of cash resources and interbank lending. Interbank lending under market conditions experienced a remarkable growth during these years (Table 3, columns (1) – (3)), centered on personal loans. Repo trading (mainly on TPNs) also increased, encouraged not only by developments in the nonbank repo market, but also because the ongoing bank solvency crisis strongly favored collateralized interbank lending. Such increases partly reflected the growing arbitrage activity of some banks that had opted for developing this line of business. The role of "finders" in the money market also expanded to the TPN market and increased in parallel with overall trading.

There was little need throughout these years to modify the essentially successful BOS settlement facility, the STMD, though its activity expanded considerably. The main novelty was that auctions of primary issues of TPNs were taken care of, as well as BOS auctions of BSMCs and repos on TPNs. Keeping the emerging book-entry system for TPNs was also a new task. Outright interbank TPN trading, plus repo trading in both BSMCs and TPNs, were also settled through it, under terms previously available for TMBs and BSCDs, namely, ensuring same-day settlement and delivery versus payment.

Third Stage, 1987–94

Government Debt Management

The main innovation during the most recent stage was a deep reform in government debt management, leading to a rapidly expanding secondary market in government securities. Techniques and experiences previously tested, on limited scales, in the monetary control sphere, the money market, and the TPNs market were now extended to the whole market for government securities, with authorities trying, however, to rectify earlier problems.

In a critical departure from past practice, legal authorization was introduced to issue all government securities under book-entry form, and to trade them, under such a form, over the counter. This was shortly followed by the introduction of a formal and general book-entry depository for government securities, managed by the BOS (April 1987). Most negotiable securities were soon under book-entry form and consequently could be traded over the counter. The BOS, in coordination with the finance ministry and (after its creation in 1988) with the specialized supervisory agency of the capital market, was entrusted with the responsibility for the organization and management of the primary and secondary markets for government securities, as well as for their supervision.

As soon as the depository was in place, the government completely reshaped its issuing policy. To encourage the development of active secondary markets, newly issued securities were restricted to a very limited range of standard instruments, lacking any fiscal privilege and issued through auctions. Central to the new policy were 12-month discount "Letras del Tesoro" or treasury bills (TBs), which from the very beginning attracted strong demand (Table 2, column (6)). Shorter maturities were refused by the government, for reasons already noted concerning the accounting of cost and competition with bank deposits—despite the fact that almost simultaneously (March 1987), the last controls on short-term bank deposit rates were removed. Limited issues of three- and six-month TBs have taken place, however, since late 1991, although a regular issue program is still pending reform. As to bonds, only three-year bonds were initially offered, the government now rejecting the need to pay the premia required by the market over longer maturities. As inflation subsided, issues of five- and ten-year bonds started in 1989, to grow significantly after 1991. Fifteen-year bonds were introduced by end-1993. With a view to increasing the size of outstanding issues, by encouraging the development of a secondary market, the same bonds have been repeatedly auctioned up to some informally set large minimum volume. By the end of 1993, outstanding bonds exceeded TBs for the first time. The reshaping of government issues also allowed the gradual elimination of the large stock of TPNs (a growing financial, as well as political, embarrassment), replaced by the newly issued securities (Table 2, column (5)).

Since 1987, all new issues of marketable government securities have taken place through auctions, open to any investor and carried out by the BOS, following as a rule regular preannounced calendars.[19] As had been the case with TPNs, volumes offered for auction were not preannounced. The persistence of this feature can be attributed to the long BOS experience with auctions of its own instruments, in which the amounts offered were never preannounced. Final decisions on auction results are taken by the finance ministry, but a joint committee of BOS and ministry representatives must submit its formal advice.

As a result of the new issuing policy, it was possible to finance the bulk of the government debt with marketable securities (Table 2, columns (1) and (4)). The role of repos, now on any kind of government security, experienced further growth until 1989, stabilizing thereafter (Table 2, columns (9)–(13)). The absence of newly issued securities with really short maturities contributed to this trend, which was also encouraged by banks for reasons noted above. As a consequence, the pattern that had developed over the previous period remained in place, with banks refinancing a large part of their holdings through repos. Households and enterprises were initially the main nonbank holders, increasingly replaced after 1990 by mutual funds and nonresidents. Demand by mutual funds and nonresidents was stimulated by special tax concessions granted in 1990, in a departure from the tax-neutrality policy initiated in 1987. The fact that nonresidents have become major (also volatile) investors in government bonds (showing instead little interest in TBs) has created new, strong interactions between government debt management and monetary policy, centered now on external capital movements and the exchange rate.

---

[19]The system is a special combination of competitive and uniform-price auctions, introduced also in 1987 and found only in Spain. Investors asking for prices lower (yields higher) than the weighted average have to pay the bid price; those asking for higher prices pay the weighted average price. Since 1991, most auctions are immediately followed by a second-round auction, limited in volume (to 10 percent or 20 percent of previous placement) and with participation restricted to market-makers (see below).

Monetary Intervention

As soon as TB issues started, the BOS introduced three-month repos on TBs purchased from the government as a means of draining bank liquidity (see the Appendix (D.f)). Refusal by the government to issue TBs in maturities other than 12 months made this reform particularly necessary and successful. Significant amounts were issued in the years 1987–90. When, in late 1991, 3-month TBs were introduced, the BOS restricted its repos to the 1-month maturity, to avoid any overlapping with the government issuing activity, and so unnecessary conflicts.

In March 1990, the decision was made to eliminate the remunerated tranche of required reserves. However, instead of tabling its gradual reduction, it was replaced by an issue of long-term BOS bonds (see the Appendix (C.d)). The interest rate was well below market, and placement was, of course, mandatory. This measure was expected to dispel doubts about future execution of the program and, by freezing the 1990 situation, to reduce the cost impact on marginal bank business.

This, in turn, led to the simultaneous reshaping of the BOS short-term money market loans, which were now to be based on repos on BOS bonds and government securities (see the Appendix (B.c)). The BOS encouraged (and banks preferred) using for that purpose the BOS bond portfolio. Its large volume allowed banks to reduce their portfolio of government securities significantly (Table 2, column (10)). Nonetheless, subsequent large increases in BOS lending, exceeding the volume of outstanding BOS bonds, have forced banks to increase their portfolio of government securities to retain their borrowing ability. Such a large increase in BOS lending under market terms has not yet prompted a legally feasible early redemption of BOS bonds (the last significant remnant of nonmarket practices in the Spanish financial system). This is a last evidence of how much resistance the transition to a fully market-oriented monetary policy has engendered.

Government Debt and Money Markets

The general BOS book-entry depository for government securities was built in early 1987 on the experience gained from the book-entry facility for TPNs, trying to overcome its weaknesses. It has the same two-tier structure encountered in other countries, with the BOS at the core of the system and a number of "entidades gestoras," or "authorized dealers," acting as subdepositories.[20] However, it has two features that may be less

---

[20]Such institutions—selected among banks and, since 1991, securities firms created according to the 1988 capital market law—do not have any exclusive entitlement to deal in government securities, though they enjoy some practical advantages over other dealing financial institutions and include, in fact, the major dealers.

common. First, all financial institutions, and not only banks, are allowed to hold direct cash and securities accounts with the central depository, namely, the BOS, thus facilitating settlement of their trading. Second, authorized dealers are limited in number and subject to rigorous conditions, obligations, and reporting requirements. All government securities issued since 1987 have been under book-entry form, and old paper securities could be converted into book entries as well.

Although the role of banks as voluntary dealers in government securities was by then already well established, some measures were taken in 1988 to encourage this function, granting some 30 dealers a special status of "primary dealers," while a subgroup of some 12 primary dealers act as market-makers. Their main obligation is to reach certain specified volumes of primary and secondary trading, and their basic entitlement is the right to trade through four newly set private interdealer brokers operating blind, screen-based trading facilities. Market-makers have, in addition, the exclusive privilege to participate in second-round auctions for government securities and, since 1990, in BOS auctions of overnight money market loans. The latter is, in fact, their most significant privilege.

Two privately managed options and futures markets were created in November 1989 and March 1990, respectively, operating mainly in government debt. In 1992, the two markets created a new, single institution to take over all transactions in futures and options on government debt. Also, as a result of the 1988 capital market law, finders active in the government securities market have had to register as incorporated securities firms, with a limited broker status. The same applies to the new interdealer brokers.

From a practical point of view, the organization of the dealers segment of the market—as well as the support to the nondealers market—has relied on the BOS STMD facility. This facility is in charge of all communications with banks concerning government debt auctions and secondary market transactions, as well as of clearing and settling the cash component of such transactions. However, a separate facility was created to support the book-entry depository. It is in charge of keeping the government securities accounts, and of clearing and settling the security element of government debt transactions, before proceeding to settlement of the cash element. Same-day settlement, on a delivery-versus-payment basis, is insured in the dealers market for government securities, and is also available, on demand, for large nondealers transactions. As a result, the STMD has become the core of the Spanish payments system, being in charge of the final clearing and settlement of the market for government securities, the money market, and the net balances stemming from the remaining clearinghouses and multilateral netting schemes existing in the country. The basic arrangement for final settlement remains the one described in the first stage under "Government Debt and Money Markets."

As a consequence of the new approach to government issues and to trading and settlement, outright over-the-counter trading in government securities has experienced an explosive growth since 1987 (Table 3), while stock exchange trading has remained marginal.[21] The participation of dealers trading in total spot trading (Table 3, columns (6) and (7)) has remained very important, despite a downward trend stemming from the development of nondealers trading. Nondealers trading also consists mainly of wholesale trading, carried out by mutual funds, nonresident dealers, and nonresident institutional investors.[22] Forward operations, mainly among dealers, also experienced rapid growth, later displaced by transactions in the specialized futures market (Table 3, columns (11)-(12)). In 1994, total trading in derivatives exceeded for the first time spot trading. Repo trading by both banks and nonbanks (not reported in Table 3) has always reached several times the corresponding volumes of spot trading, because of the short maturities involved.

The efficiency of a market for government securities where actual transactions are highly decentralized hinges strongly on centralized sources of timely information about market developments. A daily BOS bulletin, blind brokers' screens, finders telephones, and several private information systems provide such information in the case of the wholesale market. Contrary to other countries' experience, there is also detailed information on the nondealers market.[23]

During this period the money market experienced additional growth (Table 3, columns (1)-(3)). The main novelty was that trading in derivatives of interbank loans emerged spontaneously in 1986, to experience an explosive subsequent growth.[24] The strong interaction between the money market and the market for government securities that emerged in the preceding period was now enhanced by the larger trading volumes in

---

[21]Initially, stock exchange trading almost vanished. It has recovered somewhat after the introduction, in 1992, of links between the stock exchange and the BOS depository.

[22]The high efficiency of the Spanish market for government securities is confirmed by the very sizable and active direct participation of nonresident investors and dealers, while no significant trade in Spanish government securities now takes place abroad, contrary to some earlier experience. A recent attempt to set up a futures market on Spanish bonds in London ended in failure, after the Spanish futures market revised some of its practices.

[23]This observation is based on weekly tapes that authorized dealers must supply to the BOS, listing their individualized transactions (amounts, prices, and investor codes, but not names) with third parties.

[24]Trading in forward interbank loans (never carried out, and settled through differences) expanded rapidly after agreements on standardized contracts were introduced in 1988 and improved in 1990. Special settlement facilities through the STMD were introduced at a later stage. Since 1990, the official futures market has also traded futures and options on a three-month interbank contract. Forward, future, and options trading taken together exceed interbank spot trading for comparable maturities. (Such trading is not reported in Table 3.)

both markets, and by the parallel development of markets for derivatives in both cases. In fact, boundaries between the money market and the wholesale market for government securities—with basically the same participants, common trading channels, common settlement facilities, and well-integrated interest rate developments (Charts 5 and 6)—are becoming increasingly blurred.

Coordination of Monetary and Debt Management

The preceding description may be complemented with some general observations on the coordination of monetary and debt management.

Although no details can be provided here, the Spanish transition to market-oriented monetary and government debt management was part of a general overhaul of Spanish economic policy, aimed at liberalizing an economy that for many years was overregulated and highly protected from internal and external competition. To overcome the protectionist frame of mind and the vested interests involved was a very complex task, as much in the financial sphere as elsewhere.

As a result, issues in the coordination of monetary control and debt management hinged mainly on changing and diverging attitudes about the need to play to market rules and to accept the level and evolution of market interest rates resulting from the chosen mix of monetary and fiscal policy. They were reflected basically in the different degrees of reliance on market instruments over time. Overall reliance by the BOS and the government taken together was the main issue, because the relative recourse to market instruments by each of them was usually the result of joint agreements.

Within this framework, conflicts or coordination issues of a purely technical nature were always minimized by a systematic market segmentation based on maturities. Monetary control was, as a rule, limited to overnight intervention and intervention in one additional single short maturity (in the past, up to three months; currently, ten days). On the one hand, government issuing policy was centered on maturities from six months, more recently from three months and upward. On the other hand, the features, placement, and trading techniques of market instruments issued by the BOS usually matched those of government securities as much as could be expected. This contributed to a coherent term structure of the corresponding market interest rates (Charts 5 and 6), as well as to the integration of the money market and the market for government securities.

Current trends in market interest rates were often a source of diverging BOS and government views. However, experience has distilled two conclusions accepted by now. First, that setting the short-term end of the yield curve is a responsibility of monetary policy and the BOS. The BOS considered this to offer sufficient leverage on interest rate developments, and never felt the need to counteract through intervention any market forces shaping the longer maturities of the yield curve. Second, that the ministry of finance cannot and should not try to interfere with the level of interest rates stemming from monetary policy decisions, forced as it is to achieve rather strict gross borrowing targets.[25] The need to supply securities according to a fairly stable maturity structure implies that the ministry does not have much room to exert any influence on the shape of the yield curve either. The market segmentation noted earlier helped to elicit such a conclusion and has been instrumental in its continued implementation.

There have been few formal arrangements supporting the growing coordination between monetary control and government debt management.[26] As in many countries, most relevant policy decisions have been taken in the course of informal meetings of high-level representatives of the ministry and the BOS. As a rule, the institutions have been on good terms, although frequently holding contrary views. Replacement over time of staff favoring traditional policies by those favoring more market-oriented ones increased the meeting ground. From a legal point of view, the ministry always had the upper hand, but from a technical perspective, the opposite tended to be the case. Most innovations, including many concerning government debt management, originated at the BOS, with the ministry making the decision to refuse, modify, or accept them. In recent years, conflicting views have become less momentous than in the past, but not less frequent.

Historical developments contributed in a special way to the coherence between monetary control and debt management. The reluctance of the government to issue short-term securities led the BOS to introduce different substitutes for them and placed the BOS from the very beginning at the core of the emerging markets. As a result, the money market became the training ground for the later development of the market for government securities. Auction techniques, book-entry holdings, decentralized trading, repo trading, efficient same-day settlement procedures, adequate market information, and specialized market participants were all first established in the money market, under regulations set by the BOS. When later the government accepted the need to issue its own securities,

---

[25]The recourse to auctions without a placement commitment and the ability to resort to the BOS overdraft facility allowed the ministry to hope to exert some influence of its own on the evolution of interest rates. Occasional attempts to play with this margin soon became unsustainable. On average, they proved useless as a means of reducing the cost of government finance, while they interfered with the regular supply of government securities, the expectations of market participants, and the smooth development of auctions.

[26]The formal joint auction committee mentioned earlier has played a positive role in the short-run coordination of monetary and debt management policies. A standing technical commission, with representatives of the ministry of finance, the BOS, and the capital market supervisory agency, deals with organizational and supervisory issues concerning the government debt market.

it was easy and natural to extend such features to them and to call on the BOS to play an active agency role.

This process has had a strong bearing on the final position of the BOS as a fiscal agent in relation to the market for government securities. Although the Spanish arrangements do not basically differ from those found in several other countries, the central bank's position as manager of the market is probably stronger than in most countries. This is evident in its functions concerning the book-entry depository and settlement procedures; it is even more noticeable in its supervision of dealers and market developments, where minimum requirements, reporting obligations, and inspections are on the same footing as ordinary bank supervision.

Some General Technical Observations

Finally, it may be useful to point out some salient features of the Spanish transition to market-oriented monetary and debt management that may have some general technical interest. Whether they involve lessons applicable elsewhere or accidental peculiarities of the Spanish case is left for the reader to judge.

(1) Determined to keep some monetary variables under control, but not ready to accept the full interest cost implications, both the government and the BOS fell repeatedly into the trap of mandatory investment rules. The Spanish experience proves that such rules can coexist, up to a point, with an effective monetary policy and active financial markets. However, it also illustrates how they can delay the development of markets and market-oriented financing procedures or, even worse, abort ongoing successful developments. In addition, the implicit tax on bank intermediation was certainly shifted, through distortions in interest rates, to bank borrowers and lenders (including the government and the BOS), with uncertain final effects. In any case, there is little evidence that mandatory investments were of any help in reducing the general level of market interest rates.

(2) Contrary to widespread ideas that market intervention or financing cannot proceed in the absence of developed financial markets, the Spanish experience has been that the development of both the money market and the market for government securities hinged simply on issuing appropriate instruments in significant amounts and removing any obstacles to holding or trading them. It took place with almost no positive regulation of trading arrangements. Instead, setting up simple but efficient settlement facilities was a critical step, as was the emphasis on providing markets with abundant information.

(3) The Spanish experience indicates that a few simple financial instruments are sufficient for effective market-oriented monetary and debt

management and, in addition, contribute to the creation of deep secondary markets. It shows, however, that such a simplification is hard to reach, because it intensifies the need for market-oriented management.

(4) The development of the market for government securities on the foundation of a previously developed money market was, in the Spanish case, more a historical accident than a planned strategy. However, the many positive features of such sequencing suggests its more general application to other countries.

(5) Large placements of government securities became feasible only when the government decided to issue short-term instruments clearly competitive with bank deposits, in order to tap the largest and cheapest existing financial market. This contributed significantly to reducing the cost of government financing and to creating strong links between the money market and the market for government securities. The resulting coupling of money market rates and government securities yields enhanced the effectiveness of monetary intervention and reduced its cost as well.

(6) The authorities always favored the notion of the market for government securities being a dealers market but also held to the view that the markets would create the dealers (as it happened), and not vice versa. As a result, they favored increasing competition by facilitating universal access to the primary and secondary markets for government securities over according special privileges to dealers. By the time some marginal privileges were granted, in 1988, a dealers system was already well established.

(7) Money market derivatives appeared spontaneously and bloomed as a result of the development of the spot money market. The same thing happened with derivatives on government securities and the corresponding spot market. In addition, trading in money market derivatives significantly preceded trading in government securities derivatives. This logical sequencing of events validates the attitude of the Spanish authorities, who never tried to encourage derivative markets prematurely.

(8) Success in market-oriented monetary and debt management was strongly dependent on the creation of more competitive conditions in the financial system, but it has exerted, in turn, a distinct influence on such conditions. A growing share of traditional bank operations has become linked to money market developments, while government securities compete strongly with bank credit (in banks' portfolios) and with bank deposits (in investors' portfolios). As a consequence, banks' behavior has become in every respect more market-oriented and competitive. In the early stages, this was the least-anticipated function of the new market-oriented management, though it has turned out to be a most relevant one.

Appendix

Bank of Spain Operations with Banks

A. Nonmarket Lending Instruments	a.	*Special rediscount (November 1960–June 1971)* Automatic rediscount of bills financing specific investments and exports. Subject to global but not individual quotas. Because of long maturities, slowly declining outstanding amounts remained until December 1985.
	b.	*Lombard credits on government securities issued before 1957 (1940–April 1982)* Banks were entitled to pledge them with the BOS at interest rates comparable to their nominal yield. Limited to the available stock of such securities; very slowly declining over time.
	c.	*Ordinary rediscount (1940–May 1983)* Rediscount of 3-month commercial bills, usually at below-market rates. Subject to global and individual quotas, frequently revised.
	d.	*Special bank-solvency loans (1975–92)* Ad hoc credits, with subsidized interest rates, to specific banks and to the deposit insurance agency. Granted to manage an important solvency crisis in the banking system. After peaking in 1985, full reimbursement extended until 1992.
B. Market Lending Instruments[1]	a.	*Money market loans (July 1974–August 1978)* Individual loans, secured by a general pledge on certain bank assets. Maturities from 7 to 180 days. Offered to banks according to pre-established individual quotas, at frequently revised interest rates.
	b.	*Short-term money market loans (September 1977– March 1990)* Individual loans, secured by a general pledge on certain bank assets. One- and 7-day maturities. Distributed through daily multiple-price auctions, without preannouncement of amounts offered. Replaced by item B.c.
	c.	*Repos on BOS bonds (see 4.f) and government securities (since March 1990)* Ten-day repos, distributed through multiple-price auctions held every 10 days (at the beginning of each reserve reporting period), and overnight repos auctioned daily. Participation has been, in the latter case, limited since 1990 to government debt market-makers. Amounts offered are not preannounced.

---

[1]So-called second window lending facilities, designed to resolve exceptional general liquidity shortages after normal intervention, are ignored. They have existed since 1977, under the form of overnight loans or repos on government securities, and have been subject to many changes.

Appendix *(continued)*

C. Nonmarket Borrowing Instruments

a. *Nonremunerated reserve requirement (since 1970)*
Redefined as average of daily figures in 1974. Very frequent changes led to a single uniform ratio of 5.75 percent (Oct. 1978), increased to 6.75 percent (Dec. 1982), and 7.75 percent (Aug. 1983). Changes, up to 1990, associated with those in item C.c: reduction to 5 percent (Feb. 1984), and 2.5 percent (Oct. 1985); increase to 5 percent (Aug. 1988), 6.5 percent (Feb. 1989), and 7.5 percent (July 1989); and reduction to 7 percent (Mar. 1990). Additional reductions to 5 percent (May 1990), 4.5 percent (Mar. 1992), 3 percent (Dec. 1992), and 2 percent (Sept. 1993). (On the partial treatment as a nonmarket borrowing instrument, see footnote 8 to the text.)

b. *Special remunerated deposits (January 1979–February 1984)*
Initial level 1 percent increased to 2 percent (Mar. 1979), 3 percent (Apr. 1979), and 4 percent (Apr. 1983). Balances remunerated at BOS discount rate, well below market rates. Replaced by item C.c.

c. *Special remunerated reserve requirement (February 1984–March 1990)*
Initial level 13 percent, increased to 15.5 percent (Oct. 1985), 16.5 percent (Mar. 1987), and 17 percent (Apr. 1987); reduced to 16 percent (Jan. 1988), 11.5 percent (Aug. 1988), and 9 percent (Jan. 1990); increased to 12 percent (Mar. 1990). Initial remuneration 13.5 percent, reduced to 12.5 percent (July 1984), 12.4 percent (Oct. 1984), 12.3 percent (Nov. 1984), 10 percent (Oct. 1985), 9 percent (Feb. 1986), 8.5 percent (May 1986), 8 percent (Aug. 1986), 7.75 percent (Jan. 1988). Many such changes were associated with changes in item C.a. Replaced by item C.d.

d. *Bank of Spain bonds (since March 1990)*
Ten-year 6 percent bonds, by mandate placed with banks and negotiable only among them. Fractional redemption started in 1993.

e. *Special deposits against banks' external peseta liabilities*
Several transitory episodes, with small amounts involved. Geared to exchange control, rather than monetary control aims.

D. Market Borrowing Instruments

a. *Placement of treasury monetary bonds (February 1973–February 1979)*
One-, 2-, and 3-month government bonds, with low fixed interest rates (unchanged for years), voluntarily purchased, within annual limits, by the BOS. The BOS placed them with banks at market rates, incurring a loss. Banks offered their bids, and the BOS decided on the amount and applicable uniform price. The difference with a formal auction was that

Appendix *(concluded)*

banks were later free to take the TMB or not. Replaced by item D.b.

b. *Repos on treasury monetary bonds (February 1979–April 1982)*
The same bonds as in 4.a, now placed as 1- and 3-month repos, through unlimited volume tenders at preannounced interest rates. Replaced by item D.d.

c. *Repos on BOS "certificates of deposit" (BSCD) (February 1980–April 1982)*
Features similar to item D.b, intended to supplement an insufficient volume of treasury monetary bonds. Replaced by item D.d.

d. *Placement of BOS "monetary certificates" (BSMC) (April 1982–January 1984)*
Tailored, mainly 1- and 3-month maturities. Placed through multiple-price auctions held usually every 10 days. Amounts offered were not preannounced. Replaced by item C.c.

e. *Repos on treasury promissory notes (January 1984–March 1987)*
BOS purchased TPNs by directly participating in auctions. BOS placed them with banks through 1- and 3-month repos, distributed through unlimited volume tenders at preannounced interest rates. Replaced by item D.f.

f. *Repos on government securities (since March 1987)*
BOS purchased TBs from the finance ministry, which was entitled to increase any recent issue and sell it at the weighted average price prevailing in the last auction, and placed them in the market through multiple-price auctions (held every 10 days) of 1- and 3-month repos (only 1-month repos since 1991). Infrequent recent operations are based instead on government bonds. Amounts offered are not preannounced.

13

Canada: Debt Management Policy and Operating Practices

*Robin Miller**

Typically, the major objectives of debt management policy are to raise the government's gross borrowing requirements at minimum cost and at an acceptable level of interest rate risk. To achieve these objectives, debt managers need to make important decisions on the optimal structure of the outstanding stock of debt and the design and use of instruments that will determine the character of debt issuance and the composition of the stock over the longer term. Debt management policy can be categorized into tactical and strategic aspects. In a broad sense, tactical policy is aimed at managing the stock of debt by balancing debt service costs with exposures to changes in interest rates, while strategic policy is directed at minimizing costs by promoting more liquid and efficient government securities markets.

In practice, debt managers normally set goals, both for the year ahead in the context of designing the annual financing program of budget initiatives and for the longer term regarding the structure of debt and cost-minimizing initiatives aimed at improving the liquidity and efficiency of financial markets. Performance in meeting those goals is monitored periodically.

In Canada, the debt issuance and management strategy are established each year at the time of the annual budget. At that time, the Canadian Department of Finance and Bank of Canada (BOC) jointly undertake a major review of and outlook for debt management policy. The results are summarized in a comprehensive report to the minister that sets out the long- and short-term framework for federal debt management, including the objectives and tactical and strategic measures to be taken to achieve

*The author is the former Head of Financial Market Operations and Debt Management, Department of Finance, Canada.

those objectives. It looks back one year, discussing how and the extent to which objectives were met; provides analyses and recommendations on all major decisions to be made for the upcoming fiscal year; and looks forward ten years, setting the long-term target for the structure of the debt.

The rest of this chapter discusses how policies to achieve tactical and strategic objectives of debt management are designed and implemented. The coordination with monetary management is reviewed in the last section.

Tactical Policy

Debt managers set objectives for cost minimization and assess performance in meeting those objectives. Some use portfolio management techniques to measure their performance. In many countries, this involves the development of a hypothetical standard benchmark portfolio with a chosen debt composition. Then, mark-to-market valuation is used to assess performance against the benchmark over a specific period of time.

The department of finance has concluded that such benchmarks are most suitable for sovereign borrowers with active foreign currency borrowing programs. Canada has little foreign currency debt (it borrows in foreign currencies only for augmenting foreign exchange reserves), and it is mostly hedged against foreign currency assets. Importantly, the department no longer takes a view on the future path of interest rates in setting debt management policy. Earlier attempts at forecasting interest rates proved inaccurate. Instead, decisions on the structure of debt are based on a trade-off between cost and risk, explained below.

The annual and long-term debt management strategy seeks to find an appropriate balance between *cost minimization* and *cost stability*—two debt management objectives. With a typical upward-sloping yield curve, short-term, or floating rate, debt is usually less costly than longer-term or fixed rate debt.[1] On the other hand, fixed rate debt reduces the sensitivity of debt service to changes in interest rates, providing stability to the overall fiscal plan: the government's plan for the economic welfare of the country. Thus, the advantage of extending the refinancing schedule with fixed rate debt is the reduced risk of an unforeseen financing crisis brought about by an unexpected rise in interest rates. The disadvantage is the additional cost incurred by issuing fixed versus floating rate debt, which is

---

[1]A distinction between "fixed rate debt" (debt with a term to maturity of more than one year and whose rate of interest earned is not reset within a year) and "floating rate debt" (debt with a term to maturity of less than one year or whose rate of interest earned is reset within a year) is made. Thus, instruments such as index-linked bonds, whose periodic return is linked to the inflation rate, are considered floating rate debt despite their longer term to maturity, because debt service varies with the index.

Table 1. Canada: Changes in Cost and Risk of Alternative Debt Structures Compared with Base Scenario

(For fiscal year 1994/95; in millions of Canadian dollars unless noted otherwise)

	Additional Costs or Savings			Risk of Interest Rate Shock	
Debt structure	Cost(–) or savings(+) 10th year	Cumulative cost(–) or savings(+)	Debt-service shock in 10th year	Required change in interest rates (basis points)	Probability of interest rate change
55% fixed	–340	–2,700	5,000	238	16%
60% fixed	70	0.500	5,000	287	12%
65% fixed	410	3,300	5,000	347	8%

Source: Based on the Canadian Department of Finance, *Debt Operations Report* (September 1994).

like buying insurance for protection against contingencies. Therefore, setting the amount of fixed versus floating rate debt of the outstanding stock is a key tactical decision.

To determine the cost-risk trade-off, the department uses a large detailed accounting-based model with simulation capabilities; the model uses as inputs the outstanding debt stock and the annual fiscal framework (i.e., the government's projected borrowing requirements). Then, various simulations over a ten-year time frame are used to assess how the structure of outstanding debt affects the cost and sensitivity of debt-service charges to changes in interest rates (sensitivity analysis). The various costs and savings shown in Table 1 are calculated relative to the status quo (the previous year's debt strategy (1993/94) of a ten-year target for fixed rate debt in the outstanding stock of 57 percent) and are based on the historical average spread between long- and short-term rates of about 100 basis points (1 percentage point). The fixed-to-floating-rate strategy is then evaluated by assessing the risk or probability of an interest rate shock sufficient to cause debt charges to rise by $5,000 million in the tenth year of the projection period. (All dollar amounts in this chapter are Canadian dollars.) This probability is calculated on the basis of the historical volatility of interest rates in Canada over the current ten-year period.[2]

The table shows that a 55 percent fixed rate proportion in the debt structure would save money annually over the next ten years, rising to $340 million by the tenth year for accumulative savings of $2,700 million (based on the historical average spread between long- and short-term rates of 100 basis points). However, it would take only a 238 basis point

---

[2]The model can be used to assess other kinds of event risk also, for example, the effect on debt charges of a sustained yield curve inversion or upward revision to budgetary requirements.

rise in interest rates in the tenth year to cause a $5,000 million increase in debt charges at that time; there is a 16 percent probability of this occurring. In contrast, with 65 percent of the stock in fixed rate form, it would take a 347 basis point increase in interest rates in the tenth year to increase debt charges by the same amount; there is only an 8 percent probability of this occurring. However, the 65 percent strategy costs more in debt-service charges, rising to $410 million by the tenth year for accumulative costs of $3,300 million.

For many years, the percentage of fixed rate debt in the outstanding stock in Canada was about 50 percent, compared with a percentage of fixed rate debt in a range of 70 percent to 90 percent in other countries of the Organization for Economic Cooperation and Development (OECD). The importance of increasing the amount of fixed rate debt for cost stability was dramatically illustrated in the 1989/90 fiscal year, when a $4 billion increase in the budget deficit occurred, stemming from higher debt charges due to an unexpected rise in interest rates. As a consequence, in 1990/91, the debt strategy was changed to include limiting interest rate risk (along with cost minimization) as an objective of debt management. Initially, the authorities planned to increase the proportion of fixed rate debt in the ensuing ten-year period to 60 percent of the outstanding stock. However, with rising requirements, the outstanding debt was projected to grow to higher levels than earlier forecast, thus the degree of protection against rising interest rates fell. In response, the new strategy is to increase the proportion of fixed rate debt of the outstanding stock to 65 percent in ten years.[3]

Strategic Policy

Strategic Objectives and Measures

The department pursues a policy of cost-effective debt management through developing liquidity and promoting efficiency in Canadian bond and money markets. The effectiveness of this policy in Canada is evidenced by tight bid-offer spreads, high turnover volume, the relative ease and timeliness with which transactions in large amounts can be completed, and the efficiency of clearing and settlement (Canada has an electronic book-based system). With smoothly functioning and efficient markets,

---

[3]It should be noted that there is a constraint to the amount of fixed rate debt that can be issued. For example, moving to the 65 percent fixed rate target in ten years would require an annual issuance of almost all net new debt issuance in fixed rate form. This could put pressure on the bond market and would mean little net issuance of treasury bills, which might adversely affect the bill market (although Canada has a large stock of outstanding bills and this constraint should not be a major factor for some time), complicating monetary management.

costs are reduced and liquidity risk and settlement exposure are at a minimum. A well-developed market for repurchase agreements ("repos") and a mature futures market provide opportunities to cover or hedge positions.

Strategic objectives designed to achieve cost minimization are:

- improve market liquidity and efficiency for federal securities; develop markets in related (derivative) instruments that contribute to market liquidity, including markets for repos (the lending and borrowing of securities), strip bonds, and bond and money market futures;
- develop markets by using debt management techniques such as interest rate swaps and foreign exchange swaps;
- develop cost-effective new debt instruments, such as cash management bills and index-linked Real Return Bonds, that improve market efficiency and broaden the market for federal debt; and
- promote a broad distribution of holdings of Government of Canada debt.

Strategic measures taken to achieve these cost-minimization objectives are:

- increasing systematically the size of benchmark issues to improve market liquidity;
- providing the market with a transparent calendar for bond issuance to promote market efficiency, by preannouncing issues for the next quarter and regularizing quarterly auctions of two-, five-, and ten-year bond issues;
- working with major market-makers and stock exchanges to promote and develop the futures markets for debt instruments to improve market liquidity and efficiency;
- promoting the repo market and helping to resolve tax issues in the crossborder repo market;
- promoting and using electronic book-based clearing and settlement systems;
- developing and promoting an investor relations program, including regular consultations to provide up-to-date and accurate information on Canada, and on its debt program and strategy, to market-makers, investors, Canada watchers (analysts in foreign investment firms who provide financial advice to clients), and credit rating agencies; and
- establishing the Canadian Retail Debt Agency to promote sales to the retail market and broaden the distribution of federal debt.

Special Debt Management Initiatives

The department of finance has undertaken several debt management initiatives to promote efficiency and improve the functioning of Canadian financial markets to minimize costs:

Derivatives Market

A viable futures market is an essential component of well-functioning capital markets, because it provides a low-cost means of taking or hedging positions against the cash market. The key to a viable futures market is liquidity, that is, sufficient volume to allow large positions to be taken at low cost. In the past, the Canadian Government Bond futures (CGB), which were created by and trade on the Montreal Stock Exchange, lacked volume. To improve liquidity, the department, in cooperation with the major market-makers, took direct action to increase CGB trading by recommending monthly quotas for dealers, and following up on their performance. The department, along with the BOC and the stock exchange, also initiated information sessions and seminars with major institutions and associations that were potential users of the futures market to encourage their participation. These actions increased liquidity substantially.

In addition, to assist in the development and improve liquidity of the strip bond market, the department encouraged the Canadian Depository for Securities to modify their systems so as to enable the recording and settling of these transactions electronically.[4]

Bond Market

The government has promoted the building of benchmark bonds at key maturities, and the size of individual outstanding issues has risen substantially from a few years ago. Large outstanding issues are more liquid and trade at tighter bid-offer spreads, promoting efficiency in the bond market and reducing issuing costs for the government. While it was always the policy to reopen and build issues, there was some concern that the government would not obtain the best price if reopenings required lower discount pricing. There was also some concern about refunding the large-scale maturing benchmark issues. These concerns have proven to be unfounded because several factors have facilitated the building and management of larger benchmark issues, including a move to all auctions (away from a fixed price syndicated distribution method); growing sophistication and deepening of markets; and the use of cash management bills to fund temporarily large-scale maturities (usually twice the new issue size).

---

[4]In Canada, investment dealers separate interest payments from principal payments on underlying bonds issued by the federal or provincial governments. A strip bond entitles the holder to an investment in either the amount payable as principal, or payable as interest in respect of the underlying bond. The purchase price or present value of a strip bond is determined by discounting the amount of the payment to be received on the interest payment or maturity date by the market interest rate. For the investor, strip bonds remove reinvestment risk. For the government, the strip market adds to the demand for longer-term bonds.

Another initiative taken by the department to promote efficient bond markets concerned facilitating electronic book-entry clearing and settlement of securities. By issuing a global security (a single certificate) for all new domestic bond issues and registering them in the name of the depository as nominee, the securities are held in batches in the depository's vaults, and computer entries can then be used to clear and settle transactions among depository members without any movement of physical securities. This immobilization of physical securities promotes the move toward a fully electronic, book-based system for clearing and settlement of marketable securities.

Treasury Bill Market

To improve liquidity, the department initiated a reopening of the one-year treasury bill to build a larger single benchmark maturity. Prior to this, a new maturity was auctioned every week; now, the same maturity is offered consecutively at two weekly auctions.

Development of New Products

Cash Management Bills

Cash management bills—typically 1–31 days to maturity and sold on auction—were introduced several years ago to help manage cash balances. They are sold to the market on an ad hoc basis, sometimes with as little as 24 hours' notice, although two days' notice is the norm. The extent to which these bills are used is influenced by the rate of interest earned on government term deposits when proceeds from their sale lead to a buildup in cash balances. Rates paid are often somewhat higher than on regular 91-day instruments, owing to limited interest in the bills (mainly banks); but because of their much shorter term (say, 21 days), their actual cost to the government is less than if the funds had been raised for an unnecessarily longer time through the issue of 91-day bills, and the government carried surplus cash balances.

Real Return Bonds (RRBs)

First offered in November 1991, RRBs pay a fixed rate of return (currently 4.25 percent) on a principal adjusted for inflation. Canada has been able to market these bonds cost-effectively, largely because of a good marketing effort through information sessions prior to their introduction and consultation with investment dealers on the development of the bonds. Unlike other bonds that are sold at auction, RRBs have been distributed through a select syndicate of investment dealers. To ensure that the government has a group of dedicated investment dealers to market this new and somewhat controversial instrument (demand was unsure and needed to be developed), a syndicate was assembled through a competitive selection process based on an assessment of dealer capabilities and commitment to the distribution of the new instrument.

The return on the RRB comprises both a semiannual return, adjusted for inflation, plus inflation compensation for the principal value, which is paid along with the principal at maturity. These inflation-adjusted returns are set in relation to changes in the Consumer Price Index (CPI) for Canada. The semiannual return is adjusted by multiplying the fixed (real) rate (divided by two for semiannual payments) by the principal adjusted for inflation compensation as follows:

$$
\begin{array}{c} \text{Semiannual} \\ \text{return} \\ \text{(date)} \end{array} = \frac{4.25\%}{2} \times \left[\text{Principal} + \begin{array}{c} \text{Inflation} \\ \text{compensation} \\ \text{(date)} \end{array} \right]
$$

$$
\text{Inflation compensation (date)} = \frac{\text{Principal} \times \text{Reference CPI (date)}}{\text{Reference CPI (base)}}
$$

Final payment at maturity consists of the last semiannual return plus principal and its inflation compensation component accruing from issue date:

$$
\begin{array}{c} \text{Final payment} \\ \text{at maturity} \end{array} = \begin{array}{c} \text{Semiannual} \\ \text{return} \end{array} + \text{Principal} + \begin{array}{c} \text{Inflation} \\ \text{compensation} \\ \text{(maturity date)} \end{array}
$$

The reference CPI for calculation purposes is the CPI for the third preceding calendar month. For example, the reference CPI for December 1 is the CPI for the preceding September (published in October).

RRBs are attractive to tax-exempt institutional investors whose long-term liabilities are related to the rate of inflation (like pension funds). They are also popular with individual investors for their self-directed retirement savings plans. Recently, two $100 million tranches were set aside for the retail investor and were repackaged into RRB strips designed for retail retirement savings plans by a syndicate of investment dealers. Although starting on a small scale, this derivative product has immense potential because it removes inflation and reinvestment risk for retirement savings.

RRBs have been cost-effective because the real return has been lower than that on conventional bonds. For the fixed-to-floating ratio, RRBs are viewed as floating rate debt because they vary with inflation with about the same degree of variability as treasury bills.

Derivative Products

Derivative products such as the swaps described here add low-cost instruments and alternative avenues to complete transactions, as well as providing for deeper, broader, and more sophisticated markets, adding to market liquidity and efficiency.

Interest rate swaps provide floating rate debt for the government and, from a debt structure point of view, are direct substitutes for treasury bills but cost less. These swaps are substitutes for treasury bills because the stream of interest payments on the swap are floating rates and are based on the rate paid on 3-, 6-, or 12-month Banker's Acceptances. To meet both the financial requirements and fixed-to-floating target in a fiscal year, more bonds are issued—equal to the amount of swaps undertaken—which replace the treasury bills that would otherwise have been issued as part of the borrowing program.

Interest rate swaps cost less than treasury bills because the federal government, as the prime credit in Canada, has a relative advantage in issuing fixed rate debt (bonds) and can swap this advantage with counterparties who pay relatively low money market rates, but relatively high bond market rates, to obtain floating rate funds at rates below those on treasury bills. With a stock of over $8 billion outstanding, savings (had treasury bills been issued instead) are estimated at over $50 million annually. These swaps are low-risk, because the only cash flow is the net difference in the interest payments. No payment of principal is involved.

Exchange fund account cash management swaps are used for cash management to raise Canadian dollars for short terms and on short notice. The swap involves a spot sale of U.S. dollars from the official exchange reserves for Canadian dollars and a simultaneous forward repurchase of the U.S. dollars. These swaps work in tandem with cash management bills but can be executed on shorter notice, for smaller amounts and shorter terms. Their cost is compared with cash management bills, and they are undertaken only if cost-effective.

Foreign currency swaps have been entered into by the government with high-grade counterparties to swap both the principal and interest payments on the proceeds from a foreign currency borrowing into U.S. dollars. This provided cost-effective U.S. dollar funding for the foreign exchange reserves at a time when they needed to be built up. The credit risk in using these swaps is limited by a careful choice of counterparties and exposure limits.

U.S. dollar interest rate swaps are undertaken as part of managing foreign exchange reserves. Since most of the U.S. dollar reserve assets are invested in short-term securities, the interest payment on some longer-term U.S. dollar liabilities (borrowings) have been swapped into floating rate payments to balance U.S. dollar payments on liabilities with U.S. dollar receipts on assets. Risk is managed through careful choice of counterparties and design of swap agreements to limit a counterparty's ability to cancel swap agreements because of material change on cross default clauses. Clauses of this type, suited typically to corporations, are more difficult to define for sovereign borrowers.

Canada Bills

Canada Bills provide secure access to cost-effective, ad hoc U.S. dollar funding. Proceeds are taken into the U.S. dollar reserves where they are invested in short-term U.S. dollar assets, offsetting the cost of the program. The program has been highly successful, in part because of the care taken prior to its implementation. Careful research was done of the market. Major U.S. and Canadian dealers were invited to make a presentation on how the program should be run, and a syndicate was chosen on the basis of merit and selection criteria. Most sovereign borrowers in the U.S. money markets have their paper rated by credit rating agencies and are normally prime-rated. However, the market is nondistinct since many corporate borrowers share the same prime rating. So to fully exploit its historical advantage and prestige in the U.S. financial market, Canada decided that the program would not be credit rated as is the normal practice but would be offered in the same way that U.S. agencies (e.g., Federal National Mortgage Association, or Fannie Mae) offer their discount note programs. As a result of careful planning and management, the rate paid on Canada Bills is somewhat higher than U.S. agency notes but lower than prime rated commercial paper. Canada was the first sovereign borrower to go this route.

Retail Debt Strategy

Traditionally, the government has relied on the Canada Savings Bond as its main instrument to reach the retail market. At one time, retail holdings amounted to almost two thirds of the outstanding federal debt and Canada Savings Bonds to over 40 percent of that proportion. Recently, the share of federal debt held by the retail sector, including debt held in mutual funds and in stripped form, has fallen to just over 20 percent. This decline reflected a shrinking in the investor base for federal debt. Thus a broadening and diversifying of the investor base for federal debt would be desirable in order to increase the number of investors and economize on overall debt-service charges on account of greater demand.

Studies by consultants concluded that the government must offer a range of products to meet the retail investors' needs and achieve a broadening of the investor base. This will be accomplished in part by making existing instruments such as bonds more readily available to the small investor and, in part, by designing new instruments that take advantage of the characteristics unique to government debt instruments, including:

- safety and security (government is the prime credit);
- liquidity (large outstanding float for bonds and bills);
- an established name in the retail market with Canada Savings Bonds (brand awareness);
- the ability to index debt (tax revenues are indexed); and
- the ability to add special features, such as cashability on savings bonds.

To improve retail distribution, the government has announced a new retail debt strategy to provide Canadians better and cheaper access to a family of existing and new products. The plan is to offer a client-focused program with improved service, and cheaper and more direct access to federal securities. The new program will be run by a special operating agency called the Canadian Retail Debt Agency. The new agency is expected to market directly to investors. Although specific plans have not been announced, the agency is expected to concentrate on making marketable bonds and treasury bills easily available and, possibly, to market inflation-indexed and zero coupon bonds. In addition, the 1995 series of Canada Savings Bonds has been given direct retirement savings plans status, providing the investor with a tax deduction without having to pay an administrative fee to a financial institution for a self-directed plan. Administration will be handled by the BOC.

Consultations and the Investor Relations Program

The Investment Dealers Association (IDA) is the governing arm of the self-regulating investment dealers group. Formal meetings take place on a quarterly basis. At least once a year, senior personnel from the department and the BOC meet with the president of the IDA. Minutes of the meetings are distributed, and these are an important record of discussions on issues that have been brought up between the government and the dealers. In the planning process, policy decisions are discussed at an appropriate stage, and it is important to note that the membership of the IDA supports major decisions such as the move to a larger stock of fixed rate debt.

Primary distributors are the major investment firms in the Canadian bond market, and they have the right to bid at federal bond and treasury bill auctions; jobbers are the largest of these firms, and they are expected to perform at auctions more consistently and make markets in all securities. There are also chartered bank jobbers who bid and have responsibilities in the treasury bill market. The BOC deals exclusively with the jobbers in its monetary policy operations. Primary distributors need to meet criteria established by the department and the BOC. Both the department and the BOC consult with primary distributors on an individual basis as they are major stakeholders. There are frequent meetings with individual dealers and the exchange of information and ideas is mutually beneficial, and dealers are invited to provide input to the debt program. There are also consultations with special syndicates formed to market a particular product, such as the Real Return Bond. A code of conduct for government officials is in place to ensure that discussions are aboveboard and no dealer is provided information that gives him an advantage over another.

The Investor Relations Program, which started in 1990, is designed to regularize the provision of timely information on Canada's fiscal, monetary, and economic situation to existing and potential investors, to "Canada watchers" in the investment community, and to the rating agencies. The program works in cooperation with investment dealers, both domestic and foreign, to get this information to the proper recipients. Significant occasions, for example, are the dissemination of budget material, important statements by the minister or other government departments, and the annual *Debt Operations Report*. Key international centers are targeted for budget visits, such as London, New York, and Tokyo, by the minister and senior officials. Postbudget visits are also arranged for important cabinet ministers. Investor missions are coordinated, for example, from Japan and the United States, institutional investors come to Canada to meet with the minister, the governor of the BOC, and other senior officials. Canadian G-7 and New York finance counselors are used extensively to develop and maintain links with the international investment community and provide feedback. Budget information discussions and postbudget reviews are held with domestic and New York rating agencies.

Institutional investors are consulted individually as well as collectively through their respective associations. These meetings allow investors to comment on debt management practices and permit the department to inform them about, and seek their participation in, special initiatives, such as the five- and ten-year CGB futures and the repo market. Regular consultations (usually semiannual) are held with several associations, namely, the Canadian Bankers Association (also with their Treasury Committee); the Canadian Life and Health Insurance Association; and the Pension Investment Association of Canada.

Operating Practices

Operational Decisions and Implementation

The major operational decisions taken at the beginning of each fiscal year to achieve the cost-minimization and cost-stability objectives are discussed below.

Bond Program and Duration

A decision is made on the mix of bond maturities to be issued in the year, based on the size of the overall program, the desired duration of the bond program adopted for the targeted ratio of fixed-to-floating rate debt, and the objective of building and maintaining liquidity across the yield curve. There are some constraints to the decision. For example, given the objective of building large benchmarks and offering regular, preannounced auctions, it may be difficult to cover all maturities, such as the 3- and 30-year maturities. However, with a large debt program, this is less of a constraint. Consideration could also be given to dropping the 3-year bond because there are 2- and 5-year maturities. On the other hand, if the market wants a 3-year bond, if it helps maintain liquidity across the yield curve, and if there is room for it, it should be included in the program.

The 30-year bond has been examined in view of the higher interest rate that must be offered and the high risk premium over inflation demanded by investors. It continues to be offered because there is demand for it, it lengthens the yield curve, it provides stability to debt charges, and current rates are below the 30-year average for long-term bonds. However, the 30-year maturity represents only a small proportion of the bond program. The flagship issues, the 2-, 5-, and 10-year maturities, account for about 80 percent of new issuance. A typical bond program is set out in Table 2.

The duration of the bond program is established consistent with increasing the proportion of fixed rate debt in the debt stock and reducing the exposure to interest rate risk. Duration is used as a summary measure of the proposed program weights, rather than as a target; as long as the forecast duration is acceptable, no direct attempt is made to change it.

Benchmark Bond Issues

Decisions are made on the target size for benchmark issues, and these targets are announced to the market. In implementing the bond program and trying to meet the benchmark targets, there are some constraints. There is a limited time over which issues can be reopened, especially at the shorter maturities, as they fall out of the allotted time slots. Six months on either side of the 5- or 10-year term is considered acceptable. Total borrowing requirements in a year can also constrain targets, giving rise to the need to limit or eliminate some maturities. For fiscal 1994/95, preannounced benchmark targets were as follows: 2-year, $4 billion to $6 billion; 5-year, 10-year, and 30-year, $6 billion to $9 billion each.

Bond Calendar

A decision is made on the desired transparency of the bond calendar. Providing more transparency removes uncertainty and has been a key el-

Table 2. Canada: Typical Government Bond Program

Maturity	Planned Percentage of Issuance
2-year	22
3-year	9
5-year	27
10-year	30
30-year	12
Total	100
Duration[1]	5.45 years

Source: Canadian Department of Finance
[1]Duration measures the average life of a bond's cash flows (both principal repayment and periodic returns) weighted by their present value.

ement in improving liquidity and efficiency in the bond market. Currently, it is the practice to announce only the 2-, 5-, and 10-year bond auctions and the dates; other issues in the calendar quarter are announced ahead of the quarter. The terms of the nonquarterly issues are announced a week in advance of the auction date.

The progression toward more transparency has been well received and supported by the market. The case against full transparency is the ad hoc possibility that the market desires a different maturity or market conditions are poor on the preannounced auction date and the issuer may want the flexibility to miss that date, or issue a shorter maturity that is easier to market than long-dated maturities. Current practice is not to announce the date of the 30-year bond but to announce there will be one of these maturities each quarter.

Other key operational decisions taken at the beginning of the year and adhered to in their implementation, depending on market factors and cost considerations permitting, are outlined below.

Interest Rate Swaps

Both a volume (gross and net) target and floor interest rate swap spread target (i.e., the lowest rate at which the government is willing to transact, say, the Banker's Acceptance rate less 50 basis points) is established for this program at the beginning of the fiscal year. The volume target is consistent with the fixed-to-floating decision and maturities during the fiscal year, and is based on expectations of market demand. A floor swap spread is established to help insure that the swaps remain cost-effective over the life of the swap. Both the volume targets and spread can change, depending on demand and cost-effectiveness. Credit policy limits counterpart risk and establishes which counterparties are acceptable and how large a volume of swaps can be done with any single party.

Exchange Fund Account Swaps

A maximum dollar amount limit is established at the beginning of the fiscal year, consistent with the liquidity and total amount of official foreign exchange holdings. As in the case of interest rate swaps, counterparties must meet the criteria established by the credit policy. These swaps have proven to be very cost-effective for the government and have added liquidity to exchange markets as the accumulated amount outstanding has at times exceeded $3 billion.

Monitoring Performance

The Canadian Department of Finance and the BOC jointly implement the planned strategy, and in executing the program, officials adhere closely to the operational decisions taken at the beginning of the fiscal year and operate in a manner consistent with the objectives and risk tolerances established by decisions taken by the minister. Monitoring performance against objectives is an ongoing process.

Timely and reliable information is used to support decision making and monitor risk exposures. Day-to-day program evaluation and ex post analysis are ongoing and can result in active adjustment of programs. Internal reports on performance range from an annual formal report to the cabinet and the annual debt strategy exercise with the minister, to continual updating and analysis of data at the officer level.

Actual exposures never exceed guidelines without ministerial approval for the fixed-to-floating rate guideline, the limitation on interest rate and exchange fund cash management swaps, and counterparty exposures. Regarding the fixed-to-floating rate mix decision, this is monitored continually but is reviewed each year. The target percentage has been changed four times in the last four years because new fiscal information showed that the actual level of debt was projected to rise faster than earlier forecast, indicating a higher-than-expected exposure to interest rate volatility.

Data are maintained by officers of the department to monitor the performance of the primary distributors at both bond and treasury bill auctions. Results are also maintained on the effectiveness of the auctions by monitoring key indicators such as coverage and high and low price spreads. This data, collected at every auction, is analyzed and followed up, for example, with jobbers who are showing poor performance, as necessary. Another aspect being analyzed is the concentration of the bill market in the hands of a few major institutions. Market efficiency is measured in terms of tight bid-and-ask spreads and turnover volume, and these data are regularly collected and analyzed.

With regard to the Interest Rate Swap program, data are maintained and updated after every transaction to monitor counterpart risk and evaluate savings from the program. The same is done for the exchange fund cash management swaps. As well, information is maintained by the department to monitor the day-to-day cash management activities of the government, that is, the level of cash balances. Daily decisions are made regarding the breakdown between term and demand deposits, and a daily record of earnings is maintained on both types of balances. The overall profit or cost to the government of maintaining cash balances is monitored on a daily basis and reported regularly.

Externally, the annual *Debt Operations Report* provides a comprehensive review of debt management strategy and objectives, as well as providing investors and the general public with useful background information. There is also a quarterly *Finance Review* that provides useful economic and financial data to the general public, although it is geared specifically to investors. As mentioned earlier, the Investor Relations Program makes substantial information available externally.

Coordination of Debt and Monetary Policy

Canada has a fully developed financial market, and, as is usual under these circumstances, the government sells its debt through a network of primary distributors, being as cost-effective as possible, at interest rates established by the market as a result of monetary policy. At the same time, the BOC has access to whatever supply of debt instruments it requires in its portfolio to carry out monetary policy in the secondary markets.

Historically, the central bank has played a major role in developing both primary and secondary markets in Canada. For example, the BOC recruited, developed, and administered the primary distributor (and money market jobbers) system. In market development, the BOC was instrumental in limiting the role of the major banks in primary distribution so as to promote the development of dealers and brokers, who were the major force in developing secondary markets. Jobbers were permitted to refinance inventories of government securities with the BOC through purchase and resale agreements up to a line determined for each dealer by the bank. These actions also helped develop institutional investors outside the banking system.

In the early stages of development, the BOC had considerable influence over debt management policy. This permitted it to pursue strategies to develop the secondary market, creating, at the same time, the tools to support monetary operations. Throughout the 1980s, debt management concentrated on a prudent and conservative approach, avoiding surprises to the market and offering a well-planned mix of maturities at each syndicated offering. A large syndicate of primary distributors (over 100) spread throughout the country was carefully managed by the BOC. Commissions were paid for bond sales, and dealers were eager to become primary distributors and conform to the BOC's and the government's requirements. Fixed pricing was used for bond issues, and there was little risk for the dealers, who generally made a handsome profit from bond sales. For the government, good distribution was obtained.

As markets evolved and debt charges grew to a larger share of fiscal expenditures, the department has played an increasingly large role in debt management and the formulation of policy. With the development of deep and liquid secondary markets and the move to an all-auction distribution system for bonds (in the 1992/93 fiscal year), debt issuance is managed on a more active basis. Monetary policy is implemented mainly through the drawdown or redeposit (switching) of Government of Canada cash balances between the BOC and the financial institutions, through open market operations with dealers and banks using repurchase agreements backed by government securities and through occasional outright transactions in treasury bills. The current system, therefore, provides for an independent and active debt management policy. Debt operations are conducted with interest rate neutrality in mind, with the intent not to affect the yield curve.

The BOC has operational responsibility for the debt program. As fiscal agent to the government, it tends to all administrative aspects of managing the debt. These include conducting bond and treasury bill auctions, debt issuance, settlement, redemption, and servicing. The BOC also advises the government on all aspects of debt management, policy, and strategy. In practice, the BOC and department work together in a cordial and cooperative manner, with the BOC being part of policy and strategic decisions. The interface between the two is ongoing and at all levels. While the department is responsible for bringing proposals forward to the minister and is accountable to the minister for debt management, the bank takes part in the proposals and decisions made regarding debt management.

Legal and Institutional Framework

The legal and institutional framework should enable debt managers to carry out their functions without impediments and in the most satisfactory way. The framework should also provide utmost security for the investor by ensuring that the government's debt management objectives and instruments are implemented and issued under the due authority of the country's highest constitutional authority. This is the case in Canada.

Financial Administration Act (FAA)

As its name implies, the FAA is the statutory basis for financial administration in the government. Of interest to debt managers are the sections covering debt issuance. In the past, these sections were onerous, requiring governor in council approval of the smallest details of the terms and conditions of each issuance. This proved particularly difficult in pricing new issues, especially foreign issues for which time is of the essence because once a price has been agreed to, assuming it is based on up-to-the-moment market developments, it must be offered immediately before market conditions change.

In the early 1980s, the FAA was amended, bringing it up-to-date with modern financial markets. The amendments authorized debt issuance within certain volume, term, and price parameters (i.e., not to exceed a specified term or price, etc.) and left it up to officials to fix the final terms. The FAA was also amended to provide for the issue of derivative products, such as interest rate and currency swaps. At the time of writing, the FAA allowed debt managers to function in a satisfactory way.

Borrowing Authority

Statutory borrowing authority is required for the government to raise new money; there is standing authority in the FAA to roll over maturing debt. New borrowing authority is sought each year with a bill tabled at the same time as the budget. The borrowing bill is part of the budgetary process. The amount of borrowing authority sought is equal to the financial requirements set out in the budget. The budget papers plus the main estimates, also tabled in February, provide parliament with the background to consider the borrowing bill. The bill also seeks an additional amount, normally $3 billion, ostensibly to cover the transitional period between fiscal years (in case the new bill is not passed by April 1 of the new year). Supplementary borrowing authority has been sought in the past when financial requirements exceeded those originally sought. On most of those occasions, parliament has required a full financial and economic report.

Orders in Council

All issue of debt has to be approved by the governor in council. Although quarterly approval for treasury bill issuance has been in effect for many years, the government used to seek approval of individual bond issues and of the final terms of these issues, with the idea that this procedure gave council members an opportunity to keep abreast of the debt program. However, over time, the procedure had become a "rubber stamp." Moreover, for the department to keep track of all the authorities needed and not to exceed authorities granted, it was forced to develop a large and onerous set of procedures that had to be constantly checked. These procedures also covered other matters, such as drawings on the standby lines of credit. It became evident that the council did not need to keep abreast of all the details of debt issuance. Council approval of the bond and treasury bill programs is sought and obtained quarterly, although amendments are needed if the markets change sufficiently to make the parameters stated in the orders in council obsolete.

An annual report to the cabinet for information purposes is made in an aide-mémoire; the arrangement seems to be the most suitable for all concerned. Earlier, a memorandum to the cabinet was presented and decisions made; the intent was to provide ministers with a background against which they could approve individual debt issues. With the advent of governor in council approval of the debt program on a quarterly basis, the aide-mémoire is a more appropriate process.

14

United States: Primary Market Auctions and Government Debt Management

*Jill Ouseley**

The total U.S. treasury debt amounted to $4.7 trillion on December 31, 1994, including $2.7 trillion of marketable securities held by private investors.[1] The rest of the public debt consists of marketable treasury securities held by federal government accounts and the Federal Reserve System, nonmarketable treasury securities issued directly to U.S. government trust funds, and nonmarketable U.S. savings bonds and state and local government series securities.

Size of Borrowing Needs

The federal debt held by the public more than tripled, to $3.5 trillion, between fiscal years 1983 and 1994, when it rose to 52 percent of GDP from 34 percent of GDP.[2] The federal budget for fiscal year 1996 estimates that the federal debt held by the public will increase further, to $4.8 trillion by the end of fiscal year 2000, when the debt-to-GDP ratio is estimated to be 52 percent.

The treasury has auctioned large amounts of marketable treasury securities in the past decade. In fiscal year 1984, the treasury sold over $1 trillion gross amount of marketable treasury securities. By fiscal year 1994, this figure had increased to $2.1 trillion. As long as there is a budget deficit, the amount of securities the treasury is required to sell will tend to

---

*The author is Director, Office of Market Finance, U.S. Treasury.

[1]Privately held marketable securities exclude holdings of federal government accounts, such as the social security trust funds, and holdings of the Federal Reserve System.

[2]The federal debt includes treasury securities and a small amount of federal agency debt. The publicly held debt includes privately held securities and holdings of the Federal Reserve System.

increase, to raise funds to cover the shortfall between receipts and expenditures and to refinance maturing debt.

Growth in marketable securities has accounted for most of the growth in the privately held treasury debt since the mid-1970s. Nonmarketable securities held by private investors consist mainly of U.S. savings bonds and state and local government series securities.

Treasury Marketable Securities

The treasury issues three types of marketable securities—bills, notes, and bonds. They are direct obligations of the U.S. Government and are known commonly as marketable securities because they can be bought and sold in the secondary market at prevailing market prices through financial institutions, brokers, and dealers in government securities. Except for a few specific issues of treasury bonds that were issued prior to 1985, which can be called by the treasury, marketable treasury securities are not redeemable before maturity. All marketable treasury securities are issued only in book-entry form.

Treasury *bills* are short-term securities with original-issue maturities of 13, 26, or 52 weeks. Bills are issued at a discount from face value (par amount) and are redeemed at their face value at maturity. Bills mature on Thursday of each week. The 26-week bill is issued as an additional amount of the original-issue 52-week bill after it has been outstanding for 26 weeks, and the 13-week bill is issued as an additional amount of the 26-week bill. Bills are issued in a minimum purchase amount of $10,000 face value with larger amounts in multiples of $1,000.

Treasury *notes* have fixed maturities of more than one year and not more than ten years. They are issued with a fixed annual rate of interest (coupon rate), paid semiannually, and are redeemed at face value of maturity. The treasury currently offers notes with original-issue maturities of two, three, five, and ten years. Notes with a term of less than five years are issued in a minimum purchase amount of $5,000 face value and, for purchases above $5,000, in multiples of $1,000. Notes with a term of five years or more are issued in a minimum purchase amount of $1,000 and in multiples of $1,000.

Treasury *bonds* are long-term securities with fixed maturities of more than ten years. They are issued with a fixed rate of interest (coupon rate), paid semiannually, and are redeemed at face value maturity. The treasury currently offers 30-year bonds in February and August of each year. The treasury may reopen (that is, issue an additional amount of) an outstanding bond in order to enlarge the size of an issue and enhance its market liquidity. Bonds are issued in a minimum purchase amount of $1,000 and in multiples of $1,000.

The U.S. Treasury does not issue zero-coupon marketable securities, but permits long-term treasury notes and bonds to be stripped into their interest and principal components on the electronic book-entry system. Stripping has expanded the demand for treasury securities by permitting investors to create synthetic securities that have payment streams that best suit their needs. Stripped treasury securities may be reconstituted into whole securities through the book-entry system, a feature that provides investors with the flexibility to respond to market conditions that may favor intact securities.

Evolution of Market Borrowing Techniques

The treasury has employed auctions for treasury bills since their introduction in 1929. Since then, the only major modifications to bill auctions have been a provision for noncompetitive bids in 1947 and a change in 1983 to receiving bids on the basis of yield (bank discount basis) rather than price.

Prior to the early 1970s, the traditional methods for selling notes and bonds were subscription offerings, exchange offerings, and advance refundings. Subscriptions involved the treasury setting an interest rate on the securities to be sold and then selling (or taking subscriptions for) them at a fixed price. In exchange offerings, the treasury allowed holders of outstanding maturing securities to exchange them for new issues at an announced price and coupon rate. In some cases, new securities were issued only to holders of the specific maturing securities; in others, additional amounts of the new security were issued. Advance refundings differed from exchange offerings in that the outstanding securities could be exchanged before their maturity date.

A fundamental difficulty with subscription offerings was that market yields could change between the announcement of the offering and the deadline for subscriptions. Increased market volatility in the 1970s made fixed-price subscription offerings very risky for the treasury.

A modified auction technique was introduced in 1970, in which the fixed annual rate (coupon rate) was still preset by the treasury, and bids were made on the basis of price. Setting the coupon rate in advance, however, still involved forecasting interest rates, with the risk that the auction price could vary significantly from the par value of the securities. The treasury started to auction coupon issues on a yield basis in 1974. Bids are accepted on the basis of an annual percentage yield, with the coupon rate based on the weighted average yield of accepted competitive tenders received in the auction. Yield auctions free the treasury from having to set the coupon rate prior to the auction and ensure that the coupon rate and therefore the periodic interest payments of new note and bond issues accurately reflect actual market demand and supply conditions at the time of the auction.

Current Auction Technique

Today, all marketable treasury securities are sold in auctions, and all treasury auctions are conducted on a yield basis. The treasury sells the entire announced amount of each security offered at the yield or yields determined in the auction. It does not set a maximum acceptable yield (minimum price), nor does the treasury add to or reduce the announced size of an offering after the offering is announced. An exception to this general statement is that the treasury adds to the amounts that are announced for sale to the public the amounts awarded to refinance maturing securities held by the Federal Reserve System for the Open Market account. Awards to foreign official accounts that are held in custody at the Federal Reserve Bank of New York are also added to the amounts that are announced for sale to the public.

Ordinarily, there is a period of almost two weeks between the time a new treasury security offering is announced and the time the security is actually issued. The treasury permits trading during this period on a when-issued basis that provides for price discovery and reduces uncertainties surrounding treasury auctions. Potential competitive bidders look to when-issued trading levels as a market gauge of demand to determine how to bid at an auction. Noncompetitive bidders can use the quotes in the when-issued market to assess the likely auction average yield. Data on the dollar volumes of bids and awards in treasury auctions are released, along with the data mentioned below, about 45 minutes after the deadline for submission of competitive tenders in each auction. The data are published in the quarterly *Treasury Bulletin*.

Multiple-Price Auctions

With the exception of the two- and five-year note auctions, described below, marketable treasury security auctions are on a multiple-price basis. In a multiple-price auction, the treasury ranks the yields (bank discount rates in the case of treasury bills) that are bid from the lowest yield to the highest yield required to sell the amount offered to the public. Competitive bidders whose tenders are accepted pay the price equivalent to the yield (discount rate) that they bid.

Announcements of auction results include the average yield, high yield, and low yield of awarded tenders, the total volumes of bids and awards on competitive and noncompetitive tenders, the allocation percentage, if any, at the highest yield, and the amounts of awards to the Federal Reserve for its own and foreign official accounts. The treasury does not release information on bids of or awards to particular bidders, but does release data in the quarterly *Treasury Bulletin* regarding awards by investor class (Federal Reserve banks, commercial banks, individuals, insurance companies, mutual savings banks, corporations, private pension and retirement funds, state and local governments, nonbank dealers and brokers, and all others).

Single-Price Auctions

The treasury is experimenting with single-price auctions for monthly sales of two- and five-year notes. As with multiple-price auctions, bids in these single-price auctions are in terms of yield, and the coupon rate is determined after the auction. Bids are ranked from the lowest yield to the highest yield that is required to sell the amount offered. All awards are at the highest yield. The experiment began in September 1992. Announcements of the results of single-price auctions include information on the highest yield (at which all awards are made) and median and low yields bid as well as the other data that are released for multiple-price auctions.

Two main reasons are frequently cited in the academic literature as to why financing costs may be reduced through the use of single-price auctions; both of them result from the elimination of the so-called winner's curse. (The "winner's curse" is the risk that a bidder will pay more than others buying securities in an auction.) First, those participating in treasury auctions may bid more aggressively in a single-price auction than in a multiple-price auction. And second, more dealers and final investors may begin to take part in the auction as the threat of paying an above-market price is eliminated.

The treasury's experience with single-price auctions to June 1996 is that they appear to have neither increased nor decreased the treasury's cost of borrowing. Single-price auctions do appear, however, to have helped to broaden distribution of treasury securities. Thus, this auction technique likely has lessened the likelihood that bidders who want the securities will miss their opportunity to buy them in the auction. The treasury's evaluation of the single-price-auction results to date is summarized in the Appendix at the end of this chapter.

It is not possible to measure the change in treasury borrowing costs directly, because of market factors that may have an impact on the treasury market that are unrelated to auction format. Nevertheless, as reported in the treasury's October 1995 study "Uniform-Price Auctions: Evaluation of the Treasury Experience," the treasury has attempted to determine differences in expected revenues under the multiple-price and single-price auction formats by comparing the two techniques in terms of the average spreads of auction yield results to yields in the WI (when-issued) market. The results to date of such a comparison are that average spreads of auction yields over WI yields for uniform-price auctions are smaller than those for multiple-price auctions, but the difference is not statistically significant.

However, by examining the average auction spreads, and testing whether, for each technique, the spread is statistically distinguishable from zero, the treasury has obtained statistically significant results, which show that the average yield spread is different from zero in multiple-price auctions, whereas there is no similar evidence for the uniform-price technique. This suggests that expected revenue under the uniform-price technique is at least as great as under the multiple-price technique.

The primary reason for the lack of a statistically significant difference between auction yields and WI yields under the uniform-price auction technique is greater auction-to-auction volatility of the results with respect to the WI market. The greater volatility is partly a result of a broader and more volatile distributions of bids, and partly a result of the difference in the yield measure used to report auction results under the two techniques. In multiple-price auctions the results are based on the average of accepted bids, while in uniform-price auctions, the result is the highest accepted bid, a single number in contrast to an average, and therefore more volatile. Thus, uniform-price auctions may produce greater revenue on average, but present greater uncertainty regarding revenue at any given auction.

Market participants have observed that, although on occasion, single-price auctions may have led to higher costs to the treasury than might have occurred in multiple-price auctions, these occasions are balanced by others when there were apparent savings. In instances where single-price auctions seemed to have resulted in higher yields, the higher yield appears to have been related to the market environment at the time of the auction rather than to the auction technique. There is no clear basis to determine that single-price or multiple-price auctions would produce systematic savings to the treasury in weak market environments.

Competitive and Noncompetitive Bidding

Competitive bidders submit tenders stating the yield (discount rate for bill auctions) at which the bidder wants to purchase the securities. Noncompetitive bids from the public for up to $1 million face amount of treasury bills and up to $5 million of notes and bonds are awarded in full at the weighted average yield of accepted competitive bids. The ability to bid on a noncompetitive basis ensures that small investors, who may not have current market information, can purchase securities at a current market yield. It also helps to promote the treasury's goal of achieving a broad distribution of treasury securities.

Any entity may submit a bid in a treasury auction directly to a Federal Reserve bank, which acts as the treasury's fiscal agent, or indirectly through a dealer. The treasury permits all dealers that are registered with the Securities and Exchange Commission and all federally regulated financial institutions to submit bids in treasury auctions for their own accounts and for the account of customers. All bidders in treasury auctions—not just primary dealers and financial institutions—may bid in treasury auctions without a deposit, provided the bidder has a payment mechanism in place (an "autocharge agreement") with its Federal Reserve bank.

The treasury has facilitated purchases of treasury securities directly from the treasury in auctions by awarding securities on a noncompetitive basis and through the treasury direct book-entry system. In treasury direct, the investor holds treasury securities directly on the books of the treasury, without using the services of a financial institution or a dealer.

Auction Schedule

The treasury has a regular, predictable schedule for offering marketable securities, which is well known to market participants. The treasury makes an announcement as far in advance as is practical any time there is a change in the usual pattern, so that the market can digest the information and prepare for the offerings. The treasury also releases updated estimates of its borrowing requirements periodically during the year to permit market participants to estimate more accurately the sizes of treasury offerings.

The regular, predictable offering schedule has helped to reduce the government's borrowing costs by lessening the uncertainty surrounding treasury auctions. Disruptions in the schedule may occur when the statutory limit on the amount of debt that is authorized to be outstanding becomes binding. Disruptions tend to increase the government's financing costs, because investors may switch to alternative instruments, offerings become compressed, dealers have less time to distribute the securities to their customers, and the treasury must rely more on the dealer community to purchase and finance new issues.

The treasury sells 13- and 26-week bills every week, and 52-week bills every four weeks. Two-year and five-year notes are auctioned every month for settlement at the end of the month. Regular midquarter financings, which settle on the 15th of February, May, August, and November, typically have consisted of 3-, 10-, and 30-year issues. Beginning in August 1993, however, the treasury has sold 30-year bonds in two offerings each year, one in February and one in August. The regularly scheduled issues amount to about 151 separate auctions of securities each year.

The treasury also offers cash management bills from time to time to raise funds to cover low points in the treasury cash balance. The maturity dates for cash management bills usually coincide with the Thursday maturities of regular 13-, 26-, and 52-week bills. For example, cash management bills may be issued in early April, before the April 15 tax payment date, and mature later in April, when cash balances are at seasonal highs. Short-term cash management bills may be announced, auctioned, and settled in a period as short as one day, if necessary, to ensure that the government does not run out of cash. To shorten the time for the auction and reduce the cost of issuing short-term cash management bills, they may be issued only in large minimum purchase amounts—$1 million or more—and noncompetitive tenders are not accepted.

Decisions on Maturity Mix of New Issues

The treasury determines the maturities and amounts of new issues of treasury securities. It consults formally and informally with market participants and the Federal Reserve, which acts as the treasury's fiscal agent, regarding debt management issues.

A Treasury Borrowing Advisory Committee, composed of 20–25 members from firms that are broker/dealers (sell side) and investment firms (buy side), meets at the time of each regular midquarter refunding operation to advise the treasury on financing strategies for the immediate period and for the longer term. The treasury releases to the public all information that is given to the committee for its consideration, in advance of each meeting, and releases all committee reports and recommendations immediately upon receiving them.

Over the years, the treasury has developed regular cycles of issues of bills, notes, and bonds that place new issues of treasury debt across the spectrum from 3 months to 30 years maturity (see Chart 1). The treasury does not have a particular target for the average maturity of the debt, which was 5 years, 6 months, at the end of December 1994, compared with a high point of 6 years, 2 months, in May 1991 (see Chart 2).

Nor does the treasury have particular targets for the amounts of cash to be raised in treasury bills, notes, or bonds. The sizes of notes and bonds vary little from offering to offering, while treasury bill sizes may be changed frequently to account for seasonal swings in the treasury cash balance (see Charts 3 and 4). The fluctuations in the cash balance occur primarily because large income tax payments are received by the treasury in the middle of January, March, April, June, September, and December, while expenditures are spread more evenly throughout the year.

The treasury raised a large proportion of total new cash in five-year notes in fiscal year 1994 and is expected to do so again in fiscal year 1995. Monthly issues of five-year notes began in January 1991, replacing quarterly issues of five-year, two-month notes and quarterly issues of four-year

Chart 1. United States: Private Holdings of Treasury Marketable Debt
(Percent distribution by maturity)

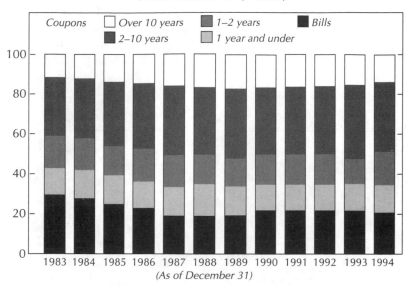

Source: U.S. Department of the Treasury, Office of Market Finance.

Chart 2. United States: Average Length of the Marketable Debt
(Privately held)

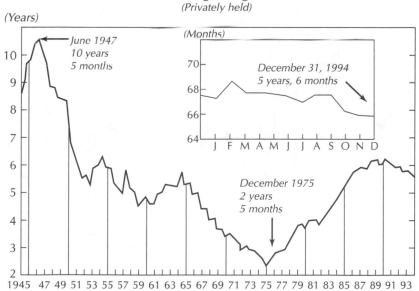

Source: U.S. Department of the Treasury, Office of Market Finance.

Chart 3. United States: Treasury Operating Cash Balance
(In billions of U.S. dollars; semimonthly data)

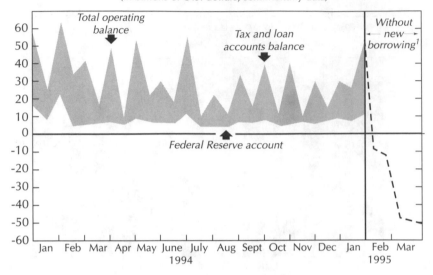

Source: U.S. Department of the Treasury, Office of Market Finance.
[1]Assumes refunding of maturing issues.

Chart 4. United States: Treasury Net Market Borrowing[1]
(In billions of U.S. dollars)

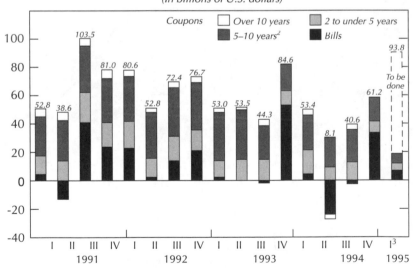

Source: U.S. Department of the Treasury, Office of Market Finance.
[1]Excludes Federal Reserve and government account transactions.
[2]Seven-year note discontinued after April 1993.
[3]Issued or announced through January 27, 1995.

notes, which were discontinued. Beginning in January 1996, the cash-raising potential of the monthly five-year notes will decline, and five-year notes that have been issued monthly since January 1991 will begin to mature. Thus, the treasury will need to adjust its offerings of new securities— for example, by increasing the size or frequency or both of new offerings or adding new types of securities—in order to raise the cash needed to refinance maturing issues and raise new money.

Auction Rules

The uniform offering circular for treasury securities, which became effective in March 1993, compiles all treasury auction rules in one document. The rules, which were written and put into effect by the treasury, set out the responsibilities of bidders and of entities that submit bids for other parties in treasury auctions and provide for certain limitations on auction awards to promote distribution of treasury securities. The Federal Reserve banks, which act as the treasury's fiscal agent, particularly the Federal Reserve Bank of New York, were consulted in the development of the uniform offering circular.

One of the significant rules is that awards to any bidder in a treasury auction may not exceed 35 percent of the amount that is offered to the public. To facilitate enforcement of this "35-percent rule," the offering circular also requires that any bidder report the amount of its net long position when the total of its bids in the auction, plus the bidder's net long position in the security being auctioned, equals or exceeds $2 billion. A bidder can acquire a net long position in a treasury security that is about to be auctioned, because the treasury permits securities to trade on a when-issued basis between the announcement and the auction. It is also possible to obtain a net long position in a security that is about to be auctioned when the new security is an additional amount of a security that is already outstanding—for example, each 13-week bill is a reopening of the 26-week bill that was issued 13 weeks before. Futures contracts in which the deliverable item is a specific three-month treasury bill are also counted in a bidder's position at the time of an auction. The maximum award that will be made to any bidder is 35 percent of the public offering, less the bidder's reported net long position.

Auction Automation

Electronic bidding in treasury auctions began with the 52-week bill auction in April 1993. The electronic bidding system, called the Treasury Automated Auction Processing System, or TAAPS, permits an entity that bids electronically to submit bids to a Federal Reserve bank by computer terminal located at the bidding entity's place of business. The TAAPS system ranks bids electronically, notifies the bidder of acceptance of bids, and facilitates electronic issuance of the securities in the commercial book-entry system (which is separate from TAAPS). All 38 primary dealers and several large investors that regularly purchase treasury securities directly in auctions, rather than through dealers, are using TAAPS. Although not every bidder has access to treasury auctions through TAAPS, a form of electronic access to treasury auctions is available for any creditworthy bidder.

Prior to the implementation of TAAPS, treasury auctions were largely paper-based, and bidding and auction result processing were done manually. Although electronic bidding accounts for most of the dollar volume of bidding, the treasury has continued to accept paper bids in order to ensure broad access to treasury auctions.

The goals of automated bidding are to increase the efficiency and accuracy of bidding and auction processing, to facilitate broader participation in auctions, and to assist in monitoring compliance with auction rules. The treasury is pleased with the results to date of auction automation through TAAPS. Bidding through TAAPS has accounted for 90 percent or more of the dollar volume of bids and awards in recent auctions. TAAPS has reduced auction processing time for most treasury auctions since its inception to about 45 minutes from one hour, although the reductions in processing time have not been consistent. TAAPS has also permitted the treasury and the Federal Reserve to ensure compliance with the treasury auction rules. For example, the bids of entities that submit tenders in treasury auctions through several dealers can be combined in a timely way to prevent awards that would exceed 35 percent of the publicly offered securities.

Treasury–Federal Reserve Relationship

The treasury and the Federal Reserve (the Fed) were established under separate federal statutes that provide for Federal Reserve management of the nation's monetary policy and U.S. Treasury management of the government's borrowing policy. The treasury is not authorized to borrow directly from the Fed. The Fed conducts transactions in treasury and other government securities in the course of managing the availability of credit in the U.S. economy. The Fed does, however, submit noncompetitive tenders in treasury auctions to purchase new securities to replace Fed-held securities that are maturing, but the amounts are limited to the maturing amounts. The Fed transfers its earnings (mostly interest on its portfolio of government securities), less federal reserve expenses, to the treasury and the transfers help to reduce the federal budget deficit.

In its capacity as the treasury's fiscal agent, the Fed conducts auctions of treasury securities, collects the proceeds of security sales, and maintains treasury securities on the commercial book-entry system for the purposes of trading and making debt-service payments. As part of administering treasury auctions, the Fed spot-checks customer bids for authenticity and receives confirmation by customers receiving large awards (over $500 million) to verify the authenticity of their bids.

The Fed also maintains the cash accounts from which treasury disbursements are made and into which tax collections and other federal receipts are deposited. The treasury and the Federal Reserve Bank of New York each independently estimates treasury near-term cash balances. Generally, cash that is not needed for treasury disbursements is transferred to accounts in commercial banks called treasury tax and loan (TT&L) accounts. Treasury deposits in TT&L accounts are fully collateralized and earn interest at a rate equal to the federal funds' rate, less one-quarter point.

There is a telephone conversation each business day between treasury staff and staff of the Federal Reserve Bank of New York to discuss the estimates and movements of cash between the treasury account at the Federal Reserve and the TT&L accounts. A buildup of the treasury balance at the Federal Reserve would absorb reserves from the banking system. If the Fed wanted to maintain a stable monetary policy posture, it would likely offset the reserve-absorbing effect of a temporary buildup in the treasury balance by taking action in the open market, such as transacting short-term repurchase agreements to supply reserves temporarily.

The treasury, Federal Reserve, Securities and Exchange Commission, and Commodities Futures Trading Commission are members of an interagency working group that monitors current conditions in the securities markets. The Federal Reserve Bank of New York, which has regular contact with market participants through open market operations, is the lead agency in obtaining and analyzing market data. If a particular security becomes expensive in the cash and financing markets, for example, the working group might discuss the reasons for the apparent shortage of the security, compare the current situation with historical patterns, and discuss whether any government actions might be warranted.

Primary Dealers in U.S. Government Securities

The primary dealers in government securities, at the time of writing 38 in number, are selected by the Federal Reserve Bank of New York. They are expected to make markets in the full range of U.S. government securities for a reasonably diverse group of customers and to participate meaningfully in treasury auctions. They are expected to be effective market-makers, to facilitate the Federal Reserve's open market operations, and to provide the central bank with information to assist it in performing its duties.

To become a primary dealer, an entity must demonstrate evidence of a strong commitment to continued participation as a market-maker over the long term; management depth and experience; a reasonable profitability record; strong internal controls; sufficient capital to support comfortably their activities; and prudent management of risk exposures.

Firms are designated primary dealers because they can be of service to the Federal Reserve Bank of New York. The designation is not an endorsement and does not entail official supervision by the Federal Reserve. The primary dealers and other dealers in U.S. government securities are subject to regulation by the Securities and Exchange Commission or a federal financial institution regulatory agency. The Federal Reserve does monitor dealer activities to determine that the primary dealer performance standards are being met and to obtain information about market developments.

Treasury Regulation of Government Market

The Government Securities Act (GSA), passed in 1986, authorized the treasury to write rules with respect to transactions in government securities effected by government securities brokers and dealers (i.e., securities firms and financial institutions) and regulations relating to the custody of government securities held by depository institutions. The legislation was enacted in response to several failures of unregulated government securities dealers between 1975 and 1985. The GSA established, for the first time, a federal system for the regulation of the entire government securities market, including previously unregulated brokers and dealers. GSA amendments in 1993 in part extended the treasury's regulatory authority for an indefinite time period.

The GSA rules were intended to prevent fraudulent and manipulative acts and practices and to protect the integrity, liquidity, and efficiency of the government securities market. Enforcement of GSA regulations is carried out by the existing regulatory authorities—the Securities and Exchange Commission and federal financial institution regulators, including the Federal Reserve—and self-regulatory organizations such as the National Association of Securities Dealers. To the extent possible, the treasury has incorporated existing regulations of the regulatory authorities into the treasury rules. The treasury consulted extensively with the Securities and Exchange Commission, the Federal Reserve, the other federal regulators of financial institutions, and market participants in the development of the rules.

Appendix

Uniform-Price Auction Results:
Summary of U.S. Treasury Evaluation

The U.S. Treasury has compared multiple-price auction results between June 1991 and August 1992 with single-price auction results between September 1992 and May 1994. Several of those comparisons are summarized below.

Large Competitive Awards to Primary Dealers and to Primary Dealers Plus Their Customers

Table 1 contains data on large competitive awards (based on bids of $1 million or greater) to primary dealers and their customers through the New York, Chicago, and San Francisco Federal Reserve Banks and branches. The data are broken out into two periods: from June 1991 to August 1992 and from September 1992 to May 1994.

The change in the shares of large competitive awards to the top primary dealers and their large customers indicates a reduction in the concentration of awards during the uniform-price auction period for the two-year and the five-year notes. Moreover, during the same time period, the concentration of awards either increased or remained essentially the same for the three-year and ten-year notes. As a result, there is evidence that the uniform-price auction technique has reduced award concentrations in treasury auctions and encouraged more aggressive bidding from a broader range of bidders.

For instance, the shares of awards going to the top five and top ten dealers decreased by a statistically significant amount for both the two-year and five-year notes during the uniform-price period. Meanwhile, the share of awards to the top bidders increased by a statistically significant amount for ten-year notes and remained essentially the same for three-year notes.

Similarly, the concentration of competitive awards to the top five and top ten dealers plus their customers was reduced or remained the same during the uniform-price period for two-year and five-year notes. At the same time, the shares remained the same or increased during the same time period for the three-year and ten-year notes.

Comparison of Auction Results to the When-Issued Market

The spreads between the auction yield results and the 1:00 p.m. when-issued (WI) bid yields for each auction, and the distribution of individual bids in terms of deviation from the average yields in the two auctions, were analyzed. It was found that under the multiple-price format, the average spreads between auction average yields and 1:00 p.m. WI bid yields are significantly different from zero. That is, there is a statistically significant premium to dealers for bidding in the auctions. By contrast, the average spreads for the uniform-price two-year and five-year auctions are smaller, and they are not significantly different from zero. That is, there is no statistically significant markup thus far in the uniform-price auctions.

**Table 1. United States: Large Competitive Awards to Primary Dealers
and Awards to Primary Dealers Plus Their Large Customers[1]**
(As a percentage of total private awards)

Maturity	Top	Dealer Own Accounts		Dealers Plus Their Large Customers	
		June 1991– Aug. 1992	Sept. 1992– May 1994	June 1991– Aug.1992	Sept. 1992– May 1994
Two-year					
note	5	32.1	24.0	43.8	40.4
	10	47.0	38.0	62.3	58.1
	All dealers	69.0	65.7	90.1	92.0
Five-year					
note	5	40.2	25.7	50.2	37.6
	10	51.3	41.6	67.4	58.5
	All dealers	68.8	67.0	89.3	92.1
Three-year					
note	5	34.6	44.2	42.9	54.5
	10	47.0	57.2	60.3	71.7
	All dealers	72.3	74.8	91.0	93.5
Ten-year					
note	5	39.3	52.1	60.2	60.1
	10	50.7	63.9	74.3	74.9
	All dealers	65.7	80.1	92.7	94.4

Source: U.S. Department of the Treasury, Office of Market Finance.

[1]Large competitive awards (based on bids greater than or equal to $1 million) to primary dealers for their own accounts and awards to their customers through the New York, Chicago, and San Francisco Federal Reserve banks and branches.

One reason is that, while the average auction spreads are comparable for the two techniques, the volatility of the auction spreads for the uniform-price auctions is greater. For 30 multiple-price two-year and five-year auctions from June 1991 to August 1992, in only one instance (September 1991 two-year note auction) did the auction average come in below the 1:00 p.m. WI yield. Otherwise, there was a relatively stable average premium under the multiple-price auction technique to successful competitive bidders. By contrast, in more than one-half (33 out of 58) of the uniform-price auctions, the auction yield has been below the 1:00 p.m. WI yield, but the auction-to-auction volatility of results has been greater.

Dispersion of Auction Yield Bids: Multiple- and Uniform-Price Auctions

One reason for greater variability in auction-to-auction results is that the average dispersion of auction bid yields under the uniform-price format is broader than that for multiple-price auctions and somewhat less stable from auction to auction. Another reason is that average yield is used to express the result in multiple-price auctions and stop-out yield is used in single-price auctions.

The distribution of the deviation from auction average of yield bids for the two-year and five-year notes under the alternate auction techniques shows that the distribution is symmetric for multiple-price auctions, as one would expect. The bids trailing off further to the right can, for the most part, be viewed as underwriting bids.[1] In contrast, there is a greater frequency of bids to the left of the auction stop in uniform-price auctions, which is also consistent with auction theory.

However, with greater uncertainty with respect to auction outcomes, the bids to the right may take on added meaning. It has been suggested that dealers may be more likely to split bids in a uniform-price auction. That is, they may place one or more bids at aggressive yields to ensure supply, and place other bids 2 to 5 basis points off the market. If awarded, experience has shown that the securities will all usually result in profits to the bidder in postauction WI trading.

The second factor contributing to the volatility of uniform-price auction results relative to 1:00 p.m. WI yields is the different yield concepts employed to report auction yield results under the two formats. In multiple-price auctions, the auction average yield is used, whereas for uniform-price auctions, a stop-out yield concept is employed. In and of itself, a single number is expected to have more volatility than an average of a relatively stable set of numbers.

---

[1]The auction tail, or the difference between average yield and highest accepted yield, for monthly multiple-price five-year auctions never exceeded 1 basis point, while that for two-year auctions had exceeded 1 basis point only once (May 1991) after 1989.

Denmark: Secondary Market for Government Securities, Public Debt Management, and Monetary Control

*Bjarne Skafte**

A primary market trade takes place when securities are sold at issue directly to an investor. A secondary market enables the original investor to sell the securities before they reach maturity. Investors are more willing to buy securities in the primary market if they know that they can reduce their holdings at a time of their choosing by trading in the secondary market. As a result, a government is able to obtain better terms for securities that are traded in an efficient secondary market.

The development of an efficient secondary market for government securities is, therefore, an essential part of government debt management. An efficient secondary market is also important for the central bank to conduct open market operations.

Structure of the Secondary Market

The efficient operation of a secondary market requires a system for bringing buyers and sellers together and for agreeing on the prices of securities. There is also a need to define a set of market participants, to set up rules concerning capitalization, skills, trading practices, rules of conduct of business, and so forth.

It may be possible to use an organized and regulated market, for example, a stock exchange or a more informal, "over-the-counter" (OTC) market. In the countries of the Organization for Economic Cooperation and Development (OECD), marketable government securities are in gen-

---

*Bjarne Skafte is Head of the Secretariat Department, National Bank of Denmark.

eral listed on a stock exchange. The listing of the securities does not necessarily mean that the stock exchange is the marketplace. The bulk of the trading may take place on a more informal basis outside the stock exchange. By developing adequate trading and information systems, some stock exchanges have, however, managed to retain an important role in the secondary markets for government securities. A stock exchange may provide a focal point for the development of a new market. It may also be well placed to carry out market surveillance, particularly in ensuring that the rules of the market are observed and unfair trading practices prevented.

Until the 1980s, membership of most stock exchanges was limited to certain brokers or stockbroking companies. Some stock exchanges had a limited number of "seats," and competition was limited through agreements between market participants. Such arrangements may be useful when only a few tradable securities are available and the market very underdeveloped. However, further development of the market requires easy access for new participants and more competition.

In some cases, regulations stipulate that securities are traded only on the stock exchange, because it is difficult to monitor the trades made elsewhere. Such a requirement may improve market surveillance, but it may also inhibit trading. For this reason, most important stock exchanges allow market participants to use the trading system they prefer.

Some countries with major government securities markets have established a system with specialized dealers in government securities (called primary dealers in the United States, specialists in treasury securities in France). These specialized dealers in the major countries are established as separate companies, but some smaller OECD countries have appointed primary dealers from among existing stockbrokers or banks. Primary dealers commit themselves to submit bids at securities auctions and are often charged with setting up an adequate trading system. They are also important contributors to the governments' marketing efforts. Primary dealers receive certain privileges as compensation for their obligations, for example, privileged access to auctions or dealer financing.

Normally, when government securities are traded on a stock exchange, all the broker-dealers (stockbrokers or banks) that are members of the exchange are able to trade securities. When a market has a low volume of outstanding securities, there is no need to establish formal categories of specialists. However, some specialization typically occurs.

Denmark has not established a system of primary dealers. Government securities are issued through the stock exchange and all broker-dealers can buy securities at issue. The broker-dealers trade government securities as well as other domestic and foreign securities because they expect to earn a profit, and the government securities market is quite active.

Trading System

Types of Trading Systems

The choice of trading and pricing techniques in the secondary market largely depends on the volume of turnover and the market structure, including the types of participants. In a market in which turnover is low and trades are small in value, trading can be carried out and prices determined by an order-matching process. It is possible for one price to be fixed for each issue for each trading session (*periodic* or *call market*). This price is set through an auction procedure according to the terms and volumes of all the buy and sell orders; at this price, the orders can be matched and executed. The price determined by this trading system can also be used as an "official" price.

In systems with order-matching and official price fixing, most trades are executed at the official price. Brokers earn a commission that is, in most cases, fixed. Order-matching is operationally inexpensive because there is no need to invest much in electronic equipment, and the time spent on each issue is limited. A number of stock exchanges still use order-matching and daily price fixing. In the early states of a secondary market, it may be sensible to limit the number of trading sessions taking place each week.

However, price fixing impedes the development of the market and is inappropriate for market participants that have a high rate of turnover and substantial transaction size, for example, institutional investors that wish to trade large volumes rapidly throughout the day. These markets have developed continuous trading during the business day. Continuous trading may take place on the stock exchange or in an OTC market.

In an efficient market, the market price of a security at any time should encompass all relevant information. The market price may be made generally known either through the publication of details of recent trades showing the price and quantity at which the last trade was made (posttrade transparency) or by reference to a firm price quoted for the next transaction (pretrade transparency).

Copenhagen Stock Exchange

Until 1986, the Copenhagen Stock Exchange (CSE) used a system of order-matching and daily fixing of securities prices on the floor of the exchange, but only a small fraction of the total trade was executed on the exchange. Reform measures were enacted in 1986 to improve the efficiency of the market and to give the stock exchange a more important role.

Today, the CSE has three electronic trading systems—the Match System, the Accept System, and the Electro Broker System. In addition, the exchange has a reporting system to which trades outside the three trading systems (i.e., generally telephone trades) must be reported. The so-called Interest System supports the telephone market. CSE members of the exchange are connected to the systems from their own offices. The trading systems are open from 9:00 a.m. to 3:30 p.m., while the Interest System is open from 8:00 a.m. to 6:00 p.m. In addition to these systems, which are reserved for members, the exchange has an information system to which anyone can subscribe. Through this system, prices and volumes from the Match, Accept, and Reporting Systems are published. In October and November 1994, 42 percent of bond trading between members of the CSE took place via the trading systems, whereas 58 percent was traded by telephone and subsequently reported.

The Match System is an automatic trading system that continuously matches "bids" (offers to buy securities) and "offers" (offers to sell securities) of all securities registered by participants in the system. When there is an offer (sell) price that is equivalent to or lower than a bid (buy) price, the Match System automatically establishes a trade. The Match System ensures that the party placing a bid/offer in the system always trades at the most advantageous price already recorded in the system. If there are several bids with the same price, the volume is divided equally among bidders. When the system has established a trade, information on the traded volume and price is generated automatically.

For each security, participants are only informed on the screen about the price of the best bid/offer and the bidder's or offerer's identity, but not about the volume behind the given bid/offer. It is possible to buy a portion of the volume offered. The smallest trading unit in the Match System is DKr 5 million ($900,000), so it is used for trading large volumes.

The Accept System is a semiautomatic trading system and can be compared to an electronic notice board on which members of the CSE can post bids and offers. The bids and offers posted include both price and volume, and all bids and offers with price and volume and the trader's identity can be seen by all participants in the system. Trades are established by a broker-dealer accepting a bid or an offer made. All trading in the Accept System is for the entire volume offered. After the trade is made, the market is informed automatically of the traded volume and price. The smallest trading unit on the Accept System is DKr 10,000 ($1,800), so it is more suitable for smaller trades than the Match System.

In September 1994, the Copenhagen Stock Exchange introduced a third trading system, the Electro Broker System. This system is like the Accept System, but broker-dealers cannot see the identity of the bidder or offerer; it is reserved for market-makers who quote two-way prices in the relevant securities.

In addition to trading via the electronic systems, it is possible to trade by telephone in the "telephone market." When securities traders agree on a bond trade by telephone, both parties must report the trade to the exchange's reporting system within 90 seconds of its conclusion. Immediately thereafter, this information is made available to the market.

To supplement the trading systems and the Reporting System, the Interest System is intended to support the telephone market. In the Interest System, broker-dealers can signal interest in trading securities by entering price and identity and possibly a comment. Participants cannot trade directly in the Interest System; the trades must be concluded by telephone and reported to the Copenhagen Stock Exchange. The indications given in the system are binding.

Market-Making in Government Securities

In most developed wholesale government bond markets, the trading system is now based on the presence of market-makers—participants who continuously quote both buying and selling prices, that is, prices at which they will always buy or sell specified amounts of particular issues. This continuous price quotation arrangement ensures that investors wishing to buy or sell government bonds can always find a counterpart among these market-makers. The market-makers may or may not quote prices for all securities.

Market-makers do not charge a commission but earn a return by selling at a price higher than that at which they buy. The spread between the dealers' selling and buying prices covers their costs and is a form of compensation for the risks they take, including the risk that prices on their unsold inventory of securities may fall below the prices paid for those securities.

Continuous trading and a market-maker system is an efficient method for large benchmark issues, but for many small, old, or infrequently traded issues of securities, it is not profitable to make markets continuously. In such cases, the government may wish to use market-making for the most important issues and an order-matching system for other securities. Moreover, in a market with a low turnover, it would be quite impractical to establish specialist market-makers. In such a situation, the government should consider identifying existing institutions or banks that may be willing to take on market-making obligations in return for being granted certain facilities.

Settlement Systems

A secure settlement system is needed to support transactions. Ideally, a settlement system should ensure that when a transaction is settled—that is, cash is exchanged for the title of the securities—the two sides of the transaction are simultaneous and irrevocable (delivery versus payment).

The attraction of any financial market will be enhanced if a secure, fast, and cheap settlement service can be offered to investors. In 1989, the Group of Thirty set out a number of principles to which settlement systems should ideally conform.

Denmark opted very early for a computer-based registration and settlement system covering all traded securities and linked to the computer system of the Copenhagen Stock Exchange. The Danish Securities Center (VP, for "Vaerdipapircentralen" in Danish) is responsible for computer registration of issues, trading, and ownership of securities listed on the Copenhagen Stock Exchange. It is a private, nonprofit organization. It services the financial sector as a whole, and about 300 banks, savings banks, stockbroking companies, mortgage-credit institutions, institutional investors, and the central bank are connected to the center. Private investors (households, companies, etc.) do not have direct access to VP, but their holdings are registered individually. The computer registration has replaced physical securities, thus eliminating the storage, security, and handling problems associated with paper securities. Payments are settled through Danmarkes Nationalbank—the Danish central bank.

Since 1983, all listed Danish bonds have been registered in the VP system. In 1988, Danish shares, investment certificates, and convertible bonds were transferred from paper to computer registration. Registration of securities denominated in foreign currency is also possible (with settlement in foreign currency).

The securities are registered on VP accounts in units of equal size (DKr 1,000 for most government securities on VP accounts). Each bank (or stockbroking company) keeps a VP account to register its own holdings. In addition, it keeps a number of VP accounts to register each of its customers. Each VP account contains information about the securities, the ownership (normally the name and address of the account holder), and a bank account to which VP can transfer payments of interest, dividends, and so forth on the holdings. Owners of securities may register in their own names or names of nominees. The latter registration implies that the name of the actual owner of the securities is known only to the nominee registered as account holder. Information about individual accounts can be retrieved only by the bank (or other institution) responsible for that customer.

Government Securities Issues and the Role of the Secondary Market

Danmarkes Nationalbank, as agent for the ministry of finance, sells government securities on the Copenhagen Stock Exchange. Government bonds (5, 10, and 30 years to maturity) and 2-year treasury notes are issued by tap sales to the market. In principle, tap sales take place every day (market conditions permitting), so that the issue of government securities is similar to the regular secondary market trading of securities. Treasury bills with three- to nine-month maturities are, however, sold at monthly auctions.

An active and efficient secondary market allows the Nationalbank to tap bonds and notes in a very smooth and cost-efficient way. The Nationalbank sells most of the government securities through the Match System because it is suited to the sale of large bond volumes, ensures all broker-dealers equal access to buy government securities (for the amount they demand), and ensures immediate dissemination of market information about the issue of government securities.

In practice, therefore, the sale of government securities begins by the Nationalbank offering an amount for sale in the Match System, after assessing whether market prices are acceptable and how much interest there is among potential buyers. The amount involved will typically be in the range of DKr 100 million to DKr 200 million. Next, broker-dealers in the system buy large or small portions of the offered amount. Normally, the securities offered are sold to several different buyers. If the market level has not changed, and there is still a selling requirement, a further amount is offered. If the market level has risen or the Nationalbank considers it appropriate, the prices for the new offering may be raised marginally. This process continues until there are no more interested buyers or the Nationalbank does not wish to sell any more securities. Usually, large amounts are involved when the Nationalbank sells government securities. The average daily sale in 1994 was just over DKr 500 million.

In practice, the Match System is predominantly used by Danmarkes Nationalbank, since most broker-dealers prefer other trading systems and (particularly) telephone trading with subsequent reporting. From July 1993 to September 1994, the Nationalbank was involved in approximately 80 percent of trading in the ten-year government bond (7 percent 2004) in the Match System. It should be noted that this bond issue accounted for only about 5 percent of total turnover between members of the Copenhagen Stock Exchange during this period.

Experience has shown that on days with falling prices, there will rarely be any real buy interest in the bond market, so that it is impossible for the Nationalbank to sell significant amounts. Furthermore, the risk cannot be ignored that because of the Nationalbank's central position in financial markets as well as the substantial size of its issuance, the Nationalbank may contribute to creating or reinforcing market trends. The Nationalbank will, therefore, typically refrain from selling government securities on days with low turnover and falling prices, although it has done so on a few occasions when it was considered necessary to stimulate sales.

To avoid creating or amplifying negative trends in the bond market, the Nationalbank will usually not underbid itself in the market over a single day. For example, if the Nationalbank begins the day selling a particular bond at DKr 99.50 per 100, it will not normally lower the price later in the day. However, offers at a lower price cannot be excluded completely if there is a general downward shift in the market (e.g., as a consequence of falling bond markets abroad), which, in reality, creates a new market situation.

Coordination of Debt Management and Monetary Control

Many OECD countries have, in recent years, reformulated the objectives of government debt management. In most cases, this has meant a narrowing of the debt management objectives to minimizing costs and the interest rate, or refinancing, risk of government deficits. Other objectives, such as support of monetary policy and promotion of household savings, have largely been abolished, or other instruments have been introduced to meet these aims.

A clear definition of the goals of government debt management facilitates both debt management and monetary policy. The scope for conflicts of interest is reduced, resulting in greater policy consistency. An efficient secondary market in government securities makes it possible to implement the separation of the tasks without any major negative consequences.

In Denmark, a clear funding rule has been agreed on by the government and the Nationalbank. The new issues of government securities on the domestic market must—on an annual basis—equal the government budget deficit plus the redemptions of domestic government securities. In addition, because Denmark borrowed abroad to finance the current account deficits of the 1970s and 1980s, the foreign government debt is reduced whenever foreign exchange reserves permit.

The issuance of government securities is implemented in a regular manner designed to fulfill the borrowing target for the fiscal year. Securities are sold even in adverse market conditions if this is necessary. The Nationalbank does not attempt through its sales to control bond yields or even to stabilize the bond market. Because the bond market is closely linked to the other government securities markets in Western Europe, attempts to control the yields would definitely fail.

The funding rule implies that government debt management does not have major repercussions on the operation of monetary policy, which is implemented predominantly via the supply of liquidity to the banking sector through two-week repurchase agreements (repos) in government securities and the sale of Nationalbank certificates of deposit (CDs). Normally, the Nationalbank fixes the interest rates for the two-week repos and the CDs and supplies adequate liquid funds to the banking sector as a whole. An interbank money market secures the efficient transmission of monetary policy changes to the financial market at large, as well as to the rest of the economy.

Conclusion

The costs of trading and handling securities are very important, and the secondary market for government securities will not fulfill its functions if the costs are too high relative to the volume of outstanding securities and transactions. The obligations of market participants and the technical "infrastructure" of the secondary market must, therefore, be developed in step with the volume of securities and transactions. In small countries, economies of scale may be obtained by using the same institutional framework and techniques for securities issued by both the private sector and the government. Finally, the development of good market skills and practices greatly promotes confidence in the market.

Glossary of Selected Technical Terms

The reader will find additional definitions in Chapter 7, Appendix 1, "Taxonomy and Organization of Market Structure and the Role of Intermediaries."

Active auctioneer: A special trader (e.g., the ministry of finance, the central bank, or specialist) who participates in trading to influence the outcome in order to achieve certain objectives for the benefit of traders— for example, price stabilization or price discovery.

Benchmark: A security used as the basis for interest rate calculations and for pricing other securities. Also denotes the most heavily traded and liquid security of a particular class.

Broker: A financial intermediary that solicits orders from buyers and sellers and then orchestrates trades, either by passing the identity of each party to the other or by making offsetting, simultaneous trades with each party. Brokers typically maintain computer screens with anonymous bid and offer quotes from dealers.

Dealer: A financial intermediary that buys and sells securities or other instruments, by setting bid and offer quotes. Dealers take positions in instruments.

Discriminatory auction: See **multiple-price auction**.

Dual-capacity broker: A broker that can trade as principal (on his or her own account), as well as on behalf of public traders.

Duration: A weighted average of the maturities of all cash flows from a debt instrument. The present values of these cash flows are used as the weights, with the yield to maturity used to compute the present values. Duration also represents the elasticity of the value of a bond with respect to changes in its yield to maturity.

Equilibrium (underlying) value: The price of a security that would emerge from a market free of trading frictions, revealing fully the under-lying demand and supply conditions.

Execution risk: The risk in executing a trade of a spurious price movement.

Fair market: A market with safeguards against fraud, manipulation of prices, and abuse by intermediaries of their position.

Gilts (or gilt-edged securities): Irish or U.K. government medium- and long-term debt securities.

GOVPX: A service in the United States that distributes real-time price and quote information for all U.S. treasury securities.

Homogeneous expectations: Where all traders agree on the relevant parameters determining a security's valuation. For example, in the context of the Capital Asset Pricing Model, investors agree on the mean, variance, and covariance characteristics of individual securities.

Immediacy: The capability of traders to execute trades immediately.

Informed traders: Traders that have superior information about a security's underlying valuation and trade on that basis (information-motivated trades).

Interdealer broker: A specialized intermediary providing trade execution services to dealers in over-the-counter markets.

Intrinsic or fundamental value: The price of a security determined in reference to a pricing model or to another market (e.g., as in the case of derivative securities).

Limit order: A buy or sell order contingent on price: minimum price in the case of a sale, and maximum price in the case of a buy.

Liquidity: The ease with which traders can buy and sell securities in desired quantities at prices (including all trading costs) that are close to underlying values.

Market-maker: A dealer that posts ongoing bid and offer quotes in a particular instrument.

Market order: A noncontingent buy or sell order that indicates only the quantity to be traded in the market.

Market structure: The organization of the secondary market including market access, order handling, the trading mechanism, transparency, the role of intermediaries, clearing and settlement services, and so forth.

Marking to market: Expressing assets or liabilities at current market rates.

Multiple-price auction: An auction in which each successful bidder pays the price bid. Also known as a discriminatory auction.

Network externalities: Positive externalities that are associated with market structures.

Price discovery: Refers to the function of securities markets of finding the prices at which trades are made. In markets with *efficient price discovery*, prices should closely track their equilibrium value.

Price stabilization: The mechanism for the reduction of large short-term (spurious) movements in transaction prices.

Primary dealers: A group of dealers in the United States with a formal, ongoing trading relationship with the Federal Reserve Bank of New York and with certain obligations in the primary and secondary markets for treasury securities; similar entities in other countries.

Primary market: The market in which a security is first sold by the issuer.

Repurchase agreements (repos): Very short-term sales of government securities through an agreement to repurchase them at a slightly higher price at a specified date. Term also applies to other securities.

Sealed-bid auction: An auction in which all bids are submitted secretly, before some deadline, with no opportunity for revision.

Secondary market: A market in which a security is sold by one investor to another, as opposed to the primary market.

Settlement risk: Risk that one party or another in a securities trade will fail to deliver, especially when the other party has already delivered.

Single-capacity broker: A broker that can act only on behalf of a client and not on his or her own account as principal.

Strip: A zero-coupon security created by the decomposition of a bond into separate securities for each coupon payment and for the final principal payment. The term comes from the U.S. Treasury acronym for "separate trading of registered interest and principal."

Syndicate: A group of intermediaries that purchase prearranged shares of a security in the primary market and sell the security to other investors.

Tap sales: Sales by a central bank of a new issue of government securities, more or less on a continuous basis ("on tap").

Thin markets: Markets characterized by few participants and infrequent trading.

Trading frictions: Costs or impediments to trading, such as commissions, intermediation (bid-offer) spreads, restrictions to market access, and information deficiencies (e.g., on prices and transactions).

Transparency: Amount and timeliness of information relevant to the trading process that is made available to the public including, for example, bids and offers, the depth of the order book (auction market), and transaction information such as prices, number of trades, and size of trades.

Uniform-price auction: An auction in which all successful bidders pay the same price, usually the price of the lowest successful bid. Sometimes called a Dutch auction.

Uninformed or liquidity traders: Non-informationally motivated traders; those trading to raise or deploy cash (liquidity).

When-issued (WI) market: The market for a security before it is sold on the primary market.

Winner's curse: Losses incurred by successful bidders at an auction, due to those bidders' having inaccurate, overoptimistic information on the value of the item auctioned.

Yield to maturity: The interest rate that makes a bond's present value equal to its market price. If the price of a bond is below/above par, the yield to maturity is greater/less than the bond's coupon rate, and the bond is said to trade at a discount/ premium.

Zero-coupon bond: A bond with no coupon, only a single principal payment at maturity.